upriver

up river

From the Sea to the Southern Alps

Colin Heinz

Quentin Wilson
PUBLISHING

Quentin Wilson
PUBLISHING

Every effort has been made to ensure that the information in this book is accurate and errors that come to the author's attention will be rectified in future editions.

Front cover: The Cook River/Weheka from its glacial sources near Aoraki/ Mt Cook to the Tasman Sea.

Andris Apse

Front flap, top: The view of the source of the Taramakau River below the junction of the Kaimatā Range and the Main Divide.

Front flap, bottom: The view of Lewis Pass/Kopi o Kaitāngata (863m) on the Main Divide from the Lewis Valley.

First published 2020 by
Quentin Wilson Publishing
105 Moncks Spur Road
Christchurch 8081
New Zealand
info@quentinwilsonpublishing.com
www.quentinwilsonpublishing.com

ISBN 978-0-9951329-3-1

A catalogue record for this book is available from the National Library of New Zealand.

Edited by: Renee Lang
Cover and book design & page layout:
Quentin Wilson Publishing

Cover & Text design:
Copyright © 2020 Quentin Wilson Publishing

Printed in Taiwan (ROC) by CHOICE Printing Inc.

contents

All the rivers run into the sea
Yet the sea is not full;
To the place from which the rivers come,
There they return again.

Ecclesiastes 1:7
(New King James Version)

Introduction

The landscapes of childhood become ingrained in the psyche. In my mind's eye I can still see the Grey River/Māwheranui flowing into the sea past my old hometown. It arises in the Southern Alps/Kā Tiritiri o te Moana (the mirages of the ocean), which rim the southern and eastern horizons. On clear days their shining summits look like a string of icebergs drifting out to sea. My father used to say that a giant had bitten the gap between the two highest peaks.

The South Island Te Waipounamu in the New Zealand Group is 151,215 square kilometres in area, which makes it the twelfth largest island in the world. It is also the largest emergent portion of a 4,920,000-square kilometre semi-submerged continent called Zealandia. The Southern Alps/Kā Tiritiri o te Moana have risen alongside the Alpine Fault, which splits that relatively thin block of continental crust in two. Its lofty watershed caps the northwest rim of South Zealandia, which is sliding past the southeast rim of North Zealandia. Recurrent earthquakes remind New Zealanders that this slow oblique collision is ongoing.

The South Island's axial watershed, the Main Divide of the Southern Alps/Kā Tiritiri o te Moana, obstructs the prevailing westerly winds in the Roaring Forties latitudes. When active fronts in that 'river of air' rise over the Alps most of the moisture in their clouds precipitates as rain or snow. Glaciers form above 2000 metres in snow accumulation zones called névés. Melt water from those rivers of ice sustain river flows during long summer droughts. When large rivers enter the sea their currents merge with the current of an offshore 'river of the ocean'. Evaporation from the ocean and moisture-laden clouds borne by onshore winds drive that never-ending, life-giving water cycle.

When I cottoned on to the fact that 24 rivers conduct all the water that runs off the Main Divide right down to the sea, I resolved to explore each river in reverse – like the early American explorers who ventured up rivers from the sea and likened them to trees with spreading branches – unsure what I would find. Whenever I reached a fork in a river, I ascended the banks of the biggest branch until I found the source of its 'master stream' on the Main Divide. The source of each river's master stream was not necessarily the farthest one from the place where the river enters the sea, but it was always near the highest cloud-catcher on the congruent section of the Main Divide. There were beautiful sights wherever I went and rock formations, landforms, and place names that revealed the longue durée history of each district. Those encounters strengthened my ties to the land and spiritual space was found in the barren places where land meets sea and sky.

The term 'landscape' was borrowed from Dutch *landshap* painters, to whom it meant 'rural district' or 'jurisdiction' as well as a picturesque scene. Place names receive considerable attention in this book because they capture the meaning and significance of landscape features that epitomise a particular area and exhibit profound respect for Nature. Recording old place names and traditions, which help us to see this country through the eyes of pioneer settlers, became the life's work of Herries Beattie (1881–1972). His publications were eye-openers for me. Ngāi Tahu's Kā Huru Manu website is a new authoritative source.

Te reo Māori place names are imbued with the traditional Pacific worldview: an ecosystem of atua, whenua, and iwi in which people, birds, trees, mountains, and rivers were kindred beings on different branches of the universal family tree that stemmed from the primal parents, Ranginui (the Sky Father) and Papatūānuku (the Earth Mother). Ranginui released mauri (the power that imparts growth and vitality) in rain and snow showers. Like water-seeking tree roots, long rivers brought mauri from the sacred summits of ancestor mountains near the heavens to human settlements near the sea and formed pathways into the interior.

The Main Divide and some long and formidable watersheds that radiate from it defined and defended the jurisdictions of tribal chiefs and papatipu rūnanga (tribal councils) empowered by inheritance and ancestral presences in territorial landmarks. The South Island's Land Registration Districts, Provinces, and Regions were based on the Crown Purchases of those chiefdoms between 1847 and 1860.

In 1840 just over 500 rangatira (hapū leaders) sought to end the spurious land sales that had fuelled the inter-tribal 'musket wars', make the 2000 foreign residents in their lands subject to British law, and gain the protection of Britain's navy by ceding kāwanatanga (governorship) through the Treaty of Waitangi to the British Monarch's local representatives.

In spite of the treaty's stipulation that rangatira would retain possession and rangatiratanga (lordship) of their lands, forests, and fisheries, Governor Grey and his successors wielded the Crown's prerogative to be the sole purchaser of Māori land and extorted the entire territory of every South Island tribe. Grey's experiences in South Australia had convinced him that wool exports would be the best way to boost New Zealand's economy and that if the vast, sparsely populated South Island grasslands were 'opened up' for sheep farms then his successors would be equipped to overcome the stiff resistance of North Island tribal leaders to further sales of their land.

In 1849 Grey extinguished Ngāi Tahu's 'customary title' to eight million hectares between the Otago and Wairau Blocks but only granted them Crown titles to 2570 hectares – a tiny fraction of the area that they had tried to retain. Most of the open country on the South Island's east coast was promptly on-sold to the British Land Settlement Companies that established the Nelson, Canterbury, and Otago Settlements.

The most distant source of the Wairau River, a tarn below Mt Dora, when I re-visited that charming spot with two of my children, Julian and Janet, and my regular tramping companion, Andrew Taylor-Perry, in March 1991. We lay on the short grass after dark, gazing up at an incredible number of stars.

Company surveyors and their provincial counterparts cut up most of the 'front country' into farm blocks with transferable Crown titles that would attract investors. Unoccupied land was usually treated as a blank canvas and peppered with English and Scottish place names as surveyors fixed the boundaries of Native Reserves and pastoral runs with similar stock capacities. Māori communities were marginalised and impoverished by the ensuing losses of land, food gathering rights, and cultural heritage.

In 1985 the New Zealand Government commissioned the Treaty of Waitangi Tribunal to address all unresolved claims against the Crown for breaches of that treaty since 1840. Most of the Crown Estate is now managed by the Department of Conservation in partnership with papatipu rūnunga. Recognition of te reo Māori as an official language in Aotearoa New Zealand and a growing list of bilingual place names signal a reappraisal of this nation's story.

The cycle of chapters in this book grounds that story in every region of the South Island Te Waipounamu and surveys its rich legacy of myths and memories through the lens of place names. Each chapter paints a full-length portrait of one of the 24 rivers that arise on this island's Main Divide, its water catchment area, and the lowest transalpine route between that river catchment and another one. The meaning and significance of the landscape features that I saw on each upriver journey are also canvassed. The Conservation Department's never-ending track maintenance work made this project possible and is greatly appreciated. I am also very grateful to my wife and other family members, my tramping and climbing companions, and my publisher and editor for their invaluable advice and support.

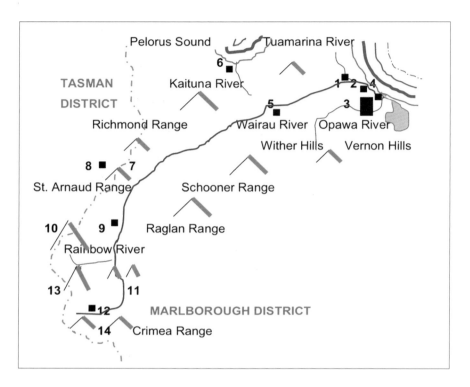

Legend

1. Tuamarina
2. Spring Creek
3. Blenheim
4. Wairau Bar
5. Renwick
6. Havelock
7. Wairau Pass/Maunga Tāwhai
8. St Arnaud village
9. Rainbow Accommodation House
10. Mt Mackay
11. Hell's Gate Gorge
12. Island Gully Hut
13. Mt Dora
14. Island Saddle

Chapter 1
The Wairau

One summer I drove to the end of Wairau Bar Road and walked along the rock training wall that directs the Wairau River into the centre of Cloudy Bay/Te Koko o Kupe. A lonely cloud on the northeast horizon hovered above a hill on the southern tip of the North Island/Te Ikanui o Māui (the great fish of Māui). A flock of kōau/shags was lined up on the opposite side of the river mouth drying their outstretched wings in the light sea breeze. That bank is the tip of the Boulder Bank/Te Pokohiwi (the shoulder), which stretches eight kilometres northward from the White Bluffs/Te Parinui o Whiti (the great cliff at the crossing over) at the seaward end of the Vernon Hills.

The stone cairn by the parking area near the Wairau River mouth marks the site of a short-lived settlement called **Wairau Bar (4)**, which sprang up in 1847 after the collapse of whale numbers and the abandonment of most of the nearby whaling stations in Port Underwood. Eight years later the magnitude 8.2 Wairarapa earthquake wrecked all its cob buildings.

There is no monument on the seven-hectare site at the tip of the Boulder Bank/Te Pokohiwi where one of the earliest settlements in this country was founded around 1280 CE. I pictured in my mind a twin-hulled waka moana crossing the Wairau Bar and anchoring in the deep side channel called Wāhanga a Tangaroa (the 'sea deity's portion') behind that spit. Every summer until the mid-fifteenth century those vessels used to cruise up and down the 'whale road' off the east coast of the North Island known as Tai Rāwhiti (the shore that received the first rays of the rising sun). At the eastern end of the inter-island strait waka helmsmen could have located the Wairau River mouth by steering to the right of White Bluff/Te Parinui o Whiti.

During the risky crossing of Cook Strait/Te Moana a Raukawa Māori seafarers used to wear kawakawa/*Macropiper excelsum* leaf blinkers to avoid the possibility of looking at the two islets named The Brothers/Ngā Whatu Kaipono, which were 'the guardian eyes' of a giant octopus named Whekenui. Meeting its baleful gaze might cause a squall that could capsize a waka.

In te reo Māori, *wai* means 'waters' and *rau* means 'leaves' or 'many'. Rangitāne elder Peter MacDonald recorded an alternative name for the Wairau River, Motukawa, and explained that the Wairau River carried kawakawa leaves from Motukawa Bush into the inter-island strait. When sea birds ate them they became drowsy and easy to catch.[1] Kawakawa wreaths are traditionally worn during funeral rites.

The Wairau River connects with Big Lagoon/Mataora and many other lagoons via Wāhanga a Tangaroa Channel. Some of those channels were dug centuries ago to snare moulting pārera/grey ducks and other native ducks in nooses that dangled from lines strung across them – and to catch tuna/eels in traps.[2]

The bones of approximately 8000 moa, native swans and geese have been found in the middens of that ancient kāinga (unfortified village). Those big heavy birds were either flightless or poor fliers and were driven to extinction within 200 years. More than 27 tonnes of pakohe/indurated siltstone flakes representing the manufacture of about 3000 stone tools have also been found on that site. Procuring blocks of that

The Wairau River mouth, where this upriver story began. The shingle spit on the opposite bank is the tip of the Boulder Bank/Te Pokohiwi. In the late 13th century a large settlement was established by a landing site on the lagoon side of this spit, which stretches eight kms south to White Bluff/Te Parinui o Whiti.

tough stone from D'Urville Island/Rangitoto ki te Tonga entailed perilous voyages out of phase with tidal rips in the inter-island strait. Finished wares were sent by sea to kith and kin in similar riparian settlements around the country. Regular manaaki (gift exchanges) strengthened ties between communities through 'munus' – the principle of reciprocity.

Gazing up the tidal reaches of the Wairau River I spotted the confluence of a navigable southern tributary called the Opawa (Ōpaoawai – 'place where water looks like smoke') River. Its dark, peat-stained current could be likened to a plume of smoke as it slowly merged with the pale, silt-laden current of the Wairau River after its upper catchment was drenched with rain.

The original names of many landmarks around Cook Strait/Te Moana a Raukawa highlight its associations with Kupe, the great trailblazing ancestor of the Kurahaupō tribes. The long promontory by the entrance to Queen Charlotte Sound/Totaranui represents his spear. Kupe immobilised the kaitiaki (guardian) of that strait, Whekenui, by hacking off its tentacles. He then steered his waka *Matahourua* into Cloudy Bay/Te Koko o Kupe to harvest clams with a koko (dredge). The chief of this island's semi-mythical first settlers, the Kāhui Tipua, furiously built a reef in front of Kupe's waka by hurling rocks from his home, Kohanga o Haumia, on White Bluff/Te Parinui o Whiti.[3]

Kupe demolished that barrier with his toki (adze), after which massive waves whipped up by those blows swept onto the land; however the Wairau Lagoons and Lake Grassmere/Kāpara o Te Haumianui (the food-stores of Hauminui, father of Haumia) remained on either side of the Vernon Hills when the sea withdrew. Arapaoa (downward strikes) was an alternative name for the South Island and the original name of Arapawa Island between the two entrances of Queen Charlotte Sound/ Tōtaranui.

Peter MacDonald also stated that giant waves had destroyed three ancient kāinga – Moua, Te Ara o Pipi, and Motueka – on the Boulder Bank/Te Pokohiwi. There is buried evidence that two huge tsunami or storm surges swamped this area around 1300 and 1500 CE.[4]

The waka *Kurahaupō* carried Kupe's son and many forebears of Ngāi Tara and Rangitāne across Te Moananui o Kiwi/the Pacific Ocean from Hawaiki by the mythical pit that Te Rā (the sun) rose from to Te Rāwhiti in Aotearoa. As the Kurahaupō tribes expanded across the lower North Island the residents of Heretaunga/Hawke's Bay, Ngāti Māmoe, were pushed south to Wairarapa. In the late fifteenth century they crossed the inter-island strait, seized control of the Wairau district, and absorbed its Waitaha residents. Rangitāne migrants from Manawatū subsequently pushed them even further south.

In 1828 Ngāti Toa warriors from the west coast of the North Island led by Te Rauparaha destroyed Rangitāne's Te Kōwhai pā near the mouth of the Wairau River and seized control of the Wairau district. In 1847 Governor George Grey arrested Te Rauparaha and negotiated the three million-acre Wairau Purchase with other Ngāti Toa rangatira for £3000. Frustrated graziers in the landlocked Nelson Settlement quickly snapped up every farm block on the plain beyond the swampy 770-acre Wairau Pā Reserve near the river mouth.

Manawhenua has been defined as the strength and authority that an established Māori community draws from its ancestral land and every past and present connection and association with it. Marlborough District Council has jurisdiction in the Wairau Catchment. Ngāti Toa Rangatira and Ngāti Rārua ki te Wairau, and Kurahaupō ki te Waipounamu representing Rangitāne o Wairau, hold manawhenua there.

After watching the Wairau River flow into the sea, I hopped into my car and followed Wairau Bar Road back along the north stopbank and over the Ferry Bridge to **Spring Creek** village **(2)**. There I turned left onto State Highway 1 and proceeded over the Opawa Bridge into **Blenheim (3)**, which has been the hub of Marlborough District and its county and provincial forerunners since the 1860s. Local wags called it Beavertown when it sprang up on a flood-prone site called Waiharakeke (flax water), which was as far as a flat-bottom scow could sail up the Opawa River. After a rail link was established with the Port of Picton in 1875 scows continued to visit Blenheim until its port status was revoked in 1967.

Under New Zealand's 1853 constitution, every province had to have a 'deep seaport'. Picton Harbour in Queen Charlotte Sound/Tōtaranui enabled the eastern half of Nelson Province to secede in 1859 and become Marlborough Province. Governor Gore Browne chose to maintain the patriotic military theme of Nelson, Wellington, and Picton by naming the new province after the Duke of Marlborough, who led the British and Dutch forces that defeated their French and Bavarian foes at Blenheim (Blindheim) in Bavaria in the War of the Spanish Succession.

The first coach road between Blenheim and Nelson opened via Rai Saddle on the Bryant Range/Maunga Tapu in 1885. However, many travellers continued to catch a ferry from Nelson to Picton and a train from there to Blenheim until the 1920s. If they were travelling to Canterbury they usually caught a train to Glenhope, a service car to

Inangahua, then another train to Greymouth and then the next day's train to Christchurch.

In May 1968 my father and I drove off the *Aramoana*, which was the first roll-on-roll-off ferry between Wellington and Picton and then followed SH1 from Picton to Blenheim and SH6 up the Wairau Valley, before it became a sea of vineyards. On the way, Dad told me about his bus trip from Hokitika to Blenheim to be inducted into the Armed Forces at Meadowbank Camp when he was my age, in 1942.

SH6 turns north in **Renwick (5)**, then crosses the Wairau River and a very low saddle on the Richmond Range and descends the Kaituna (meal of tuna/eels) Valley to **Havelock (6)** at the head of Pelorus Sound/ Te Hoiere en route to Nelson. The Kaituna River is a former tributary of the Wairau River that reversed direction when the Whanganui Basin at the western end of Cook Strait/Te Moana a Raukawa sank and the entire Marlborough Sounds Block dipped towards it. The sea invaded its valleys and turned them into Pelorus Sound/Te Hoiere and Queen Charlotte Sound/Tōtaranui.

We carried on driving up the Wairau Valley from Renwick on SH63, which crosses the Main Divide via Wairau Pass/Maunga Tāwhai and rejoins SH6 at Kawatiri Junction in the Buller/Kawatiri Valley. It follows the route of the old Wairau Stock Track from Nelson to Renwick, which was upgraded for motor traffic in 1926. The Schooner Range on the southern side of that section of the Wairau Valley consists of hard but brittle sandstone called greywacke (grauwacke in German; onawe in te reo Māori). Its grass- and scree-clad slopes contrast sharply with the more stable, bush-clad, Richmond Range on the northern side of the valley. That mountain range is part of the Marlborough Sounds Block, which consists of a harder material, low-grade schist laced here and there with seams of gold-bearing quartz.

Seventy kilometres southwest of Renwick we crossed the Wash Bridge at the base of Mount Chrome, where the Bryant Range joins the Richmond Range. High soil concentrations of nickel and magnesium on the eastern spur of Mount Chrome called Red Hills Ridge stunts the mānuka scrub on its southern slopes, which are studded with reddish outcrops of olivine-rich hartzburgerite. Chromite ore has been found there and on Dun Mountain behind Nelson, where it was mined in the 1860s.

Rushpool Quarry by the ancient Maungatapu Trail over the Bryant Range just north of Dun Mountain/Maungatapu is littered with flakes of pakohe/indurated siltstone. Māori explorers found that stone near some conspicuous reddish rock outcrops on the hills on the eastern side of Tasman Bay/Whakatū. Tough tremolite fibres had migrated into pakohe/indurated siltstone from dunite (pure olivine) rocks when they were subjected to extreme heat and pressure at great depth near the earth's mantle. The tremolite content of pakohe made it ideal for making toki (adzes). A few small lenses of a tougher stone, pounamu/nephrite, with a greater content of tremolite are also present in that area.

Many years later I hiked up a dirt road from the derelict Red Hills homestead on the eastern side of Wairau Pass/Maunga Tāwhai to the crest of Red Hills Ridge and saw olive-green rock beneath the chipped surface of a very weathered, rust-red outcrop of olivine-rich hartzburgerite where its 'mafic' (magnesium-ferrous iron) content had oxidised. Red Hills Ridge is the southernmost portion of the northern Dun Mountain Ultramafic Belt, which runs 70 kilometres due north from the Wairau Valley to D'Urville Island/Rangitoto ki te Tonga. It is a slice of the earth's deep mantle that was obducted (thrust up) to the surface about 200 million years ago when two converging blocks of Continental Crust crumpled up a forerunner of the Southern Alps/Kā Tiritiri o te Moana and obliterated an old subduction (down thrust) system, which re-formed elsewhere.

Eighty-five million years ago the crustal convergence regime in this part of the planet ran in reverse for 65 million years. Zealandia was peeled off Australia and stretched out into a less buoyant five-million-square kilometre continent, which slowly submerged. When crustal convergence was re-established Zealandia tore in half along the Alpine Fault. North Zealandia stayed on the Australian Plate, but South Zealandia was on the rotating rim of the Pacific Plate and an oblique collision ensued.

The northeast end of the Alpine Fault splays out into the Hope, Clarence, Awatere, and Wairau Faults. They sequentially 'transform' into the Hikurangi Trench off the North Island's east coast where descending slabs of basaltic Oceanic Crust, which had emerged from a mid-ocean rift, dives back to its hot viscous source. The Schooner Range is one of the high rugged ranges that have crumpled up between those four branch faults in what geologist Pat Suggate called the 'Marlborough Shear Zone'. It walls Marlborough off from other east coast districts.

Geologist Harold Wellman deduced that the Nelson and Otago Ultramafic Belts were once contiguous and had been drawn 500 kilometres apart by strike-slip (sideways) movements on the Alpine Fault, which he and David Willett had described and named in 1942. Red Hills Ridge and the Richmond Range on the northern side of the Wairau Branch of the Alpine Fault sit on the southeast rim of North Zealandia. The Schooner Range sits on the northwest rim of South Zealandia.

My father and I followed SH63 over the Wash Bridge and then up the north bank of the Wairau River and over **Wairau Pass/Maunga Tāwhai (7)** between Red Hills Ridge and the northern end of the St Arnaud Range, which is also the northern end of the Main Divide. At 695 metres above sea level, the summit of that pass is the lowest spot on the portion of the Main Divide that bounds the water catchment area of the Wairau River. We then drove on to Greymouth via Inangahua and Reefton. Twelve hours later the magnitude 7.1 Inangahua earthquake triggered massive landslides that blocked the upper Buller Gorge section of SH6 for months.

The original name of Wairau Pass/Maunga Tāwhai (tāwhai/beech mountain) referred to its two distinctive wooded sentinels: the St Arnaud Range to the south and Beebys Knob on Red Hills Ridge to the north. The Nelson Settlement, which was founded around Tasman Bay/Whakatū in 1841, was separated from the Sounds and Wairau districts by the Bryant Range/Maungatapu, which runs due north from Mount Chrome at the eastern end of Red Hills Ridge. The crest of that longitudinal barrier marked the boundary between Nelson and Marlborough Provinces from 1859 until 1876. Since 1989 it has been the boundary-marker between Tasman and Marlborough Districts.

The view of Wairau Pass/Maunga
Tāwhai (695m) on the Main Divide,
before driving across it on SH63 from
the Wairau Valley. The roadside cairn
commemorates the first Nelson settlers
to drive a mob of sheep over this pass.

Modern roads follow the routes of two ancient trails that diverged
from the Wairau Valley trail on Wairau Pass/Maunga Tāwhai. One trail
ran north to Tai o Aorere (the coast of scudding clouds); the other trail
ran west past Rotoiti (little lake) and Rotoroa (big lake) to Tai Poutini
(Poutini's Coast). Those two lakes occupy the first of many hapua
(hollows) containing springs called Kā Puna karikari a Rākaihautū that
the giant commander of the Kāhui Tipua waka *Uruao*, Rākaihautū, had
excavated with his great kō (spade) during his epic north-south journey
through the interior of this island. He was the great trailblazing ancestor
of its first residents and their descendants, the Waitaha iwi. Taare Te
Maiharoa told Herries Beattie that many of them had disembarked
from the *Uruao* at the mouth of the Wairau River. Some of Rākaihautū's
companions became tūpuna maunga (ancestor mountains). Many east
coast rivers issue from large lakes in some of the hapua that he dug
throughout the high country.

In January 1842 a local Māori guide led two Nelson surveyors, John
Cottrell and Richard Peanter, along the old trail from Tasman Bay to

Wairau Pass/Maunga Tāwhai via Big Bush in the Motupiko Branch of the Motueka Valley. Cotterill subsequently crossed and re-named that pass and descended the Wairau Valley to the east coast. He died a year later at **Tuamarina (1)** by the lower Wairau River when the New Zealand Land Company's Nelson agent, Colonel William Wakefield, led a party of surveyors with an armed escort of 'special constables' to the Wairau Plain, which the company coveted but had not formally purchased. Ngāti Toa rangatira Te Rangihaeata and his veteran warriors confronted them and 23 Nelson settlers, including Wakefield, were killed in the ensuing battle.

As soon as the Wairau Purchase was finalised in 1847 Nelson-based surveyors carved up the Wairau Plain into 150-acre farm blocks and the Wairau Trail became a busy drove road. A stone cairn beside SH63 commemorates two squatters, John Cooper and Nathaniel Morse, who pastured the first sheep in the Wairau Valley in 1846.

SH63 follows Black Valley Stream down the gentle western slopes of Wairau Pass/Maunga Tāwhai to Lake Rotoiti and then follows the banks of the Buller/Kawatiri River to the confluence of the Hope River at Kawatiri Junction, where it rejoins SH6. Lake Rotoiti laps the terminal moraine that the Buller Glacier had deposited during the Ōtira Glaciation, or 'Ice Age', which lasted about 60,000 years and ended 13,000 years ago. About 220,000 years ago, in the Waimea Glaciation, the Buller Glacier had pushed through the pass and merged with the Wairau Glacier, which extended to the base of Mount Chrome.

In January 1993 my wife Evelyn and I spent a week in **St Arnaud village (8)** on the southern shore of Lake Rotoiti. John Cotterill had surveyed it in 1842 and climbed a peak on the St Arnaud Range to look for a gap in the rugged mountains on the southern border of the Nelson Settlement. His Māori guide did not tell him about the old Kopi o Uenuku trail to the Amuri Plain, which was rediscovered in 1855. The Rainbow Road follows the route of that trail along the banks of the upper Wairau River. It flows northward until the Wairau Branch of the Alpine Fault deflects it onto a north-easterly course towards the inter-island strait from the base of Wairau Pass/Maunga Tāwhai. The furthest source of the Wairau River was an easy hike from the Rainbow Road so I obtained permission from Rainbow Run holders Phillip and Allison Graham to cycle along it. The public section of that road ended at a locked gate by the turn-off to the Rainbow Ski Area. I lifted my bicycle over it and pedalled on through a tāwhai/beech enclave of Rainbow State Forest.

The forerunner of the Rainbow Road was the Amuri stock track from Wairau Pass to the Hanmer and Amuri Plains, which was constructed in the 1860s. It was upgraded to a road in the 1950s to erect and service the 220-kilovolt transmission lines that plug Buller and Tasman Districts into the national grid. The 'hydro camp' in Dip Flat was built to house the pylon riggers. In 1958 the Animal Control Section of the Forest Service turned it into a training camp for deer cullers. The Rainbow Road also improved access to the Rainbow Run, which was part of the 26,000-hectare Rainbow Station in the 1990s. It is now the Rainbow Recreation Reserve.

The air temperature rose as the sun climbed into a clear blue sky. I picked a cupful of raspberries that had spread along the roadside from an old garden and consumed them under the veranda of the 1874 **Rainbow Accommodation House (9)** in Irishmans Flat. Cattle had evidently tasted traces of salt in the building's cob walls and had licked some deep grooves in them.

At the top of Irishmans Flat the road crossed the boulder-studded terminal moraine that the Wairau Glacier had deposited during the Ōtira Glaciation. Just beyond that ridge lay the site of the first Rainbow hostel, which burned down. After skirting Connor Bluff the road entered Rainbow Flat where the Wairau River is joined by a large tributary called the Rainbow River. The Wairau River enters this flat through **Hell's Gate Gorge/Kopi o Uenuku (11)** between the Raglan Range and a spur of the Crimea Range called Turk Ridge.

Nelson lawyer, ex-soldier, and amateur naturalist William Travers maintained the military theme of colonial place names at the top of the South Island by naming the Raglan and St Arnaud Ranges on either side of the upper Wairau River after the commanders of the British and French armies that invaded Crimea in 1854 to deter Czar Nicholas I of Russia from expanding his empire into the Balkans and the Middle East.

The Crimean port Sebastopol was still under siege when Travers explored this area with Robert Strange in the autumn of 1855. His Ngāti Toa guide, Nopera, told him that the Wairau Gorge and the adjacent Tarndale-Wairau Saddle was called Kopi o Uenuku (Gorge of

Uenuku).[5] The appearance of that ancestral spirit's aria (epiphany), a giant rainbow, behind a war party was a tohu pai (good omen). Some said that Rainbow Flat was named after a drover who left 8000 ewes there. When he returned they had all disappeared.[6]

I crossed the Wairau River via a concrete bridge to Rainbow Station's old bull paddock at the eastern end of Rainbow Flat and then followed the Rainbow Road into Hell's Gate Gorge. That name, which was written on a signpost, originally referred to the portal to the underworld at Cumae in Italy in John Dryden's translation of Virgil's Latin poem 'The Aeneid':

> The Gates of Hell stand open night and day;
> Smooth the descent and easy is the way;
> But to return and view the cheerful skies,
> In this, the task and mighty labour lies.

After negotiating Hell's Gate Gorge/Kopi o Uenuku, I followed the Rainbow Road back across the Wairau River and then up onto a high terrace covered with pātiti/silver tussock, which rippled in the warm nor'west breeze. From that height I could peer over Tarndale-Wairau Saddle at the head of that gorge into Tarndale, which is in the Acheron Catchment of the Clarence River/Waiau toa. The upper Wairau River flows along the crush zone of the Awatere Fault between the Crimea Range and Turk Ridge until the Raglan Fault re-directs it onto a northward course at the base of that saddle. The Awatere Fault line carries straight on through Tarndale and the Awatere Valley to the inter-island strait. During the Last Ōtira Glaciation, silt-laden meltwater from the Wairau Glacier carved Hell's Gate Gorge.

When Travers was planning to search for potential routes through the mountain ranges at the head of the Wairau Valley the superintendent of Nelson Province asked his friend Frederick Weld to follow up persistent reports of an ancient trail from the head of the Wairau Valley to grassy inland plains in the southern sector of Nelson Province known as the Amuri District. Pastoral runs had been surveyed there but the only stock route from Nelson that drovers were aware of crossed Wairau Pass/Maunga Tāwhai and ran down the Wairau Valley to the east coast, then up the Awatere Valley, down the Acheron Valley and over Jollies

Pass/Ōmiromiro to the Hanmer and Amuri Plains. Weld and his cousin, Alphonso Clifford, climbed Mount Turk from Rainbow Flat and spied a grassy basin dotted with lakelets, which Weld named Tarndale.

A few days later Travers' party waded through Hell's Gate Gorge/ Kopi o Uenuku. His Māori guide, Nopera, had followed the elusive inland trail to the Amuri Plain with a band of Ngāti Koata warriors led by Te Whare o Te Riri in the summer of 1831–32. Their Rangitāne guides had scores of their own to settle with Ngāi Tahu. At the end of that journey they had joined a band of Ngāti Rārua warriors led by Te Niho, who had crossed an alpine pass from the west coast, and a sea-borne host from Kāpiti Island led by Ngāti Toa war-leader Te Rauparaha. The combined forces proceeded to attack the Kaiapoi stronghold of Ngāi Tahu's paramount chief Te Maiharanui.

In the 1880s a chain of cob accommodation houses was built beside the Rainbow Track between Tophouse Hotel on Wairau Pass/Maunga Tāwhai and Jollies Pass Hotel. The distance between these hostels reflected the average distance that sheep could be driven in one day. Local run holders agreed to service these properties in exchange for additional grazing rights. In 1880 the Hell's Gate section of the so-called 'Main South Road' from Nelson was upgraded, however, it was still too rough for passenger coaches. Tarndale experiences approximately 260 frosts per year so the Tarndale Accommodation House beside Lake Sedgemere on the Tarndale-Wairau Saddle was sorely missed after it burnt down.

I carried on cycling along the Rainbow Road, which had returned to the south bank of the Wairau River. After passing the base of Mount Balaclava it ascended Island Gully, which was named after a rock outcrop, to **Island Saddle (14)** on the Crimea Range en route to the Clarence/Waiau toa Valley. **Island Gully Hut (12)** at the bottom of that gully was built by the Forest Service for its deer cullers and has been well maintained by members of the fishing fraternity.

After hiding my bike in the tall haumata/snow tussock or 'elephant grass' behind Island Gully Hut I continued my journey to the source of the Wairau River on foot. On the way I spied a rare penwiper/ *Notothlaspi rosulatum* plant with fragrant flowers in the gap that the river had carved through an 11,500-year-old terminal moraine in the centre of a long flat. Cows and their calves were grazing nearby. At the top of the flat I climbed a steep cattle track next to a waterfall and entered a narrow glen between the Crimea Range and Turk Ridge, which unite on **Mt Dora (13)**; the Crimea Range joins the Main Divide on Mount Belvedere. Pressing on through the tall tussock, I flushed a Canada goose and nearly stood on a hedgehog.

The 169-kilometre continuous above-ground course of the Wairau River began at the end of a trail of boulders. They had tumbled out of the valley's head cirque, which had once held the névé of the Wairau Glacier. When the ice that steadily accumulated in that basin during one of the glaciations descended against the basin's back wall, rocks were plucked off it until parts of that wall collapsed. Geologists have concluded that this mechanism usually prevents mountains from exceeding a height of 600 metres above the highest cirque on their flanks.[7]

When I reached the top of the trail of boulders I saw the infant Wairau River emerge from a string of small tarns in the valley's head cirque. Mount Dora towered 600 metres above it. Daylight was swiftly fading and I failed to notice that dark clouds had filled the sky until raindrops began to splatter on my head. I found a cubbyhole under a giant boulder and spent a dry but sleepless night tucked up inside it.

At dawn there was a short lull in the storm and I managed to reach Island Gully Hut before the next bout of driving rain and gale-force winds. The sky cleared overnight. Ten minutes after leaving the hut I had to push my bike over a huge pile of shingle that floodwater had sluiced out of the Rag and Famish Gully during yesterday's storm. I wondered what lay around the next bend.

After closing the gate between Molesworth and Rainbow Stations I spotted the figure of an elderly man lying beside the road. Sitting up as I drew closer, he explained in a shaky voice that he had spent a sleepless night under a bush after abandoning his car when it became stuck in the bed of a swollen side stream. He had driven over Jacks Pass and mistakenly turned left and headed up the Rainbow Road instead of turning right onto his intended route, the Molesworth Road. I lent him my parka for warmth and biked back to a farm cottage that I had passed a short time ago. Luckily a fencer and his wife happened to be staying there and they were able to pick up the distressed traveller in their ute

Mt Mackay (2,300m) with a cap of snow
on the Main Divide above the head
cirque of the Rainbow Valley. The infant
Rainbow River, which is the master stream
of the Wairau River, cascaded past my
campsite in the last grove of trees.

and drive him to the medical centre in Hanmer Springs. His car was engulfed up to its axles in the bed of Judges Creek when I rode past it.

When Evelyn and I stayed in St Arnaud village in 1991 I ventured up the banks of the Rainbow River, which is the master stream (principal headwater) of the Wairau River and arises on the Main Divide. Sometime in the future, when Alpine Fault movements have dragged the Raglan and St Arnaud Ranges 10 kilometres southwestward, the Rainbow River may become the master stream of the Buller River/Kawatiri on the west coast.

I cycled to Rainbow Flat, stowed my bicycle behind a big boulder, and then headed up the Rainbow Valley on 'shanks' pony'. Three stoats crouching under a tumatakuru/matagouri bush were the only animals that I spotted on that long grassy flat. At the top of that flat I picked up a bulldozed stock track and followed it around a short gorge to the high summer pastures that the Swiss-German word Alpen (Alps) primarily refers to. Two tributaries joined the Rainbow River above that gorge: Paske Stream on the left drained the grassy slopes below Paske Saddle on the Crimea Range; Begley Stream on the right drained the wooded flanks of the northern portion of the Main Divide called the St Arnaud Range.

The Rainbow River approached that double confluence though a gap in a terminal moraine that the Rainbow Glacier had deposited after the Ōtira Glaciation. I pressed on through the tāwhairauriki/mountain beech woods on its east bank. An hour later I spied the infant Rainbow River cascading out of the valley's head cirque at the base of **Mt Mackay (10)**. At 2300 metres above sea level, the summit of that peak is the highest point in the water catchment area of the Wairau River and on the portion of the Main Divide that bounds it. I pitched my little tent by the last grove of trees just before the sun disappeared behind the Main Divide.

In the morning I took the route up the eastern side of Mount Mackay that Barrie Preston had described in the Nelson Lakes National Park Handbook. From the top of the grassy spur behind my campsite I crossed a scree slope below a line of bluffs, then traversed a rock ledge and scrambled up the next scree to the crest of the Main Divide. Stepping cautiously on unstable, frost-shattered rocks and patches of soft snow, I followed that watershed southward to the summit of Mount Mackay.

In 1857 Poutini Ngāi Tahu hapū leaders sent a letter to Governor Grey that included a list of pou rāhui (boundary markers) on the rohe (boundary) of their northern domains on the west coast. They asserted that they had re-established manawhenua there after the withdrawal of Ngāti Rārua and Ngāti Tama forces.[8] The place name Waripa, which appeared on that list between Maruia and Matakitaki, could be a contraction of Whā ripa (four ridges). If that were the case then it could refer to the contiguous Freyberg and Spenser Ranges and three other western components of the nexus of lofty ridges called the Spenser Knot plus all its peaks. Three of the nine major east coast rivers that I wanted to trace back to their alpine sources arise in that 'horst block', which is being squeezed up like a pip between the Wairau, Raglan, and Awatere Faults.

James Mackay acquired the 1500-acre Farewell Spit Run after the Pakawau Purchase was finalised by Major Richmond in 1853. Mackay's knowledge of the backcountry and fluency in te reo Māori led to his appointment as the first warden of the Aorere Goldfield in 1858. He was subsequently appointed Assistant Native Secretary to Governor Gore Browne, who sent him to the west coast in 1860 to conduct the Arahura Purchase negotiations on behalf of the Crown. He set off from Nelson and caught up with two young geologists, James Burnett and Julius Haast, by the outlet of Lake Rotoiti. They had been sent to survey the economic resources of the southwestern portion of Nelson Province. Haast named Mount Mackay when he climbed a mountain near Lake Rotoroa to view the lie of the land.

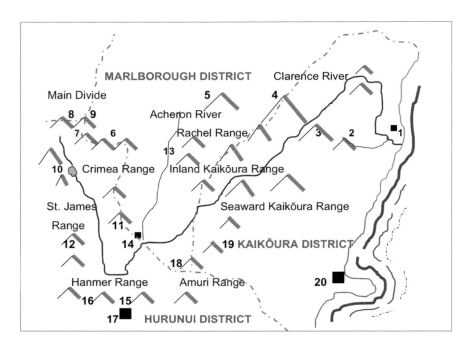

Legend

1. Clarence
2. Puhi Saddle
3. Te Ao Whekere
4. Tapuwae o Uenuku
5. Maungatere/Shingle Peak
6. Island Saddle
7. Mt Guinevere
8. Clarence Pass
9. Belvedere Peak
10. Maling Pass
11. Five Mile Saddle
12. Peters Pass
13. Wards Pass
14. Acheron Accommodation House
15. Jollies Pass/Ōmiromiro
16. Jacks Pass
17. Hanmer Springs
18. Mt Lyford
19. Blind Saddle
20. Kaikōura

Chapter 2
The Clarence / Waiau toa

In May 1997 my friend Andrew Taylor-Perry and his daughter Natasha joined me in Hanmer Springs (17) for a transalpine trip from the Clarence River/Waiau toa Valley to Lake Rotoroa in the Buller/Kawatiri Valley via Clarence Pass. My daughter Janet very kindly agreed to meet us in Sabine Forks Hut on the other side of the Main Divide in order to drive us back to our starting point.

Next day we drove over **Jacks Pass (16)** on the Hanmer Range portion of the long fold range between the Hope and Clarence faults in the Marlborough Shear Zone (see Page 20). On the other side of that pass we turned left and followed the Rainbow Road up the true right bank of the section of the Clarence River/Waiau toa that follows the crush zone of the Elliot branch of the Clarence Fault. The river valley veered north by the site of the first St James homestead but the Elliot Fault maintained its south-westward course and crossed **Peters Pass (11)** on the St James Range to the Edwards Branch of the Waiau uwha Valley, where it reunited with the Clarence Fault.

The upper Clarence River flows southward from its Main Divide source flanked by the St James Range to the west and the Crimea and Boddington Ranges to the east until the Elliot branch of the Clarence Fault redirects that river onto a northeastward course towards the Pacific Ocean. The surface trace of main Clarence Fault crosses **Five Mile Saddle (12)** on the Boddington Range and Edwards Pass on the St James Range.

That northeast-southwest alignments of rivers and ranges in the Marlborough Shear Zone contrasts sharply with the north-south alignments of the majority of rivers and ranges that radiate from the Main Divide. The latter pattern reflects the angle at which the greywacke basement rock had rumpled up like a rug between 145 and 100 million years ago during the major mountain-building era called the Rangitata Orogeny. Those precursors of the Southern Alps/Kā Tiri o te Moana were scraped off the basalt basement of the Pacific Plate as it slipped into a subduction zone under the rim of Gondwanaland. The superimposed northeast-southwest array of fault lines and fold ranges reflects the more oblique angle of impact of the Pacific Plate on the Australian Plate during the Kaikōura Orogeny, which is on-going.

The upper Clarence River/Waiau toa marks the boundary between Molesworth Station, which was redesignated as a Recreation Reserve in 2015, and St James Station, which became a Conservation Area in 2008. We drove past Fowlers Hut at the base of a 1296-metre dip on the St James Range called Fowlers Pass. In the 1870s William Fowler drove his sheep over that pass from Stanleyvale Station in the upper Waiau uwha Valley to a pen beside his Clarence Valley woolshed where they were shorn. Fowlers Hut was built on that site to accommodate the fencer who maintained part of the rabbit-proof fence that once stretched 174 kilometres from Lake Tennyson/Rangatahi to the Waiau uwha River mouth.

The Awatere Fault splits into two branches in the upper Wairau Valley. One branch crosses a dip on the Crimea Range between Mount Maling and Crystal Peak; the other branch crosses 1347-metre **Island Saddle (6)** on the same range. The two branches reunite in a small flat by the outlet of Lake Tennyson/Rangitahi in the upper Waiau uwha Valley and then cross **Maling Pass (10)** on the St James Range to the upper Waiau uwha Valley.

James Mackay recorded the original name of Lake Tennyson/ Rangitahi (one day) on the Kaikōura Purchase deed. It was the third puna (spring or waterhole) that the Waitaha ancestor Rākaihautū had dug on his journey through the island's interior (see Page 21). In the autumn of 1855 Frederick Weld crossed Tarndale and continued his search for potential stock routes between Nelson and Canterbury with an employee named McCabe, who had joined him in the Acheron Valley after Clifford's departure (see Page 24).

They subsequently explored the upper Clarence/Waiau toa Valley, which Weld had glimpsed from a hilltop near Five Mile Saddle on his first venture into the maze of ranges beyond the head of the Awatere Valley. He was so disorientated at the time that he thought he was gazing into the Leader Branch of the Waiau uwha Valley and called the valley on the other side of that pass the Leaderdale. Before he and McCabe returned to Nelson via Island Saddle, they visited the lake called Rangitahi, which was dotted with pūtangitangi/paradise shelducks, kōwhiowhio/blue ducks, and tete/grey teal.[9] Weld renamed it after England's poet-laureate, Alfred Tennyson, and the high mountain behind it after Tennyson's poem 'The Princess', which sings of the horns of Elfland faintly blowing among crags and waterfalls. A subsidiary peak was named after McCabe.

Low terminal moraine ridges hem the southern shore of Lake Tennyson/Rangitahi, which filled part of the vacant bed of the Clarence Glacier at the end of the Ōtira Glaciation.

We left our vehicle in the frosty car park by the outlet of that lake and followed fresh cattle tracks along its partly wooded eastern shore. The only birds that we saw there were Canada geese; high country farmers call them 'flying rabbits'. After skirting the lake shore we weaved our way between haumata/snow tussocks and thorny tumatakuru/matagouri bushes on the banks of the diminutive Clarence River. A few cattle eyed us from the last grove of tāwhairauriki/mountain beech trees.

We then crossed the low terminal moraine that the re-invigorated

Clarence Glacier had left at the bases of Mounts Guinevere and Dora about 1500 years after the Ōtira Glaciation. Shortly afterwards the sun dipped behind the St James Range and the air temperature dropped. A talus slope below a formidable line of bluffs confronted us at the head of the valley. The infant Clarence River/Waiau toa trickled over a low bluff to the right of the scree at the start of its 230-kilometre journey to the sea.

Clarence (1) place names in Australia and New Zealand ultimately refer to the 1362 nuptials of Lionel of Antwerp, the third son of King Edward III, and Elizabeth de Burgh, heiress to the Clare estate in West Suffolk, which bore the old Celtic river-name Clare or Clere (bright stream). Lionel became the first *Dux Clarensis* (Duke of Clarence). Another Duke of Clarence was the third son of George III, the Earl of Munster, who became King William IV in 1830. He joined the Royal Navy at the age of 13 and was popular with seafarers.

The first European settlers usually called this river the Waipapa or Big River. Frederick Weld advocated renaming it the Clarence River. Its original name, Waiau toa, means 'male fast-flowing water' – beware!

An Aeromacchi jet trainer screamed overhead as we slogged up the snow-covered scree slope until we gained enough height to sidle into the boulder-filled head cirque above the bluff on the right. The west face of **Belvedere Peak (9)** at the head of that basin was bathed in bright sunlight that streamed through a dip on the Main Divide called **Clarence Pass (8)**. At 1850 metres above sea level, it is the lowest point on the three-kilometre portion of the Main Divide in the centre of the 'Spenser Knot' that bounds the water catchment of the Clarence River. The highest point is the 2114-metre summit of Belvedere Peak. The boundary between Marlborough District and Canterbury Region follows the crests of the Inland Kaikōura, Boddington, and Crimea Ranges and joins the Main Divide on Belvedere Peak.

As we approached the crest of Clarence Pass my boots kept slipping on ice underneath 20 centimetres of powder snow. The sun slipped below the western skyline for the second time that day when we stepped onto the Main Divide. We wasted no time in descending the comparatively bare slopes on the far side to the banks of the infant East Sabine tributary of the Buller/Kawatiri River, which arose at the

Belvedere Pk (2,114m) and Clarence
Pass (1,850m) on the Main Divide
before I crossed it with Andrew and
his daughter Natasha from the head
cirque of the Clarence/Waiau toa
Valley where this river arises.

base of Mount Mackay. After following it by torchlight for an hour we
eventually found a level campsite.

Mount Dora and **Mount Guinevere (7),** the twin apices of the Crimea
Range, are separated from Mount Belvedere (beautiful outlook) by
Paske Saddle, which connects with the Rainbow Branch of the Wairau
Valley. Dora and Guinevere were the titles of two long poems by Alfred
Tennyson. The name Dora also calls to mind the actress Dora Jordan
who lived with the Duke of Clarence for 20 years. Their 10 children
were surnamed FitzClarence. A 10-member Tararua Tramping Club
party made the first recorded crossing of Clarence Pass en route from
Lake Rotoiti to Hanmer Springs in the summer of 1948–49.[10]

In October 2014 Evelyn and I embarked on a family rafting trip down the
Clarence River/Waiau toa. The Clarence River Rafting Company provided

the rafts and guides; we provided the paddle-power. Ellis Emmett was the trip leader. On day one we drove to **Hanmer Springs (17)**, then over **Jacks Pass (16)** on the Hanmer Range and down the Molesworth Road to the Acheron Bridge by the confluence of the Acheron River. The old cob **Acheron Accommodation House (14)** on the opposite bank was used by drovers on the forerunner of this road, the Awatere Stock Track over **Wards Pass (13)** on the Rachel Range and **Jollies Pass/Ōmiromiro (15)** on the Hanmer Range. Its identifier, Ōmiromiro (haunt of tomtits), is the prominent peak on its eastern side. William Hamilton, the cartographer on the survey ship *Acheron,* obtained a list of landmarks on the old inland trail between Kaiapoi and Kapara Te Hau/Lake Grassmere from an unidentified resident of the Awatere district. It ascended the Awatere Valley and crossed the Hanmer Range via Jollies Pass or Hossack Saddle on either side of Ōmiromiro.[11]

When all the food and gear was stowed on the two rafts we cast off. After drifting past the confluences of the Dillon and Hossack Rivers, the current of the Clarence River/Waiau toa drew us into the first gorge, which bisects a northern spur of the Amuri Range near **Mount Lyford (18)**. Shooting the rapids in that canyon was our first test in co-ordinated paddling. We managed to stay afloat and later set up our first camp on the eastern side of that spur, which was named the Bullen Hills after local run holders.

On day two we watched tarapiroe/black-fronted terns swoop back and forth across the river catching insects. After traversing the sinuous second gorge between two basalt outcrops called The Observatory and The Warder, we pitched our tents in Quail Flat then inspected the old Warden homestead and its large outdoor oven. The residents measured the passage of time by the positions of shadows on Clockface Hill on the opposite side of the river. Behind that homestead rose the Gridiron Hills, which are roasting hot in high summer. They contain cretaceous land and marine sediments and basalt extrusions. The highest Inland Kaikōura peaks are remnants of the magma chamber!

Koreke/native quail became extinct about ten years after Joseph Ward took up the Warden Run. Californian quail were subsequently introduced and a much-vilified neighbour released grey warren rabbits for sport shooting. Stoats and ferrets were released in this district 30 years later in a desperate but futile attempt to counter the plague of 'underground mutton'.

The only access track to the old Warden Station from the Inland Road to **Kaikōura (20)** crossed **Blind Saddle (19)** on the Seaward Kaikōura Range. In 1861 Joseph Ward's manager, Robert Palmer, stocked Warden Station with 1600 sheep and subsequently spent three cold and lonely winters there. During the Long Depression in the 1880s the uneconomic, rabbit-ridden Warden, Tyler, and Jam Runs were returned to the Crown Reserve of unoccupied pastoral runs and most of their half-starved, scab-ridden sheep were slaughtered. Later on the Clarence Reserve was contract-grazed from Bluff Station. [12]

In 1922 the owners of Woodbank Station by the mouth of the Clarence River/Waiau toa re-grassed and restocked the 80,000-hectare Bluff Station. Every week a team of seven or eight pack mules spent six days trotting up and down the 48-mile (a bit more than 77 kilometres) access track from Kekerengū. Sixty years later 18,000 hectares were split off Bluff Station to create Muzzle Station. The 2007 land tenure review reduced it to about 8000 hectares. The remainder was added to the Clarence Reserve of relinquished pastoral runs to create the 90,000-hectare Kā Whata Tū o Rakihouia Conservation Park. Quail and Horse Flats continued to be contract grazed to check the spread of weeds.

Next day we drifted past the old cob homestead of Muzzle Station, which was hidden by a windbreak of Lombardy poplars. Before the 2016 Kaikōura earthquake the journey from Kekerengū in a four-wheel drive vehicle took at least four hours – if the dirt road was in good condition. The rough road over Blind Saddle to Kaikōura subsequently became the easiest option.

The surface trace of the Clarence Fault was hidden behind a limestone ridge that rose between the river and steep eastern spurs of the Inland Kaikōura Mountains, which culminated in Mount Alarm and **Tapuwae o Uenuku (4)**. On the opposite side of the valley, bare rock spurs soared up to the snowy summits of Manukau and **Te Ao Whekere (3)** on the Seaward Kaikōura Mountains, which my son Adam and I had climbed from **Puhi Saddle (2)** in 1990. The active Kekeremgū Branch of the Hope Fault lurks beneath their eastern flanks. Rakihouia gathered eggs up there in pākaha/Hutton's shearwater burrows when he sailed down the east coast. Te Whata Tū o Te Rakihouia (the high

The grandstand view across the Clarence/Waiau toa Valley of Tapuwae o Uenuku (2,885m) and Mt Alarm on the Inland Kaikōura Mountains, when my son Adam and I climbed Te Ao Whekere on the Seaward Kaikōura Mountains from Puhi Saddle in 1990.

food platforms of Te Rakihouia) included the sea cliffs around Kaikōura (meal of kōura/crayfish) Peninsula.

Although no ice is visible in the Kaikōura Mountains, glaciologist Trevor Chinn identified eight 'rock glaciers' on their upper slopes.[13] Crescent-shaped terminal moraines disclose the presence of those slowly moving amalgams of ice and frost-shattered rock. Cessation of subduction south of Clifford Bay and low rainfall have allowed compressive forces in the earth's crust and erosion by the elements to attain equilibrium at a higher altitude in these mountains than anywhere else in the upper South Island.

The South Australian explorer, Edward Eyre, attempted to climb Tapuwae o Uenuku in 1849 to see the lie of the land when he and the cartographer on the survey ship *Acheron,* William Hamilton, followed up reports that an ancient trail from Kāpara Te Hau/Lake Grassmere to the Canterbury Plain/Waitaha crossed a large inland plain behind the Kaikōura Mountains. Eyre turned back '300 yards' from the summit when one of his Ngāti Toa guides slipped on frozen snow and fell to his death. [14] When Terry Richardson, Andrew and I followed Eyre's route up the Hodder Branch of the Awatere Valley in October 1986 the summit was encased in cloud. I neither saw nor understood very much at the time.

Tapuwae o Uenuku on the Inland Kaikōura Range and **Maungatere/ Shingle Peak (5)** on the Schooner Range represent two great men that came ashore in Waipapa Bay from the Kāhui Tipua waka *Arai Te Uru* (path to the west), also known as *Te Ara Tāwhao* (the path of driftwood), which brought the first seed kūmara/sweet potatoes from the far-off land called Hawaiki. A terrible north wind drove that legendary waka down the east coast and onto the rocks at Shag Point/Matakāea in North Otago. Ngāti Māmoe ancestor Rongo-ī-tua had constructed that waka from a massive log that he had found on a North Island beach and sailed it back to Hawaiki to fetch those nutritious tubers. Before then the only edible plants in this country were the fibrous roots of aruhe/bracken ferns and tī kouka (cabbage trees), which were reputedly imported on the waka *Uruao* by ancestors of the Waitaha iwi.

Tapuwae o Uenuku on the Inland Kaikōura Range and Hell's Gate Gorge/Kopi o Uenuku flag the two important overland routes between the Wairau and Amuri Plains.[15] The place name Tapuwae o Uenuku (sacred footsteps of Uenuku) alludes to the wisdom and foresight of the high chief Uenuku, who led his family to safety on the upper slopes of Hikurangi, a lofty mountain in Hawaiki, before a catastrophic sea-rise called Te Huripureiata destroyed that country's coastal settlements. Uenuku's son Paikia was transported to Tai Rāwhiti on the back of a whale; his descendant Tahu Pōtiki was the eponymous ancestor of Kāi Tahu. Other descendants of Uenuku sailed there in the waka *Takitimu* and *Hourata.*[16] In perilous times Uenuku's wairua (spirit) manifested to his descendants as a giant rainbow. This pēpeha (proverb) proclaims his mana:

Haere e whai i te waewae o Uenuku,
kia ora ai te tāngata.
(By walking in the footsteps of Uenuku,
people can survive and live well.)

Tapuwae o Uenuku is the tipua ancestor mountain of the indigenous residents of this district. The summits of such mountains represent the tapu heads of great ancestors of the local iwi and bind them to their land. Some lofty mountains were the residences of atua and sacred thresholds of the heavenly realm of Ranginui.

The summits of Tapuwae o Uenuku and 13 other wāhi tapu (hallowed places) in the Kāi Tahu rohe were accorded tōpuni (overlay of traditional spiritual values) status in the 1998 Kāi Tahu Deed of Settlement. Climbers are requested to refrain from 'standing on the very top of these sacred mountains (because it) denigrates their tapu status'. Marlborough and Kaikōura District Councils have jurisdiction over the upper and lower halves of the Clarence/Waiau toa Catchment respectively. Te Rūnunga o Kaikōura representing Ngāti Kuri, and Kurahaupō ki Waipounamu have overlapping manawhenua there.

The Ngāti Māmoe-Waitaha residents of Kaikōura district were pushed further south by the Ngāti Kuri vanguard of the Ngāi Tahu migration. Ngāti Māmoe's Matariki pā in the contested border zone between Wairau and Kaikōura chiefdoms was defended on the seaward side by the Clarence River/Waiau toa before its mouth shifted southward. Traces of garden walls mark the site of an old Waitaha kāinga on the southern side of the river delta near the safe beach landing in Waipapa Bay in the lee of Ōhau Point. Until recently fishing boats were hauled up that beach by an old bulldozer. The old Kaikōura Track around Ōhau Point was not upgraded into a road until the 1920s. The last gap in the South Island Main Trunk Railway Line was closed around that bold headland in 1945.

As we approached the Sawtooth Gorge between the Sawtooth and Seaward Kaikōura Mountains the riverbanks became steeper and more thickly vegetated. We spotted several feral goats on the bluffs and spent the third night in a private hut below the exciting Jawbreaker Rapid. On day four we emerged from that gorge and drifted southward for a few

My wife Evelyn and me and our fellow rafters and guides at the mouth of the Clarence River/Waiau toa on Waipapa Point, after travelling down this river from the Acheron Bridge on the Molesworth Road north of Hanmer Springs for four days in October 2014.

Photo credit: E. Emmett

more hours until we reached our final campsite behind a small beach below Matai Flat. On day five we drifted past limestone cliffs and then shot a string of rapids below the new concrete bridge to Glen Alton and Waiau Toa Stations. The devastating 2016 Kaikōura earthquake sequence destroyed that bridge and created a steep rapid over a new escarpment where the Papatea Branch of the Kekerengu Fault crossed the Clarence/Waiau toa Riverbed. Similar earthquakes in the past had raised the tall alluvial terrace between there and the sea.

After drifting under the Clarence Bridge on SH1 and the parallel railway bridge we beached the two rafts beside the mouth of the Clarence River/Waiau toa on Waipapa Point. It is the tip of that river's broad delta called Waipapa (or Woodbank) Flat. Frederick Trolove established Woodbank Station on the northern side of the river mouth in 1853; Waipapa Station was on the southern side. A vehicle was waiting to transport us to the raft company's headquarters in an old railway settlement on the north bank named **Clarence (1)** by the site of Matariki pā. We were blessed with sunny skies and no head winds for the entire trip.

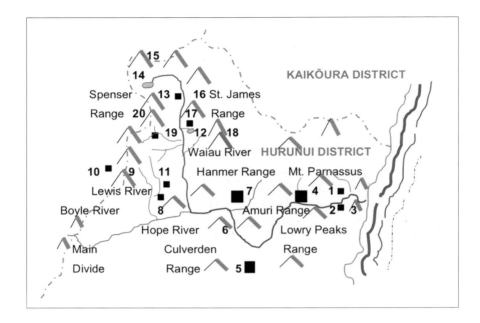

Legend

1. Parnassus
2. Spotswood
3. Mt Beautiful
4. Waiau village
5. Culverden
6. Marble Point
7. Hanmer Springs
8. Boyle Huts
9. Lewis Pass/Kopi o Kai Tāngata
10. Maruia Springs
11. Rockeby Hut
12. Lake Guyon Hut
13. Caroline Bivouac
14. Thompson Pass
15. Waiau Pass
16. Maling Pass
17. Mt Stanley
18. Fowlers Pass
19. Christopher Hut
20. Mt Una

Chapter 3
The Waiau uwha

In October 1989 my son Julian and I embarked on an overnight trip to the mouth of the Waiau uwha River. We left SH1 at Spotswood (2) at the southern end of the lower Waiau Bridge and followed Waiau East Road across a flat to a farm on the Seaward Range. The 'spring monsoon' was melting the high country snow and Canterbury's alpine rivers were in full spate.

The landowner, Lionel Wilkinson, gave us permission to follow a farm track over Mount Eleanor and down Barnes Gully to a small riverside terrace in the gorge that the Waiau uwha River had carved through the Seaward Range. The lower Hurunui River marked the old boundary between Cheviot Hills Station and Hawkswood Station, which was on the north bank.

The view of the Waiau uwha River
mouth when I followed a farm track from
Cheviot to Mount Beautiful in 1990. This
upriver story began a year earlier when
my son Julian and I walked to that spot
via a farm track from Spotswood.

We pushed on through regenerating tōtara-matai bush in a 39-hectare
conservation area towards the next riverside terrace on which stood
two corrugated iron huts. The largest one was locked, but the door of
the other stood ajar. One of its piles had been washed away and the
unsupported corner sagged over the riverbank. Inside there were two
empty swallow nests on the walls. We dusted off two of the canvas
bunks, laid our sleeping bags on them, and then sat outside in the warm
sun watching Welcome swallows zip back and forth across the river.

In the morning we walked around a backwater and then to the end
of a shingle spit to watch the rain-swollen Waiau uwha River rush into
the sea. On the way back I peered around a rocky point and startled a

young bull kēkeno/seal with a raw wound on its flank. It gave a loud bark, then dashed into the surf. When we headed back to the car we saw two fishermen turn up in a mud-splattered ute. Snow chains had been fitted onto its tyres to improve traction on the clay access road from Cheviot, which descended a long spur beside **Mt Beautiful (3)**.

That prominent hill and an adjacent sea-stack called Shag Rock might well be the two seamarks that Rawiri Te Maire mentioned when he told Judge Frederick Chapman that Te Whaka Hinu and Otara came ashore from the legendary waka *Arai Te Uru* by the Waiau River mouth and turned into 'a mountain and a bluff or rock'.[17] Archaeologists have found traces of a fourteenth-century nohoanga (intermittently occupied camp) by the Waiau uwha River mouth. Hurunui District Council has jurisdiction over the Waiau uwha Catchment. Te Rūnunga o Kaikōura representing the Ngāti Kuri hapū of Kāi Tahu holds manawhenua there.

This particular 'Waiau' is an abbreviation of Waiau uwha (female river with a strong current). Wellington historian Percy Smith recorded a folk tale that explains the meaning of this river name as well as the original name of the Clarence River, Waiau toa (male river with a strong current). 'Waiau toa and Waiau uwha were the male and female spirits of the mountains at the sources of those rivers. When Waiau uwha laments for her separation from her lord it is known by the warm rain that melts the snow on the hills where those rivers rise.'[18] Although the sources of the Waiau and Clarence River are close to each other on the eastern side of the Main Divide the Waiau uwha drains an 80-kilometre portion of that watershed, so it swells a lot more than the Waiau toa when heavy rain drenches the Alps.

The pēpeha 'Kā tangi o Waiau uwha' (the lamentations of Waiau-uwha) refers to the flash floods that race down this river; floods in the Waitaki River are 'nā Aoraki i riringi' (tears shed by Aoraki/Mount Cook). The Waiau uwha River may have been characterised as female because it quietly meanders towards the coast unlike the Clarence River/Waiau toa, which races through rapids right down to the sea. The generally calm sea off the east coast was 'female' whereas the generally rough sea off the west coast was 'male'. Settlers from small Pacific islands lacked terms for rivers so they co-opted *awa* (reef channel) and *waiau* (swirling stream).

In October 2014, Evelyn and I spent a night in Cheviot before we embarked on a raft trip down the Clarence River/Waiau toa. Next day we followed SH1 over the lower Waiau Bridge to **Parnassus (1)**. The parallel railway bridge, which was built in 1911, was also used by vehicles until the road bridge opened in 1940. Before 1961, when trucking was deregulated, sheep and cattle from local farms were driven to the stockyards next to Parnassus Station and railed to the Addington sale-yards in Christchurch.

Cheviot, Spotswood, and Parnassus lie in the Cheviot Trough between the Seaward Range and the Lowry Peaks Range, which is traversed by SH1 and the South Island Main Trunk Railway Line. While these parallel fold ranges slowly rose on either side of the Kaiwhara Fault, the Waiau uwha River maintained its course to the sea by down-cutting two gorges straight through them. Leader Road climbs over Leader Saddle on the northern side of Mount Parnassus to bypass the gorge that the river had carved through the Lowry Peaks Range.

The two men that drove the first mob of sheep from Nelson to the Amuri district, Edward Lee and Edward Jollie, acquired Mount Parnassus Run in 1853. Near the sea, the Waiau uwha River marked the boundary between John Caverhill's Hawkswood Station and William Robinson's 34,000-hectare Cheviot Hills Station, which was split up into 150 small-to-medium-size farms after his death in 1893.

We left SH1 just north of Parnassus and followed Leader East Road up the banks of the Leader/Tuahuka (snow ahead) tributary, which Caverhill renamed after a tributary of the Tweed River on the Scottish Border. After crossing Leader Saddle we followed Leader West Road down the Stanton Valley and then up the north bank of the Waiau uwha River to **Waiau village (4)** by the confluence of the Mason River. It sprang up at the junction of the Inland Kaikōura Road (SH70), which was the terminus of the Waiau Branch Line from 1919 until 1978. SH70 was the only access road to Kaikōura after the 7.8 magnitude Kaikōura earthquake sequence in 2016.

After visiting the local farmers' market and enjoying a coffee break in the old Waiau Hotel, which was severely damaged two years later by the 2016 earthquake, we followed SH70 over the old Waiau Road-Rail

Bridge and then across the Amuri Plain/Pūkāhu (hawk's home) in the Culverden Basin to Red Post Corner, three kilometres east of **Culverden (5)**. We turned right at that road junction and followed SH7 through the gorge that the Waiau uwha River had carved between the Leslie Hills and the Culverden Range.

We emerged from this gorge on a tall terrace overlooking the Hanmer Plain/Mānia Rauhea, which was surveyed by Thomas Hanmer and Edward Jollie. It lies in the depressed 'pull-apart' Hanmer Basin between the Hope Fault and its divergent Hanmer branch at the base of the Hanmer Range where the well-known spa town of **Hanmer Springs (7)** has developed around a hot spring. That town is also the southern gateway to the Marlborough high country.

Although the whole Waiau uwha Valley had been allocated to Nelson Province it is now in Canterbury Region. In January 1989, Evelyn and I took the inland route from Christchurch to Nelson. We left SH1 in Waipara and followed SH7 through Culverden on the Amuri Plain and then up the south bank of the Waiau uwha River. After skirting the southern side of the Hanmer Plain the highway entered the corridor of the Hope Fault, where the Waiau uwha River flows between 100 metre-high gravel terraces at the bases of the Glynn Wye Range/Whakarewa (to raise up) and the Hanmer Range. Those elevated 'drift' terraces are remnants of the thick alluvial outwash surface that formed below a set of terminal moraine ridges, now capped by pine windbreaks, that the Hope Glacier had deposited during the Ōtira Glaciation. A pine shelterbelt on one of those ridges was visible on top of the south bank terrace behind the old Glynn Wye homestead near the confluence of the Waiau uwha and Hope Rivers.

The Waiau uwha River flows southward through a long gorge between the Hanmer and Poplars Ranges until it enters the Hope Fault corridor, which redirects it on a north-easterly course towards the Hanmer Basin. In 1860 Gerald Ducarel acquired Glynn Wye (Wye Valley) Station, which then encompassed the Hope Catchment. In 1912 that 80,000-hectare sheep and cattle station was split up into Glynn Wye, Glen Hope, and Poplars Stations.

After crossing the Poplars Bridge over the Hope River, we followed SH7 past the old Poplar Station homestead and then northward up the Boyle Branch of the Hope Valley, which is parallel to the upper Waiau uwha Valley. Fifteen kilometres further on, the upper Boyle River emerged

The view of Lewis Pass/ Kopi o Kaitāngata (863m) on the Main Divide from the Lewis Valley. I followed SH7 over this pass after driving up the Waiau uwha Valley and its Hope branch and then the Boyle Valley and its Lewis branch.

from the northeast-southwest corridor of the Clarence Fault between the Poplars Range and the southern tip of the Libretto Range. There it is joined by the Lewis River, which flows down the north branch of the Boyle Valley. We followed the highway up the east bank of the Lewis River between the Sylvia Tops and the Libretto Range to **Lewis Pass/Kopi o Kai Tāngata (7)** on the Main Divide. On the far side of the pass I saw its identifier, Cannibal Gorge/Kopi o Kai Tāngata (the gorge where human flesh was eaten) in the Maruia Valley, which is the longest branch of the Buller/Kawatiri Valley. The summit of Mount Gloriana at the head of that valley is the tri-point where the boundaries of Canterbury, West Coast, and Nelson-Marlborough Regions meet.

At 863 metres above sea level, the summit of Lewis Pass/Kopi o Kai Tāngata is the lowest point on the portion of the Main Divide that bounds the Waiau uwha Catchment. It also lies within the Marlborough Shear Zone (see Page 20). Ada, Amuri, and Hope Passes mark the places where the Awatere Fault and two branches of the Clarence Fault cross the Main Divide. During the Ōtira Glaciation melt water from the vanished Maruia Glacier carved Cannibal Gorge/Kopi o Kai Tāngata in the crush zone of the Awatere Fault between the Freyberg Range and the Main Divide. When that glacier disappeared, the Maruia tributary of the Buller River/Kawatiri captured the source of the Lewis River through that gap in the old Main Divide, which is called the Freyberg Range. The adjacent portion of the Lewis Valley became a low pass on the new Main Divide on the eastern side of Cannibal Gorge/Kopi o Kai Tāngata.

In 1873, Land Commissioner Alexander Mackay was told that a band of Kāi Tahu warriors from Kaiapoi had taken a cross-country route over 'the pass of Kai Tangata' to attack a Ngāti Tūmata Kokiriri enclave on the northern west coast.[19] Werita Tainui was referring to the alpine passes at the headwaters of the Waiau uwha River when he stated that 'war parties … simply followed up the Mawhera or some other river to its source, and then popping over the saddle, followed a stream flowing the other way'.[20] In the autumn of 1860 Nelson surveyor Henry Lewis and his two field assistants, Christopher Maling and D Stewart, crossed Maling and Ada Passes to the upper Maruia Valley and then crossed a low saddle into the valley that was later named after Lewis. He realised that the river that they had followed from Ada Pass must have been the Maruia because it turned west. The Doubtful tributary of the Lewis River indicates that Lewis had doubts that the Grey River/Māwheranui arose on the other side of that low saddle, which was later renamed Lewis Pass. During the Great Depression an unemployment relief workforce built a road over this pass alongside the old Rolleston Stock Track. It opened in 1937.

The last week of my summer holiday in 1989 was reserved for a solo tramping trip to the source of the Waiau uwha River and so on the way back from Nelson Evelyn dropped me off at the **Boyle Huts (8)** by the confluence of the Boyle and Lewis Rivers, which is the southern terminus of the 66-kilometre St James Walkway. It bypasses the first Waiau uwha Gorge via Anne Saddle on the Opera Range, then crosses Ada Pass on the Main Divide and descends the upper Maruia Valley to **Lewis Pass/Kopi o Kai Tangata (9)**. I followed the walkway through tāwhairauriki/mountain beech woodland in the upper Boyle Valley and spent the first night in the rickety old **Rockeby Hut (11)**. Clouds were slowly thickening overhead.

Rain set in next morning as I crossed Anne Saddle and descended the Anne Branch of the Henry Valley to Anne Hut.

The Marlborough Shear Zone is a geographical maze that perplexed many Nelson explorers. In the summer of 1859–60 William Travers and cadet surveyor Christopher Maling searched for a potential road line through the upper Wairau and Waiau uwha Valleys between Nelson and Grey District on the west coast. They explored the upper Waiau uwha Valley and climbed onto the Opera Range to gain their bearings. Travers mistook the Libretto Range on the other side of the upper Boyle Valley for the Main Divide and assumed that the Grey River/ Māwheranui flowed south-westward on the other side of it from a source on the Spenser Range. His report in the *Nelson Examiner* stated that he had named the Ada, Henry, Anne and Boyle tributaries of the Waiau uwha River.[21] Anne and Henry were the names of his children; General Boyle Travers was his father; Ada was his cousin.

The original names of the Henry River and its Anne tributary, Otaku and Otukawa, which appear on the 1864 'Stanford Map' of Nelson Province, imply that hunters and cross-country travellers used the snow-free passes in this area long before Travers rediscovered them. Territorial disputes between Kāi Tahu and Ngāti Tūmata Kokiri from Whakatū/Nelson resulted in the feast of human flesh that the original name of Lewis Pass/Nōti Kai Tāngata referred to. The Henry River arises below Henry Saddle on the Main Divide and joins the Waiau uwha River in Henry Flat. 'The Downs' on that flat are vestiges of the terminal moraine that the vanished Waiau Glacier had deposited during the Ōtira Glaciation.

After a lunch stop in Anne Hut I followed the St James Walkway down the grassy north bank of the Henry tributary of the Waiau uwha River and then around the base of Mount Federation to Ada Flat, where the Ada River joins the Waiau uwha and the walkway heads west up the Ada Valley en route to Ada Pass. I headed north across that flat, giving the old Ada homestead a wide berth as the landowner had requested. My plan was to spend the next night or two in the old Forest Service hut by Lake Guyon, which was located on the opposite side of the valley, so I followed vehicle tracks to a vehicle ford in the Waiau uwha Riverbed.

When I reached the opposite bank two tarapiroe/black fronted terns dived at my head. The reason became clear when I spied four grey chicks scrambling over the ubiquitous greywacke cobbles. I took off along a farm track that zigzagged up a steep slope, then crossed the outlet of Lake Guyon and skirted its northern shore to an old Forest Service hut. The only signs of the sod homestead of Lake Guyon Station, which originally stood on that site, were an old Lombardy poplar windbreak and some gooseberry bushes and strawberry plants in the long grass.

Heavy rain pounded on the hut's iron roof during the night, but I stayed dry. I decided to spend an extra night in **Lake Guyon Hut (12)** to allow the river to drop further and give me the opportunity to visit an old hut in Glenrae Flat on the opposite side of the saddle behind Lake Guyon. That hut occupied the site of the old sod homestead of Stanleyvale Station, which was still marked by gooseberry bushes and a few wizened old rowan trees.

On the way back I spotted what looked like four white poles at the foot of a hillside several hundred metres from the lake, but they turned out to be the stiff legs of a dead horse. Not long after I met a couple of trampers who gave me the background story, which was that the animal had been ridden over Fowlers Pass on a hot day and collapsed when it was led into Lake Guyon to cool off after that trek. A fortnight later two goose shooters found the carcass floating in the lake and dragged it out with their Land Rover.

Lake Guyon fills the hollow in the wide hanging valley between Lake Hill and **Mount Stanley (17)** that an arm of the vanished Waiau Glacier had occupied during the Ōtira Glaciation. Tāwhairauriki/mountain beech woodland on the lower slopes of Mount Stanley swept down to the lakeshore near Lake Guyon Hut. William Travers acquired Lake Guyon Station, which included Ada Flat, and built a homestead by Lake Guyon for its manager in 1864. Two years later William Fowler and his wife built their homestead on Stanleyvale Station and raised seven children there. Mounts Clara, Laura, and Maria were named after their daughters. One of their sons, William (Chook) Fowler, became a packer on St James Station and is still remembered for the feat of dragging an ex-army wagon over the St James Range with a team of horses.

During the Long Depression of the 1880s the New Zealand Loan and Mercantile Agency Company repossessed seven small, snowbound, rabbit-infested runs in the upper Waiau uwha and Clarence/Waiau toa

Valleys and created the 78,000-hectare St James Station, which became New Zealand's largest farm. Only farm hacks and cattle were grazed there after the winter of 1941, when two-thirds of the sheep flock perished in snowdrifts. In 2008 the Department of Conservation acquired St James Station, then destocked it (apart from a small breeding herd of horses) and re-designated it as the St James Conservation Area.

The next day was cool and overcast. I forded the Waiau uwha River without difficulty and followed the St James Station's main access road further up the west bank. As I approached them, a herd of grazing horses lifted their heads, flicked their tails and cantered off with their manes flying. I followed the farm road across the river but when it climbed towards **Maling Pass (16)** en route to the Clarence/Waiau toa Valley I carried on tramping up the east bank and forded the river once again at the bottom of the next flat. The terminal moraine that the re-invigorated Waiau Glacier had deposited about 1500 years after the Ōtira Glaciation crossed the middle of that flat. I sat on top of it and ate handfuls of tapuka/snowberries, which are southern *Ericaceae* (heathers).

An hour later I dropped my pack in the two-bunk **Caroline Bivouac (13)** by the confluence of Caroline Creek, which Willliam Travers may have named after his wife. At dusk I heard a faint scream and saw something move on the riverbank. I got there just in time to see a doe rabbit hop away from the lifeless body of one of her offspring. A stoat had just killed it.

Next day the sun rose into a clear blue sky. I forded Caroline Creek and followed an overgrown track up the true right bank of the Waiau uwha River. When it reached the tree line the track switched to the opposite bank and then ascended a steep slope covered in tūpare/ *Olearia colensoi* or 'leatherwood'. I emerged from this 'monkey scrub' on the lip of the valley's head cirque, which the Main Divide looped around, and saw the infant Waiau uwha River tumble over a line of bluffs to the left. Beyond that escarpment I saw a groove running up to **Thompson Pass (14)**. It was evidently the trace of a small fault because a similar groove ran up the opposite side of the cirque towards **Waiau Pass (15)**. According to folklore, the source of the Waiau uwha is the peak at the head of this cirque, Mount Mahanga (bird snare), which is in love with the source of the Waiau toa, Belvidere Peak.

Scrambling up that couloir to Thompson Pass, I peered down the other side of the Main Divide into the head of the D'Urville Valley.

Dave Clark standing by the Lake
Thompson source of the Waiau uwha
River when he and Andrew Taylor-Perry
crossed Wairau and Thompson passes
a few years after I visited this spot.

Photo credit: D. Clark

The D'Urville and East and West Sabine Rivers on either side of Mount
Franklin unite in Lake Rotorua in the Buller/Kawatiri Catchment on the
west coast. When I turned around I spotted the ultimate source of the
Wairau uwha River, Lake Thompson, in a hollow above the escarpment
on the southern side of the cirque. Two trampers from Wellington met
me on the lakeshore and after we had exchanged greetings they told me
that they had bivouacked on Waiau Pass after hiking up the West Sabine
Valley and were now heading back to Lake Rotoroa via Thompson Pass
and the D'Urville Valley.

The Waiau uwha River commences its 169-kilometre journey to
the sea at the waterfall-outlet of Lake Thompson. Although its source
is only seven kilometres from the source of the Clarence River/Waiau
toa, the mouths of those two rivers are 135 kilometres apart on the

section of the east coast between Banks Peninsula/Horomaka and the inter-island strait. It was named Te Tai o Marokura after the atua that had stocked it with abundant kai moana (sea food) and constructed Kaikōura (meal of kōura/crayfish) Peninsula. In the autumn of 1884 two Nelson surveyors, James Park and Frederick Thompson, ascended the upper Waiau uwha Valley and climbed Mount Māhanga, which they mistook for Mount Franklin. The nearby lake and pass were named after Frederick's son Hugh Thompson, who had died of exposure when Frank Smyth's survey party was caught by a blizzard on **Fowlers Pass (18)** in 1866.

From Thompson Pass I sidled across snow-covered scree slopes and bare rock ledges at the base of Mount Māhanga to the 1870-metre Wairau Pass where Te Araroa, the Cape Reinga-to-Bluff Walkway, crosses the Main Divide between the West Sabine Branch of the Buller/Kawatiri Valley and the upper Waiau uwha Valley. Following snow stakes down the steep southern slopes of that pass I overtook two Danish trampers and accompanied them to the first grove of tāwhairauriki/mountain beech trees, where they decided to erect their tent. I stopped to have a cup of tea with them and managed to reach Caroline Bivouac just before dark.

Next day a gusty nor'wester propelled me up the 500-metre eastern side of Maling Pass. The Lake Tennyson car park on the other side was only 200 metres lower. The only vehicle in it was a minibus that had been hired by a party of Japanese botanists. They kindly gave me a lift to **Hanmer Springs (7)** where I caught a bus back to Christchurch.

Six months later my son Adam and I cycled up the farm road to Maling Pass and then walked southward along the crest of the St James Range to the broad summit of Mount Stanley. We were rewarded with a panoramic view of the Spenser Range and its apex, **Mount Una (20)**. At 2300 metres above sea level, the summit of this Main Divide is the highest point within the water catchment area of the Waiau uwha River. Like its lofty neighbours, Mount Gloriana and Faerie Queene, Mount Una rises on the northern side of the Awatere Fault, which strikes south-westward across the upper Waiau uwha Valley towards Ada Pass at the end of the Spenser Range after crossing Maling and

The view of Mt Una (2,300m) on
the Main Divide when my son Adam
and I climbed Mt Stanley on the St
James Range from the farm track over
Maling Pass in midwinter 1989.

Island Passes on two other mountain ranges that unite in the Spenser
Knot (see Page 29).

It was snowing lightly when my friend Andrew and I crossed Fowler
Pass en route to Ada Hut in May 1994. Next day we climbed Mount
Una via the West Christopher branch of the Ada Valley under a clear
blue sky. I was woken that night by the patter of rain on our tent and it
was snowing quite heavily at times when we tramped back over Fowler
Pass.

William Travers named the section of the Main Divide that bordered
his Lake Guyon Run after English poet Edmund Spenser – and some
of its peaks after the title and chief protagonists of Spenser's paean to
Queen Elizabeth I of England, *The Faerie Queene*. Gloriana represented
the queen. When Duessa (duplicity) captured Una (unity), the Red Cross
Knight (St George), representing the Church of England, managed to
rescue her and restore peace with the help of Sir Guyon (the Knight of
Temperance), a noble lion, and some loyal fauns and satyrs.

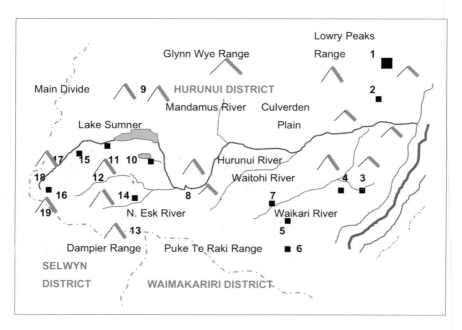

Legend

1. Cheviot
2. Domett
3. Greta Valley village
4. Scargill
5. Waikari
6. Waipara
7. Hawarden
8. Māori Gully
9. Kiwi Saddle
10. Number One Hut
11. Number Two Hut
12. Terrible Knob
13. Mt Crossley
14. Bush Camp Hut
15. Number Three Hut
16. Harper Pass Bivouac
17. Mt Drake
18. Harper Pass/Nōti Taramakau
19. Point 1725

Chapter 4
The Hurunui

One beautiful spring day Evelyn and I left SH1 by an old train stop called Domett (2), between the Hurunui Bridge and Cheviot (1), and then followed Hurunui Mouth Road down to a cluster of fishing huts by the sea. Parking about one kilometre further north, we walked down a track to the current site of the river mouth where a keen whitebaiter was scooping a hand-held set net into the incoming wavelets. There were almost as many willow leaves as mata/whitebait (inanga/*galaxiidae* fry) in his catch bucket.

The Hurunui Huts occupy the site of an old nohoaka. Many years ago a cache of toki (adzes) and an 84-kilogram block of matā tūhua/ obsidian or 'volcanic glass' were ploughed up by a farmer in a nearby field. In the fourteenth and fifteenth centuries, fresh maripi (sharp

A whitebaiter emptying his net by the Hurunui River mouth, where this upriver story began, when this spot was a kilometre north of the Hurunui Huts.

blades) were knapped off blocks of matā tūhua/obsidian from Tūhua/Mayor Island off the upper North Island and delivered by sea to riparian settlements right around the country. In 1852 Governor Grey decreed that the Hurunui River would mark the northeast boundary between Canterbury and Nelson Provinces. It marked the boundary between Amuri and Waipara Counties until 1989, when they were amalgamated to form Hurunui District. Its council has jurisdiction over the Hurunui Catchment. Kāi Tū Ahuriri Rūnunga and Te Rūnunga o Kaikōura hold manawhenua there.

The Hurunui River flowed northward behind a long shingle spit before it entered the sea. The long-shore drift sweeps sand and shingle onto that spit and gradually lengthens it until a major flood in the Hurunui River punches a direct outlet into the sea. The old river channel then becomes a quiet hapua (lagoon) until a new spit begins to form and the river mouth moves north again. That cycle is endlessly repeated at river mouths all the way along the east coast.

Kāi Tahu elder Teone Tikao told Herries Beattie that the Hurunui River was probably named after the dense thickets of mānuka and kānuka that used to cover its banks.[22] They were one of the proverbial Obstructions of Tū. These small, wiry trees are the only indigenous members of the 'tea tree' group of *Myrtaceae*, which is more widely represented in Australia. Percy Smith opined that the place name Hurunui means 'contractions or gorges'. It also means long flowing hair, which was the name of Kupe's kuri (dog). He left it to guard the hospitable districts that he had discovered when he sailed back to Hawaiki.

The Hurunui River has maintained a straight course to the sea by carving gorges through two parallel, slowly rising fold ranges: the Lowry Peaks-Black Hills and the parallel white limestone hills to the east. They are separated by the Kaiwhara Fault, which strikes south-westward through the Waikari Valley from the Cheviot Trough (see Page 46). The Hurunui River marked the boundary between Stonyhurst Station, which Frederick Weld and Charles Clifford leased in 1851, and Cheviot Hills Station, which was initially leased by John Caverhill and then freeholded by William 'Ready-Money' Robinson.

The Main Trunk Railway Line traverses the gorge that the Hurunui River has carved through the limestone ridge on the eastern side of the Kaiwahara Fault to an old train stop called Kaiwhara (meal of kōwharawhara/*Astelia banksii* roots) and then crosses the river to Scargill in the Waikari (Waikare – 'rippling water') branch of the Hurunui Valley, after which it crosses a low saddle on the limestone ridge to the Ōmihi Branch of the Waipara Valley. We followed SH1 across the Hurunui Bridge just below that gorge and up Greta Valley to **Greta Valley** village **(3)** and then drove down Tipapa Valley Road to visit friends in **Scargill (4)**.

We returned to SH1 via Waikari Valley Road and SH7, which leaves the Hurunui Catchment via Weka Pass on the limestone ridge east of **Waikari (5)**, and rejoins SH1 at **Waipara (6)** by the confluence of the Ōmihi River and the Waipara River, which marked the northern boundary of the original Canterbury Settlement.

In January 1988 I drove north over Weka Pass to **Waikari (5)** and then headed west along the base of the limestone ridge to **Hawarden (7)**. I then drove northward again on Horsley Down Road. After passing an isolated hill called Horsley Down/Te Kati on Horsley Down Station, I turned left and drove up the south bank of the Waitohi tributary of the Hurunui River on Waitohi Gorge Road, which was flanked by an 1880s-era rabbit-proof fence. The deep topsoil on the south bank of the Hurunui River had been removed from the opposite side of the river by nor'west gales. Although Balmoral Station on the north bank had light stony soils that encouraged shallow rooting it became a large state *Pinus radiata* plantation. It was plagued by extensive wind-throws and is being returned to pastureland.

This road became Lake Sumner Road and tar seal was replaced by shingle beyond the Waitohi Gorge Bridge. A few kilometres further on, that road left the banks of the Waitohi River and climbed over Jacks Saddle on the Seven Hills Ridge. The mānuka scrub on its flanks was smothered with white flowers. The sun was low on the skyline and I had to wipe dust off the windscreen several times to avoid sun-strike.

On the far side of Jacks Saddle, Lake Sumner Road returned to the south bank of the Hurunui River and entered a narrow gorge called **Māori Gully (8)** between the Puke Te Raki (hill that props up the sky)[23] Range and the Hooligan spur of the Glynn Wye Range/Whakarewa (to raise up).

The manager of Horsley Down Station, George Mason, had named Māori Gully in 1857 when he found some vine ladders that a Kāi Tahu party had constructed in a difficult section. A few months later he guided Canterbury's first Provincial Engineer, Edward Dobson, and three prospective run-holders – Christopher Dampier, John Mallock and Henry Taylor – through Māori Gully to Lake Sumner. They reached a Main Divide pass, which they called Hurunui Saddle, and gazed into the Taramakau Valley on the far side.

Two months later Ihaia Tainui reluctantly agreed to guide the new Anglican Bishop's son Leonard Harper and his friend Adolphus (or Edwin) Lock to the west coast via that Main Divide pass, which was thereafter called Harper Pass.[24] In bygone times it was the busiest route between the east and west coasts. Three ancient names have been recorded for it: Nōti Taramakau, Te Rakamaunikura, and Te Rau o Tama (the leaves of Tama). The latter refers to the vegetation that sprouted from shreds of Tama-nui-a-Raki's pōkeka (grass and flax leaf rain cape) when he hacked his way through the thorny tumatakuru/matagouri scrub that used to blanket river flats on the eastern side of the Main Divide.

Tama was often away from his home in Ōmihi on the Kaikōura Coast on long hunting expeditions. During one of those absences Tama's erstwhile friend, Tū Te Koropānga (Tū the obstructer), eloped to the west coast with Tama's beautiful wife Rukutia (melancholy Tia). Tū barricaded his remote hideout with wild waves on the seaward side and thickets of mānuka, tataramoa/'bush lawyer', tumatakuru/matagouri or 'wild Irishman', and taramea/speargrass or 'wild Spaniard' on the landward side. Tama followed their tracks through the western mountains, overcoming the 'Obstructions of Tū' on the way. To cut a long story short, Tama won Rukutia back after visiting the underworld through a hidden portal behind those mountains. There he met his ancestor, Ūe, who gave him a red feather korowai (cloak) that befitted an ariki (high chief) and tattooed his face with the first moko worn by a mortal man.[25] That myth echoes the story about Kupe's elopement with his friend's wife to the west coast of Aotearoa, which he fenced with the 'Obstructions of Kupe'.

In December 1849 William Hamilton heard that a large Kāti Waewae party from the west coast had walked over a pass at the head of the Hurunui Valley to Kaiapoi to collect their share of the Kemp Purchase payment. Te Hua took Hamilton up the last section of that trail to the southern end of the inland plain that he and Eyre had failed to find. When gold was found on the west coast in the spring of 1864 Horomona Taupaki carried a bag of mail along that trail to Christchurch in just five days.[26]

The Provincial Council's first response to the news of the gold strike was to ask Edwin Blake to upgrade the track that Dobson's party had blazed through Maori Gully Gorge. Every week over the following summer and autumn more than a thousand gold diggers, peddlers, and drovers walked, rode on horseback or travelled by coach up 'Mason's Road' over Weka Pass to the Hurunui Hotel by the Hurunui Ford, and then up Horsley Down Road to a bustling camp below the Waitohi Gorge. 'Blake's Road' ran from there to the head of Lake Sumner via Māori Gully; 'Howitt's Track' carried on to Harper Pass/Nōti Taramakau. The number of travellers on that trail fell sharply in the autumn of 1866 when the first road to the west coast opened – via Arthur's Pass near the head of the Waimakariri Valley. In 1927 the upper Hurunui run-holders banded together to construct a dray road through Māori Gully and maintained it for the next 40 years.

When Lake Sumner Road emerged from Māori Gully I crossed the South Branch of the Hurunui River and passed a short section of 'Blake's Road, which was marked by a commemorative plaque. A few kilometres further on, the road left the bank of the Hurunui River and ascended the south bank of Sisters Stream to **Number One Hut (10)** on the shore of Lake Taylor. It was the first of five public huts that the Internal Affairs Department built at intervals along the Hurunui Track in the 1930s.

I lifted my bicycle out of the van and over a locked gate and then pedalled up the farm road through Lake Taylor Station, which more or less follows the line of the 'paper' extension of Lake Sumner Road to **Number Two Hut (11)**. That old hut burned down in 1996 and was replaced; Number One Hut was removed after vandals damaged it.

The farm road skirted the western shore of Lake Taylor and then crossed a low rise to Loch Katrine at the base of the Brothers Range. The row of huts on its eastern shore occupy an old boat landing reserve. Henry Taylor named this antipodean loch after his wife Katharina and a scenic gem in the Scottish Highlands. Boats can negotiate the short passage called The Canal that connects it to Lake Sumner/Hokakura.

George Mason and Henry Taylor acquired the original pastoral run in the upper Hurunui Valley, which they called The Lakes Station, and stocked it via the Hope Valley and **Kiwi Saddle (9)**. When it was split into Lake Sumner Station (between Lakes Sumner and Taylor) and Lake Taylor Station (between Lake Taylor and the South Branch), Taylor acquired the latter but drowned in 1867 on a cattle drive to the west coast via Harper Pass/Nōti Taramakau.

The surface of the dirt road deteriorated as it climbed onto a lateral moraine bench above the western shore of Loch Katrine. Daylight was fading as I followed that road down to Homestead Bay at the head of Lake Sumner/Hokakura, which is a remnant of the 'proglacial' lake that filled the vacant bed of the Hurunui Glacier when the Ōtira Glaciation ended 13,000 years ago. Lakes Taylor and Sheppard, which are the twin sources of Sisters Stream, filled portions of the vacant bed of the western arm of that glacier. It was almost dark when I reached Number Two Hut. A searchlight-wielding helicopter was prowling Macs Knob,

I suspect illegally, on the opposite side of the lake next to Kiwi Saddle.

Lake Sumner's original name may refer to a decoy of 'kura' red feathers that lured kākā/'bush parrots' into the spear range of a hunter who was concealed in a hoka (hide). It was the fourth waterhole that Rākaihatū dug when he explored this island's interior. Some say that Hokakura was the name one of his companions. This lake was renamed after John Sumner who was the Archbishop of Canterbury from 1848 until 1862. He chaired the first public meeting of the Canterbury Association in London.

Today a stockyard and Lombardy poplar windbreak mark the site of Lake Station's first homestead. A bit further on I passed a hut on the site of Dreardon's Accommodation House on the track that Charlton Howitt cut at the behest of the Canterbury Provincial Government in the summer of 1862–63.

In the morning I headed up the Hurunui (or Howitt's) Track, which initially ran through magnificent tāwhairaunui/red beech woodland at the base of the Crawford Range. After about an hour it skirted a small bluff and when I put my hand on it for support, warm water trickled over my fingers. I dropped my pack, scrambled up the side of the bluff, and discovered a very small steaming pool fed by a very hot spring which, unfortunately, could only accommodate my bare feet. (A few years later some off-road vehicle enthusiasts build a concrete wall around that pool and three people can now sit in it.) An hour later the track left the trees and I briefly lost my bearings in a maze of huge tumatakuru/matagouri bushes. Eventually I spotted the red roof of **Number Three Hut (15)** and made a beeline for it.

Shortly afterwards I entered Cameron Flat and saw **Harper Pass/ Nōti Taramakau (18)** for the first time. At 962 metres above sea level, the summit of this pass is the lowest spot on the portion of the Main Divide that bounds the water catchment area of the Hurunui River. A pair of pūtangitangi/paradise shelducks flew around me in wide circles emitting plaintive cries. After a short rest in Cameron Hut I followed the next section of the track through mossy tāwhairauriki/mountain beech woodland to **Harper Pass Bivouac (16)**. James Drake surveyed the track lines that Charlton Howitt's gang cut from this pass to the sea in the summer of 1862–63.

I dropped my pack in the two-bunk bivvy, then forded the river and scrambled up a dry streambed to a 1425-metre knoll named **Mount**

Drake (17) on the grassy tops of the relatively low section of the Main Divide between Hope Pass and Harper Pass/Nōti Taramakau. Hurunui run-holders called it the Nelson Tops because a Nelson Land District grazing licence was required to run sheep up there.

The Crawford Range on the southern side of the upper Hurunui Valley meets the Main Divide on an unnamed 1725-metre summit referred to as **Point 1725 (19)**, which is the highest point on the 24-kilometre section of the Main Divide that bounds the Hurunui Catchment. The Hurunui River commences its 138-kilometre journey to the east coast from numerous seeps on its northeast slopes.

In April 1865 Julius Haast crossed Harper Pass/Nōti Taramakau, which in his view was where the Southern Alps ended, to conduct a geological survey of 'West Canterbury'[27]. Haast may have named the watershed between the North and South Branches of the Hurunui Valley after Wellington's Provincial Geologist, James Crawford, who had endorsed his conclusion that the ubiquitous greywacke rocks in Canterbury east of the Main Divide were not gold bearing.[28] The relatively low 50-kilometre section of the Main Divide between Point

My first view of Harper Pass/Nōti Taramakau (962m) on the Main Divide from Cameron Flat when I tramped to the head of the Hurunui Valley.

The view across Harper Pass/Nōti
Taramakau of Pt 1725 on the Main
Divide when I climbed Mt Drake on the
'Nelson Tops' section of that watershed.

1730 and Mount Gloriana on the Spenser Range lies in the Marlborough
Shear Zone (see Page 20).[29]

I spotted a large cylindrical stone cairn on a low eminence at the
junction of the Nelson Tops and the Kaimatā Range and found that
it commanded great views of the upper Taramakau and Hurunui
Valleys on one side and the Tutaekuri Branch of the Ahaura Valley on
the other. I surmised that George Roberts' chainmen had erected that
cairn around 1890 to support a beacon flag when he connected the
Canterbury and Westland geodesic surveys through Harper Pass/Nōti
Taramakau. On the western side of that knoll countless rills coalesced
in an eroded hollow or 'draw' to form the infant Taramakau River. At
the base of Harper Pass/Nōti Taramakau it veered right and flowed in
a south-westerly direction through the Hope Fault corridor towards
the Tasman Sea. Hope Pass was visible at the head of the Tutaekuri
Valley in the parallel Clarence Fault corridor on the northern side of
the Nelson Tops.

I scrub-bashed down to the Harper Pass Track and stepped sideways into a small clearing to take a photograph. When I looked down I saw the old iron survey peg that marked the point where the common boundary between the old Nelson and Canterbury Land Districts crossed the Main Divide. Looking eastward I saw the gap between Macs Knob and the Nelson Tops where the Hope Fault corridor connects the upper Hurunui Valley and the Hope Valley. From 1852 until 1876 the boundary between Nelson and Canterbury Provinces followed the beds of the Hurunui and upper Taramakau Rivers.

A kōparapara/bellbird chorus roused me in time to climb Point 1730 before I tramped back to Lake Taylor. I boulder-hopped up the riverbed for a while, passing a kōwhiowhio/blue duck that was dabbling in a small pool. When a waterfall barred the way forward, I clambered up a steep pitch covered with tūpare/leatherwood and carried on climbing through alpine grasslands and herb fields. One of the rills that I crossed was the farthest source of the Hurunui River from the sea. After a short walk along the crest of the Crawford Range I reached Point 1725 and discovered that it was capped by another tall cylindrical stone cairn.

A white sea of 'fine weather fog' covered the floor of the Taramakau

The distant view of Mt Crossley (1,980m) on the Dampier Range through a dip in the Studleigh Range when I climbed Terrible Knob on the Crawford Range from Number Two Hut.

Valley and lapped the western flanks of the Main Divide – a layer of cool, moist air was trapped underneath the pressurized centre of an anticyclone while a finger of fog extended through Harper Pass/Nōti Taramakau into the Hurunui Valley where it rapidly warmed and dissipated. It had been a very long day indeed, so I flopped onto a bunk in Number One Hut and slept like a log before driving back to Christchurch.

On an earlier solo trip up the Hurunui Valley I had followed an old drove track from Number Two Hut onto the Crawford Tops and obtained a panoramic view of the upper Hurunui Catchment from **Terrible Knob (12)**.

A line of deer hoofprints crossed its snow-capped summit and headed down a steep spur towards the upper Hurunui Valley. Gazing in the opposite direction across the South Branch of the Hurunui Valley, I saw three snow-capped summits on the Dampier Range through a dip in the Studleigh Range. The highest one was **Mount Crossley (13)**. At 1980 metres above sea level its summit is the highest point within the water catchment area of the Hurunui River.

Two pastoral runs in the South Branch of the Hurunui Valley make up the 16,000-hectare Esk Head Station. Canterbury Association solicitor Christopher Dampier acquired them in 1859 and 1863. His son Crosleigh, who managed that sheep station, changed his surname to Dampier-Crossley and drove the first mob of sheep over Harper Pass/ Nōti Taramakau to the Arahura Saleyard in 1864.[30] In March 1932 the Christchurch Lands and Survey Office's chief draughtsman, Charles Ellis, and five companions completed the topographical survey of the water catchment area of the Poulter tributary of the Waimakariri River. Ellis named its watershed with the Hurunui Catchment and the highest peak on that mountain range after Esk Head run-holder H M C Dampier-Crossley.[31] In November 1990 the farm manager gave Andrew and me permission to follow a track up the North Esk Valley and climb Mount Crossley. It was a long day so we had a nap in the dilapidated **Bush Camp Hut (14)**. We were rudely woken that night by mice nibbling our hair.

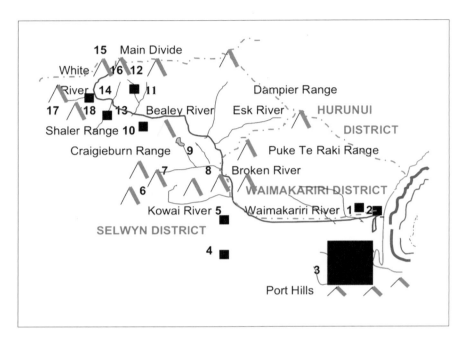

Legend

1. Kaiapoi
2. Kairaki
3. Christchurch
4. Darfield
5. Springfield
6. Porters Pass
7. Castle Hill/Te Kura Tāwhiti
8. Avoca
9. Lake Pearson

10. Bealey Hotel
11. Arthur's Pass village
12. Arthur's Pass
13. Anticrow Hut
14. Carrington Memorial Hut
15. Mt Armstrong
16. Mt Rolleston
17. Mt Murchison
18. Mt A.P. Harper

Chapter 5
The Waimakariri

One spring afternoon when the rivers were relatively low I followed the Old Main North Road from Christchurch (3) to Kaiapoi (1) via the 'Old Waimak Bridge'. 'Old Kaiapoi' was the Kāi Tū Ahuriri stronghold 10 kilometres further north near the foot of their tupuna maunga Mangatere/Mount Grey. A Ngāti toa-led host destroyed that large pā in the summer of 1831–32. The auxiliary scow *Tuhoe* was berthed at the town wharf on the Kaiapoi branch of the Waimakariri River. A fleet of small scows shuttled between Kaiapoi and Lyttelton before the first Waimakariri Railway Bridge opened in 1872.

After crossing the Kaiapoi River I turned right and followed Beach Road to a seaside village named **Kairaki (2)** by the site of an old nohoaka on the northern side of the Waimakariri River mouth.

A whitebaiter monitoring his set net
by the mouth of the Waimakariri River,
where this upriver story began.

A few whitebaiters were patiently waiting for a shoal of whitebait to swim into their nets. Sea haze hid Banks Peninsula/Horomaka at the southern end of Pegasus Bay. Christchurch's port in Lyttelton Harbour/ Whakaraupō, the northern caldera of that pair of extinct volcanoes (the other one is Akaroa Harbour), is the only deep-water port between Picton and Timaru linked to the Main Trunk Railway Line. The once busy Lyttelton-Wellington passenger ferry service ceased in 1976.

One of several old names for the South Island, Te Waka a Māui identifies it as the gigantic waka from which the Polynesian trickster-hero fished up the Te Ikanui a Māui (the North Island). In southern tribal lore the Sky Father Rakinui's son, Aoraki, had descended from the heavens in that waka but failed to return. Its broken hull rests on the semi-submerged body of the Earth Mother, Papatūānuku. Taare Te Maiharoa told Herries Beattie that Banks Peninsula/Horomaka was the largest of several coastal promontories the atua Tū Te Rakiwhānoa, son of Aoraki, and his assistants had built along this coast with fragments of Te Waka a Aoraki's hull and clay from the sea floor. Another atua, Kahukura, whose name became attached to some hills on this peninsula, cloaked them with vegetation.[32] Its ancient names, Horomaka (falling streams) and Kā Whata Tū a Rakihouia (the high food platform of Rakihouia, son of Rākaihautū), refer to its fringe of sea cliffs and the seabirds that nested on them and in burrows on the ridges behind them.

Banks Peninsula/Horomaka's two shield volcanoes were active between six and 12 million years ago. It was an island before the Ōtira Glaciation. The growing deltas of the Rakaia and Waimakariri Rivers connected it to the Canterbury Plain/Kā Pākihi Whakatekateka a Waitaha. The eponymous ancestor of its original residents, the Waitaha iwi, was a descendant of Rākaihautū named Waitaha ariki. Captain James Cook mistook this peninsula for an island and renamed it after the Royal Society's representative, Joseph Banks, on the Royal Navy's first expedition to the South Pacific. In 1809 Samuel Chase tried to sail around 'Banks Island' in the sealing brig *Pegasus* and almost ran aground in Pegasus Bay.

Waimakariri (cold water) is aptly named and may also be an after-naming of a cold stream named Vaima'ariri in Tahiti. The Canterbury Association's chief surveyor, Joseph Thomas, renamed it after one of the company's directors, William Courtney, Earl of Devon, however that name failed to stick.

The northward longshore drift curls around Banks Peninsula/ Horomaka and forms a huge eddy in Pegasus Bay. The Waimakariri River's outflow is captured by that eddy, which drives its fine sediments onto the beach. Strong easterly winds pile them up into parallel rows of sand dunes, which have dammed the outlets of streams behind the bay and caused them to back up in swampy swales, most of which are now drained, between parallel sand ridges.

SH1 follows the line of an ancient track along dry sand ridges from the site of Kaiapoi pā near the estuary of the Ashley River/Rakahuri to (New) Kaiapoi beside the former North Branch of the Waimakariri, which is called the Kaiapoi River. This river port was established between the original wharf and a Kāi Tū Ahuriri village named Kāikanui when point-to-point shipping was the most efficient way to move goods around the country. The *Tuhoe* was the last of many scows that used to pick up wool bales in small east coast ports and deliver them to the Kaiapoi woollen mill. Every year she sailed to Lyttelton to undergo a marine survey. On the return voyage in 2015 she was wrecked on the Waimakariri Bar.

Parallel sand ridges mark progressive stages in the eastward movement of the Pegasus Bay shoreline over the last 5000 years. When moa hunters camped in Moa Point Cave on the northern side of Banks Peninsula the Waimakariri River mouth was right beside it. After the major Alpine Fault movement in 1460 CE a massive quantity of sand and shingle was flushed down the Waimakariri riverbed and formed New Brighton Spit/Karoro Kōrero and Ihutai/the Estuary of the Heathcote and Avon/Ōtakao Rivers. In the sixteenth century the Waimakariri River flowed south into Te Waihora/Lake Ellesmere for a while via the bed of the Halswell River/Awa a maka (riri), then it began to flow east towards Kairaki.[33]

In the 1930s Wright's Cut was dug through Kaiapoi Island and a second cut was dug through the former North Spit to straighten the Waimakariri River's course into Pegasus Bay; its old bed became Brooklands Lagoon. Those projects were designed to help the river's current to flush sand and shingle out to sea. A double row of stop-banks also reduced the risk of this river re-entering an old flood channel occupied by the Avon River/Ōtakaro, which flows through the centre of Christchurch City. The broad South Branch of the Waimakariri River, which was spanned by the 1908 Empire Bridge, became farmland after Wrights Cut and the 'Old Waimak Bridge' eliminated Kaiapoi Island.

As soon as the Wairau Purchase was finalised Governor Grey instructed his Assistant Native Secretary, Henry Kemp, to negotiate the Crown purchase of 5,484,000 hectares of land between the Wairau and Otago Blocks. 'Kemp's Purchase' was hastily finalised in the winter of 1849 on board the Royal Navy sloop *Fly* in Akaroa Harbour. The Kāi Tahu negotiators were all too aware that 18 years earlier, their archenemy Te Rauparaha had lured their paramount chief Te Maiharanui onto the Australian trading ship *Elizabeth* when it was anchored near the same spot. The ship then sailed to Kāpiti Island where Te Maiharanui was killed. The Compaigne Francais de la Nouvelle Zelande, which was based in the port cities of Nantes and Bordeaux in France, had purchased 102,000 hectares on Banks Peninsula in 1839 and established the South Island's first planned colonial settlement in Akaroa Harbour in August 1840. The Crown's Akaroa Purchase was finalised in 1856.

The City of **Christchurch (3)**, or Ōtautahi, which incorporates Banks Peninsula/Horomaka, is the largest metropolis in the South Island. It was established by an offshoot of the New Zealand Land Company called the Canterbury Association in 1850 near an old Kāi

Tahu kāika site called Ōtautahi. It was as far as a whale boat could travel up the Avon River/Ōtakaro, which is fed by an aquifer from the Waimakariri River. Te Pōtiki Tautahi, who was a great-grandson of Tū Ahuriri, had established that kāika and subsequently married the daughter of a local rangatira who lived further up the river in an old Waitaha-Kāti Māmoe kāika named Pūari. Tautahi had joined the band of high-ranking Kāi Tahu warriors led by Moki that had wrested control of Banks Peninsula along with the rich fowling and fishing grounds on the surrounding lakes, estuaries, and wetlands from Kāti Māmoe rangatira.[34] Christchurch City, Waimakariri District, and Selwyn District Councils have jurisdiction over the Waimakariri Catchment. Kāi Tū Ahuriri Rūnunga, which is based at Tuahiwi near the site of Kaiapoi pā, holds manawhenua there.

Christchurch was the capital of Canterbury Province from 1852, when Provincial Governments were constituted, until 1876, when they were disestablished. It became New Zealand's first city in 1856 when Queen Victoria made Henry Harper the first Anglican bishop of the antipodean Diocese of Canterbury. This metropolis and its cathedral were named after Oxford University's Christ Church College and its large chapel, which is Oxford's cathedral. Twenty-six founding members of the 'Association for Founding the Settlement of Canterbury in New Zealand' had been students at that college.

In 1848, which was the year of revolutions in Europe, they resolved to address England's dire problems of poverty and unemployment by establishing a well-endowed agricultural settlement on a Netherland-sized plain that the Crown had just bought in New Zealand. They named it Canterbury after the archbishop who had agreed to chair their first public meeting. Lord George Lyttelton was the Canterbury Association's second chairman and a key financial supporter. The first contingent of their 'Canterbury Pilgrims' landed in the port town of Lyttelton in December 1850.

My four maternal great-grandparents immigrated through Lyttelton and settled in Canterbury. Rebecca Bennison arrived with her parents from East Yorkshire on the *Captain Cook* in 1863. Twenty passengers had died at sea so the rest had to spend four weeks in the new Camp Bay

Quarantine Station. Rebecca grew up on farms that her father worked on near Mayfield and married an ex-seaman from North Wales, Richard Jones. My grandmother, Emily Jones, grew up on their small farm at Glenroy and married Rolf Shillito who was born in South Yorkshire. He arrived in 1899 with his parents, Robert and Fanny Shillito, who had been crop farming in Tasmania for ten years. Rolf opened a garden shop in Christchurch, 'the Garden City', where my mother, Kathleen Shillito, and my children grew up.

In February 1984, when the third 243-kilometre coast-to-coast race was about to take place over Goat Pass at the head of the Mingha branch of the Waimakariri Valley, my friend Andrew and I embarked on a transalpine trip over Waimakariri Col above the source of the Waimakariri River. We boarded a westbound railcar in Christchurch on Thursday evening and had crossed the broad Canterbury Plain by nightfall. The Staircase and Broken River Viaducts and 15 short tunnels in the Waimakariri Gorge passed unseen in the dark.

Major advances of the Waimakariri Glacier during the Ōtarama, Woodstock and Avoca Glaciations (which correspond to the Waimea, Waimaunga and Porika Glaciations on the west coast[35]) had carved the Waimakariri Gorge between the Puke Te Raki Range and the Torlesse Range/Te Whata a Rama (the high food platform of Rama) where the Waitaha hunter Rama slew its fierce guardian, a huge bird of prey named Pouakai.[36] Canterbury's chief surveyor, Thomas Cass, renamed this 'front range' behind the Canterbury Plain after Charles Torlesse who had climbed his namesake peak with a local guide, George Tūwhai, in 1849. Torlesse renamed **Castle Hill/Kura Tāwhiti (7)**, which is studded with limestone tors, in the fault angle depression behind the Torlesse Range when he surveyed the upper Waimakariri runs in 1857. It represents Te Kura Tāwhiti (the treasure from afar) who came ashore from the waka *Arai Te Uru*.[37] That old place name also alludes to the folktale in which an early voyager mistook crimson forest flowers on these shores for red bird feathers, which were highly prized. They were sought from kea/mountain parrots in this area and attached to cloaks worn by high-ranking chiefs.

In 1857, Joseph Pearson and John Sidebottom sidled above the

Waimakariri Gorge with two packhorses. After fording (and naming) the Broken River, which drains Castle Hill Basin, they ascended an old glacial outflow channel occupied by Slovens Stream and explored the Cass Basin. Torlesse divided it into Craigieburn and Grasmere Runs on either side of Lake Pearson/Moana Rua ('two seas' – a large shingle fan nearly splits it in two). Between 1858 and 1860 the Porter brothers took up Castle Hill Station, Joseph Hawdon took up Craigieburn and Grasmere stations, and the Goldney brothers took up Cora Lynn Station beyond the Cass River.

After passing through **Darfield (4)**, Sheffield and **Springfield (5)** on the Canterbury Plain, SH73 enters the high country via the 939-metre 'high stile' called **Porters Pass (6)** between the Torlesse and Big Ben Ranges. The railway exits the Waimakariri Gorge via the Broken River and Slovens Stream valleys and re-accompanies SH73 through the Cass Basin and around the Waimakariri Bluffs at the eastern end of the Black Range.

After hopping off the railcar at the request stop by the rail bridge over the Bealey River, we crossed the 'Bealey' road bridge over the Waimakariri River and followed O'Malley's Track up the true right bank. We lost the track on Turkey Flat when the batteries in our sole torch died. Light rain had set in but just enough moonlight filtered through the clouds for us to navigate the maze of tumatakuru/'matagouri' thorn bushes. Eventually, we reached the tāwhai/beech trees on the far side of Turkey Flat and followed the edge of the woods to **Anticrow Hut (13)**.

The rain stopped before dawn and the cloud base was beginning to lift when we left the hut and followed a cairned route over a smooth rock outcrop that the vanished Waimakariri Glacier had scraped over. Clouds concealed the glacial source of the Crow River on **Mount Rolleston (16)** on the opposite side of the valley. The Canterbury Museum's taxidermist, Andreas Reischek had shot and skinned two orange-wattled kōkako/crows over there in 1879. After fording the Anticrow tributary we ascended the broad shingle bed of the Waimakariri River to **Carrington Memorial Hut (14)** by the confluence of the White River. Its milky hue was due to a suspension of 'rock flour' ground out by six small glaciers on the Shaler Range.

The view of the head cirque of the
Waimakariri River below Waimakariri
Col on the Main Divide from the
head of the White Valley, when Dave
Murchison and I returned to Barker
Hut after climbing Mt Murchison.

Above the White Confluence the Waimakariri River flowed southward at the base of the Main Divide. We followed a track through tāwhairauriki/ mountain beech woodland on its true right bank and left the shelter of the trees below Campbell Pass, which communicates with the Taipō Valley on the western side of the Main Divide. Back in 1867 one of the Campbell brothers that acquired Craigieburn Station had climbed onto it to see if there was any sheep country on the other side.[38]

The infant Waimakariri River plunged over a high bluff from this valley's head cirque, which was encased in cloud. We climbed the steep track beside the lower waterfall and then a side gully on the opposite side of the upper waterfall. The roar of that waterfall guided us through the mist to Waimakariri Falls Hut, which the Canterbury Mountaineering Club had erected near the lip of that cirque in 1944.

Next day the cloud base rose a little, but the mountaintops remained clagged in. We postponed the crossing of Waimakariri Col for a day and enjoyed an easy scramble through swirling mist to the summit of Carrington Peak on the adjacent section of the Main Divide. That night the sky cleared but more rain was forecast so we made an early start.

On the way up to Waimakariri Col we saw the Waimakariri River emerge from a tongue of old avalanche snow below the vestigial Waimakariri Glacier on the western side of Mount Rolleston. At 2275 metres above sea level, the summit of that peak is the highest point on the Main Divide in the water catchment area of the Waimakariri River. Canterbury's chief surveyor, Thomas Cass, named it after William Rolleston (pronounced with two syllables) who was Canterbury's Provincial Secretary when the Arthur's Pass route was selected for the West Coast Road. After climbing a flight of ice-worn greywacke ledges we stepped onto the col, then turned left and cramponed up a lightly crévassed slope to the summit of **Mount Armstrong (15)**.

From that vantage point we gazed southward along the crest of the Main Divide between the Waimakariri Catchment and the Taipō Branch of the Taramakau Catchment on the west coast. Beyond Carrington Peak rose the snowy summits of Mounts Davie and Isobel, where the watershed between the Waimakariri and Rakaia Catchments meets the Main Divide. Geological Survey Director James Bell renamed it the Shaler Range after the Professor of Geology at Harvard University in the United States. He also renamed its apex after Christina Murchison, who was the daughter of the owner of Glenthorne Station.

The view of Mt Rolleston (2,275m) on the Main Divide and the vestigial Waimakariri Glacier, which is the source of the Waimakariri River, when Andrew Taylor-Perry and I climbed Mt Armstrong from Waimak Falls Hut.

That peak's previous name, Mount Greenlaw, was subsequently transferred to the apex of the contiguous Birdswood Range. Bell visited Glenthorne Homestead several times when he was conducting a geological survey of the Hokitika Subdivision in 1905. At 2408 metres above sea level, the summit of **Mount Murchison (17)** is the highest point in the Waimakariri Catchment and Arthur's Pass National Park. In the summer of 1864–65, Canterbury's Chief Surveyor, Cyrus Davie, sent two of his staff, R. Armstrong and J. Browning, and two civil engineers, R. J. S. Harman and E. J. Cahill, to the head of the Waimakariri Valley to look for potential road lines to the west coast.

We cramponed down a couloir filled with frozen snow on the northern side of Mount Armstrong, bagging Anderson Peak on the way, then skirted Lake Florence and scrambled down an old scrub-covered lateral moraine wall to the Rolleston Valley Track. When I paused for a breather halfway down that slope, an inquisitive kea/'mountain parrot' left the alpine tōtara berries that it had been feeding on and pecked at my red bootlaces. We raced on to Otira Station and reached the platform just in time to catch the afternoon railcar back to Christchurch.

In August 1969 I caught the evening railcar to the west coast at Christchurch Station with three friends from Dunedin. We hopped off at the request stop by the Bealey Railway Bridge, seven kilometres south of **Arthur's Pass village (11)**, switched on our torches and tramped to the Forest Service's **Anticrow Hut (13)**. A fleeter tramping party had placed a lighted candle on the windowsill to guide us there in the dark. The next night was spent in the Canterbury Mountaineering Club's second **Carrington Memorial Hut (14)**, which was built in 1941. Its forerunner was built in 1926 as a memorial to the club's founder, Gerard Carrington, who had drowned on a rafting trip through the Waimakariri Gorge.

John Harris and I set off before dawn and ascended the rocky banks of the White River by torchlight. We bypassed a big bluff by cramponing up a ribbon of frozen snow and searched for the Canterbury Mountaineering Club's Neville Barker Memorial Hut, which was built on top of that bluff in 1945. John spotted the gable of its orange roof and the handle of a shovel attached to its door in the middle of a snowdrift. The adjacent White Glacier was a smooth white road running straight up to Kahutea (white cloak) Col on the southern shoulder of **Mount Murchison (17)**. We skirted a small icefall and kicked steps in firm snow up the final pitch to the summit ridge. Fortunately for us, a fragile cornice of wind-driven snow did not overhang it.

In the summer of 1984–85 a young climber died when a snow cornice on the summit ridge of Mount Murchison collapsed without warning. A week after that terrible accident Andrew and I drove to the car park at Klondyke Corner and hiked up to the new Barker Hut. Every bunk was occupied so we slept on the floor. Condensation trickled down the heavily insulated walls all night, even though the window was open.

We climbed onto White Col, where the Birdwood Range joins the Shaler Range, and then took turns plugging steps up a rapidly softening snow slope on the western side of **Mount A.P. Harper (18)**. From the summit we enjoyed a panoramic view of Mounts Murchison, Davie and Isobel above the White, Marmaduke Dixon, Cahill and Kilmarnock

Glacier sources of the White River. Part of O'Malley's Track was visible near the top of a talus slope above the north bank of the White River.

In 1912 a party led by Arthur Paul Harper, who in 1891 had co-founded the New Zealand Alpine Club in Christchurch with George Mannering, climbed the peak that now bears his name. This was just before he left his legal practice in Greymouth and moved to Wellington. In 1913 Arthur Talbot and Charles Ward, who also hailed from Greymouth, accomplished the first ascent of Mount Murchison (which they called Mount Greenlaw) via the White Glacier.[39] Talbot also accomplished some notable first ascents in northern Fiordland before he enlisted in the Army and died in World War I.

After descending to Barker Hut we picked up O'Malley's Track and followed it down to an old rock cairn on the bank of the stream that issues from the Kilmarnock Waterfall. The proprietor of the old **Bealey Hotel (10)** by the Waimakariri Ford (which the Bealey Bridge replaced in 1936), James O'Malley, named that waterfall after the label on a bottle of whiskey. He reputedly concealed it nearby for use if an emergency occurred when we guided his guests up that track to see the glaciers.[40]

The view of Mt Murchison (2,408m) on the Shaler Range from Mt A. P. Harper, when Andrew and I climbed it from Barker Hut.

I travelled back and forth between Christchurch and Greymouth on the Midland Railway Line innumerable times during the 1950s and 60s. The 8.5-kilometre Ōtira Tunnel takes it under **Arthur's Pass (12)** between Ōtira village in the Ōtira branch of the Taramakau Valley and **Arthur's Pass village (11)**, which is 737 metres above sea level, in the Bealey branch of the Waimakariri Valley. At 920 metres above sea level, the broad summit of Arthur's Pass is the lowest spot on the portion of the Main Divide that bounds the Waimakariri Catchment. That deep gap was formed when the southern arm of the now almost non-existent Rolleston Glacier gouged out the crush zone of the Scott Fault between Mount Rolleston's Goldney Ridge and the West Ridge of Phipps Peak.

In August 1963 I attended a 'Winter Snow Camp' led by Doc Martin in the Youth Hostel in Arthur's Pass village. Rain was forecast on the second day so we caught a railcar to Ōtira and hiked back to the hostel via the 15-kilometre gravel road over Arthur's Pass. I walked under Reid's Falls in the Ōtira Gorge, through Candy's Ford, and up the periodically extended zigzag that enabled the road to cross a fairly stable section of the enormous Ōtira Slip. It formed 2000 years ago when half of Hills Peak collapsed into the gorge, probably during an earthquake.[41] Rain set in at that point and my brand-new nylon parka leaked like a sieve.

A thousand-strong workforce managed to complete the construction of the West Coast Road over Arthur's Pass in March 1866 before a particularly harsh winter set in. The west coast goldfields were booming and the Superintendent of Canterbury Province, Samuel Bealey, hoped (in vain) that a coach road between the provincial capital and West Canterbury District would redirect gold exports through Lyttelton rather than Nelson.[42] The west coast's economy was revitalised when the Midland Railway Line opened in 1923.

Arthur Dobson was commissioned to survey the northern coastline of West Canterbury District in 1864 and decided to take two packhorses over the Alps to speed up that project. The paramount Kāti Waewae rangatira on the west coast, Tarapuhi, had told him that there was a low alpine pass between the upper Taramakau and the Waimakariri Valleys. Arthur thought that its identifier, Kaimatau (Kaimatā), was Mount Rolleston, however it was probably the apex of the Kaimatā

Range, Mount Alexander, which is much more conspicuous on the west coast and is also visible from the summit of Arthur's Pass.

In March, Arthur and his brother Edward rode up the Waimakariri Riverbed from Francis and George Goldney's homestead in the Cass Basin to Bealey Junction Flat to examine a low alpine pass that Samuel Butler had spied at the head of an adjacent side valley. The original name of that flat, Te Pākihi Tikumu (open flat where tikumu/*Celmisia semicordata* – 'large mountain daisies' grow[43]), told Māori travellers where they could line their flax sandals with the soft woolly leaves of those large native daisies. The Dobsons hobbled their horses in Daisy Flat at the head of the Bealey Valley and bush-bashed up to the pass from the Bealey Gorge. Rain set in when they reached the summit so they retreated to Cora Lynn Homestead in case rising rivers cut them off.

Arthur was determined to cross that pass when the weather improved. However, Edward had promised to help his brother George survey a road line over Porters Pass so Arthur recruited Francis Goldney, who wanted to search for more grazing land, and his head shepherd, John Marshall. The trio returned to the pass and descended the Ōtira Gorge with considerable difficulty. Log-ladders had to be constructed to circumvent a few waterfalls and eventually they emerged from the gorge onto a scrubby flat, which Arthur thought might be in the Arahura Valley. The route they had taken was clearly impracticable for horses and rain was setting in again so they turned back at that point.

After reporting his findings to Thomas Cass, Arthur took his pack-horses to the west coast via Harper Pass/Nōti Taramakau. On the way down the Taramakau Valley he ventured up its Ōtira branch and recognised the point that he had reached from the Bealey Valley.[44] Leonard Harper noted that his guide, Ihaia Tainui, on the Taramakau-Hurunui trail had called the upper Hurunui Valley on the eastern side of the Main Divide the Taramakau so the Bealey Valley may have likewise been called the Ōtira (food gathering place for a party of travellers). The Ōtira-Waimakariri trail was impractical for porters carrying heavy loads of pounamu/nephrite to Kaiapoi so few parties used it.[45]

In the summer of 1864–65, Arthur's brother George was asked to determine which Main Divide pass in the Waimakariri Catchment was the best route for a road to connect Christchurch with the newly discovered West Canterbury goldfields. He rejected them all, however his father, Provincial Engineer Edward Dobson, chose 'Arthur's Pass'

Arthur's Pass (920m) on the Main
Divide from Arthur's Pass Village,
after a light snowfall in August 1991.
Evelyn is holding Sybil and mist is
emerging from the Otira Rail Tunnel.

and that name stuck. The New Zealand Geographic Board bowed to
public pressure and endorsed the exceptional use of an apostrophe in
that place name.

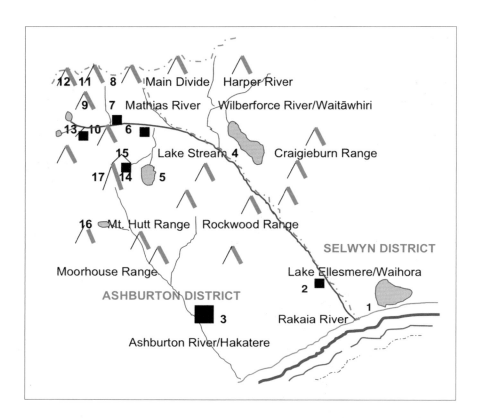

Legend

1. Taumutu
2. Rakaia
3. Mount Somers village
4. Lake Coleridge/Whakamatau
5. Lake Heron
6. Washbourne Hut
7. Lauper Bivouac
8. Whitcombe Pass
9. Mt Ramsay
10. Meins Knob
11. Mt Butler
12. Mt Whitcombe
13. Lyell Hut
14. Cameron Hut
15. Tent Peak
16. Lake Clearwater
17. Mt Arrowsmith

Chapter 6
The Rakaia

In October 1996 my friend Andrew and I took the Main South Road out of Christchurch with our ears glued to the car radio. Each successive weather forecast sounded worse than the last so when we reached the end of the Rakaia Bridge, the backcountry trip that we had planned was ditched in a favour of a walk to the mouth of the Rakaia River. We left SH1 in Rakaia village (2) and drove down Acton and Kingsbury Roads to the South Rakaia Huts, which are encircled by a high earth embankment. Canterbury Regional Council continues to warn the residents that an exceptionally big flood could breech that barrier.

We parked near the huts and followed quad bike tracks along a four-kilometre shingle spit to 'Suicide Point' on the southern side of the Rakaia River mouth, where we watched its fast silt-laden current race

Salmon anglers picketing the Rakaia
River mouth, where this upriver story
began, when this spot was more than a
kilometre north of the South Rakaia Huts.

into the surf. The North Rakaia Huts are located at the head of the
lagoon behind a similar spit on the northern side of the river mouth.
Both hut compounds occupy the sites of nohoaka that date back to the
fourteenth century. On this occasion salmon anglers were lined up on
both sides of the river mouth, staying a safe distance from the water's
edge in case the river surged.

The Rakaia River flushes enormous quantities of sand and shingle
into the sea each year. The longshore drift sweeps pea-gravel onto the
broad 26-kilometre Kaitōrete Spit. When it formed around 6000 years
ago, 'Te Waihora (the spreading water) Bay' became the estuary of the
Waimakariri River until that river changed its course and its estuary
became a lake. Its remaining inflows, the Selwyn River/Waikirikiri
and Halswell River/Awa a maka, were too small to keep its outlet open
and its waters nearly backed up to Lincoln before the local authorities
began to re-dig an outlet through the spit near Taumutu several times
a year to lower the lake level and create more farmland. Faecal and

fertiliser run-off into this lake have resulted in toxic algae blooms and reduced the Taumutu Māori community's ability to harvest tuna/eels in spillways on that spit. Once known as Rākaihautū's kete (food basket), Te Waihora/Lake Ellesmere was the last in the string of lagoons in the hapua (hollows) that Rākaihautū excavated as he walked up the east coast. The handle of his giant kō (spade) is represented by Mount Bossu beside Akaroa Harbour, where his journey ended.

Canterbury's Chief Surveyor, Joseph Thomas, renamed that lake after a prominent member of the Canterbury Association, Francis Egerton, Earl of Ellesmere. On one old map the delta of the Rakaia River is labelled 'Cape Ortegal, the antipodes nearly of Cape Ortegal (in the Bay of Biscay) in Spain'.

The earliest residents of this district lived on the flat between Te Waihora/Lake Ellesmere and Little Rakaia Lagoon on the northern side of the Rakaia River mouth. They engaged in fowling and eeling on those bodies of water and gathered eggs from seabird nests in a portion of the Rakaia riverbed called Huatau (egg season). Bands of moa hunters roamed the hinterland and sent gutted carcasses down the river on mōkihī (rafts) to a large earth-oven complex near the river mouth. In the fourteenth and fifteenth centuries, wildfires fanned by nor'west gales raged across the plains and destroyed most of its dry woodlands dominated by kānuka/'tea tree', totara and pōkaka. Moa preferred to browse houhi/ ribbonwood, koromiko, and makomako/wineberry, which grew on the peninsula and the western foothills where rain is more plentiful. After those devastating wildfires the dry plains became semi-open mānuka, pātiti/silver tussock, and hard fern heathland.

In the mid-eighteenth century Te Ruahikihiki, son of Manawa, built Ōrariki pā on a low sand ridge at **Taumutu (1)** by the southern shore of Te Waihora/Lake Ellesmere after wresting control of the Taumutu (end of the ridge) district from Kāti Māmoe rangatira Te Rakitamau. The latter had given sanctuary to his cousin, Tukiauau, who had mortally wounded Manawa, son of Kuri, at Pari Whakatau pā in Kaikōura district. Manawa and his brother-in-law Maru, son of Purahonui, had spearheaded the migration of the Ngāti Kuri hapū of Kāi Tahu from the southern tip of the North Island to the Kaikōura coast. Te Ruahikihiki's sons Moki and Taoka harried Kāti Māmoe communities south of the Rakaia River from their Taumutu stronghold.[46] Later, in the late 1820s, Kāi Te Ruahikihiki and Kāi Tū Ahuriri became embroiled in a bitter feud. Newly acquired firearms took a terrible toll of both hapū and impaired their ability to resist Ngāti Toa incursions in the next decade. Selwyn and Ashburton District Councils have jurisdiction over the Rakaia Catchment. Te Taumutu Rūnunga representing Kāti Moki holds manawhenua on a large part of Te Waihora/Lake Ellesmere and the Rakaia Valley. Te Wairewa Management Board representing six other Kāi Tahu rūnunga with ties to this lake holds manawhenua on the other part.

Twenty kilometres south of the Selwyn Bridge, SH1 crosses the 1.7-kilometre Rakaia Bridge, which opened in 1939. The road and railway bridges over this river's broad shingle bed are the longest of their kind in New Zealand, replacing the timber truss Rakaia road-rail Bridge, which opened in 1873. Between 1858 and 1873 coach runs between Ashburton and Christchurch stopped at the North and South Rakaia Hotels on the respective sides of Durford's Crossing in the Rakaia Riverbed. Passengers then transferred to a bullock wagon, which took them through small channels in this braided river, after which a punt-ferry took them across the main channel. Because the Rakaia River drains a long section of the Main Divide, some coach passengers had to spend several days in those hotels waiting for bank-to-bank floods to subside.

Rakaia or Ōrakaia has been translated as 'watercourse spread out'. It is also the southern dialectal version of Rangaia ('to form a rank' – the traditional way to ford this island's big braided rivers). In 1844, Edward Shortland forded the Rakaia River and described how his Māori-led party gripped a long tūwhana (fording pole) and moved together in a line with the sturdiest person at the upstream end to break the current.[47]

In April 1985 a slow-moving anticyclone spreading onto the South Island at the beginning of the Easter holidays was a golden opportunity for my friend Wayne Butt and me to explore the upper Rakaia Valley. We left SH1 in **Rakaia** village **(2)** and followed Rakaia-Barrhill-Methven Road, Rakaia River Road and Mount Hutt Station Road up the south bank of the Rakaia River. We then followed SH77 over the partly buried set of terminal moraine ridges that the Rakaia Glacier had deposited during the Ōtira Glaciation. Before SH77 crossed the Gorge Bridge we turned left onto Blackford Road and drove through Blackford Station on a 150-metre-high terrace on the southern side of a broad gap in the front ranges. My great-grandfather, Richard Jones, had a small farm and postal agency at Glenroy on the northern side of that gap and worked part-time on the adjacent Terrace Station.

The origin-story of the Rakaia Gorge relates to the eternal strife between the atua of the four winds, Tāwhiri Matea, whom irreverent yachters and mountaineers call Hughey, and his brother Tāne, the atua of birds and trees. Nor'west gales sent by Tāwhiri toppled trees and scattered the birds in the woodland around the confluence of the Acheron and Rakaia Rivers so the tipua-warden of that area piled up huge boulders to form a windbreak across this bottleneck in the Rakaia Valley. He enabled the river to escape via a gorge by dislodging a massive boulder named Marutaomu (Goat Island) at the end of it.[48]

Beyond Terrible Gully Blackford Road became Double Hill Road, which crosses Double Hill Station where the Rakaia Basin opens out and the Rakaia River is joined by a large tributary, the Wilberforce River/Waitāwhiri, near an isolated landmark called Double Hill/ Tokanui. **Lake Coleridge/Whakamatau (4)** fills the long hollow on the opposite side of the Rakaia Valley that was excavated by the vanished Wilberforce Glacier during the Ōtira Glaciation. It was said to be one of the waterholes that Rākaihautū dug when he explored the high country. The outflow from Lake Coleridge/Whakamatau entered the Harper tributary of the Wilberforce River until 1914, when it was redirected into the Rakaia River via a hydroelectric power station to generate electricity for the City of Christchurch.

The 'Maori Plan of the Rakaia River System' in Julius Haast's papers records the original names of the three principal tributaries of the Rakaia River: the upper Rakaia River (Rakaia Waiki —'deep water'), the Mathias River/Rakaia Waipākihi (dried-up water), and the Wilberforce River/ Waitāwhiri (raging water). The source of the large tributary called Lake Stream **Lake Heron (5)** is labelled Ōtūroto, while the 'high mountain Unuroa', which rises on the eastern side of Ōtūroto, is probably Mount Sugarloaf. Haast thought that Unuroa was the name of the apex of the Arrowsmith Range, which rises on the opposite side of that lake.[49] On the 1880 Taiaroa Map, the Mathias River is labelled Orikaroro.

Double Hill Road ended at the entrance to Glenfalloch Station. We parked beside a vehicle shed, shouldered our packs, and then followed wheel tracks across the stony Rakaia Riverbed and through the thigh-deep vehicle ford to Manuka Point Station, which had been split off Double Point Station. On the opposite bank I spotted a karoro/seagull feasting on a salmon carcass.

The water was clear, but fast moving. The manager, Jim Morris, told us that the river was running against Tōtara Bluff so we would have to climb over it. Two hours later we reached the base of the bluff and searched in vain for a bypass track. After thrashing through swathes of mānuka and tūpare/leatherwood scrub, we slid our packs over a small bluff and scrub-bashed down to Cattle Creek Flat. It was nearly dark when we reached **Lauper Bivouac (7)** near Lauper Steam.

William Gerald acquired Double Hill Station in 1874 and burnt off the river flats on its Manuka Point Block before he stocked it with cattle. In 1895 C O Digby replaced the stock on Cattle Creek Flat between Tōtara Bluff and Lauper Stream with 2000 sheep. Unfortunately, most of them were smothered by snow the following winter. His shepherd on that block, Duncan McLeod, had to be dug out of his tōtara slab hut by Cattle Creek.[50]

Lauper Stream drains the eastern slopes of **Whitcombe Pass (8)**. At 1239 metres above sea level, the summit of that pass is the lowest spot on the portion of the Main Divide that bounds the Rakaia Catchment. Julius Haast explored that area in 1866 and named the peak on the northern side of Whitcombe Pass Mount Martius after a German botanist. The lofty peak on the southern side of the pass, which Haast had named Mount Whitcombe, was renamed (and misspelled) after Henry Whitcombe's Swiss guide Jakob Lauper, who had accompanied the young Canterbury surveyor on his transalpine journey over this pass in 1864. Tragically, Whitcombe drowned when he tried to cross the Taramakau River mouth on the west coast in an old, partly rotten canoe shortly after they set off on the return journey to Christchurch via Harper Pass/Noti Taramakau.[51]

On the 1880 Taiaroa Map, Whitcombe Pass appears to be labelled Rurumataikau, which Herries Beattie thought might mean seeking the only place up there that is sheltered from the wind.[52] Māori travellers were unlikely to have picked this long, arduous route to the west coast when there was a much easier alternative, Browning Pass/Noti Raureka at the head of the Wilberforce/Waitāwhiri Valley.

The view of Whitcombe Pass (1,239m)
and Lauper Pk on the Main Divide
when Duncan Williams and I tramped
to the head of the Rakaia Valley.

Two years before Whitcombe's death and the naming of Whitcombe
Pass, Canterbury surveyor John Baker and Rangitata run-holder Samuel
Butler had spotted it from Butler Saddle at the head of the Lawrence
branch of the Rangitata Valley. They subsequently rode up the Rakaia
Valley and walked up to its summit. As a matter of interest, Butler
noted in one of his diaries that those trips had inspired the account of
an alpine crossing to a remote utopia called Erewhon (from 'nowhere'
spelled backwards; *outopia* means 'nowhere' in Greek) in his satirical
novel *Erewhon*.

In 1865 Richard Harman cut the first track down the Whitcombe
Branch of the Hokitika Valley on the far side of that pass.

In the morning we ascended the banks of Lauper Stream and a tussock-covered terrace on the eastern side of the Butler Range to reach the boulder-strewn crest of Whitcombe Pass. The sky was clear and the air was still. On the northern side of the pass, I saw the nascent Whitcombe River emerge from the shrunken Sale Glacier behind a tall, crescent-shaped terminal moraine at the base of Lauper Peak. It meandered northward across a stony outwash surface and disappeared into a gorge between the Katzenbach Ridge and Mount Neave on the Main Divide.

Next day Wayne and I forded Lauper Stream and scrambled up a talus slope to the flat summit of Jims Knob at the southern end of the Butler Range, which meets the Main Divide on Lauper Peak. We then headed north along the snowy crest of that range until we reached the summit of **Mount Butler (11)**. A wonderful panorama unfolded from there of the arc of Main Divide peaks around the eight-kilometre Ramsey Glacier culminating in the High Peak of **Mount Whitcombe (12)**. At 2,650 metres above sea level, its summit is the highest point on the portion of the Main Divide that bounds the Rakaia Catchment. Westland surveyor George Roberts erected a trigonometric station on top of Mount Butler in 1880 and transferred the name Mount Whitcombe to that peak from Lauper Peak (which he renamed but misspelled 'Louper').[53]

In May 1970 I visited the headwaters of the Rakaia River with two fellow students at Otago University, Mace Ramsay and Doug Warren. We followed SH1 from Christchurch to **Rakaia (2)**, then Thompson's Track, which was named after a bullock wagon driver, to **Mount Somers village (3)**. On the way we made a detour to the Methven telephone exchange and used its radio-telephone to tell the manager of Upper Lake Heron Station, John Rowse, who was aware of our imminent arrival, that we would not arrive until well after dark. He said that it would be a very frosty night and we could sleep in the hay barn.

After driving through Mount Somers village we followed Ashburton Gorge Road further up the banks of the Ashburton River/Hakatere, over Blowing Point Bridge, and then through a short gorge between the Moorhouse Range and the Clent Hills. Above leaving the gorge we turned right at Hakatere Junction and followed Hakatere-Lake Heron

Road across Hakatere Flat. The wire fence alongside it now marks the boundary between Lake Heron Station and Clent Hills Conservation Park. After skirting **Lake Heron (6)** we crossed Lake Stream and parked by the hay barn near Lower Lake Heron homestead.

Upper Lake Heron Station comprises five pastoral runs and covers 17,000 hectares on the south bank of the Rakaia River between Reischek Stream and Lake Stream, which marked its boundary with Double Hill Station before Glenfalloch Station was split off it. The Cameron River marks its boundary with Mount Arrowsmith Station (formerly Lower Lake Heron Station). Henry Washbourne acquired Upper Lake Heron Station in 1861 and built a hut beside Washbourn Stream on the far side of Prospect Hill. Burn-offs are now banned in the Upper Rakaia Valley and its flats are reverting to tumatakuru/'matagouri' scrubland.

In the morning we had to scrape a rime of ice off the car's windscreen, before we could drive along the dirt road on the true right bank of Lake Stream to the footbridge. We then shouldered our packs, walked across the bridge, and followed a bulldozed stock track down the opposite bank to Downs Hut.

The next section of the track climbed 200 metres onto the broad summit of Prospect Hill, which is directly across the Rakaia Riverbed from Tōtara Bluff. The Rakaia Glacier left a terminal moraine on top of this hill at the end of a Little Ice Age 11,500 years ago. As we crossed the summit a number of merino sheep streamed down an adjacent mountain and lined up beside the track, evidently expecting to be mustered; they stared blankly at us we strode past. On the other side of the hill we forded Washbourne Creek and had lunch in Thompson's Hut.

We reached **Washbourne Hut (6)** just before the sun slipped behind the Main Divide and the temperature began to plummet. Many names and messages, including those of a 1911 mustering party, which made it the oldest, had been scratched on the old sheet of Redcliffe corrugated iron next to the door. Among those from the end of the first half of the twentieth century, I spotted two familiar names and a message: 'W E Heinz, W F Heinz, P Fox, 1949. Departing for Whitcombe Pass'. Missing from this list was the name of the fourth member of that party, Max Gage. One of them told me that that the river was high on that occasion so they had stuck to the south bank all the way to Lyell Hut. Next day they forded the Lyell River and crossed the pass.

The Lyell Glacier source of the Lyell
River, which is the most distant source
of the Rakaia River, below Malcolm
Pk, when Mace Ramsay, Doug Warren
and I visited Lyell Hut in May 1970. The
nominal source of the Rakaia River is
the nearby confluence of the Lyell and
Ramsay rivers at the base of Meins Knob.

Next morning we passed the first patches of snow on the river flats near the South Canterbury Deerstalkers Association's Reischek Hut on the sunny side of a knoll covered with thin-barked tōtara and pāhautea/ mountain cedar. An hour later we reached the base of **Meins Knob (10)** where an aluminium ladder gave access to a rock ledge that led to a swing bridge over the Lyell tributary of the Rakaia River. Once on the other bank we scrambled along the old terminal moraine of the Ramsay Glacier and forded the Lyell River on the other side of Meins Knob to **Lyell Hut (13)**, which the Canterbury Mountaineering Club had built in 1933.

Julius Haast named the nearby peak, tributary, and glacier after the British Geological Survey's Director-General, Andrew Ramsay, and the farthest glacial source of the Rakaia River after the famous Scottish geologist, Charles Lyell, whose 1830 opus, *Principles of Geology,* had a strong influence on Charles Darwin.

In the afternoon I walked up the south bank of the Lyell River and around a frozen proglacial lake to the tongue of the Lyell Glacier. The nominal source of the Rakaia River is the confluence of the Lyell and Ramsay Rivers. The larger but shorter Ramsay River, which issues from the Ramsay Glacier, is the Rakaia's master stream. The Lyell Névé was bathed in bright sunlight, which streamed through Rangitata Col between Mount Nicholson on the Armoury Range and Malcolm Peak on the Main Divide.

Noting a plume of white ice entering the upper Lyell Glacier from the Heim Icefall, which lay out of sight on its eastern flank, I ascended the rubble-covered glacier's tongue. Eventually I was high enough to gaze up its large northern tributary, the Cockayne Glacier, which descends from a névé on the southeast flank of **Mount Ramsay (9)**. That glacier was named after Canterbury botanist Leonard Cockayne, who explored the upper Rakaia Valley in 1909 with Robert Speight, Professor of Geology at Canterbury University at the time.

That night Lyell Hut turned into an icebox after the fire went out. I shivered all night in my sleeping bag, despite having all my clothes on. A loud bang at first light made me sit up with a jolt. Mace sheepishly explained that he had attempted to shoot a mouse that was sitting on the doorstep but had missed. After breakfast he carried his rifle up the sunny slopes above Meins Knob to hunt bigger game while Doug and I set off in the opposite direction.

The Ramsay Glacier, source of the Ramsay River, which is the master stream of the Rakaia River, below Mt Whitcombe (2,650m) on the Main Divide, when Andrew Taylor-Perry, Cam Odlin, Duncan Williams and I skirted its terminal lake en route to Whitcombe Pass in January 2001.

We forded the icy Lyell River in our spare socks in order to keep our boots dry and avoid getting frostbite later in the day. After stumbling over countless concealed boulders on the snow-covered Ramsay Glacier we climbed onto a ridge next to its icefall and obtained a fine view of that glacier's extensive névé between Lauper Peak and Mount Whitcombe.

The Ramsay Glacier began to retreat a few years after Doug and I ventured up it. A slowly enlarging 'proglacial lake' appeared below its terminal face in the 1970s. The lateral moraine on the adjacent flanks of Mount Kinsey and Ramsay is slowly collapsing into this lake. Boulder-hopping along its western shore exposes climbers to significant risks from rock falls, especially after heavy rain. One life has been lost there.

The barren trim line that is visible on the lower flanks of those peaks marks the height of the Ramsay Glacier during the 'Little Ice Age' from the fifteenth to the nineteenth century.

When Julius Haast explored this area in 1866 the terminal face of this glacier almost butted against Meins Knob, which is on the opposite side of the valley from Jims Knob. During the Ōtira Glaciation the united Ramsay and Lyell Glaciers over-rode those tough greywacke outcrops and planed their flat summits.

Thirty years later my friend Duncan Williams and I left Reischek Hut and skirted the proglacial lake below the terminus of the Ramsay Glacier. When we reached the junction of the Clarke Valley we stowed our bivvy gear in an orange pack liner, placed it on a pile of rocks, and then climbed onto Strachan Pass via a snow-filled gully in the lateral moraine wall that towered over the down-wasted tongue of the Clarke Glacier. On the western side of that Main Divide pass lay the remote Lambert Branch of the Whanganui Valley. We arrived back at nightfall and searched in vain by torchlight for our orange bag, which was indistinguishable from grey rocks in the dark. We had to sleep rough that night.

In March 1987 Andrew and I drove to **Lake Heron (5)** and parked in the front paddock of Mount Arrowsmith Station at the request of the farm manager and then headed up the stock track on the true right bank of the Cameron tributary of Lake Stream. Four hours later we climbed over a tall terminal moraine ridge and dropped our packs in the Canterbury Mountaineering Club's **Cameron Hut (14)**. A stony outwash surface stretched from the hut to the terminal face of the Cameron Glacier, which is the receptacle of all the snow and ice that slides off the southeast face of **Mount Arrowsmith (17)**. At 2,781 metres above sea level, the summit of that great peak is the highest point in the Rakaia Catchment.

Next day Andrew and I forded the Cameron River below the retreating terminus of this glacier and scaled an old lateral moraine wall to enter the Peg Valley. The enormous scree on the left descended from the summit ridge of **Tent Peak (15)**. We slogged halfway up it, three steps up and one step back, ad infinitum. When we were halfway up we heard a loud report followed by the sight of some big rocks cartwheeling down the scree about 200 metres away. There was nowhere to hide so we carried on cramponing up a snow-filled couloir to reach the comparative safety of the slowly disintegrating summit ridge after which we took turns belaying each other along the ridge until we reached the summit. It offered a panoramic view of the arc of high peaks around the two tributaries of the Cameron Glacier. The South Cameron Glacier on the flank of **Mount Arrowsmith (17)** had recently become disconnected from the heavily crévassed tongue of the North Cameron Glacier, which descended from a small névé between Tent Peak and the precipitous east face of Jagged Peak. One of the climbers that accomplished the first traverse of the ridge between Jagged Peak and Mount Arrowsmith, Bruce Naylor, happened to be also staying in Cameron Hut with us so we discussed all the routes up Mount Arrowsmith with him. Two years later Andrew, Dave Clark, and I took the road to **Lake Clearwater (16)** and then tramped up the Lawrence Valley and climbed that great peak's South Ridge from a campsite on Moses Rock. The only problems that we encountered were a gusty wind and many tottering piles of fractured greywacke, which climbers call 'weetbix'.

Julius Haast visited the glacial source of the Cameron River in 1864 and named it after his companion, the visiting Speaker of the South Australian Parliament, George Hawker. The glacier was subsequently renamed after the river, which Haast may have named after General Duncan Cameron, who had sent 12,000 Imperial troops to 'pacify' the northern Waikatō district in 1863.

Haast's son-in-law, Arthur Dobson, told Professor Arnold Wall that Haast had named Mount Arrowsmith after his camp cook when he explored this area in 1861.[54] However Wall's poem *Arrowsmith* states that this peak was named after John Whitcombe's cook. It is likely that Haast had initially named this mountain after the London map publisher, John Arrowsmith, but later declined to acknowledge the fact. In a letter to Sir Joseph Hooker, Haast expressed his disappointment that Arrowsmith had not replied to his letter that had enclosed a copy of his 1867 Central South Island map, which had the place name Mount Arrowsmith inscribed on it. [55]

Frederick Chapman obtained Mount Arrowsmith's original name

The view across the Cameron Glacier of
Mt Arrowsmith (2,781m) on the Arrowsmith
Range, when Andrew and I climbed
Tent Pk from Cameron Hut in 1987.

from Rawiri Te Maire, who related the saga of the waka *Arai Te Uru*
to him. As it passed the mouth of the Ashburton River/Hakatere,
Putea whatiia 'went over, and after him was named the mountain at
the source of the Hakatere'. Mount Somers represents Te Koikoi, who
followed him ashore.[56]

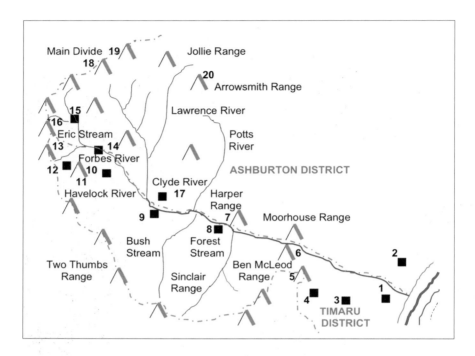

Legend

1. Ealing
2. Hinds
3. Arundel
4. Peel Forest village
5. Mt Peel/Tara Haoa
6. Coal Hill
7. Mt Harper/Mahaanui
8. Mesopotamia homestead
9. Black Mountain Hut
10. Findlay Face Hut
11. Findlay's Hill
12. Forbes Bivouac
13. Mt D'Archiac
14. McDonald Hut
15. Eric Bivouac
16. Dennistoun Pass
17. Erewhon homestead
18. Baker Peak
19. Newton Peak
20. Mt Arrowsmith

Chapter 7
The Rangitata (Rakitata)

Canterbury's Anniversary Day in November 1990 was earmarked for a family camping trip to Peel Forest in South Canterbury on the south bank of the Rangitata River. On the way there we left SH1 in Hinds (2) and drove down Coldstream and Wren Roads to see where the Rangitata River runs into the sea.

Kāti Huirapa elders told William Taylor that Rangitata (Rakitata in the southern brogue) means 'shrouded peak' or 'day of lowering clouds'. The original name of the tupuna mountain of their Arowhenua community, Tara Haoa/Mount Peel, means 'enclosed peak'. Hekao (descending clouds) is the cognate name of the Hinds River, which arises in the Moorhouse Range on the northern side of the Rangitata Gorge. Low clouds borne by onshore breezes bank up on the front ranges of Mid and South Canterbury, which are only 20 kilometres from the sea.

I waded through a shallow backwater near the North Rangitata Huts, which occupy the site of an old nohoaka named Te Maru Raki, and joined a group of anglers that had gathered to watch a large fish being landed by the Rangitata River mouth. It turned out to be a kahawai, which was promptly tossed back into the sea. An elderly fisherman told me that people had to shout across the mouth of this river before 1945, when the opening of the 67-kilometre Rangitata-to-Rakaia Diversion Race reduced its flow. People could now hold normal conversations across it.

Canterbury Regional Council (ECAN) has ruled that the minimum flow at this river mouth must not fall below 15 cumecs – a measure of flow abbreviated from cubic metres per second (m^3/s) in June and 40 cumecs in December. Ashburton and Timaru District Councils have jurisdiction over the Rangitata Catchment. Te Rūnaka o Arowhenua, which is based in Arowhenua by the confluence of the Temuka and Ōpihi Rivers, holds manawhenua there. This district's Kāti Huirapa, Ngāti Māmoe, and Waitaha-ki-te-Toka residents escaped involvement in the musket wars that raged across the northern half of the South Island in the 1820s and 30s.

After that detour we followed Ealing Road to its junction with SH1 at the site of an old postal agency called **Ealing (1)**. We carried on driving up the north bank of the Rangitata River on Withells Road until it joined SH72, which crosses the Upper Rangitata Bridge to **Arundel (3)**. From there we followed Coopers Creek-Peel Forest Road up the south bank to **Peel Forest village (4)** and its camping ground by the Peel Forest Conservation Area. Next day we trooped up Little Mount Peel.

The Rangitata and Waipara Rivers marked the boundaries of the original Canterbury Settlement; the Rangitata and Hinds/Hekao River mouths were the boundary markers of the original Coldstream Station. By 1900, serial subdivisions of that 51,000-acre sheep station had reduced it to 18,000 acres; 10,000 acres were subsequently split up for close settlement and sold to experienced farm workers. The low country of South Canterbury between the Rangitata and Waitaki Rivers was cut up into licenced pastoral runs in 1852. Some of them were snapped up by 'shagroons' (Canterbury sheepmen who came from a place other than Britain, in this case from the drought-stricken Australian Colony of Victoria, where a million sheep had recently perished in the Black Friday bushfire). The Macdonald brothers acquired Ōrari Station near

The view looking east across the
Canterbury Plain of the Rangitata
River mouth, where this upriver
story began, when I climbed Little
Mt Peel from Peel Forest.

the Rangitata River mouth in 1853 and allegedly created Rangitata Island by diverting part of the Rangitata River into 'Rangitata Creek' to prevent their sheep from straying.[57] The forerunner of SH1 ended at the North Rangitata Landing of Ward's Ferry until 1875, when a road-rail bridge replaced that punt-ferry. The parallel Lower Rangitata Bridge on SH1 opened in 1939.

The first road between Ashburton and Timaru was the old mail coach road called the Timaru Track that now joins SH72 in Mayfield. SH72 crosses the Upper Rangitata Bridge, which replaced Marshall's Ferry in 1872, and then follows the route of the Timaru Track along the old boundary line between Francis Jollie's and the Macdonald brothers' sheep stations. In 1903 George Dennistoun bought the 3000-hectare homestead block of Peel Forest Station, which he had managed after Jollie's death. My great-great-grandfather William Bennison, who emigrated from Yorkshire in 1863, worked on sheep farms around Mayfield on the other side of the Rangitata River until the 1880s, when he was balloted to buy a 70-acre farm near Dipton in Southland.

Peel Forest stretched from Tara Haoa/Mount Peel to the site of Arundel village in 1849, when Captain John Stokes of the Royal Navy's survey ship *Acheron* named that prominent landmark after Britain's Tory Prime Minister Robert Peel. While that vessel was anchored in Lyttelton Harbour/Whakaraupō, Stokes obtained a lot of topographical information about North and South Canterbury from his cartographer, William Hamilton, and a Canterbury Association surveyor, Charles Torlesse, who had scouted the latter area with a local guide from Arowhenua. Tara Haoa/Mount Peel on the Tara Haoa Range and the Four Peaks Range on the opposite side of the Ōrari Valley respectively represent Tara Haoa and Ōhuatekerekere who came ashore from the legendary waka *Arai Te Uru*.[58]

In April 1995 Adam and I embarked on a transalpine trip from Christchurch to the west coast via Dennistoun Pass near the head of the Havelock branch of the Rangitata Valley. Andrew was unable to come but he kindly agreed to drive us to the road-end on the south bank of the Rangitata River. His route took us through Peel Forest, then up Rangitata Gorge Road past the Mount Peel Station homestead at the foot of **Tara Haoa/Mount Peel (5)** and then over the flat, fogbound summit of **Coal Hill (6)** alongside the Rangitata Gorge. Thin coal seams are exposed beneath a limestone bed on the side of this hill, but cannot be seen from the road.

We emerged from the mist on the south bank of the Rangitata River above the Rangitata Gorge, near the confluence of Forest Creek. Terminal moraine ridges that the Rangitata Glacier had deposited during the Ōtira Glaciation were visible nearby. Looking west across Forest Creek I could see the jagged skyline of the Two Thumbs Range and the twin peaks that inspired its name, which tower above the Sinclair Range. A large *Pinus radiata* plantation blanketed its northern slopes. **Mount Harper/Mahaanui (7)** soared into a low-hanging cloud on the northern side of the Rangitata River. That island mountain, which was surrounded by ice during the Ōtira Glaciation, was said to be the waka that Māui and his brothers had taken on the fishing expedition when they discovered the wrecked hull of Te Waka a Aoraki, now commonly known as the South Island (see Page 70). The seaboard and inshore waters of Canterbury/Waitaha between Banks Peninsula/Horomaka and the Waitaki River mouth were called Te Tai o Mahaanui.

In 1860 Samuel Butler explored the grassy basin above the Rangitata Gorge and found an unsurveyed 2000-hectare run around the headwaters of Bush Stream on the southern side of the Sinclair Range. Butler's lawyer registered his client's pre-emptive right to purchase 250 acres around a homestead site near the Rangitata River just one day before a local squatter, John Caton, reached the Christchurch Land Office and tried to lodge a prior claim to it. Butler subsequently bought out Caton and acquired the whole pastoral block bounded by Forest Creek and the Rangitata River. Calling it Mesopotamia (land between the rivers), usually abbreviated to 'Messie', he built a thatched cottage on the homestead block below the sunny northern slopes of the Sinclair Range. Following Mesopotamia Station's tenure review in 2009, 5500 hectares of farmland near the river was free-holded and 21,000 hectares of high tussock land was transferred to the 93,000-hectare Two Thumbs/ Te Kāhui Kaupeka Conservation Park.

The sou'west front that had been battering the west coast was soon to be followed by a ridge of high pressure. The clouds were beginning to lift but my heart sank when I saw the height of the Rangitata River; it was almost bank-to-bank above the gorge. As I walked up the driveway to **Mesopotamia homestead (8)** to talk to Laurie Prouting, I saw the foundations of Butler's cob house. Laurie doubted that we would get very far tomorrow. We decided to carry on and skirted the flooded flats by sidling along the base of Black Mountain and spent the first night in **Black Mountain Hut (9)**.

On day two a couple of problems that threatened to bring this trip to a premature end were solved in quick succession after we passed Findlays Bush in the Havelock Branch of the Rangitata Valley. The first was our success in managing to ford the murky but fast-falling Havelock River via a shallow shingle weir just above the confluence of the Forbes River. A resolution to problem number two, which began when Adam noticed that the sole of one of his boots was beginning to peel off, was sorted by the discovery of some old floorboards stacked outside the nearby South Canterbury Deerstalker Association's **McDonald Hut (14)**. After rummaging through them, I extracted a few short nails and used them to repair the flapping sole.

Dennistoun Pass (1,899m) on the Main Divide when my son Adam and I crossed it from the Eric Branch of the Havelock Valley in 1995. The nominal source of the Rangitata River is the confluence of the Havelock and Clyde Rivers.

We stuck to the true left bank of the Havelock River until we were past the big bluff on the opposite bank, then forded one of the river's braided channels to a scrub-covered terminal moraine mound called Agony Island, which may be a relic of the Little Ice Age about 11,500 years ago. In 1948 the Canterbury Mountaineering Club built **Eric Bivouac (15)** on top of that island using recycled timber from an old musterers' hut. A notice inside it stated that its historic intentions book had been archived in Canterbury Museum. We had a tight schedule to keep so we forded the other river channel and tramped up the banks of Eric Stream until dusk.

At first light next morning a flock of kea watched us eat breakfast and pack up. Then, after boulder bashing up the valley for an hour, we stepped onto a tongue of old avalanche snow that covered a vestige of the Eric Glacier and slogged up it to Dennistoun Pass under a clear sky. To remind us of just how cold it was, near the top I spotted the frozen corpse of a little bird that had been blown over the pass during a storm. From the summit we gazed straight down the Perth Branch of the Whataroa Valley to the west coast.

At 1899 metres above sea level, the summit of **Dennistoun Pass (16)** is the lowest spot on the section of the Main Divide that bounds the water catchment of the Rangitata River. In the summer of 1887–88 South Canterbury surveyor Gordon McClure explored the two main branches of the Rangitata Valley, but failed to find a Main Divide pass at the head of either of them. The identity of the water catchment on the opposite side of the Main Divide remained uncertain for the next 30 years. In the summer of 1907–08 George Dennistoun's son Jim from Peel Forest Station and his friend Eric Harper took up the quest for a Main Divide pass at the head of the Havelock Valley. They failed to reach that watershed from the Havelock Glacier so they backtracked five kilometres and pitched their tent on the bank of a western tributary of the Havelock River, which Dennistoun named Eric Stream.

Next day the pair ascended its banks and spotted a Main Divide pass at the head of the Eric Glacier, which had been hidden behind the northeast ridge of McClure Peak. They reached it without difficulty and then gingerly descended the bluff on the other side and followed the banks of Bettison Stream into a deep gorge. The onset of rain that night and a lack of food forced them to turn back before they could identify which river catchment they were in.

Instead of following Dennistoun and Harper's direct route down the bluff on the western side of that pass, we climbed over the knoll on the northern side of the pass and then scrambled down a rubble-filled couloir to a grassy glen at the head of the Bettison Valley. Passing an empty tahr hunters' tent, we sidled further north along the base of a line of bluffs, sticking roughly to the same contour line. When the sun went down we camped in a dry streambed high above the Bettison Gorge.

In the morning we continued sidling at the same height until we picked up a line of stone cairns on a broad fan of large boulders. They led to a recently recut track, which we followed down a wooded spur to a swing bridge over Scone Creek. Shortly afterwards we reached Scone Hut by the confluence of Scone Creek and the Perth River, where we took a break for lunch, before following the Perth Track down the true left bank of that river. The Perth Track consisted of long riverside beaches interspersed with short steep climbs over bush-covered bluffs. After crossing Nolans Flat the track climbed 50 metres onto the large bush-covered terrace. We camped for the night on the far edge of that terrace above the confluence of the Perth and Whataroa Rivers. Our mountain radio was useful for contacting a relative in Whataroa, who had agreed to meet us at the road end the next day and put us on a bus to Greymouth that connected with the TranzAlpine train to Christchurch.

In December 1993 Andrew and I tramped up the lower Havelock Valley and followed a short track through Findlays Bush to **Findlay Face Hut (10)**, which the Forestry Department had built for its deer cullers. Findlay was a fencing contractor who had cut totara fence posts in that patch of bush in the nineteenth century.[59] We left at dawn and ascended the bed of the next side stream, then slogged up a long narrow scree that slashed through the subalpine scrub zone. From the top of the scree we sidled across the tussock face above Murphy Stream and then plugged steps up a couloir filled with soft snow to the summit of **Findlays Hill (11)**. There we obtained a grandstand view of the Two

The spectacular view of Mt D'Archiac
(2,875m) on the Two Thumbs Range
and McClure Pk, where it joins the Main
Divide, when Andrew Taylor-Perry and
I climbed Findlays Hill from Findlay
Face Hut in the Havelock Valley.

Thumbs Range from the Two Thumbs to Mount McClure, where that
range of mountains meets the Main Divide, and its majestic apex,
Mount D'Archiac (13). At 2875 metres above sea level, the summit of
that great peak is the highest point in the Rangitata Catchment.

We could see the route that we had taken up the South Forbes
Glacier with Neil Harding-Roberts and Terry Richardson just before
Easter 1984. After a cavalier start from the **Forbes Bivouac (12)** we
reached the summit of Mount D'Archiac just in time to see the sun set
in the west over the Tasman Sea, which was blanketed with pink fog.
An almost full moon immediately rose in the east and illuminated our
route down to the bivvy site on the glacier where we had stashed our
sleeping bags. A veteran mountaineer once said that you do not really
know a mountain until you have slept on it.

When Julius Haast conducted his geological survey of Canterbury
Province in the 1860s he named that great peak Mount Forbes after
the Professor of Natural Philosophy at Edinburgh University who had

studied the motion of glaciers and was an accomplished mountaineer. However, on Haast's 1870 Central Southern Alps Map, it was relabelled Mount D'Archiac after the Professor of Palaeontology at the Paris Museum of Natural History, Vicomte d'Archiac, who had read one of his papers at a meeting of the Geological Society of France. The name Mount Forbes was transferred to the next peak on the Two Thumbs Range, but the Forbes Glacier and River beneath Mount D'Archiac retained their names.

Mount D'Archiac is a conspicuous sight from Lake Clearwater and is also visible from the Canterbury Plain. Herries Beattie tentatively identified the place name Te Kāhui Kaupeka with Mount D'Archiac, however I suspect that it was primarily attached to the lofty section of the Two Thumbs Range between that peak and Mount Sibbald, which appears to be the apex on the Two Thumbs Range from Lake Tekapo and is only 64 metres lower than Mount D'Archiac.

Te Kāhui Kaupeka may be a local version of Whiti Kaupeka (the East Polynesian name of the steering star Spica, which is the brightest star in Virgo). Whiti Kaupeka precedes Te Rā (the sun) along the ecliptic circle in summer; Matariki/the Pleiades takes over that role in winter. Whiti Kaupeka and Mauka Kukutu, were said to be two men that came ashore from the waka *Arai Te Uru* and were represented by peaks or ridges near the source of the Rangitata River. Mauka Kukuta (mountain where kukuta/club rushes grow) was the original name of the portion of the Two Thumbs Range that ends on Mount Ross and the adjacent Macaulay River, which flows into the head of Lake Tekapo.[60]

The nominal source of the Rangitata River is the confluence of the Clyde and Havelock Rivers at the southern end of the Cloudy Peak Range, directly opposite Black Mountain Hut. When Edward Shortland forded the Rangitata River with his guide, Tarawhata, he was told that it arose in three hapua (hollows) called One (sand), Kiri-oneone (shingle and sand), and Ōtama-tako. The Havelock River approaches that confluence between the Two Thumbs and Cloudy Peak Ranges. Its original name, Te Awa o Tukua (the river of Tukua), commemorates a Waitaha ancestor.[61] Julius Haast renamed it after Major General Henry Havelock, who had commanded the relief force that fought their way into the besieged city of Cawnpore during the great Indian uprising against the British East India Company in 1857. A year later it relinquished its governance of India to the British Crown. Havelock's men were trapped there for seven weeks until a second relief force led by General Colin Campbell raised the siege but Havelock died of dysentery a few hours later. Campbell survived and was awarded the title Baron Clyde of Clydebank, where he was born. The Lawrence Branch of the Clyde Valley on the western side of **Mount Arrowsmith (19)** was named after the Governor of Oude Province who was killed during that uprising.

As a matter of interest, Samuel Butler based the topography in his satirical novel *Erewhon* on his observations when he rode past the Rangitata Gorge and up that long side-valley between the Jollie and Arrowsmith Ranges in 1861 (see Page 91).

In April 1990 Andrew and I decided to visit the headwaters of the Clyde River, which is the master stream of the Rangitata River. We drove to **Erewhon homestead (17)**, discussed our plans with Colin Urquhart, and slept under a *Pinus radiata* windbreak on the other side of a knobbly ridge called the Jumped-up Downs, which the Clyde Glacier had once over-ridden.

In the morning we tramped up the broad shingle bed of the Clyde River between the Cloudy Peak Range and the Jollie and Armoury Ranges. After about five hours we stopped for lunch at McCoy Hut on a grassy flat called the Bay of Plenty near the confluence of McCoy Stream and the Frances River, which is the nominal source of the Clyde River. A hundred years ago visitors used to arrive on horseback and leave their hobbled mounts to graze while they hiked further up the riverbed to see the Clyde Glaciers.

In 1880 John Acland made his last trip from Mount Peel Station to the Clyde Glaciers with his daughter, Agnes, and his neighbour's daughter, Frances Tripp, from Ōrari Gorge Station. A century later the wooden ladder that Acland's party had used to climb onto the Frances Glacier was rediscovered under a rock overhang. Acland renamed the Clyde Glacier at the head of the Clyde Valley – and the river that issued from it – after Frances, and a glacier that almost joined the Frances Glacier's tongue after Agnes.[62] The original name of the Clyde River was Te Awa a Moinaina (the river of Moinaina).[63]

The Frances River rushes through Sewer Gorge between the Cloudy

Peak Range and a spur of the Armoury Range called the Froude Range. The upper Frances Valley veered right and ran north-eastward between the Main Divide and the Froude Range. Barren trim lines on the adjacent mountainsides revealed how much ice the Frances Glacier had lost since the climax of the 'Little Ice Age' in the middle of the eighteenth century.

Wet to the waist after wading through the gorge, we stumbled on for more than two kilometres over piles of surface moraine, which had settled on the ground when that glacier's tongue melted. Eventually, we pitched our tent on a patch of taru/carpet grass by the terminal lake of a former tributary, the Colin Campbell Glacier, which poured through a gap on the Main Divide between Baker and Newton Peaks from the Garden of Eden Ice Plateau.

In 1861 Julius Haast clambered over the terminal moraine ridge that barricaded the head of the Frances Valley and walked up the rubble-covered tongue of the 'Clyde Glacier'. The Main Divide must have been continuously obscured by cloud because he assumed that both the Havelock and the Clyde Glaciers descended from a huge mountain. He named it after Professor John Tyndall of London's Royal Institute who had published *The Glaciers of the Alps* in 1860 and deduced that gigantic glaciers had excavated the beds of Switzerland's great lakes during an 'Ice Age'.

When I tried to skirt the right-hand side of the lake a kōwhiowhio/blue duck dashed out of a gap between two boulders to check on me. I then struck a patch of quicksand on the left-hand side, but managed to carry on up the valley to the rubble-covered terminus of the Frances Glacier, which descended from its sunlit névé on the southern flanks of Malcolm Peak between Rangitata Col on the Froude Range and Lambert Col on the Main Divide. A pennant of mist streamed through the latter col from the Lambert branch of the Whanganui Valley on the West Coast.

In the morning Andrew and I ascended a rubble-filled gutter beside the tongue of the Colin Campbell Glacier and then headed up a side valley towards a former tributary called the Wee McGregor Glacier. An icefall barred access to its névé so we climbed a small unnamed glacier

Above: The view across the névé of the Colin Campbell Glacier of Newton Pk (2,543m) on the Main Divide and Mt Tyndall (on the left) when Andrew and I climbed Baker Pk from a campsite by this glacier's terminal lake in 1990.

Left: The view of the rubble-covered tongue of the Colin Campbell Glacier from Baker Pk on the Main Divide. This glacier is the principal source of the Clyde River, which is the master stream of the Rangitata River.

The view across the Rangitata
Catchment from Newton Pk (far left)
to Mt Arrowsmith (far right) when we
summited Mt D'Archiac just before sunset.

Photo credit: A. Taylor-Perry

on the left, which had few crevasses. When we had gained enough
height we crossed the Wee McGregor Névé to the 2018-metre crest of
Perth Col on the Main Divide. Peering down the other side, I saw a
row of icefalls spilling over the southern rim of the Garden of Eden Ice
Plateau. Beneath them lay a shrivelled remnant of the Perth Glacier,
which is the repository for all the snow, ice, and rocks that slips off
the surrounding mountains and is the most distant source of the Perth
tributary of the Whataroa River.

In December 1934 Duncan Hall, Gavin Malcomson, John Pascoe
and Priestly Thomson crossed Perth Col and descended the Perth and
Whataroa Valleys to the west coast. Thomson coined the name 'Garden
of Eden' for the névé of the Adams, Perth, and Colin Campbell Glaciers
because it lay on the Adams Range. Westland's chief surveyor, George
Roberts, had named that range after Warren Adams, who had helped
him to link the Westland and Canterbury geodesic surveys through

Strachan Pass in 1881. Sticking to the biblical theme, Pascoe named the Eve, Cain, Abel, and Serpent Icefalls, which used to augment the tongue of the Perth Glacier.[64]

The flat summit of **Baker Peak (18)** on the northern side of Perth Col had clearly been planed off by moving ice. Climbing onto it, we caught a glimpse of Adams Col just before a bank of mist blotted out the view across the Garden of Eden. The Adams Glacier pours into the Adams Branch of the Whanganui Valley through that col between the Adams Range and Pascoe Ridge, which joins the Main Divide on **Newton Peak (19)**.

Hokitika surgeon Ebenezer Teichelmann named that peak after his former climbing companion, the Anglican vicar of South Westland, Henry Newton, who had at that time recently returned to England.[65] At 2543 metres, the summit of Newton Peak is the highest point on the portion of the Main Divide that bounds the Rangitata Catchment. Its near neighbour, Mount Tyndall, is just 26 metres lower. Looking east, I saw the jagged skyline of the Armoury Range beyond the Froude Range, which was named after a shepherd. The day was still young, but Andrew had to attend a meeting the following afternoon so we reluctantly turned back.

In 1910 Jim Dennistoun and his guide, Jack Clarke, travelled up the Clyde Valley and climbed Mount Nicholson, where the Froude Range joins the Armoury Range. Dennistoun named that peak after the Brigadier General who had lifted the siege of Delhi in 1857. When Haast explored the Rakaia Valley he also mistook that peak for 'Mount Tyndall'. From the summit of Mount Nicholson, Dennistoun scanned the Main Divide and identified the real Mount Tyndall on the Main Divide above the Colin Campbell Icefall.[66]

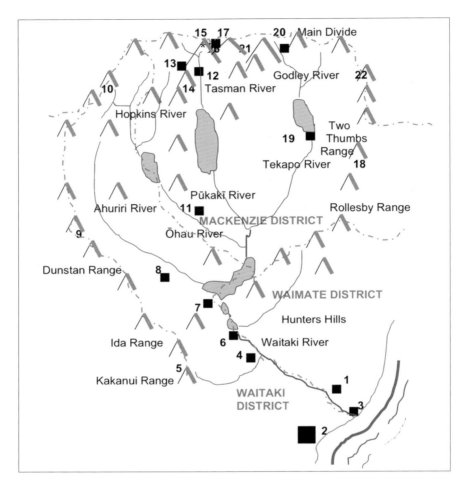

Legend

1. Glenavy	12. Aoraki/Mt Cook village
2. Oamaru	13. Mueller Hut
3. Glenavy Fishing Reserve	14. Mt Sealy
4. Duntroon	15. Aoraki/Mt Cook
5. Danseys Pass	16. Plateau Hut
6. Kurow	17. Mt Tasman/Horo Kōau
7. Ōtematata	18. Burkes Pass
8. Omarama	19. Tekapo village
9. Lindis Pass	20. Godley Hut
10. Brodrick Pass	21. Mt Malte Brun
11. Twizel	22. Stag Pass

Chapter 8
The Waitaki

In January 2002 Evelyn and I returned to Christchurch from Central Otago via 'The Pigroot' (SH85), which joins SH1 in Palmerston. Heavy rain had drenched the east coast and SH1 was blocked by floodwaters south of this town. Luckily for us, we were heading north. After crossing the Waitaki Bridge, we turned right at Glenavy (1) and drove down Fisheries Road to the Glenavy Fishing Reserve (3), which was established on Canterbury Point when the government broke up Waikakahi Station in 1898. Walking down to the river mouth, we watched it surge into the surf; all was greyness: sea, shore, and sky. The Waitaki River's 11,822-square-kilometre water catchment area is the second-largest in the South Island and its greatest recorded flood, back in 1878, was estimated to have been 4000 cumecs.

The Waitaki River mouth from the Glenavy
Huts, where this upriver story began.

A fourteenth-century kāika, Korotuaheka (Kolotuahek), on the
southern side of the Waitaki River mouth, was said to have been
occupied by the Kā Puhi descendants of a Waitaha ancestor named
Puhirere or Te Rapuwai. Although floods had scoured away part of that
60-hectare site, archaeologists who excavated it in the 1930s estimated
that about 100,000 moa legs had been steam-cooked in up to 1200
umu (earth oven) pits. Its population peaked in summer when roving
bands of moa hunters in the upper Waitaki Catchment sent gutted moa
carcasses downriver to family members in Korotuaheka. Cooked moa
meat could be preserved in fat for two to three years in airtight pōhā
rimu (bull kelp bags).

Waitaki is the southern dialectal version of Waitangi (wailing water),
which relates to the following pēpeha: Ko Waitaki nā Aoraki i riringi
(Waitaki is the river, the tears shed by Aoraki) and to Te Whakatiki ā
Tārehu who fell off the waka *Arai Te Uru* and became a semi-submerged
rock off the Waitaki River mouth. Her grieving brother, Mauka-atua,
became a mountain range near Aoraki/Mount Cook, which is the tipuna
maunga of every tribe.[67]

Te Taki o Maru/Danger Reef, 60 kilometres south of the Waitaki River mouth, represents that waka's broken hull off Shag Point/Matakāea. Many of the survivors headed up the Waitaki Valley and metamorphosed into other mountains. The seaboard and inshore waters south of the Waitaki River mouth were called Te Tai o Arai Te Uru.

Archaeologist David Simmons concluded that the Waitaki River mouth was the main distribution centre of koha-i-raki/silcrete maripi (knives), which have turned up in most early settlement sites.[68] The largest quarry of this quartz-rich stone was at Ōtekaike in the Waitaki Valley. Maripi and pōhā containing preserved meat were gifted to kith and kin when hunters returned to their northern homes before winter. In return the recipients would probably have gifted them new waka and toki (adzes).

According to local tradition the Waitaki Riverbed is the huge riu (hold) of the waka *Uruao*. Its last commander, Rakihouia, left it there when he joined his father, Rākaihautū, on the northward leg of his long journey when he pioneered the east coast trail from Murihiku south of the Waitaki River. On the way, Rākaihautū scooped out the beds of Wainono, Waitarakao, Ōtaio, Waihora, and Wairewa Lagoons. His son caught tuna/eels in them so they were collectively called Kā Poupou a Te Rakihouia (the tuna/eel weir posts of Te Rakihouia). [69]

After two centuries of sustained hunting with kuri/dogs, and devastating wildfires, this district's moa and kēkeno/seal populations collapsed and Korotuaheka and a satellite settlement by the mouth of the Shag River just south of Shag Point/Matakāea were abandoned. Fishing and fowling in the wetlands on the northern side of the Waitaki River mouth, where shingle discharged by that river had dammed the outlets of streams, sustained a small community of the Waitaha descendants of the earliest settlers, who were later joined by Kāti Māmoe and Kāi Huirapa migrants from northern regions. The few wetlands that have not been drained now receive the runoff from numerous dairy farms.

Members of that community continued to travel to the high country lakes every summer to trap tuna/eels and moulting ducks and exchange gifts with visitors from the west coast, who brought pounamu/nephrite items and kiwi and kākāpō feathers. In the autumn they caught weka/'wood hens' and preserved the cooked meat in fat for winter consumption.

In 1853 the Filleul brothers acquired Papakaio Station, which lay between the Waitaki River mouth and Boundary (or Landon) Creek, from the Otago Wastelands Board. Hugh Robison acquired the adjoining run between Boundary Creek and Awamoa Stream, which became the site of Oamaru township. In bygone times this area was a good source of aruhe/bracken fern roots and the sweet piths of tī kouka/'cabbage trees', which were harvested in autumn and baked in long umu for winter consumption. Firewood was sourced from a tree grove called Papakaio (flat area where ngaio/*Myoporum laetum* grow), but timber for buildings and fences had to be sourced further afield.

Early European travellers were ferried across the Waitaki River by the head of the local Māori community, Te Huruhuru, who had two residences 20 kilometres up the Waitaki Valley at Puna a Maru (Maru's spring) on the south bank near Georgetown and Te Kapa Tauhinu kāika on the north bank. Before the 1107-metre Waitaki Bridge replaced a punt-ferry in 1876, the Timaru coach turned around at North Waitaki Landing at the end of the Ferry Road, which branches off the Glenavy-Tawai Road. The first Waitaki Bridge carried SH1 and the Main Trunk Railway Line over this river until the parallel road bridge opened in 1956. The lower Waitaki River marks the boundary between Waimate and Waitaki Districts. Waitaki, Waimate, and Mackenzie District Councils have jurisdiction over the Waitaki Catchment. Te Rūnaka o Arowhenua, Kāti Huirapa Rūnaka, and Moeraki Rūnaka hold manawhenua there.

Fifteen kilometres south of the Waitaki Bridge, SH1 passes through **Oamaru (2)**, the hub of Waitaki District. It sprang up in 1858 around the Oamaru Landing Store, which opened in 1858 behind Friendly Bay on the leeside of Cape Wanbrow (spelt 'Wanhou' in Mantell's first report). The town site was originally named Ma Kōtukutuku (Manga Kōtukutuku – 'tree fuchsia stream'). Oamaru is a contraction of Te koha a Maru ('the gift of Maru', who was the atua guardian of this area and its offshore fishing grounds[70]).

In the 1870s, construction of a long breakwater created a sheltered harbour on the northern side of Cape Wanbrow. However, ship visits declined when rail links were established between Oamaru and the larger ports in Timaru and Dunedin. The Port of Oamaru closed in 1978 and is now only used by fishing boats.

The harbour-side precinct of Victorian shops and warehouses, much admired today especially by visitors to the town, was built of cream

'Oamaru stone' from the Ōtotara limestone quarry. About 25 million years ago, when warm seas transgressed over most of Zealandia, Ōtotara Limestone was a Bryozoan coral reef around a chain of extinct volcanic islands.

In April 1970 I embarked on a transalpine trip from Dunedin to the west coast via Brodrick Pass with my friends John Harris and Ken Mason, whose brother Bruce kindly agreed to drive us to the road end in the Hopkins Valley. After driving 130 kilometres up the east coast on SH1 we turned left just north of **Oamaru (2)**, at Pukeuri Junction. From there we followed SH83 up the south bank of the lower Waitaki River. It flows along the crush zone of the Waitaki Fault between the Hunters Hills and the Kakanui (Kakaunui) Mountains, which represent the huge wave that sealed the fate of the *Arai Te Uru* by carrying away its kakaunui – 'steering oar'. Pukeuri (Pukeure) Hill by that road junction represents one of the passengers on that waka. Walter Mantell was told that travellers left gifts of food and seaweed for the spirit of this area, presumably Maru, at an uruuruwhenua site below that hill.[71]

Thirty-five kilometres up the Waitaki Valley, we passed the junction of the **Danseys Pass (5)** Road to Naseby in Central Otago, then crossed a tributary named Maerewhenua (Tama-haere-whenua – 'son who travels the country', presumably Tamatea[72]) and entered **Duntroon (4)** – Dùn Treoin in Gaelic. The Ōtekaike tributary marked the boundary between Maerewhenua and Ōtekaike Stations. William Dansey acquired the latter in 1857 after he had crossed his namesake pass between the Kakanui (Kakaunui) Mountains and the Ida Range/Ō Te Ake in the Hawkdun/Ōteake Conservation Park. The second owner of Ōtekaike Station, Robert Campbell, built a Scottish-style baronial mansion called Duntroon using limestone from a local quarry.

Many limestone bluffs and overhangs, some of which are decorated with ancient korowai/red ochre-charcoal drawings, line SH83 between Duntroon and **Kurow (6)**. Teone Tikao recorded the saga of the waka *Takitimu*, which partly echoes the saga of the *Arai Te Uru* and describes the origin of this thick bed of creamy limestone. After a storm drove the *Takitimu* ashore on the south coast its commander, Tamatea, and crew trekked north to Lyttelton Harbour/Whakaraupō. Tamatea carried a hollow stick, probably filled with dry smouldering bracket fungus, which he used to ignite a fire each night, but accidentally dropped it in the lower Waitaki Valley where the precious embers sank into the ground and smouldered away in the underworld. The limestone outcrops in that area represent the ash that was generated by that subterranean fire.[73] Tamatea was the great trail-blazing ancestor of the Takitimu tribes. His original fire stick is represented by Green Island in Foveaux Strait. Spontaneously burning coal seams in South Canterbury and South Otago were called Te Āhi a Ūe (the fires of Ūe – Māui's companion who reputedly lit the wildfires that destroyed most of the woodlands on the east coast).[74]

Kurow, the name of the small town some 60 kilometres northwest of Oamaru, is a corruption of Kohurau ('many mists' or 'roofed in mists'[75]), which was the original name of Kurow Hill/Te Kohurau and the St Mary Range/Kohurau. The Oamaru-Kurow mail coach run was inaugurated in 1867. From 1881 until 1983 Kurow was the terminus of the Kurow Branch Railway Line.

This township sprang up in the 1860s around Christian Hille's accommodation house and punt-ferry over the Waitaki River – the first Hakataramea Bridge replaced his ferry in 1881. Te Warekorariho had initiated the ferry service at that crossing point, which was close to his residence in Hakataramea (taramea/speargrass valley) kāika by the confluence of its namesake river. He took the Southern Land District's Commissioner of Crown Lands, Walter Mantell, across the Waitaki River in the summer of 1852–53 and showed him a seam of lignite beside Coal Stream. At Mantell's request, Te Warekorariho sent some trial 100-pound consignments of coal down to the coast on mōkihī (reed rafts).

The Waitaki River generates a quarter of this country's electric power through the three huge hydroelectric power stations that have been built in the narrow section of the Waitaki Valley between the St Mary Range/Kohurau and the Kirkliston Range/Taumata o Patuki (summit of Patuki). In earlier years Kurow had housed the workforce that built the Waitaki Dam during the Great Depression. Two decades after it was commissioned in 1936, another 'hydro town' called **Ōtematata (7)** was established 20 kilometres further up the Waitaki Valley to house the workforce that built the Aviemore Dam. When that project was completed, work began on the Benmore Dam a bit further up the valley at Black Jack's Point. Shortly after it was commissioned in 1965, power began to flow through the first Cook Strait cable and the national electricity grid was finally in place.

The 75-square kilometre hydro lake behind the Benmore Dam was officially named Lake Benmore/Te Ao Mārama. Its southwest arm drowned the confluence of the Waitaki and Ahuriri (shingle weir) Rivers.

After driving through Ōtematata, the four of us crossed the Ōtematata (place of the matata/fern bird) River and then headed up the true right bank of the Ahuriri River to Omarama township. The Ōtamapaio tributary of the Ahuriri River marked the old boundary between Ōtematata and Omarama Stations.

Walter Mantell allocated a 60-hectare Native Reserve in the Hakataramea Valley to Kāti Huirapa, however it was unaccountably added to a pastoral run. The run-holder banned the traditional autumn weka/'wood hen' hunt carried out by Kāti Huirapa fowlers who used kuri/dogs to catch those flightless birds just like the moa hunters, who evidently used them too. Rabbit poison eliminated the weka, introduced trout displaced most of the native fish, and Māori fishermen could be prosecuted if introduced trout were found in their tuna/eel traps.

In 1868 the government offered this Kāi Tahu hapū 198 hectares of stony land around the site of Korotuaheka. In protest, the prophet and head of the Waitaki Māori community, Hipa Te Maiharoa, led their occupation of the lambing block on Omarama Station. This was one of their traditional food-gathering sites in Te Ao Mārama (the light-filled middle world), abbreviated to Omarama, where the Tāhu a Arapaoa trail left the often cloudy valley and entered the sunny uplands of the Waitaki Basin. Travellers would catch weka there and replenish their supplies of baked aruhe/bracken fern roots. The government feared that giving concessions to that hapū would strengthen the concurrent resistance of Taranaki iwi to land confiscations. Armed constables ended the peaceful occupation of Te Ao Mārama in 1879.[76]

SH8 follows the route of the Tāhu a Arapaoa trail and a nineteenth-century bullock track over the 960-metre **Lindis Pass (9)** between the Dunstan and Grandview/Tatara Kai Moko Ranges to the upper Clutha River/

Mata-au Basin. The Osler Fault strikes west beneath a clay escarpment on the east bank of the Ahuriri River called Paritea (white cliffs) and the Landslip Valley and Lindis Valleys on either side of that pass. On the 1880 'Taiaroa Map' Landslip Creek is Maka Tipua; Lindis Pass is Ōmako [haunt of makomako/bellbirds – when this was bushland]. Otago surveyor John Thomson crossed that pass in the summer of 1857–58 and renamed it after the small castle on Beblowe Craig on Lindisfarne Island because it looked like Double Hill next to Lindis Pass. Lindisfarne probably means 'wayfarers from Lindsey (North Lincolnshire)'.[77] Landslip Creek marked the old boundary between Omarama and Dalrachney Stations. It initially took the run holders in this area two weeks to transport bales of wool to the Oamaru Landing on bullock-drawn sledges.

When we reached the junction of SH83 and SH8 by the old Omarama Hotel we turned right, crossed the Ahuriri Bridge, and drove eastward across the Waitaki Basin. We left SH8 near Benmore homestead at the base of the Benmore Range and then followed the dusty Lake Ōhau Road over the escarpment of the Ostler Fault and some low terminal moraines that the Hopkins Glacier had deposited during the Ōtira Glaciation.

The next stretch of the road hugged the western shore of Lake Ōhau, which filled part of the vacant bed of that glacier at the end of that 'Ice Age', approximately 13,000 years ago. A tier of tawny tussock-covered terraces on Benmore Station at the base of the snow-streaked Barrier Range was matched by another tier of terraces on Ben Ohau Station at the base of the Ben Ohau Range on the other side of Lake Ōhau.

Alexander McMurdo and his partner, George Hopkinson, took up the huge Benmore Station between the Ahuriri and Ōhau tributaries of the Waitaki River in 1857. It was reputedly the first prize in a horse race between McMurdo and Hugh Fraser. The consolation prize for Hugh and his brother Samuel was Ben Ohau Station between the Ōhau and Twizel Rivers. They coined its name from Ben (Beinn – 'hill' in Gaelic) and Ōhau or Ōhou (belonging to Hou). Hou accompanied Rākaihautū when he excavated the beds of all the lakes in the Waitaki Basin.[78] Mount Ruataniwha and Tari o Mauka Atua (the Ben Ohau Range) represent two brothers that survived the wreck of the *Arai Te Uru*. The

The view of the tongue of the Godley Glacier from the shore of its terminal lake when I visited Godley Hut with a Christchurch Tramping Club party in October 1992. This glacier is the source of the Godley River, which is the most distant source of Waitaki River.

portion of the Main Divide at the head of the Hopkins Valley represents another survivor, Hape-ki-Tuaraki.[79]

Members of the Waitaki Māori community spent the summer months in fowling and fishing camps by tōtara groves beside Lake Ōhau. Nowadays the nearby 1316-hectare Ruataniwha Conservation Area contains the last sizable tōtara grove in this area. In the eighteenth century Kāi Tahu raiders from Kaiapoi sacked Kāti Mamoe's Ōhinetū nohoaka by a pā tuna (eel weir) at the outlet of Lake Ōhau.

The Dobson River joins the Hopkins River just before it enters Lake Ōhau. Their valleys are separated by the Neumann Range, which meets the Main Divide on Mount Hopkins. The 25,000-hectare Ōhau Conservation Area embraces most of the Hopkins Valley. When

Canterbury's Provincial Geologist, Julius Haast, explored this area in 1862 he named the Neumann Range after German mineralogist C F Naumann, the river on its western side after British geologist William Hopkins, and the river on its eastern side after his future father-in-law, Edward Dobson. On the 1880 Taiaroa Map, those rivers are labelled Te Awa Aruhe (the river of aruhe/bracken fern) and Ōtao (place of cooking), respectively. Baked, pounded, and sun-dried aruhe roots were essential provisions for early Māori travellers.

Governor Grey followed traditional English precedents when he decreed in 1852 that the boundary between Otago and Canterbury Provinces would ascend 'the Waitangi River to its (unspecified) source' then proceed by a right line to the source of the 'Awarura' river, which was mistakenly depicted on Edward Sortland's map flowing into Big Bay on the West Coast. 'Te Kapo' (Tekapo) was inscribed by the alpine source of the Waitaki on that map, which was based on information supplied by Te Huruhuru and a sealer named Meurant.

When Otago's chief surveyor John Thomson surveyed that 'right line' between Otago and Canterbury in the summer of 1857–58 he named the Twizel tributary of the Ohau River after the old stone bridge over the River Till by the border between Scotland and England. Thomson was the first European to see both Aoraki/Mount Cook and Mount Aspiring/Tititea from the east. He presumed that the Waitaki River arose at the base of the former peak and that the 'Awarua River' arose at the base of the latter. Canterbury's chief surveyor counter-claimed that the true source of the Waitaki River was the source of the Ahuriri River. In 1861 the General Assembly passed a compromise motion that the source of the Waitaki River was the confluence of the Ōhau and Pūkakī Rivers. A dike and ditch were subsequently dug across the Ahuriri Valley to mark the inter-provincial boundary line.[80]

After provinces were abolished in 1876 the Hopkins River and the Ōhau and lower Waitaki Rivers marked the border between Waitaki and Mackenzie Counties and Districts.

Bruce dropped us near Monument Hut on the west bank of the Hopkins River and drove back to Dunedin while we headed up the Hopkins Valley Track in the cool shade of tāwhai/southern beech trees, which

My first view of Brodrick Pass (1,639m) on
the Main Divide when I followed the track
up the North Branch of the Hopkins Valley.

British settlers called 'birches'. After crossing the high suspension bridge over the tributary that Julius Haast had renamed after English biologist Thomas Huxley, we followed a side track through a long grassy flat, crossed another swing bridge, and then tramped up to the wooded true right bank of the North Branch of the Huxley River at the base of Mount Strauchon. The contiguous Grandview and Barrier Ranges join the Main Divide on the summit of that peak, which is therefore the tri-point between Canterbury, Otago, and West Coast Regions.

We spent the first night in Brodrick Hut at the base of **Brodrick Pass (10)**, which is flanked by Mounts Strauchon and McKenzie and connects with the Landsborough branch of the Haast/Awarua Valley on the west coast. At 1639 metres above sea level, the summit of this pass is the lowest spot on the portion of the Main Divide that bounds the Waitaki Catchment.

Herries Beattie adduced from the 1880 Taiaroa map that the original name of the Huxley River was Tirau (many tī kouaka/'cabbage trees'), Mount Strauchon was Mauka Tirau and Strauchon Pass was Tarahaka Tirau.[81] The existence of an ancient trail from Lake Ōhau to the west coast was reported in an article in the *Timaru Herald* on August 12, 1865. William Taylor was informed that Tamatea had pioneered it.[82]

In 1887 Westland's Chief Surveyor, Gerhard Mueller, and his assistant, Charlie Douglas, climbed onto the Solution Range and spotted Brodrick Pass on the opposite side of the Landsborough Valley. Mueller thought that the Hunter branch of the Clutha River/Mata-au Valley lay on the eastern side of that pass. He named all the Main Divide peaks that he could see on either side of it after his colleagues including Westland's Commissioner of Crown Lands, John Strauchon, and the Minister of Lands, John McKenzie.[83]

Three years later South Canterbury District Surveyor Noel Brodrick and his assistant Louis Sladden crossed Brodrick Pass from the Huxley Valley to Creswick Flat in the Landsborough Valley. Five years after that journey Dougal Matheson led two packhorses over Brodrick Pass and left them to graze in the glen at the head of Mackenzie Creek while he crossed the Landsborough Valley to the Solution Range and peered into the Paringa Valley from Mount Matheson on the Hooker Range. He suggested in a letter to the Survey Department that a pack track could be constructed over Brodrick and Lower Ōtoko Passes to enable fit tourists to hike from Lake Ōhau to the west coast. Brodrick followed that route in both directions under very adverse conditions and reported that it was quite impracticable.[84]

After imbibing the views from Mount McKenzie we descended to the source of McKenzie Stream in the glen on the western side of Brodrick Pass. We left its banks before it tumbled into a gorge and sidled across the haumata/snow tussock-covered slopes on the western side of Mount McKenzie to a prominent spur that ran down to Creswick Flat. When we reached the tree line, John and I set up the tent while Ken searched for water. He came back with just enough to make three cups of tea. While we were waiting for the billy to boil a ruru/'morepork' owl glided silently over our heads.

A pair of kākā/'bush parrots' escorted us down to the flat next morning. After boiling the billy for a decent brew of tea in Creswick Hut we forded the Landsborough River and ascended the opposite bank to Toetoe Flat where the feathery kakaho (seed heads) of toetoe grasses nodded in a light northerly breeze. We pitched our tent under a tarpaulin that deer shooters had slung between two tāwhairauriki/ mountain beech trees, both of which had been badly scorched when Toetoe Flat Hut burned down a year ago. An abandoned packhorse eyed us warily from the edge of the woods, but I heard later on that it had been subsequently shot by a hunter who mistook it for a deer.

Next day we explored the upper Landsborough Valley as far as Zora Creek in Hind Flat. On the fifth day we descended the banks of the Landsborough River to its confluence with the Haast River in Pleasant Flat, where we planned to catch a bus to Wānaka. Because there had been no rain for two weeks the Landsborough River was quite low and we were able to ford it 13 times in the long gorge between the Solution Range and the Main Divide. On the way we watched a kākā rip up a rotten tree trunk in search of grubs. When it moved on a flock of mohua/ yellowheads or 'bush canaries' began to pick over the ransacked wood.

Right on the scheduled time, a bus pulled into the rest area by the Pleasant Flat Bridge on SH6 and the passengers alighted to stretch their legs. I asked the driver if it was the Railway Road Services bus from Fox Glacier. 'No, that's it,' he said pointing to a fast-approaching Bedford bus, which zoomed straight past. Unfortunately, the next Road Services bus was not due for another two days – and the only tour bus that stopped that day had no empty seats.

Ken managed to hitch a lift in one of the few cars that were heading east, but John and I were not so lucky. We paced up and down for the rest of the afternoon to keep the namu/sandflies at bay and then, early in the evening, we met a kind fisherman who invited us to spend the night in a nearby hut, which belonged to the Central Otago Deerstalkers Association. Back we went to the lay-by near the bridge the next morning and around noon another tour bus halted. The driver told us he had two empty seats and after consulting the passengers he agreed to take us to Wānaka where we stayed in a cabin in the lakeside motor camp. The next day we caught the morning Road Services bus to Dunedin.

In October 1969 John and I hitched a ride from Dunedin to Aoraki/ Mount Cook village with Keith McIvor and his climbing partner who planned to reconnoitre the south face of Aoraki/Mount Cook. Our modest objective was Mount Sealy at the northern end of the Ben Ohau Range. We bought fish and chips in Oamaru and drove through **Omarama (8)** after dark.

After crossing the Ōhau Bridge we saw the lights of a new hydro town by the name of **Twizel (11)** that had arisen by the confluence of the Twizel and Ōhau Rivers to house part of the workforce that was being assembled to construct the huge Upper Waitaki Hydroelectric Scheme. That area was initially claimed by Otago Province. The place name Twizel (junction of two streams) was originally attached to the confluence of the Rivers Till and Tweed near Coldstream village on Scotland's contentious border with England.

A cold southerly front overtook us near the SH80 (the Pūkakī-Hermitage Road) turn-off and so, when Ken had to stop and change a flat tyre by torchlight a few kilometres up that road, he had to do it in driving rain. An hour later we reached the New Zealand Alpine Club's Unwin Hut near Aoraki/Mount Cook Airport.

Although the rain stopped before dawn and the wind dropped away the clouds took a long time to lift. However, fine weather was forecast for the next two days so we drove through **Aoraki/Mount Cook** village **(12)** and parked near the terminus of the Mueller Glacier. Keith and his partner then headed up the Hooker Valley while John and I climbed the steep track to the second **Mueller Hut (13)**, which was built on the tip

The stunning view of the Tasman and
Hooker Glacier sources of the Tasman
tributary of the Pūkakī River below
Aoraki/Mt Cook when John Harris
and I climbed Mt Sealy in 1969. The
nominal source of the Waitaki River is
the confluence of its master stream, the
Pūkakī River, and the Tekapo River.

of the Ben Ōhau Range in 1955. An avalanche had destroyed the first
Mueller Hut, which was built on a lateral moraine bench beside the
Mueller Glacier in 1915. We had to shovel a large snowdrift out of the
hut's porch before we could open the door.

Julius Haast named the adjacent portion of the Main Divide,
which culminates in Mount Sefton/Kakīroa, after Superintendent
of Canterbury Province, William Sefton Moorhouse. The arc of high
peaks that surrounds the Mueller Glacier, is punctuated by Barron

Saddle and Fyfe Pass, which connect with the heads of the Dobson and Landsborough Valleys respectively. Mount Sealy on the southern side of that arc is labelled Te Aopoka (the pierced cloud[85]) on the 1880 Taiaroa Map.

The panorama that I saw from the summit of **Mount Sealy (14)**, where the Ben Ōhau Range joins the Main Divide spur called the Sealy Range, encompassed the 72,160 hectares of Aoraki/Mount Cook National Park and its colossal centrepiece, **Aoraki/Mount Cook (15)**. At 3724 metres above sea level, the summit of its High Peak is the highest point in Australasia as well as the Waitaki Catchment. It is two kilometres north of the 3505-metre Low Peak, which is the only portion of the summit ridge of this massif that is visible from The Hermitage. Interestingly, the height difference between the High Peak and Unwin Hut is only 500 metres less than the difference in height between the summit of Mount Everest and Everest Base Camp on the Khumbu Glacier in Nepal.

The Tasman and Hooker Glaciers on either side of the Aoraki/Mount Cook Range were thinning but had not begun to retreat that year. The tip of the Hooker Glacier's tongue almost touched the tip of the Mueller Glacier until 1973, when 'proglacial lakes' began to form in front of the Tasman and Hooker Glaciers.

In the summer of 1872–73, Governor George Bowen and his wife enjoyed a camping holiday at Governors Bush near the present site of The Hermitage. He was so enchanted by the scenery that he offered to support any member of the London-based Alpine Club who wanted to climb Aoraki/Mount Cook. Irish clergyman William Green took up the challenge and sailed to New Zealand in the autumn of 1882 with two Swiss guides, Emil Boss and Ulrich Kaufman. They climbed onto the Grand Plateau on the eastern side of the mountain from the Tasman Glacier and then ascended the Linda Glacier, which Green had named after his wife, until they were confronted by a deep crévasse. It was an hour before dark and the weather was deteriorating so they prudently turned back about 70 metres below the High Peak.

In the 1920s and 30s Kāi Tahu alpine guides George Bannister and Joe Fluerty refrained from stepping onto the highest point of Aoraki/Mount Cook. The summit of this sacred mountain is tapu and has been designated a tōpuni area.[86]

Captain James Cook renamed the South Island's lofty axial watershed the Southern Alps when he cruised up the west coast in HMS

Endeavour in 1770. Eighty years later Captain John Stokes completed Cook's maritime chart of this island when he circumnavigated it in HM Survey Ship *Acheron* and bestowed Cook's name on its highest peak.

Taare Te Maiharoa told Herries Beattie that Aoraki/Mount Cook and three mountains to the north represent four sons of Rakinui and his first wife, Poharua-o-te-Pō. Those atua had descended from the heavens to visit their father's second wife, Papatūānuku, and now sit on the raised washboard of Aoraki's wrecked waka, which rests on a submerged portion of her immense body.[87] Māui called that row of shining ice-capped peaks Kā Tiritiri o te Moana (the mirages of the ocean) when he sighted it from the west on a fishing trip in the waka *Mahaanui* from a land on that side of the great ocean. Most authorities associate this story with Waitaha and the story of the passengers on the waka *Arai Te Uru* with Kāti Māmoe. In one version of the latter story, Aoraki/Mount Cook and the ridge that runs southward from its base to the junction of the Hooker and Tasman Valleys represents the two highest-ranking members of the party of shipwreck survivors that headed up the Waitaki Valley. The above-mentioned ridge is Kirikiri-katata 'who carries his grandchild (Aoraki) on his back, hence his greater height'.[88] Aoraki's mana was so great that the ground in that area would have become tapu if his feet had touched it. Suspended rock flour in the glacier-fed Tasman River produces Lake Pūkakī's remarkable turquoise hue. It was said to carry grit away from a parahoaka (grind stone) used by Kirikiri-katata.[89]

William Wilson's West Coast informants said that Aoraki means 'above the clouds'.[90] Several high peaks in Polynesia bear the same name, for example Aolaga in Samoa and Aora'i in Tahiti.

Julius Haast examined the four large valley glaciers at the head of the Tasman Valley for the first time in 1862 and named them after the director of the Kew Royal Botanical Garden, William Hooker, the director of the Melbourne Botanical Garden, Ferdinand von Müller (or Mueller), the director of the British Geological Survey, Roderick Murchison, and the Dutch United East India Company's Captain Abel Janzoon Tasman, who had cruised past the western shores of New Zealand and charted them for the first time in 1642.

Frank Huddlestone established the original Hermitage Accommodation House in 1884 on the grassy flat below the huge terminal moraine of the Mueller Glacier. The first Mount Cook Coaching Company passengers arrived from Timaru the following year. The government purchased that hotel in 1895, however a flash flood destroyed it in 1913. The Department of Tourist and Health Resorts then built the second Hermitage Hotel on an elevated site on the alluvial fan of Kitchener Steam by Governors Bush. It burned down in 1957 and was replaced by the third Hermitage Hotel.

In 1953 the Department of Lands and Survey acquired Birch Hill Station, which was then destocked and amalgamated with Mount Cook Recreational Reserve to create Aoraki/Mount Cook National Park. Birch Hill homestead by an 11,500-year-old Little Ice Age terminal moraine became the park's first headquarters. Birch Hill Stream marks the park's boundary with Glentanner Station.

In January 1985 I drove to Tekapo to join my friends Andrew Taylor-Perry and Terry Richardson on a climbing trip up the Tasman Glacier. I left SHI at the southern end of the Rangitata Bridge and followed SH79 through Geraldine to Fairlie, then I turned right onto SH8 and followed it up the Opihi Valley to Burkes Pass village at the foot of Burkes Pass/Te Kopi o Pihi (the gorge of Pihi). Michael Burke of Raincliff Station between the Ōpihi and Ōpuha Rivers drove the first bullock wagon over this pass between the Rollesby Range and the southern end of the Two Thumbs Range/Te Aruhe Pora.

In the autumn of 1855 one of the Rhodes brothers' shepherds, Jock Mackenzie, stole a large mob of sheep from their Levels Station near Arowhenua and attempted to drive them to Southland via a secret inland route. A posse led by George Rhodes tracked them up the Tengawai (Te Ana Wai) branch of the Ōpihi Valley and arrested Mackenzie on the northern side of Mackenzie Pass/Manahuna between the Rollesby and Kirkliston Ranges. They were astonished to see a vast tract of open country, soon to be called the Mackenzie Country, beyond the 'Snowy Mountains'. In 1856 Frank and Mary Sinclair acquired the first pastoral run in that area, Mary's Range Station by the southern shore of Lake Pūkakī.

Beyond **Burkes Pass (18)**, rainbow-hued Russell lupins/*Lupinus polyphyllus* festooned the verges of SH8 as it arrowed across Sawdon Station towards Lake Tekapo. Before the practice was discouraged, many motorists would buy packets of lupin seeds in Fairlie and strew them out the window as they drove across the Mackenzie Country.

After crossing a series of stony outwash surfaces and the terminal moraine that the Godley Glacier had deposited during the Ōtira Glaciation I entered **Tekapo village (19)** by the outlet of its namesake lake. On a separate trip in 1992 to **Godley Hut (20)** I visited the Godley Glacier source of the Godley River, which flows into Lake Tekapo (see Page 274). It is the farthest source of the Waitaki River.

Every summer members of the Arowhenua-based Kāti Huirapa community would trek to their nohoaka beside the Waitaki lakes via Mackenzie Pass/Manahuna to hunt weka and catch tuna/eels and moulting ducks. Herries Beattie's informants called the inhospitable alpine zone beyond the Waitaki Basin Te Whenua o Atua (the land of powerful spirits). Hawaiians attached a similar term to the tapu heights of their volcanoes, Wao Ākea (the bright heavenly world); the fertile seaboard was called Wao Kanaka (abode of mankind). Kaitiaki (guardians) could lift the tapu for the seasonal harvesting of food in an intermediate zone called Wao Kele. Its South Island counterpart was the zone of high country basins called Te Whenua o Te Kāhui Tipua (the land of the Tipua folk).[91]

Tekapo (Takapō – 'to move about in the night') is the name of this lake's tipua-guardian. Taare Te Maiharoa told Maud Hayter that Takapō occasionally roamed its shore on moonlit nights. He was well disposed to the residents of an old Waitaha kāika on Take Karara Island in Lake Tekapo (Takapō) and warned them of impending dangers.[92] Some of Herries Beattie's informants said that the Kāhui Tipua (or Kui) folk retreated to Te Pō (the dark underworld) when the Kurahaupō and Takitimu folk arrived on this island. Like Hawaii's secretive Menehune folk, the Kāhui Tipua who had arrived on the *Uruao* and *Arai Te Uru* performed marvellous deeds at night but would turn into stone if they were accidentally exposed to sunlight.

Terry and his family were staying in a bach in Tekapo village; Andrew was there, too. In the morning we hopped into Andrew's car and drove east on SH8. It crosses the Tekapo hydro canal, which takes most of this lake's outflow and drops it 147 metres through two penstocks into the Tekapo B Power Station beside Lake Pūkakī, which is the largest reservoir in the Upper Waitaki Hydroelectric Power Scheme. Most of the outflow from this lake has been diverted into the next canal, which debouches into a purpose-built rowing venue called Lake Ruataniwha and then plunges 47 metres through another set of penstocks to the Ōhau B and C Power Stations at the head of the north arm of Lake Benmore.

Pūkakī (swollen neck) is named after the shape of its outlet before the level of this lake was raised by a control dam in the gorge that the Pūkakī River had carved in the huge terminal moraine that had impounded its waters since the Ōtira Glaciation. The nominal source of the Waitaki River is the confluence of the Pūkakī and Tekapo Rivers. Since the Pūkakī River is the largest afferent, the Tasman River must be the master stream of the Waitaki River. On the 1880 Taiaroa Map that river is labelled Te Awa Whaka Mau (river that carries things); Kamau Te Uru is an alternative name. John Thompson called it the Upper Waitaki River. Its principal source is the Tasman Glacier (Haupapa – 'ice'), which is fed by numerous tributary glaciers and icefalls. The largest one is the Hochstetter Icefall, which drains the east faces of New Zealand's two highest mountains, Aoraki/Mount Cook and **Mount Tasman/Horo Kōau (17)**.

Although the surface of the Tasman Glacier has been dropping at an average rate of one metre per year since 1890, its terminal face did not begin to retreat until 1973. An eight-kilometre proglacial lake, which will probably double its current length before it stabilises, is lapping and undermining the ice at the glacier's terminal face, which originated as snow on its main névé near Lendenfeld Saddle about 400 years ago. Before 1973, the Tasman Glacier was three kilometres wide and 29 kilometres long. Julius Haast examined this glacier around the end of a 400-year 'Little Ice Age' and saw rocks and melt-water sliding off its surface, which then bulged above the western lateral moraine bench. The rise in atmospheric levels of the 'greenhouse gas' carbon dioxide since then has mirrored the global rise of air and sea temperatures since the industrial revolution and the rate at which glaciers are melting.

After crossing the control dam at the outlet of Lake Pūkakī we turned right and headed north on SH80 along the 37-kilometre eastern shore of that lake and then up the Tasman Valley to Aoraki/Mount Cook village.

After registering our intentions at the park headquarters we drove to the Husky Flat car park near the small lake that had recently formed below the terminus of the Tasman Glacier. Keas had ripped up the seat of a motorbike that was parked there so that foam chips littered the ground. We had to walk up the last section of Tasman Valley Road, which ended at Ball Hut, before slumping of the lateral moraine wall resulted in its closure and the demolition of that hut in 1978.

Governor Onslow had opened the first Ball Hut on the lateral

The spectacle across the Tasman Glacier of Mt Tasman/Horo Kōau (3,497m) on the Main Divide and Aoraki/Mt Cook (3,754m) on the Aoraki/Mt Cook Range above the Hochstetter Icefall when Andrew Taylor-Perry, Terry Richardson and I climbed Mt Malte Brun in 1985.

Photo credit: A. Taylor-Perry

moraine bench beside the confluence of the Ball Glacier in 1891. It had six bunks for men, a four-bunk annex for women and a drystone corral for horses. In 1925 an avalanche demolished both huts. Five years later unemployment relief workers extended Tasman Valley Road to the new Ball Hut. However, motorists were required to pay a one-pound toll to drive there.

From the site of that hut we scrambled down 'Garbage Gully' and then crossed the chaotic surface of the Ball Glacier and headed for the smooth white ice in the centre of the Tasman Glacier en route to the five year-old Beetham Hut, which had replaced the second Malte Brun Hut that had opened in 1930 but was threatened by ground subsidence; an avalanche destroyed the new hut in 1995. Next day we scaled the West Ridge of **Mount Malte Brun (21)** on the Malte Brun Range, which Haast had named after the Secretary-General of the French Geographical Society.

When we reached the summit a magnificent panorama unfolded across the Tasman Glacier of Aoraki/Mount Cook, which is an outlier of the Main Divide, and the highest point on that axial watershed, the shining white 3497-metre summit of Mount Tasman/Horo Kōau. James Cowan noted that it was called Horo Kōau 'because it resembled the swelling in the long neck of a shag (kōau) when it is swallowing a fish'. Haast named the great icefall that emerged from the névé – called The Grand Plateau below the east faces of those ice-clad peaks – after his mentor, the Austrian geologist Ferdinand Hochstetter.

I followed with my eyes the Haast Ridge route that Ron Hay and I had taken past that icefall to **Plateau Hut (16)** in 1970 to meet fellow students Doug Warren and Terry Richardson. Next day Terry's climbing partner Rob Brown paired up with me for an ascent of Mount Tasman/ Horo Kōau. The weather was impeccable and the views were superb, but two problems preoccupied me that day: sustrugi – horizontal spikes of water ice, which repeatedly snagged the climbing rope – and my new alloy crampons. The right one snapped over the boot's instep on the way up and was successfully converted into a hinged crampon with spare cord. The left one snapped on the summit and I had to focus hard on supporting myself with my ice axe and digging the heel spikes of the crampons into the frozen snow, step by step, all the way down.

William Green named the tributaries of the Tasman Glacier on either side of that icefall after the Under-Secretary for the Colonies, John Ball, who was elected president of the London-based Alpine Club at its first meeting in 1857, and its current president, Douglas Freshfield.

The precipitous east faces of Mounts Tasman/Horo Kōau and Aoraki/Mount Cook, which soar above the Grand Plateau, and Mount Sefton/Kakīroa, are segments of the 60-kilometre-long hanging wall of the Main Divide Thrust Fault, which rebounds off the eastern rim of the Australian tectonic plate between Fyfe Pass and Lendenfeld Saddle. Its fault plane is roughly congruent with the weathered, slightly reddish greywacke crests of the Sealy and Malte Brun Ranges and the southern portion of the Aoraki/Mount Cook Range.[93]

On a dark, moonless night in December 1991, the tip of the old High Peak of Aoraki/Mount Cook collapsed. Twelve million cubic metres of pulverised greywacke plunged 2720 meters onto the Tasman Glacier. At 3724 metres above sea level, the new High Peak is 30 metres lower and 10 metres further south than the old High Peak. Since this portion of the Southern Alps/Kā Tiritiri o te Moana is rising at the average rate of one centimetre per year, Aoraki/Mount Cook's lost height ought to be restored in a few thousand years.

Legend

1. Milton
2. Lawrence
3. Cromwell
4. Queenstown
5. Arrowtown
6. Macetown
7. Glenorchy
8. Esquilant Bivouac
9. Mt Earnslaw/Pikirakatahi
10. Popes Nose
11. Sisyphus Peak
12. Mt Alfred/Ari
13. Lindis Pass
14. Hāwea
15. Wānaka
16. Haast Pass/Tiori Pātea
17. Makarora Hut
18. Clyde
19. Alexandra
20. Kaitāngata
21. Balclutha
22. Kākā Pt

Chapter 9
The Clutha/Mata-au

Although most of our family summer holidays were spent in the north of
the South Island, some were spent somewhere down south. In January
1991 Evelyn, Francis, Janet, Julian, Sybil, and I headed south to the Lake
Hawea Holiday Park. We took the shortest route from Christchurch, via
the Mackenzie Country and Lindis Pass (13) between the Hawkdun/
Oteake Mountains and the Grandview Mountains/Tatara Kai Moko,
which form part of the watershed between the Waitaki and Clutha/
Mata-au Catchments. The forerunner of the old stock track over that
pass, which became SH8, was the ancient Tahu a Arapaoa trail from the
Waitaki River mouth to the Central Otago lakes.[94] Quartz chips in the tar
seal and the absence of shingle screes on the western side of Lindis Pass
indicated that we had not only crossed the regional boundary between

Canterbury and Otago on this major watershed but also the geological boundary between Torlesse greywacke and Haast schist, which is more highly metamorphosed and richly gold bearing in certain places.

On the way down the Lindis Valley we passed the ruins of Lindis Pass Hotel in a grove of trees and then, a bit further on, we passed the old Morven Hills homestead. An old photograph in the Tarras tearooms showed the last cavalcade of bullock-drawn wool wagons from Morven Hills Station trundling up the open Lindis Valley in 1894 en route to Kurow. Sheepmen followed the old Scottish crofters' practice of 'burning off' inedible tussocks in autumn so that sheep could feed on their tender new leaves in the spring, however warren rabbits flourished on them too. Central Otago's extensive tussocklands suffered badly and became infested with exotic sweetbriar rose/*Rosa rubignosa* and wild thyme/*Thymus vulgaris*.

In the summer of 1857–58, two years after the Mackenzie Country was cut up into pastoral runs, Jock McLean retraced the steps of Otago's Chief Surveyor, John Thomson, over Lindis Pass, down the Lindis Valley, and then up Mount Grandview. From the summit he spotted a potential pastoral run between Longslip Station on the eastern side of the Grandview Range/Tatara Kai Moko and the upper Clutha River/Mata-au. Under the 1856 Waste Land Regulations, 14-year Crown leases on huge pastoral runs could be acquired for 10 shillings per acre if certain conditions were met. McLean bought a licence to graze sheep on a huge 150,000-hectare run, to which he gave the anglicised name Morven Hills after Clan McLean's Mhorbhairn estate in West Scotland where he was born.

We left SH8 just west of Tarras and drove northward across Hāwea Flat on Bell's Lane (SH8a) and the Luggate-Hāwea Road to **Hāwea** village **(14)**, then crossed the control dam at the outlet of Lake Hāwea to Lake Hawea Holiday Park. That dam was built in the early 1960s to maintain the flow of the Clutha River/Mata-au and the electricity output of the Roxburgh Hydro Dam when there is insufficient rainfall about the river's headwaters. Lake Hāwea's control dam raised its mean level by 20 metres and kept it 70 metres above the mean level of Lake Wānaka. A plan to build a similar dam at the outlet of Lake Wānaka, 12 kilometres to the west, was stymied in the 1970s by the HOWL (Hands Off Wānaka Lake) campaign.

In 1858 John Wilkin bought a 14-year grazing licence on a 100,000-hectare pastoral run on the opposite bank of the Clutha River/ Mata-au between the confluences of the Hāwea and Kawarau Rivers. He named it The Forks Station and built his first homestead near the site of an old nohoaka called Kahuika by the Hāwea Confluence. In 1862 the original pastoral runs were split up into smaller units. In 1878 Ewan Cameron stocked the remote Matukituki (Mātakitaki – 'to gaze at') Valley behind Lake Wānaka's West Arm with several thousand sheep, but he lost a lot of them in the big snow of 1886. John Aspinal acquired Mt Aspiring Station in 1920. More than forty years later his son Jerry returned 20,235 hectares of it to the Crown to add to Mount Aspiring National Park when it was established in 1963.

During the Arrow gold rush near Queenstown a small settlement sprang up between Wilkin's first homestead site and the western landing of Hassing's Ferry (which was replaced by a bridge in 1930) across the Clutha River/Mata-au. It was named Albert Town after Queen Victoria's husband, who had recently died in London. A township named Pembroke, after a British Colonial Secretary, arose in the 1890s on the site of Para Karehu kāika on the southern shore of Lake Wānaka. However, in 1940 the Geographic Board bowed to public pressure and renamed it **Wānaka (15)**.

Lakes Wānaka and Hāwea filled the vacant beds of the Makarora and Hunter Glaciers after they retreated at the end of the Ōtira Glaciation. Rākaihautū was said to have excavated the parallel beds of those two lakes with his enormous kō (digging stick).[95] Lake Hāwea and one of the sounds in Fiordland were named after Hāwea-ī-te-Raki, son of Waitaha-ariki. He was the eponymous ancestor of the southern hapū of the Waitaha iwi, Kā Hāwea, which eventually melded with Kāti Māmoe. Teone Tikao told Herries Beattie that the forebears of Kā Hāwea had arrived in Cloudy Bay/Te Koko a Kupe in the waka *Kapakitua* under the leadership of Taiehu and subsequently settled around the shores of Ōtākou (Otago) Harbour. Their main inland nohoaka was Te Tāwaha o Hāwea by the outlet of Lake Hāwea and Manuhaea on the shore of Isthmus Inlet near the head of that lake. Most of the adjacent Manuhaere Reserve, which was returned to Kāi Tahu in 1866, disappeared when the lake level was raised.

On Te Huruhuru's sketch map of the interior of Te Waipounamu/the South Island, which Edward Shortland published in 1851, Lake Wānaka is labelled Ōanaka'. Teone Tikao spelled that place name Wānaka ('place of a wānanga' – school of sacred teachings) and explained that it referred to the learning of 'speeches, debating or genealogies'.[96]

In the late eighteenth century Kāi Tahu warriors launched a number of attacks on Ngāti Māmoe settlements in the island's southernmost region, Murihiku. Many raiding parties followed old inland trails through the upper Waitaki and Clutha/Mata-au Basins to avoid detection until peace was sealed. Ngāti Tama rangatira Te Puoho led the last Murihiku raid in 1834. His taua marched down the west coast from Golden Bay/Mohua and crossed Haast Pass/Tiori Pātea to Lake Wānaka. From there they crossed a natural rock bridge in the Kawerau Gorge and Nevis Saddle to the Mataura Valley. The paramount southern Kāi Tahu rangatira, Tūhawaiki, received advance warning and slew Te Puoho at Tuturau.

In the spring of 1853, Reko and Kaikōura agreed to guide Nathaniel Chambers from Tuturau to Canterbury via an old inland route. When Chambers fell ill near Lake Hāwea his guides constructed a mōkihī (raft) and transported him down the Clutha River/Mata-au to a settlement near the coast.

After a couple of cool drizzly days fine settled weather returned. I decided to take the three older children on an overnight hike from Davis Flat on the western side of Haast Pass/Tiori Pātea to Makarora Hut. We headed north on SH6 up the western shore of Lake Hāwea to Isthmus Inlet, then over The Neck, and up the steep eastern shore of Lake Wānaka. Halfway along it we crossed Boundary Creek, which marked the boundary between Otago and Canterbury Provinces from 1861 until 1876 (see Page 126).

Lake Wānaka is the nominal source of the Clutha River/Mata-au, which is the country's largest river by volume. The largest and longest inflow into that 40-kilometre lake is the Makarora River, which is the master stream and the most distant source of the Clutha River/Mata-au.

Makarora Bush in the Makarora (Makarore – 'to set a trap') Valley is a remnant of the mixed conifer-broadleaf-tāwhairaunui/red beech

The view of Haast Pass/Tiori Pātea (562m)
on the Main Divide below Mt Brewster
from Cameron Flat when I followed SH6
across it from the Makarora Valley.

woodland that used to flank the lower Makarora River. In the 1860s
logging gangs began to clear-fell that bush and float trimmed logs down
to the Luggate sawmill south of Wānaka. Mount Shrimpton, on the
Young Range on the eastern side of the Makarora Valley, was named
after the brothers who acquired Makarora Station around that time and
increased the area in pasture as Makarora Bush diminished in size. The
original name of that bush, Kāika Paekai (village with abundant food),
highlights its importance for early travellers on the trail between Lake
Hāwea and the west coast.

At the top of Millionaire Flat we entered Mount Aspiring National Park
and the road became a leafy tunnel through tāwhai/beech woods. When
we entered Cameron Flat, **Haast Pass/Tiori Pātea (16)** came into view on
the Main Divide between Cameron Peak and Boundary Spur. The usual
meanings of tiori and pātea are 'to shout' and 'lay down burdens'. The
Waipounamu circa 1840 Infomap has two alternatives: 'hold up to view'
and 'cloak known as a pātea' (perhaps Brewster Glacier).[97]

At 542 metres above sea level the summit of Haast Pass/Tiori Pātea is not only the lowest point on the portion of the Main Divide that bounds the Clutha River/Mata-au Catchment, but also the lowest point on that entire watershed. Just north of Haast Pass/Tiori Pātea, the Main Divide soars to the identifier of this pass, the icy 2423-metre summit of Mount Brewster, which appears to be labelled 'Mount Tiori Patea' on the 1860 deed map attached to the Arahura Purchase. The *Waipounamu circa 1840 Infomap* labels that peak Haumia tiketike (the atua who presides over aruhe/fern root' – a staple food for travellers of those times). During the Ōtira Glaciation, an arm of the Brewster Glacier evidently gouged out this gap in the Main Divide and merged with the Makarora Glacier.

Haast Pass/Tiori Pātea and a couple of other negotiable passes punctuate a relatively low section of the Main Divide called Taikawariki between Mount Brewster/Haumia Tiketike (or Tiori Pātea) and the lofty peaks around Mount Aspiring/Tititea. The nigh impassable section of the Main Divide to the south of them was called Taumaro (a strong string stretched out). The commander of the waka *Takitimu*, Tamatea, reputedly pioneered the important transalpine trail over Haast Pass/ Tiori Pātea when he explored this island after his vessel was wrecked on the south coast.

After inspecting Whitcombe Pass in the Rakaia Valley with Samuel Butler in the autumn of 1861, John Baker conducted a preliminary survey of the Makarora Valley with Edward Owen. Edward Jollie and William Young simultaneously surveyed the upper Matukituki Valley, which at that time was also located in Canterbury Province. Baker climbed onto Haast Pass/Tiori Pātea and peered into upper Haast/Awarua Valley, but the only observation relating to the climb to be found in his memoirs was that there was no sheep country on the other side.

In the summer of 1862–63 Canterbury's Provincial Geologist Julius Haast and surveyor William Young conducted a topographical and geological survey of the Makarora and Haast/Awarua Valleys. Three porters were engaged to carry their provisions. Haast was determined to follow his namesake river all the way down to the sea.[98]

Haast's party approached his namesake pass via the Fish River Canyon. When it veered west they climbed out of that ravine and walked up a gentle wooded slope until they noticed a small northward-flowing stream which they followed down to Blue Duck Flat where it joined the infant Haast River/Awarua. Its farthest source is in a hollow on the western side of the Main Divide near the junction of Boundary Spur. Between 1875 and 1880 Vincent County Council built the Makarora Bridle Track up the eastern side of the Fish Canyon from Davis Flat to the summit of Haast Pass/Tiori Pātea. That section of the Makarora-Haast Bridle Track is now a 4-kilometre walkway.

Westland County Council extended the Makarora Bridle Track through Blue Duck Flat and down the western side of the Haast/Awarua Gorge to Pleasant Flat. SH6 sidles the western side of Fish Canyon and then roughly follows the route of the old stock track through the Haast/Awarua Gorge. Between the Great Depression and World War II, a 400-strong Public Works Department workforce pushed the Wānaka-Makarora Road end over Haast Pass/Tiori Pātea to Pleasant Flat.

Janet, Julian, Francis and I hopped out of the car by the Davis Flat Bridge and headed up the Makarora Gorge Track while Evelyn drove back to Lake Hāwea with two-year-old Sybil. The first section of our track climbed 400 metres through mossy tāwhairauriki/mountain beech woods to the southern lip of the Makarora Gorge. Patches of crimson petals on the track flagged the presence of epiphytic red pirita/mistletoe in the treetops, which rang with makomako/bellbird calls. Chocolate stops at half-hour intervals helped us to stay on schedule; after 10 stops we emerged from the gorge and two stops later we reached **Makarora Hut (17).**

In the morning Janet minded the two boys while I made a short sortie to the head of the valley. At the top of the flat I pushed through a belt of sub-alpine scrub next to a cascade and emerged in the head cirque of the Makarora Valley. Waterfalls tumbled down its sheer walls from hidden snowfields. The sun-kissed summit of Mount Brewster, where the Young Range joined the Main Divide, soared into the clear blue sky above a huge tongue of old avalanche snow that extended to the floor of this huge amphitheatre. It was the repository for all the ice and snow that falls from remnants of the Makarora Glacier on the southeast flank of Mount Brewster.

The infant Makarora tributary of the Clutha River/Mata-au emerged from the tip of that tongue of avalanche débris. The smooth rock knoll

The Makarora Glacier source of the Makarora River, which is the master stream of the Clutha River/Mata-au, at the base of Mt Brewster when I visited this spot from Makarora Hut in 1991.

on which I rested had been over-ridden long ago by the Makarora Glacier and contained a smooth cavity called a 'glacial mill' where an entrapped boulder had been tumbled around by a vigorous melt-stream.

In April 2005 Andrew, Cam Odlin and I drove up the Matukituki (Mātakitaki – 'fine river view') Valley hoping to view some of the highest peaks in the Clutha River/Mata-au Catchment. They had remained hidden in a blanket of cloud since we arrived at the Glendhu Bay Camping Ground on the western shore of Lake Wānaka. We shouldered our packs in the Raspberry Hut car park in the West Branch of the Matukituki Valley and then crossed a footbridge over the river and headed east to Homestead Flat in the East Matukituki Valley where the old Mount Aspiring homestead stood.

We carried on across Cameron Flat and followed a track through tāwhairauriki/mountain beech woodland to Junction Flat and then ascended a steep side track beside the Kitchener tributary of the East Matukituki River to Aspiring (or Kitchener) Flat in a huge cirque above the Kitchener Gorge. Flocks of Canada geese and putangitangi/Paradise shelducks heralded our arrival with a cacophony of honks. A recent slip at the top of this gorge had dammed the Kitchener River and turned the southern half of the flat into a shallow lake fringed by dead or dying trees.

After skirting its western shore we found the stone cairn that marked the start of a short track to the Rock of Ages bivouac. Someone had left a Gideon's Bible lying on a dry ledge at the back of that overhang, which was large enough to accommodate both of our tents.

The mountaintops were still clagged in when we woke up, however the sky cleared completely as we ascended the Rainbow Valley on the opposite side of Aspiring Flat. A huge pile of old snow in the middle of that side valley was a timely reminder that we were in an avalanche hazard zone. At the head of the Rainbow Valley we scrambled up to Wilmot Pass on a short spur of the Main Divide between a fortress-like peak named Fastness and an outlier named **Sisyphus Peak (11)**.

From the summit of Sisyphus Peak we obtained a panoramic view of the Main Divide between Picklehaube and **Popes Nose (10)**. Beyond that watershed, the bare northeast face of Mount Aspiring/Tititea soared above the head of the Waiatoto Valley. Its Cockscomb Ridge

The dramatic view of Popes Nose (2,700m) on the Main Divide and the northeast face of Mt Aspiring/Tititea (on the right) beyond that watershed, when Andrew Taylor-Perry, Cam Odlin and I climbed Sisyphus Pk from the East Matukituki Valley.

joined the Main Divide on Popes Nose (from the south it looks like the tail of a cooked chicken), which soared above the head of the Kitchener Valley. At 2700 metres above sea level, the summit of Popes Nose is the highest point on the portion of the Main Divide that bounds the water catchments of the Clutha River/Mata-au on the east coast and the Arawhata and Waiatoto Rivers on the west coast.

Wilmot Saddle was named after Otago surveyor Ernest Wilmot, while Sisyphus Peak was named after the cruel tyrant of Corinth in Greece whom the gods posthumously sentenced to push a huge boulder up a mountain. Whenever he reached the summit the stone rolled down to the bottom and he had to repeat the same exercise, ad infinitum.

After our tramping trip up the Makarora Valley, Evelyn, Francis, Janet, Julian, Sybil, and I left the Lake Hawea Holiday Park and drove over the Albert Town Bridge to **Wānaka (15)** and then followed SH6 down the true right bank of the Clutha River/Mata-au at the base of the Pisa Range to **Cromwell (3)**. On the way we bought a box of ripe apricots from a roadside packing shed and consumed them by the stone towers of Cromwell's old suspension bridge, which spanned the clear blue Clutha River/Mata-au before it mingled with the brown, silt-laden Kawarau River. The bridge's deck had been removed in preparation for the commissioning of the Clyde Hydro Dam and the filling of Lake Dunstan, which would soon submerge part of the town's main street. Some of the old stone stores that used to line it had already been moved to higher ground.

Floods destroyed the first two Cromwell bridges, which back then only carried foot traffic. They were built to encourage the stream of diggers that were heading to the Arrow and Shotover Goldfields in the 1860s to take the Kawarau Gorge route and buy food and equipment in Cromwell, rather than catch the punt ferry to Albert Town and then climb over the Crown Range to **Arrowtown (5)**. The third Cromwell Bridge, which opened in 1866, was much stronger and carried horse-drawn vehicles until 1891, when the imposing Cromwell suspension bridge replaced it. The Dunedin-Cromwell coach service was extended to Arrowtown and Queenstown via the Kawarau Gorge after a roadway was blasted around Nevis Bluff in 1869. Side roads were then cut through the Arrow Gorge to **Macetown (6)**, which still contains a few stone buildings, and through the formidable Shotover Gorge to Skippers.

The Clutha River/Mata-au has carved the Cromwell Gorge between the Dunstan Mountains and the Cairnmuir (stony moor) Mountains. The old Hawksburn Track from Dunstan to Kawerau Station and the Bannockburn Diggings on the south bank of the Kawerau River bypassed that gorge over the Cairnmuir Mountains. The Clyde Dam at the southern end of the Cromwell Gorge was completed in 1991, however it took another three years to rebuild SH8 on a higher contour line and construct drainage tunnels and rock buttresses to stabilise 10 slow-moving slips in the gorge. Lake Dunstan could not be filled until those projects were completed.

Clyde (18) is the oldest town in Central Otago and was initially named Dunstan. The Clyde Dam dominates the view looking northward up its main street. Eighteen months after the first Otago gold rush, at Tuapeka, two Californian gold prospectors struck a bonanza on a beach in the Cromwell Gorge in the very cold winter of 1862 when the river level was particularly low. William Fraser of Earnscleugh Station saved the vanguard of the horde of gold diggers that rushed to Dunstan from starvation by slaughtering some of his sheep in Muttontown Gully. Clyde became the hub of Vincent County, which was named after the Otago Goldfields' Secretary and Parliamentary Representative, Vincent Pyke, whose lobbying ensured that the boundary between Lake and Vincent Counties crossed the Kawerau Gorge and followed the crest of the Pisa Range/Tara Puta instead of crossing the Cromwell Gorge and following the crest of the Dunstan Mountains. That meant that Cromwell remained in Vincent County, which was incorporated into Central Otago District in the 1989 local government reforms.

Matakanui (Matakinui – 'gaze at a big object) was the original name of Castle Rock near the western end of the Dunstan Mountains by the Cromwell Gorge. The other end of that range near Lindis Pass was called Kura Matakitaki (treasured view).[99] John Thomson renamed the whole mountain range after Dunstanburgh Castle on the Northumberland Coast by the contested border between England and Scotland. The adjacent Ida Range was named after Bamburgh (Bebban Burgh) or 'King Ida's Castle' on a Northumbrian promontory opposite Lindisfarne Island, which Thomson could see from his childhood home. Ida and his wife Bebba built a fort on that promontory after they came ashore with an Anglian army from Denmark in 547 CE. Ida became the first king of the early English kingdom in northern Northumbria called Bernicia.[100] Thomson renamed the Pisa Range/Tara Puta after a schist tor on its crest that reminded him of the Leaning Tower of Pisa in Italy.

We crossed the new Cromwell Bridge at Deadmans Point and then followed SH8 on its new high route through the Cromwell Gorge and past the soon-to-be commissioned Clyde Dam to the old township of Clyde (formerly Upper Dunstan). The next section of SH8 accompanied the disused Central Otago railway track across Dunstan Flat to **Alexandra (19)**, the hub of Central Otago District, where SH8 from Milton intersects with SH85 from Palmerston in North Otago.

The railhead of the Central Otago Branch Line from Dunedin was pushed through the Upper Taieri Gorge to Middlemarch in 1892. Before then, heavy freight had to be hauled to the Dunstan Goldfield from Palmerston on horse-drawn wagons via the Pigroot Track. The railhead reached Clyde in 1907 and Cromwell in 1921 and although the last passenger train rolled into Clyde Station in 1976, freight trains continued to arrive until the last batch of concrete was poured for the Clyde Dam in 1990. The railway track beyond Middlemarch was subsequently removed and the Department of Conservation converted the bare rail bed into the enormously popular 150-kilometre cycleway known as the Central Otago Rail Trail.

At the height of the Dunstan gold rush a town named Lower Dunstan sprang up at the southern end of Dunstan Flat by the confluence of the Clutha River/Mata-au and the Manuherikia ('a bird tethered' – to lure other birds into spear range). Fires lit by moa hunters to clear trails through dense scrub and flush out flightless birds also destroyed the vegetation on which those birds browsed. Dunstan Flat was originally called Moutere (island) or Kā Moana Haehae (the divided waters). [101] In 1863 Lower Dunstan was renamed Alexandra to commemorate that popular Danish princess's marriage to Queen Victoria's eldest son and heir; the town has since gained fame through its popular blossom festival which has been held each spring since the 1940s. In 1958 a steel truss bridge replaced the 73-year-old Alexandra suspension bridge that had replaced the original punt-ferry.

The Dunstan, Cromwell and Maniatoto Basins have dry continental-type climates because they are situated so far from the sea and lie in the rain shadows of many mountain ranges. In 1995 New Zealand's biggest annual air temperature range, 55.4 degrees Celsius, was recorded at Ophir in the Manuherikia Valley. The lowest air temperature, minus 25.6 degrees Celsius, was recorded at Ranfurly in July 1903.[102] The lowest annual rainfall, 211 millimetres, was recorded at Alexandra in 1964.

After the shallow gold claims in the Dunstan Basin were worked out they were taken over by mining companies, which sank deep shafts and built water races from dammed-up mountain streams to drive hydraulic elevators that raised 'pay dirt' from formerly inaccessible alluvial deposits. Around the same time, coal-fired bucket line dredges began to extract detrital gold from the bed of the Clutha River/Mata-au. In the first half of the twentieth century, huge gold dredges excavated deep gravel beds beneath the riverbanks. The last gold dredges were decommissioned at Alexandra and Cromwell in the 1960s. When the Dunstan Goldfield was exhausted the abandoned water races were used to irrigate orchards and vineyards, the longest of which is the 123-kilometre Mount Ida Race.

In December 1857 Alexander and Watson Sheenan ventured up the east bank of the Clutha River/Mata-au from John Cargill's Tuapeka Station on Millers Flat. They climbed over the Knobby Range to avoid the Roxburgh Gorge and saw grassy flats beyond that barrier. Alexander Garvie was dispatched from Dunedin to survey the Dunstan Basin and cut it up into pastoral runs. The Sheehan brothers promptly bought grazing licences for Galloway and Moutere Stations on either side of the lower Manuherikia River and stocked them with sheep, which were driven up the Teviot Track from Balclutha to Millers Flat and then over the Knobbys to Dunstan Flat.

The first wool clips from Galloway and Moutere Stations were dragged to Dunedin on bullock-drawn sledges via the Mountain Track, which avoided the Ida and Taieri Gorges by crossing the Raggedy, Rough Ridge/Ōturehua, and Lammermoor Ranges to the punt ferry at Outram on the Taieri River. The Old Man Range/Kopuwai and the Raggedy and Rough Ranges represent the three giant waves that drove the legendary waka *Arai Te Uru* onto Shag Point/Matakaea.

Passenger coaches from Dunedin plied the Mountain Track at the start of the Dunstan Gold Rush, however it was blocked by snowdrifts during the harsh winter of 1863. Many of the gold seekers that trudged along that route at the time perished from exposure. Coach services subsequently switched to the Pigroot Track over Taieri Ridge from Palmerston, which the Sheehan brothers had also pioneered. The routes of the Knobbys, Mountain, and Pigroot Tracks to Central Otago were all labelled 'Native paths' on Walter Mantell's 1848 map of the 'South part of the Middle Island of New Zealand'.

In 1871 The Knobbys Track was replaced by the forerunner of the section of SH8 at the base of the Old Man Range/Kopuwai on the opposite side of the Roxburgh Gorge. Gold diggers called the prominent 27-metre schist tor on the crest of that range 'The Old Man' or 'The Obelisk'. According to folklore it is the petrified body of Kopuwai (water-swallower), one of the giant Kāhui Tipua that drank rivers dry during summer droughts. The tale about the escape of a Rapuwai woman whom Kopuwai had captured and his subsequent death in a fire lit by her relatives may be a folk-memory to the firestorms that ravaged Otago in ancient times. The Stuart Mountains on the western shore of Lake Te Anau represent Kopuwai's hunting dogs. Leaning Rock at the end of the Dunstan (or Old Woman) Mountains was called 'The Old Woman'. Its original name, Haehaeata (split in the morning), refers to it being hit by the first rays of the rising sun.[103]

In the 1990s geologist Chuck Landis concluded that the high plateaux of Central Otago were remnants of a 23–30 million-year-old wave-cut marine platform called the Waipounamu Erosion Surface. It was the worn-down terrain of the slowly sinking continent called Zealandia, which became almost completely submerged by the sea around that time. Some of its archaic fauna and flora evidently survived on a chain of small islands stretching northward to New Caledonia. Plants and animals spread southward when compression and uplift along the Alpine Fault line created the New Zealand archipelago, which is just a tenth of Zealandia.[104]

Hydraulic sluicing by gold diggers in Conroys Gully removed an ancient bed of red clay and exposed part of the underlying 5600 square-kilometre bed of Lake Manuherikia, which was the original source of the Mataura River in Southland. Its buried sediments contain fossils of the New Caledonia-type fauna and flora of this area when it re-emerged from the sea: eucalyptus, she-oak, and wattle tree leaves, fresh water crocodile teeth, and turtle, tuatara, and bat bones.

After crossing the Alexandra Bridge over the Clutha River/Mata-au we followed SH8 up the sunny north-facing slopes of the Old Man Range/Kopuwai, which were dotted with vineyards and stone fruit orchards, and parked beside Butchers Dam, which had drowned the old gold workings in Conroys Gully, where my great-great grandfather, George Orams, and his partners had a gold claim in 1862. We walked across the dam to examine a thick bed of ancient red clay in a 'hydraulicked' side gully. The tall drystone wall on the other side had been built by a Chinese market gardener.

Long ago the Clutha River/Mata-au had captured the north-eastern headwaters of the Mataura River when it carved Roxburgh Gorge in the Teviot Fault Zone between the Lammerlaw Range and the Old Man Range/Kopuwai. The Roxburgh Dam at the bottom of its namesake gorge was commissioned in 1956. John Cargill – who acquired the first sheep run in Central Otago, the 40,000-hectare Teviot Station on Millars Flat and the Lammerlaw Range – and Walter Millar explored the Clutha/Mata-au Valley up to this gorge in 1857.

After passing the Roxburgh Dam we drove through a sea of apricot orchards near Roxburgh township, which was named after a strong castle on the Scottish Border. A bit further on we passed Raes Junction, where SH90 peels off towards its junction with SH1 in Gore. Below the 1887 Beaumont Bridge, the Clutha River/Mata-au leaves the Tuapeka Fault Zone and races through a series of rapids at the base of the Blue Mountains. Settlers from Australia renamed the Blue Mountains after the barrier range behind the Sydney Basin in New South Wales. The original name of the apex of Otago's Blue Mountains, 'Tapanui', is a corrupt version of Tapuwae o Uenuku (sacred footsteps of Uenuku – see Page 39), which implies that it is a tupuna maunga like Tapuwae o Uenuku near Kaikōura.

The Clutha River/Mata-au flows on towards the coast between rolling schist and sandstone downs. Just before SH8 crossed the Beaumont Bridge en route to its junction with SH1 in **Milton (1)** we turned right and followed Rongahere Road further down the river's south bank, passing New Zealand's last working punt-ferry by the confluence of the Tuapeka (concealed) tributary in a farming district called Rangahere. Clutha District Council maintains that ferry as a heritage project; every day, between 3 and 5pm, it is propelled across the river by water pressure on its two slightly divergent hulls. The once-busy road from the ferry's north landing leads to **Lawrence (2)**, which was the bustling hub of the Tuapeka and Waitahuna goldfields in the nineteenth century. Paddle steamers used to shuttle back and forth between Tuapeka Mouth Landing and Port Molyneaux by the mouth of the Clutha River/Mata-au from 1863 until 1939, when the Clydevale Bridge replaced another old punt-ferry 10 kilometres down-river.

We crossed the Clydevale Bridge and then followed Clutha Valley Road 22 kilometres further down the north bank of the Clutha River/Mata-au to its junction with SH1 at the northern end of the Balclutha Bridge. Carrying on driving along the river's north bank on SH9, which passed through Stirling, we came to an old coal-mining township called **Kaitāngata (20)**.

Balclutha (21), at the southern end of the Balclutha Bridge, sprang up in 1863 by an accommodation house beside the southern landing of the 10-year-old Clutha punt ferry on the Main South Road from Dunedin. The first bridge opened in 1868 but was destroyed by debris from the first Beaumont Bridge, which was swept away by the great flood of 1878. The second Balclutha Bridge opened three years later, but was replaced in 1935 by a ferro-concrete 'bowstring' bridge that survived yet another '100-year flood' in 1978. The lower Clutha River/Mata-au marked the boundary between Clutha and Bruce Counties until 1989, when they were amalgamated to form Clutha District and Balclutha became its hub.

Below the Balclutha Bridge the river splits into a northern branch, the Matau, and a southern branch, the Kōau ('shag' – one of these birds with a fish in its beak symbolised a successful raid). The ancestral spirit Maru, who was invoked by warriors and fishermen, could manifest as a solitary kōau. Between the Mata-au and Kōau branches lies the large island named Inch Clutha (*inch* means 'island' or 'riverside meadows' and *bal* means 'homestead' in Gaelic).

The Otago Association , which founded the Scottish Otago Settlement in 1848, named this great river the Clutha after Scotland's largest river, the Clyde (Chluaidh in Gaelic), which flows past Glasgow. Those three names derive from the Old Cumbic-Welsh word clotā (washer).[105] The original name of Otago's Clutha was spelled 'Waimatahu' on the 1841 Halswell Map of the South Island. There are two versions of its second element: Matau (shaped like a fishhook, referring to the old course of the river's east branch) and Mata-au (surface current that was moving faster than the bottom current').[106]

In 1844 Fredrick Tuckett found the Taratū Coal Measures on Coal Point, just east of Kaitangata. The thick coal seam at Kaitāngata is approximately the same age as the coal measures near Ohai in Southland and others near Greymouth and Westport on the west coast, all of which were laid down approximately 60 million years ago in fault-angle depressions as the spreading floor of the Tasman Basin thrust Zealandia away from Australia.

In 1861 coal began to be railed from a pit on Coal Point to a jetty on the Kōau branch of the Clutha River/Mata-au. In 1876, 34 miners were killed when a methane explosion ripped through the new Kaitāngata coal mine. In the same year a branch line from Stirling linked that mine to the advancing railhead of the Main South Line from Dunedin. The nearby pipe clay pits and glazed pottery kiln at Benhar were also connected to it. In 1879 the last gap in the Dunedin-Invercargill Line was closed when the Balclutha Rail Bridge opened.

Kaitāngata (Kaitākata – 'where human flesh was eaten') Hill above the mine represented a survivor from the wreck of the *Arai Te Uru* who had found maukoroa (red ochre) there. Te Rapuwai (Te Pātea or Kā Puhi) were said to have settled nearby. Everywhere on this island apart from the upper west coast they were absorbed into the Waitaha iwi, which established Mataipipi and Ōtūpatu kāika near the mouth of the Clutha River/Mata-au and were in turn absorbed into Kāti Māmoe. Kāi Tahu migrants established Kotore a Hinau pā near the future site of Kaitāngata and clashed with the Kāti Māmoe residents of Taratū pā near the future site of Benhar over eeling rights in Lakes Kaitākata and Tuakitoto. Kāi Tahu suffered a severe setback in a subsequent battle on the future site of Balclutha, which became known as Te Iwi Kā Tea (the bleached bones).[107] The Clutha River/Mata-au marked the armistice line between these feuding tribes when hostilities ceased. Once peace was restored and sealed through intermarriage, this river marked the rohe between the jurisdictions of Ōtākou Rūnaka to the north and Hokanui Rūnaka to the south.

After driving through Kaitāngata we followed Summerhill Road onto the crest of Coal Point and then walked down a dirt road to a cluster of fishing cribs (huts) beside the Mata-au branch of the Clutha River/Mata-au, which glided into Molyneaux Bay. I walked on to the river mouth and gazed down the long sweep of white quartz sand on the seaward side of Inch Clutha to **Kākā Point (22)**, where the river's Kōau branch entered the sea. Nugget Point/Kā Toka tā at the far end of Molyneaux Bay was faintly visible through the sea haze.

Waves were breaking on offshore shoals. The Clutha River/Mata-au's two branches drop sand and silt on the floor of Molyneaux Bay as their currents slow and start to merge with the north-flowing 'river of the ocean' called the Southland Current. From time to time a stack of those sediments avalanches down a sinuous groove in the seafloor known as the Bounty Channel. A side channel from the mouth of the Waitaki River joins the Bounty Channel before it reaches the edge of the continental shelf. There are no definitive answers to the questions: Where precisely does a river begin and end, and do you ever step into the same river twice?

Captain James Cook and his sailing master on HMS *Endeavour*, Robert Molineaux (or Molyneaux), were cruising well offshore when they passed the mouth of the Clutha River/Mata-au in March 1770 and failed to spot it. The feature that Cook labelled 'Molineaux's Bay' lies 50 kilometres further south. It was renamed Porpoise Bay after a naval draughtsman subsequently mis-labelled the long coastal indentation between Coal Point and Kākā Point 'Molyneaux Bay'.[108]

The Clutha River/Maua-au's 21,960-square kilometre water catchment area is the largest in the South Island. Its great 1878 flood was estimated to have been 5700 cumecs. Before then the Kōau and Mata-au branches of the Clutha River/Mata-au used to unite in a lagoon and enter the sea between the tip of a very long sand spit, called Ōtauira, and Kākā Point. Small steamers could cross the shoals outside the river mouth at high tide. During the 1878 flood the Mata-au branch punched its current outlet through the base of that sand spit by Coal Point. The outlet of the Kōau branch was subsequently too shallow for ships to enter, but the fate of Port Molyneux had already been sealed with the opening of the railway line between Stirling and Dunedin in 1876. The capitals of

My daughters Janet and Sybil by
some fishing cribs near the mouth of
the Clutha River/Mata-au at the end
of our road trip down the banks of
this river from its nominal source, the
outlet of Lake Wānaka, in 1991.

the Otago and Canterbury Settlements, Dunedin (Dùn Éideann in Gaelic;
Edinburgh in English) and Christchurch, were sensibly founded near
deep sheltered inlets on Otago and Banks Peninsulas, rather than the
treacherous mouths of large east coast rivers.

Hone Tūhawaiki headed the Murihiku (Southland) community
during the turbulent 1830s. Born in Maranuku pā on Inch Clutha, he
had residences in Murikauhaka kāika by Kākā Point and on Ruapuke
Island in Foveaux Strait. He and his cousin Te Matenga Taiaroa, who
was the head of the Ōtākou (Otago) community, had the tactical skills
and military resources to roll back the Ngāti Toa offensives in Kaikōura,
Kaiapoi, and Akaroa.

Tūhawaiki later declared that liquor and infectious diseases
introduced by pākehā were 'a worse enemy than even Te Rauparaha'.[109]
The influenza and measles epidemics of 1836 and 1838 decimated his
hapū and wiped out the Tokomairaro Māori community at Measley
Beach near Milton. In January 1840 Tūhawaiki sold a block of land,
a bit over 50 square kilometres, behind Molyneaux Bay to Sydney
entrepreneur Thomas Jones. Five months later Jones chartered the brig

Portenia and sailed to Wilsher Bay near Kākā Point with his agent, George Wilsher, and three prospective farmers. After the Crown purchased the 215,702-hectare Otago Block Tūhawaiki's hapū was allocated the 259-hectare Te Kororo Māori Reserve behind an abandoned whaling station on the southern side of Kākā Point. Wellington magistrate John Symonds negotiated 'Symond's Purchase' (the Otago Block) with 25 Kāi Tahu rangatira on the shore of Ōtākou (Otago) Harbour in 1844.

Governor Grey promptly on-sold that block to the New Zealand Land Company and its northern boundary became the southeast boundary of the 1848 'Kemp's Purchase' (the 8 million–hectare Canterbury Block) which ran from Mauka Atua on the eastern side of the Taieri Valley to Heyward Point/Purehurehu by the entrance to Otago Harbour. The southern boundary of Symond's Purchase became the northeast boundary of the Murihiku (tail of the fish) Purchase, which ran along the crest of the Kaihiku (to eat the fish's tail) Range from Tapuwae o Uenuku/the Blue Mountains to Nugget Point/Kā Toka tā. Clutha, Central Otago, and Queenstown Lakes District Councils have jurisdiction in the three sectors of the Clutha/Mata-au Catchment. Te Rūnaka Ōtākou representing the Kāti Te Ruahikihiki hapū of Kāi Tahu holds manawhenua there.

Captain Edward Cattlin took Tūhawaiki and Taiaroa to Sydney to confer with his lawyers and press the Governor of New South Wales, George Gipps, to ratify his purchase of The Catlins Block and Johnny Jones and William Wentworth's purported purchase of most of the South Island between Murihiku and the New Zealand Company's enormous land purchases in 1839 from Te Āti Awa and Ngāti Toa rangatira, which had increased their offensive capabilities. The Kāi Tahu rangatira evidently hoped that a cordon of pākehā settlements protected by British armed forces between their core southern territory and their northern foes would bring peace and prosperity. They presumed that they would retain their customary hunting and food gathering rights on unoccupied land within their rohe.

On January 14, 1840, Governor Gipps banned further purchases of Māori land by British subjects and issued an 'anticipatory proclamation' that New Zealand would shortly become a Dependency of New South Wales. He also decreed that the Crown would only ratify prior land purchases in New Zealand if they complied with Australian regulations, which restricted free holdings to a maximum of 2650 acres. Old Land

Claim Commissioners appointed by the Colonial Office in London dismissed Jones' and Wentworth's land claims and reduced Cattlin's claim to 93 hectares. Russell and Wilsher gained freehold titles to their smallholdings in Molyneaux Bay.

In November 2000 Evelyn and I followed SH6 through the Kawarau Gorge from **Cromwell (3)** to **Queenstown (4)** and spent a week there with our friends Cam and Liz. One day Cam and I drove up the eastern side of Lake Wakatipu to **Glenorchy (7)** to see some of the abandoned scheelite mines on Mount Judah at the southern end of the Richardson Mountains. Scheelite or 'white gold' contains tungsten, which is added to iron to make armament-grade steel; unsurprisingly there was high demand for it during World War II and the Korean War. Next day we all drove to Glenorchy and walked to Sylvan Lake in the Dart Valley. A noisy flock of kākāriki/parakeets passed us on the woodland track. After that hike we visited Liz's friend Tommy Thomson, who had been the mining engineer in charge of the local scheelite mines during World War II after a remarkable escape from Malaya at the start of the Japanese invasion. After the war he bought Mount Earnslaw Station. When we met him, he told us that he'd picked the road line on the eastern side of the lake when he sailed past on TSS *Earnslaw*. That road has subsequently been named the Tommy Thomson Scenic Drive.

On the last day, Evelyn dropped me at the start of the bush track that zigzags up the western side of Mount Alfred/Ari. From the summit I gazed northward across Paradise Flat and watched a small cloud drift away to reveal the twin summits of **Mount Earnslaw/Pikirakatahi (9)** above the dazzling white Earnslaw Glacier. On my 21st birthday in 1969 I had climbed its East Peak from **Esquilant Bivouac (8)** on the opposite side of the mountain with three friends from Dunedin: Dick Brazier, Peter Douglas, and Ken Gousmet. The sky was cloudless all day, but when we woke up next morning it was snowing.

The mountain-name Pikirakatahi (flax cloak with an ornamental border) was also attached to the entire Forbes Range. James McKerrow renamed it Mount Earnslaw (hill of the eagle) after a hill farm near Coldstream on the Scottish Border that had belonged to the grandfather of his boss, Otago's Chief Surveyor, John Thompson.[110]

The view of Mt Earnslaw/Pikirakatahi
(2,830m) on the Forbes Range when
I climbed Mt Alfred/Ari from the
Dart/Te Awa Whakatipu Valley.

Some mountains represented great ancestors of the indigenous
inhabitants of this island or their waka or special implements; others
represented the atua or tipua guardians of important local resources.
Personal links to those wāhi tapu (hallowed places) instilled deep
connections with the land. The apex of the Forbes Mountains, Mount
Earnslaw/Pikirakatahi, was the tipua guardian of the precious Te Koroka
pounamu/nephrite outcrop in the Dart/Te Awa Whakatipu Valley. The
summit ridge of that great mountain has been designated a tōpuni area.
Pounamu was classed as fish that had swum to Te Waipounamu/the

South Island from Hawaiki and would turn into that hard green stone when they were pulled out of the water. Some said that Te Koroka had been swallowed and regurgitated by Pikirakatahi.

Edward Shortland noted that Waitaki rangatira Te Huruhuru called Lake Wakatipu 'Whakatipua', which gives some credence to the well-publicised story that the Whakatipu Lakebed preserves the impression of the body of a giant tipua that was burnt in a fire. The surrounding mountain ranges were said to be sleeping tipua, although whaka (hollow or harbour) is usually rendered haka or aka in the southern dialect. For Teone Tikao, Whakatipu was the correct spelling and meant 'regeneration of families', which had retreated there a long time ago after a great disaster.[111] James Cowan recorded a long version, Te Roto Whakatipu Whenua, which supports that interpretation.

Core samples from the bed of Diamond Lake on Paradise Flat reveal that disastrous bushfires had destroyed the woodlands around the head of Lake Whakatipu around 1460 CE. Huge wildfires rampaged across Central Otago and along the east coasts of the North and South Islands during the fourteenth and fifteenth centuries.

Lake Wakatipu is labelled 'Wakatipua (the famed Waipounamu)' on Edward Shortland's 1844 map of the lakes in the Interior of the South Island. The label 'Wahipounamu' (place of pounamu/nephrite or 'greenstone') appears beside "Wakatipu wai maori (fresh water Whakatipu)' on Walter Mantell's 1848 map of the lower South Island. Otago surveyor James McKerrow must have been aware of those associations when he named the Greenstone River, which flows into the head of Lake Wakatipu.

When Captain Cook learned through his Tahitian interpreter Tupai'a that a precious green stone was obtained from Tovy poenammoo (Te Wa'i pounamu or Te Wāhi pounamu) he wrote in his logbook that 'all agree that it is fished out of a large lake or collection of waters, the most probable conjecture is that it is brought from the mountain and deposited in the water by the torrents. This lake is called by the natives Tavai Poennammoo – that is, The Water of Green Talc; and it is only the adjoining part of the country, not the whole southern island of New Zealand, that is known to them by the name which hath been given to it on my chart'.[112]

Green pebbles of takiwai/serpentine, which is softer than pounamu/nephrite but hardens in a fire, have been found in the Greenstone

Riverbed. 'Te Wāhi Pounamu' may be the small lens of pounamu/ nephrite called Te Koroka in the Greenstone Melange containing olivine-rich rocks in the Humboldt Mountains/Kā Mauka Whakatipu. It is part of the Otago section of the Dun Mountain Ophiolite Belt, which was separated and drawn far away from the Nelson section by successive movements of the Alpine Fault (see Page 19).

In 1860 Walter Rees and his friend Nicholas von Tunzelmann followed an ancient trail from the outlet of Lake Wānaka up the Cardrona/Ōrau Valley and over the Crown Range/Tititea, which appeared to culminate in Mount Aspiring/Tititea, to Arrow Flat near the outlet of Lake Wakatipu. The original name of the Cardrona Valley means 'belonging to Rau', grandson of a Waitaha ancestor named Tititea (shining peak); Mount Alfred/Ari was originally named after another grandson of Tititea. Rees and his two business partners obtained a 14-year licence to graze sheep on a 100,000-hectare pastoral run on the eastern sides of the Kawarau River and Lake Wakatipu and stocked it a year later. When the Arrow Branch of the Kawarau Valley was proclaimed a goldfield in 1863, the Otago Provincial Council rescinded the partners' grazing licence on the southern half of their run and paid them £10,000 compensation.

Rees retained Buckler Burn Run between Simpson's (or Twenty Five Mile) Creek and the Dart River/Te Awa Whakatipu. He renamed that river after a swift tributary of the Exe River in Devon, England, which was the subject of this dirge: 'River of Dart, oh River of Dart, every year thou claimest a heart'. Alfred Duncan and George Simpson drove the first sheep up to the head of the lake in 1862. When Rees' licence expired in 1875, Buckler Burn Station was split into Mount Earnslaw, Rees Valley, and Temple Peak Stations. The boundaries of Nicholas von Tunzelmann's Fernhills Station were the Von River, Dart River/Te Awa Whakatipu, and the Humboldt Mountains/Kā Mauka Whakatipu, which Otago surveyor James McKerrow renamed after the famous Prussian geographer Alexander von Humboldt.

Glenorchy lies at the base of the Richardson Mountains/Whaka-ari, which McKerrow renamed after the Superintendent of Otago Province, John Larkins Richardson. The Rees River/Pua Hiri (a tree frequented by birds, sought by people for that reason[113]) flows southward between the Richardson and Forbes Mountains towards Lake Wakatipu. McKerrow named the mountain range between the Rees and Dart/Te

Awa Whakatipu Valleys after the Professor of Natural Philosophy at Edinburgh University, James Forbes. He had studied Switzerland's Valais glaciers and concluded that they flowed like particularly viscous liquids. His book *Travels through the Alps of Savoy*, which was published in 1843, earned him the epithet 'Father of British Mountaineering'.

During the Ōtira Glaciation the Dart Glacier excavated the beds of Lake Wakatipu and Lake Hayes in Arrow Flat. After those lakes had filled the glacier's vacated bed, the Arrow tributary of the Kawarau River captured the Nevis River, which had formerly flowed into the Frankton arm of Lake Wakatipu. When that river flowed in the opposite direction the lake level dropped 60 metres, its old outflow channel into the Mataura River, which flows to the south coast, dried up, and the Kawarau River's ultimate source became the Dart Glacier. Incorporation of the Kawarau Catchment made the water catchment area of the Clutha River/Mata-au New Zealand's largest river catchment and the East Peak of Mount Earnslaw/Pikirakatahi, which is 2830 metres above sea level, became its highest point.[114]

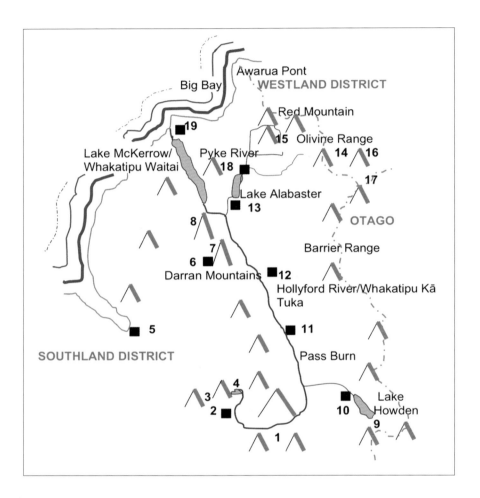

Legend

1. The Divide
2. Homer Hut
3. Homer Tunnel
4. Gertrude Saddle
5. Milford Sound Hotel
6. Turner's Bivouac Rock
7. Mt Madeline
8. Mt Tūtoko
9. Greenstone Saddle
10. Howden Hut
11. Hollyford Motor Camp
12. Hidden Falls Hut
13. Pyke Lodge
14. Forgotten River Col
15. Four Brothers Pass
16. Blockade Peak
17. Albert Peak
18. Olivine Hut
19. Martins Bay Hut
20. Big Bay Hut

Chapter 10

The Hollyford/Whakatipu Kā Tuka

Every summer morning tour buses stream out of Queenstown and head south along the eastern shore of Lake Wakatipu. When they reach the Five Rivers Plain they turn right and follow SH94 (the Gore-Milford Road) through the gap between the Takitimu Mountains, which represent the famous waka, and the Eyre Mountains/Taka Rā Haka to Te Anau village near the outlet of Lake Te Anau, which is this island's largest lake. The buses then head north up the Eglinton Valley between the granodiorite Earl Mountains in Fiordland and the Livingston Mountains, which are relics of ancient volcanoes. At the head of this valley they follow SH94 over a 532-metre saddle called The Divide (1) to the upper Hollyford/Whakatipu Kā Tuka Valley. At the head of that valley they follow the highway through the Homer

Tunnel (3) and then down the Cleddau Valley to the shore of Milford Sound/Piopiotahi.

One summer morning in 1994 I drove to the Fiordland National Park headquarters in Te Anau village and registered my intention to climb onto **Gertrude Saddle (4)**, at the head of the Hollyford/Whakatipu Kā Tuka Valley, on the opposite side of Mount Talbot to Homer Saddle, which is directly above the Homer Tunnel. Although neither pass can be crossed, in the 1930s Kurtz Suter guided competent parties up to Homer Saddle and then over Mount Macpherson to the Gulliver Branch of the Cleddau Valley. The popular Milford Track over Mackinnon Pass in the Earl Mountains from the western shore of Lake Te Anau is a much easier alternative. The tourist hotel at the head of Milford Sound/Piopiotahi opened in 1954 in conjunction with the long-delayed opening of the Homer Tunnel.

I parked beside the New Zealand Alpine Club's **Homer Hut (2)** at the base of Mount Talbot and walked a little further up the Hollyford/Whakatipu Kā Tuka Valley. Near the base of Barrier Knob I turned left and shinned up the gritty, moderately pitched granodiorite slabs beside the infant river, which cascaded out of Black Lake. A wire rope bolted onto the rock provided moral and physical support until I reached Gertrude Saddle between Mount Talbot and Barrier Knob.

Peering down the sheer northern side of that saddle, I saw the head of the Gulliver Branch of the Cleddau Valley and the distant blue waters of Milford Sound/Piopiotahi. I crossed the smooth rock knob on the left to find a large tarn above Black Lake. Melt water trickled into it from patches of snow on Mount Talbot and the Hollyford River/Whakatipu Kā Tuka commenced its 72-kilometre journey to the sea from its outlet. Near the tarn I spotted an orange object and on closer inspection I was surprised to discover that it was a pair of overalls stuffed with straw. I made a mental note to ask a DOC member of staff about them.

Later that day I drove to the Hollyford Motor Camp and asked the proprietor, Murray Gunn, if I could buy a cold drink. He pointed outside to a pile of soft drink cans over which cold water was trickling from a hose – a novel way of keeping them cool. Later, while passing through Te Anau village, I told a DOC officer about my find on Gertrude Saddle

The tarn source of the Hollyford River/Whakatipu Kā Tuka below Mt Talbot, when I climbed onto Gertrude Saddle from Homer Hut in 1994.

and learned that it was a dummy that searchers had missed when an avalanche rescue exercise had been held there last winter. Avalanche warning signs beside SH94 remind motorists that loaded snowfields lurk above the sheer bluffs near the entrance to Homer Tunnel.

In January 1999 Andrew, Adam, Janet and I caught an Intercity bus from Christchurch to Queenstown. However, the afternoon shuttle bus that we had planned to catch from there to the start of the Greenstone Track at the head of Lake Wakatipu had been cancelled, so Janet talked to the owner of a fishing charter boat who agreed to ferry us to Elfin Bay for a comparable fare. As we had to reach our pick-up point at the road end in South Westland in eight days' time, we could not afford any delays.

Lake Wakatipu was as calm as a millpond with Mount Earnslaw/ Pikirakatahi mirrored in its glassy waters as the boat sped northwards. We disembarked on the beach at Elfin Bay and followed the track on the true left bank of the Greenstone River into a gorge between the Thompson and Humboldt Mountains/Kā Mauka Whakatipu. At the top of that gorge we crossed the Caples tributary and pitched our two tents

Greenstone Saddle (698m) on the Main Divide when I crossed it from the Greenstone Valley with Andrew Taylor-Perry and two of my children, Janet and Adam, en route to Martins Bay in January 1999.

in Slip Flat. The only other tent there belonged to an American angler who was frying a brown trout in front of it.

Next day we followed the Greenstone Track through a gorge between the Thompson and Ailsa Mountains and then along the fringes of a series of grassy flats. While the sun was high in the sky we endeavoured to stay in the shade of the tāwhai/beech trees at the base of the Ailsa Mountains. Shadows were lengthening when we reached McKellar Hut near the outlet of Lake McKellar.

At the bottom of the next flat we passed a grove of sweetly scented whauwhi/eastern mountain ribbonwood trees and saw **Greenstone Saddle (9)** between Key Summit and the southern tip of the Barrier Range, which is the southernmost section of the Main Divide. At 698 metres above sea level, the summit of that saddle is the lowest spot on the portion of the Main Divide that bounds the Hollyford River/ Whakatipu Kā Tuka Catchment. On the 1860 Arahura Purchase deed plan, the nigh impassable section of the Main Divide behind the upper headwaters of the Dart River/Te Awa Whakatipu was labelled Taumaro, which means 'a strong string stretched out'. Greenstone Saddle was not named on that map, but its identifier at the end of the Main Divide was labelled 'Mount Taumaro'.

We followed a track over that indistinct saddle and descended a wooded slope to **Howden Hut (10)** on the shore of Lake Howden/ Hunaiti (little hidden lake[115]). The Pass Creek/Tuketuke (bird snares) tributary of the Hollyford River/Whakatipu Kā Tuka, which issues from that lake, is that river's most distant source on the Main Divide.

In 1861 two sheepmen, David McKellar and George Gunn, rode up the Mararoa Valley from Lake Te Anau to the Mavora (M'fhiorgh rá) Lakes, which McKellar renamed in Gaelic after his horse. They crossed a wooded saddle at the head of this valley to the upper Greenstone Valley, and climbed onto Key Summit from the low saddle at the head of that valley. From there McKellar gazed down the Hollyford/Whakatipu Kā Tuka Valley and spied Lake McKerrow/Whakatipu Waitai, which he mistook for Milford Sound/Piopiotahi.

In 1865 Otago Provincial Councillors proposed the establishment of a new port town for the Otago goldfields near the mouth of the Hollyford River/Whakatipu Kā Tuka in Martins Bay. Francis Howden surveyed the route of a track from Lake Wakatipu (or Whakatipu Wai Māori – 'freshwater Whakatipu') to Martins Bay via the Greenstone Valley and Saddle, however that track was not completed until 1881. Construction of a side track from the Dart Valley via the Routeburn Valley and Harris Saddle/Tarahaka Whakatipu was delayed by World War I, so the first Howden Hut did not open until 1918. The last Martins Bay farmer, Davey Gunn, drove cattle over Greenstone Saddle and down the Greenstone Track to Elfin Bay near the head of Lake Wakatipu from 1926 until 1938, when unemployment relief workers pushed the Gore-Milford Road end up the Eglinton Valley from Te Anau to The Divide.

In the autumn of 1863 a lone gold prospector, Patrick Caples, tramped up the Greenstone Valley from Elfin Bay, over Greenstone Saddle, and then all the way down the banks of the Hollyford River/ Whakatipu Kā Tuka to the sea. According to his diary he was too afraid to visit Te Keri Tūtoko who lived at the southern end of Martins Bay, even though he had very little food and could not light a fire. Caples renamed Whakatipu Kā Tuka after the Hollyford River in County

Tipperary, Ireland and Whakatipu Waitai (salt water Whakatipu), where this river's fresh water enters the tapu realm of the sea atua Tangaroa, after James McKerrow, who had given him a sketch map of that area.[116] After talking to Tūtoko, James Hector labelled this river 'Koduku' (Whakatipu Kōtuku would correspond to Lake Brunner/Moana Kōtuku – white heron sea, which is further up the west coast). Herries Beattie proffered a different translation, 'descending from Whakatipu'.

The poorly drafted 'Kemp's Purchase' deed stated that the southern boundary of the eight million-hectare block of Kāi Tahu territory that the Crown bought in 1848 ran from 'the mountains of Kaihiku (which reach the east coast at Nugget Point/Kā Toka tā) … to the other ocean at Wakatipu Waitai'. Charles Heaphy and Walter Mantell assumed that 'Whakatipu Waitai' was the original name of Milford Sound/Piopiotahi and labelled it as such on their 1848 maps of the South Island.

From Howden Hut we followed an old stock track down the west bank of Pass Creek to the Hollyford Road and bought some more provisions from Murray Gunn at the **Hollyford Motor Camp (11)**. The museum attached to his store contained a carved post from Kōtuku Whakaoho pā in Martins Bay and some artefacts from the failed Jamestown Settlement on the shore of Lake McKerrow/Whakatipu Waitai. While there I bought a piece of takiwai/bowenite from Murray's claim at Anita Bay. The brown mare grazing outside was a descendant of Arawhata Bill's packhorse 'Dolly' and was the only horse permitted to live in Fiordland National Park. The word COW was painted in big white letters on her flanks to ensure that hunters did not mistake her for a deer. After we left the store a kind motorist gave us a lift to the end of the road, which enabled us to reach **Hidden Falls Hut (12)** before dark.

The largest tributary of the Hollyford River/Whakatipu Kā Tuka was named after the Otago goldfields secretary Vincent Pyke. The only tributary of the Pyke River that drains the Main Divide is the Olivine River. On a lengthy trip to the Olivine Range with Adam and Ken Mason in 1992 I caught fleeting glimpses of the source of the Olivine River on the cloud-bound southwest flank of **Albert Peak (17)** from **Blockade Peak (16)** which we had climbed after jet boating up the Pyke River to **Olivine Hut (18)** and crossing **Four Brothers Pass (15)** and **Forgotten**

River Col (14) from the Diorite Valley. We popped up to Beresford Pass from there and saw the astonishing bare red flanks of Little Red Hill and Red Mountain in the Dun Mountain Ultramafic Belt, which the Olivine Range derives its name from.

Our tight schedule meant that we had to catch the big jet boat that leaves for Martins Bay at 11am each morning from its landing on the south bank of the Pyke River near **Pyke Lodge (13).** We made an early start from Hidden Falls Hut and reached the Pyke landing in time to have a dip in the river before boarding the jet boat. When all of the passengers were seated it roared into the main river, slalomed down a long stretch of rapids and then sped down Lake McKerrow/ Whakatipu Waitai. Before we entered the final stretch of the Hollyford River/Whakatipu Kā Tuka the skipper approached the beach in Half Moon Bay, lowered the gangway, and then waited while the passengers inspected the overgrown site of Jamestown. The only traces of Otago Superintendent James Macandrew's failed scheme that I spotted were two wizened apple trees and a cast iron stove.

Jamestown was founded in 1870 on the delta of Hokuri (shout at a dog) Creek near the government store that James Hector's party had built in 1863 on the eastern shore of Lake McKerrow/Whakatipu Waitai. Otago surveyor John Strauchon surveyed nine streets on that site. After several ships struck sunken logs in the lower Hollyford River/ Whakatipu Kā Tuka, between the sea and the lake, Jamestown's port status was revoked and the pilot station on Long Reef Point/Aturere was removed. Every three months until World War II a lighter from the government steamer that serviced remote lighthouses would leave mail and supplies in a landing shed near the Mackenzie homestead at the southern end of Martins Bay.

Most of the boat's passengers disembarked at private jetties on the final six-kilometre stretch of the Hollyford River/Whakatipu Kā Tuka. In the 1950s many meat workers with seasonal jobs came here and built huts and jetties along its banks. They would spend the spring 'whitebait season' netting shoals of inanga/galaxiidae fry, which were sealed into large tins and flown out by floatplanes.

We disembarked on the north bank near the river mouth and followed a short track to **Martins Bay Hut (19)**. After dinner we walked to Long Reef Point/Aturere, which separates Martins Bay from Big Bay/ Hokiauau (a Hāwea chief who had died there), where we saw kēkeno/ seal pups playing in a rock pool and a fishing boat crossing the bar on the flood tide. During the Ōtira Glaciation the Hollyford and Pyke Glaciers merged beyond this point to form a 'piedmont' ice sheet that extended from Awarua Point/Te Hōkai at the northern end of Big Bay/ Hokiauau to Konini Point at the southern end of Martins Bay, which was originally called Ōkare or Te Remu (the lower end). It was probably renamed after the leader of a sealing gang.

The summits of the May Hills/Hokau behind Konini Point were clagged by low clouds, which turned pink as the sun slipped over the western horizon. Over the next four days we tramped around Long Reef Point/Aturere to **Big Bay Hut (20)** and on to Barn Bay/Kaiwai and then up a tractor track to our pick-up point by the Cascade Ford.

The name of the Martins Bay pā, Kōtuku Whakaoho (aroused by the call of the kōtuku/white heron), may also have been attached to the short stretch of the Hollyford River/Whaktipu Kā Tuka between Lake McKerrow/Whakatipu Waitai and the sea since the Arnold River/Kōtuku Whakaoho issues from Lake Brunner/Moana Kōtuku 300 kilometres up the coast. Pale kēhua (ghosts) called Tūrehu or Pākehakeha were said to haunt the misty hills beside both lakes. At the time of first contact, Europeans were often regarded as dangerous 'pākehā' beings, rather than 'māori' (normal human beings).

The original name of the mountain range on the eastern side of Lake McKerrow/Whakatipu Waitai was Tokopa. Captain Alabaster renamed it after his mate 'Skipper' Duncan when he visited Martins Bay.[117] The Alpine Fault strikes south-westward through Jamestown Saddle between those mountains and the Sara Hills/Hokau and an unnamed saddle between the Darran Mountains and the May Hills. Sara (Hera) and May (Mahi) were the Christian names that Captain Alabaster gave to Tūtoko's daughters Kawaipatiere and Te Ruaakeake.[118]

Thirty kilometres south of Martins Bay, the Alpine Fault leaves the continental shelf at the entrance to Milford Sound/Piopiotahi and transforms into the Puysegur Oceanic Trench. Lateral pressure from

Adam standing on Long Reef Point
watching a fishing boat exit the mouth of
the Hollyford River/Whakatipu Kā Tuka.
Photo credit: J. Heinz

the steeply dipping Puysegur Subduction Zone, which begins at the
bottom of that trench, and the Fiordland Boundary Fault beneath the
Waiau Valley is slowly squeezing up the incompressible 'big brick'
called Fiordland. It consists of a Palaeozoic suite of metamorphosed
basement rocks plus the Darran Diorite Belt, which derived from
oceanic crust in a subduction system under the rim of the Gondwana
Supercontinent. Subduction was disrupted there 200–140 million
years ago when Mesozoic mudstone and sandstone on the converging
Pacific Plate crumpled up into a mountain range and molten diorite
and gabbro intruded its core.[119] Alpine Fault movements split that belt
off the Rotoroa Complex around Lake Rotoroa in Tasman District and
dragged it 480 kilometres southwestward. It has become the southern
rim of the Hollyford/Whakatipu Kā Tuka Valley while the southern
section of the Dun Mountain Ultramafic Belt (see Page 19), has become
the northern rim of the Pyke Valley.

Kōtuku Whakaoho pā at Martins Bay was once an important waka
construction site and collection point for kākāpō, kākā, and kiwi
feathers, takiwai/bowenite from Anita Bay/Hūpōkeka to the south and

pounamu/nephrite from Barn Bay/Kaiwai to the north. A sixteenth-century pounamu/nephrite workshop has been excavated on the site of Puia kāika at the head of Lake Wakatipu. Herries Beattie was told that long ago a large boulder of takiwai/bowenite was transported to Murihiku in a Te Rapuwai (Pātea) waka. Porters lugged this precious stone over Harris Saddle/Tarahaka Whakatipu and Greenstone Saddle to Lake Wakatipu, North Mavora Lake/Hikurangi, and South Mavora Lake/Manawapore. Waitaha-Pātea-Kāti Māmoe families from Murihiku/Southland spent summers beside those lakes fowling and fishing. It was a convenient time and place to receive visits from kith and kin in northern chiefdoms, arrange marriages, and exchange gifts, which circulated like breaths in hongi greetings.

Pounamu/nephrite bore an otherworldly aura from its source in hard-to-reach, far-western places associated with the dark spirit world called Te Pō. Murihiku rangatira controlled much of the northward traffic in pounamu/nephrite before Kāi Tahu rangatira in Kaikōura and Kaiapoi established transalpine links with the Arahura district to the north. Kōtuku Whakaoho pā was abandoned after a violent confrontation with an Australian sealing gang; Tūtoko's family settled there in the 1830s when the sealing era was almost over and kept the 'fire of occupation' burning until 1864.

Anita Bay/Hūpōkeka on the southern side of the entrance to Milford Sound/Piopiotahi was Te Wāhi Takiwai (the place of takiwai/bowenite) where Tama-ki-te-Raki's wife Hine Te Kokotakiwai had turned into a reef of that beautiful green stone.[120] The original name of that bay refers to a man who was killed there and fallen shreds of Tama-ki-te-Raki's pōkeha (rain cape) when he searched the shores of the fiords for his missing wives. The other wives were eventually found further up the west coast. In 1842, Captain Anglem took two vessels, the *Anita* and *Royal Mail*, to that bay and loaded them with 10 tons of takiwai/bowenite that he had blasted from the outcrop but found it was too shattered to export to China. Kokotakiwai ear pendants were made of that semi-translucent green stone, which was not as hard as pounamu/nephrite.[121]

Some old west coast place names allude to the ancient myth about Tama-nui-a-Raki's sun-wise journey to the underworld from his home in the east (see Page 61). Taking the form of a kōtuku/white heron he flew to the shore of a remote lake where he met Tū Mauka's granddaughter, Te Kohiwai. She led him to a deep pit near the place of the sunset through which Tama descended to Rarohenga (the underworld). There he met his ancestor Ūe who gave him a prestigious kahukura (red feather cloak) and the first facial moko (tattoo) worn by a living man. The Murihiku elders that related this story to Johann Wohlers commented that that their ancestors' sprits dwelt on the shore of a large lake that was surrounded by hills. Two ancient names for Fiordland, Te Rua o Te Moko (the pit of the tattoo) and Te Atawhenua (the shadow land), appear to relate to that myth and parts of the Tamatea saga that echo it.

The South Island's earliest settlers, who had followed the sun's path from the lower tip of the North Island, probably shared the old Tahitian belief that the spirits of deceased rangatira followed Te Waewae o Te Rā (the ecliptic path of the sun) to Te Rua o Te Rā, the deep pit where the sun began its nightly journey through the underworld. The cardinal direction for Polynesian voyagers was the western horizon, which the sun and stars and the tropical winds and currents travel towards. Herries Beattie was told that the mistress of the underworld, Hinenui Te Pō, had infested Fiordland with namu/sandflies and keroa/mosquitos to drive people away from her domain.[122]

The original name of Milford Sound/Piopiotahi (one piopio/thrush) may refer to Maui's pet bird, which called for him in vain after he was squeezed to death between the colossal thighs of Hinenui Te Pō, who was the underworld's first and oldest inhabitant.[123] Sydney sealer John Grono found that fiord, which Cook had missed, and renamed it Milford Haven after the estuary of the Cleddau (sword) River near his birthplace in Pembrokeshire, Wales.[124]

In February 1986, Andrew, Terry and I left Christchurch after dinner and took turns driving through the night to Te Anau village, via Dunedin and Gore. For an hour after midnight we were entertained by an aurora australis on the southern horizon.

After registering our climbing intentions at the Fiordland National Park headquarters we followed SH94 up the Eglinton Valley and over **The Divide** (1) to the upper Hollyford/Whakatipu Kā Tuka Valley, We then drove through the **Homer Tunnel** (3) and down the Cleddau Valley, stopping by the Tūtoko tributary of the Cleddau River/Te Awa Piopiotahi to stash our packs behind a fallen tree before driving the last six kilometres to a public car park near **Milford Sound Hotel (5)** at the head of Milford Sound/Piopiotahi.

We made it a sea-to-summit trip by dipping our boots in the tide before we walked back to the Tūtoko Bridge, then we shouldered our heavy packs, and headed up the muddy track on the true right bank of the Tūtoko River. Two hours later we emerged from the moss-draped tāwhai/beech woods and were confronted by a huge amphitheatre with 1500-metre granodiorite walls. The one on the right was the base of the cloud-capped southwest ridge of **Mount Tūtoko (8)**. We forded the Tūtoko River and ascended the bed of its Leader tributary on the other side of that ridge, bypassed the Leader Falls via a short track, and spent the first night out in a rock bivouac in a cirque above that waterfall. Leader Creek thundered out of the terminal face of the Age Glacier, which was perched on top of the rear wall of that cirque.

In the morning the clouds lifted and we spied the snowy summit of Mount Tūtoko for the first time under a roof of grey altostratus cloud. According to my copy of *Moir's Guidebook*, the route to **Turner's Bivouac Rock (6)** ran up the steep rock slabs at the back of the cirque. However, we found a safer route about 200 metres up the dry creek bed behind the rock bivouac and traversed a line of grassy ledges until it intersected the cairned route well above the rock slabs. The line of cairns guided us to a roomy rain-proof recess beneath Turner's Rock on a grassy bench approximately 1600 metres above sea level.

Eastbound passenger ships from Australia began to visit Milford Sound/Piopiotahi after its tourist facilities were upgraded in conjunction with the opening of the Milford Track from Lake Te Anau. In 1895 the owner of Melbourne's *Age* and *Leader* newspapers agreed to publicise that track by sponsoring Kenneth and Malcolm Ross's attempt to climb Mount Tūtoko from Milford Sound with an experienced guide, Tom Fyffe. They ascended the bed of Leader Creek and the Age Glacier, which they named after both newspapers, but mistook Mount Madeline for Mount Tūtoko. Malcolm Ross called the real Mount Tūtoko 'Mount Fosbery' and named a nearby peak Mount Syme after the newspapers' owner. In 1919 a party of climbers led by Samuel Turner ensconced themselves under his namesake rock and climbed the peak that he presumed was Mount Tūtoko. Duncan Macpherson subsequently sorted out the topography and renamed that peak after Turner's daughter Madeline.

The view of Mt Tūtoko (2,723m) on
the Darran Range when Andrew, Terry
Richardson and I climbed Mt Madeline
from Turner's Bivouac Rock in 1986.

The 40-metre wire aerial of our mountain radio enabled us to pick up the weather forecast from the Invercargill transmitter and hear that rain was on the way, which we already knew because it was raining outside our shelter. Next day we took advantage of a short lull in the weather to reconnoitre the route onto the Age Glacier's southern névé called the Madeline Ice Plateau between Mount Syme and **Mount Madeline (7)**.

Two days later a ridge of high pressure approached Fiordland. The cloud base lifted, but a blustery sou'wester continued to buffet the tops. We climbed back up to the Madeline Plateau and sheltered from the strong wind behind a rock pinnacle at the end of the west ridge of Mount Madeline. While we were weighing our options the wind dropped and patches of blue sky began to appear overhead.

Without further ado we plugged steps up the long snow slope on the opposite side of the west ridge, then shinned up a short bluff and traversed a snow arête to the summit of Mount Madeline. At this point we had climbed 2536 metres from the shore of Milford Sound/Piopiotahi. Mount Tūtoko dominated the view to the north. It cleaved the clouds that scudded past us on either side of Mount Madeline. At 2723 metres above sea level, the summit of Mount Tūtoko is the highest point in Fiordland and the water catchment area of the Hollyford River/Whakatipu Kā Tuka.

We traversed Mount Madeline by descending its south ridge and negotiating a field of crevasses to the saddle between that peak and Mount Syme. The westering sun conjured 'Broken Spectre' halos around the shadows of our heads in a bank of mist on the eastern side of the saddle.

On the way down the Leader Valley I sat on a log and watched a few namu/sandflies gather on my legs. Then to my amazement a big black fly with ribbed wings landed behind one of those pests, grabbed it with two forelimbs and proceeded to eat it! It was my sole sighting of the rare 'bat-wing fly'.

Taare Te Maiharoa told Herries Beattie that the atua Tū Te Rakiwhānoa, son of Aoraki, had carved the fiords in the stern of Te Waka a Aoraki with his huge toki (adze). Milford Sound/Piopiotahi was his masterwork.[125]

Rākaihautū dug the line of hollows filled by the Mavora Lakes, Lake McKellar, Lake Howden/Hunaiti, and Lake McKerrow/Whakatipu Waitai when he made a detour to the west coast. He then dug the line of hollows filled by Lakes Te Anau (Te Ana-au) and Manapouri/Roto Ua en route to the south coast where the high country leg of his great journey of exploration ended and the last leg up the east coast began.[126]

One of Herries Beattie's Murihiku sources told him that a member of a party of Waitaha explorers had bestowed Mount Tūtoko's original name. Unfortunately he could not recall it, however he did remember that Mount Madeline was named Mate Heraki (death a day before it was expected) after a member of the same party and that the southern end of Darran Mountains was named after her companion, Paritata.[127] Since the 1930s, nine other Darran peaks have been named after Ngāi Tahu rangatira: Apirana, Karetai, Makere, Patuki, Taiaroa, Tarewai, Te Wera, Tūhawaiki, and Waitere.

Beattie was informed that the name Ōtukerau ('belonging to Tukerau' or 'place of many bird snares') once applied to the entire Darran Mountains. In olden times a mountain range and its highest peak commonly shared the same name, so Ōtukerau could be an alternative name for Mount Tūtoko. This great peak may have been regarded as the atua of mountains, Tū-maunga, and also as one of the tū-toko (posts) that were said to prop up the heavens to maintain this light-filled middle world where life can flourish. Tū-maunga's granddaughter Te Kohiwai (misty water) guided Tama-nui-a-Raki to a western entrance to the underworld.[128]

Mount Tūtoko was the kaitiaki (guardian) of this district and a direct connection with the heavens.[129] Its sublime summit ridge has been designated a tōpuni area. Southland Regional Council and the Department of Conservation have jurisdiction over the Hollyford/ Whakatipu Kā Tuka Catchment. Rūnaka Makaawhio, representing Kāti Māhaki ki Makaawhio on the southern west coast, holds manawhenua there. Mount Tūtoko is named as their tūpuna mountain in the following pēpeha, which is is displayed in the Haast Visitor Centre:

> Uruao te waka
> Rākaihautū te tāngata
> Tūtoko te maunga
> Maitahi te awa
> Poutini te whenua
> Ngāti Māmoe–Ngāi Tahu te iwi.

The dawn view across the Hollyford/ Whakatipu Kā Tuka Valley of Albert Pk (2,353m) on the Main Divide and Mt Aspiring/Tititea (just to the right) from Turner Pass, after Gary Dickson guided me up the southeast ridge of Mt Tūtoko in 1997.

Southland historian John Hall-Jones concluded that the Welsh-born captain of HMSS *Acheron*, John Stokes, had probably renamed the Darran Mountains after a prominent crag in Glamorganshire called Y Darren Wildon (the rock of sighs).[130] Stokes renamed the Manu Upokorua mountains northeast of the Darran Mountains after the Bryneira (snowy) Mountains in Wales. Fellow Welshman John Grono had set a precedent by renaming Piopiotahi after Milford Haven in Pembrokeshire.

Eleven years later I climbed the southwest ridge of Mount Tūtoko from Turners Bivouac Rock with an alpine guide, Gary Dickson, and Kevin who was in training. We turned back 115 metres below the summit when an ugly bergschrund barred the way forward. As the old saying goes, 'you do not conquer mountains, they permit you to climb them – sometimes'. They demand respect. We descended to Turners Pass and bivouacked there overnight. At daybreak a glorious vista unfolded to the east. Fleecy white fog covered the floor of the Hollyford/Whakatipu Kā Tuka Valley like a rug. On the opposite side of the valley a tier of three watersheds towered above the fog, one behind the other: the dark Bryneira Mountains/Manu-upoko-rua, the snow-capped Barrier Range culminating in **Albert Peak (17)**, and lastly the Forbes Range culminating in Mount Earnslaw/Pikirakatahi.

At 2353 metres above sea level, the summit of Albert Peak is the highest point on the portion of the Main Divide that bounds the Hollyford River/Whakatipu Kā Tuka Catchment. It is also the tri-point where the Otago, Southland, and West Coast regional boundaries meet.

Between 1881 and 1889 Ernest Wilmot surveyed the Hollyford River/Whakatipu Kā Tuka Catchment and named many of its peaks, but the apex of the Barrier Range was still unnamed when Jack Holloway, David Albert Jackson, and E Lilley climbed it in the summer of 1934–35. The New Zealand Geographic Board declined the name that Holloway had proposed, which was Mount David, and substituted David's middle name, Albert, presumably because there was a Mount David elsewhere and a Mount Victoria nearby on the Barrier Range.

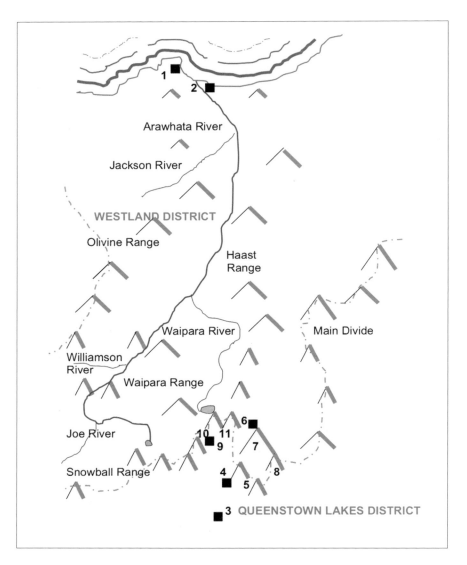

Legend

1.	Jackson Bay/Ōkahu	7.	Mt Aspiring/Tititea
2.	Neils Beach	8.	Popes Nose
3.	Aspiring Hut	9.	Liverpool Bivouac
4.	French Ridge (Lucas-Trotter) Hut	10.	Arawhata Saddle
5.	Quarterdeck Pass	11.	Hector Col
6.	Colin Todd Memorial Hut		

Chapter 11

The Arawhata

When my father and I drove from Picton to Dunedin via the new Haast Highway in 1968 we detoured down to Jackson Bay/Ōkahu village (1) to visit a retired road worker and ferryman, Dan Greaney, whom Dad called 'the mayor of Jackson Bay'. I was very impressed to hear that he knew the famous gold prospector Arawhata Bill. Dan's brother Alec had worked alongside Dad on the *Grey River Argus* linotype machines in Greymouth. A pīwakawaka/fantail fluttered around Dan's doorway as we talked.

Forty years later I drove down a side road behind **Neils Beach (2)** and parked by the old South Landing of the Arawhata Ferry. Neil Carmichael operated that ferry from 1874 until 1878; in 1944 a concrete bridge replaced it 10 kilometres upriver. Today, however, two anglers

Two anglers in a dinghy near the
mouth of the Arawhata River,
where this upriver story began.

were rowing a dinghy across the estuary's silvery waters, which mirrored the overcast sky. An isolated hill on the opposite shore named Mount McLean towered above the Burmeister Morass, which drains into the Arawhata Estuary via Barton Creek and also into the Waiatoto Estuary via the Dawn Rivulet on the seaward side of Mount McLean, which was named after the captain of the steamer *Alhambra*, Jack 'Hellfire' McLean.

Te Arawhata (the food store ladder) was said to be the name of a warrior who was killed at Jackson Bay/Ōkahu. Many old west coast river names were memento mori of deaths due to drowning or fighting.[131] Jackson Bay/Ōkahu ('belonging to Kahu' – a chief who died there) in the lee of Jackson Head is one of the safest anchorages on the west coast. It may have been renamed after the whaler James Jackson who was stationed there for a while. The Arawhata was also called the Jackson River before that name was transferred to a tributary. Captain Cook gave the name Open Bay to the broad indentation between Jackson Head and Arnott Point.

Ōkahu pā was located behind Neils Beach by the Arawhata River mouth, which is 10 kilometres from the bridge. Pounamu/nephrite stone workers resided there and also in a satellite kāinga further down the coast at Barn Bay/Kaiwai. After a large Ngāi Tahu taua from Ōtākou led by Te Matehaere had harried the west coast, a Ngāi Tahu taua from Kaiapoi and Waipara crossed Harper Pass/Nōti Taramakau and seized control of the entire region. The leader of its Ngāti Tuke contingent, Wharetai, settled at Ōkahu pā with his slave, Te Kanau, who was said to be the last Ngāti Wairangi tohunga. When Wharetai's strained relations with the sealers hit a low point in 1826 his warriors raided their base on Arnott Point. The sealers destroyed the pā and killed many of its residents in retaliation.

Westland District Council and the Conservation Department have jurisdiction over southern West Coast Region from Awarua Point/Te Hōkai to the Taramakau River. Rūnaka Makaawhio holds manawhenua between Milford Sound/Piopiotahi and the Hokitika River.

In 1869, Westland County Council asked its chief surveyor, Gerhard Mueller, to lay out a 'Special Settlement' with a jetty in Jackson Bay/Ōkahu and a township called Arawata four kilometres away behind Neils Beach. It was founded in 1874 but failed, like Jamestown, basically due to the lack of port facilities. A few families stayed on. The Nolans acquired the Jackson, Collins, and Callery partnership's Arawhata Run and Fraser's Cascade Run and slowly turned their fortunes around. The settlement's jetty was finally built in 1938.

The Burmeister Tops between the Jackson Valley and Jackson Head was the massive lateral moraine of the Arawhata Glacier during the Ōtira Glaciation. William Burmeister was an early settler and Arawhata ferryman in the 1870s; 'Arawhata Bill' (William O'Leary) was the ferryman for a while in the 1920s.

A 50-kilometre-wide piedmont ice sheet consisting of the amalgamated tongues of the Arawhata, Waiatoto, Turnbull, Okuru, and Haast Glaciers formed on the western side of the Alpine Fault during during the Ōtira Glaciation. When it ended 13,000 years ago, the sea level rose until it lapped the western spurs of the Southern Alps/Kā Tiritiri o te Moana. Silt-laden melt water from retreating valley glaciers and debris from massive slips caused by Alpine Fault movements built expanding river deltas, which eventually amalgamated to form the Haast Plain. Parallel swales between bush-covered sand ridges mark stages in the westward advance of the Open Bay shoreline over the last 6000 years.

In April 1969 I accompanied three friends from the Otago Tramping and Mountaineering Club – Ken Gousmet, Bruce Mason and Roger Conroy – on our initial attempt to climb **Mount Aspiring/Tititea (7)**. We spent the first night with another party of trampers in Jerry Aspinall's hay barn on Cameron Flat in the Matukituki Valley after the long drive from Dunedin. Next day we tramped up the grassy flats on the true right bank of the West Branch of the Matukituki River to the New Zealand Alpine Club's **Aspiring Hut (3)**, which opened in 1949 on the first site in that valley with a view of that mountain.

Mount Aspiring/Tititea is the only 3000-metre peak in New Zealand outside Aoraki/Mount Cook National Park. At 3033 metres above sea level, its summit is the highest point in the water catchment areas of the Arawhata and Waiatoto Rivers and has been designated a tōpuni area. Its southeast Coxcomb Ridge meets the Main Divide on **Popes Nose (8)**, which at 2700 metres above sea level is the highest point on the portion of the Main Divide that bounds the water catchments of the Arawhata, Waiatoto and Clutha/Mata-au Rivers.

Otago surveyor John Thompson coined the name Mount Aspiring when he spied it from Mount Grandview near Lake Hāwea in 1857. Rawiri Te Maire stated that 'the whole range east of Lake Wakatipu, and round the head of the Shotover River to Lake Wanaka' was called Tititea, which means 'white peak or peaks' (see Page 164). Two other names of that great peak have been recorded: Ōtapahū (belonging to Tapahū) and Te Matakahi o Tū Te Rakiwhānoa (the wedge of Tū Te Rakiwhānoa).[132]

In the summer of 1949–50 Dunedin-born poet James Keir Baxter spent a month in Aspiring Hut with a New Zealand Film Unit team that was preparing to make a documentary provisionally titled *Ascent of Aspiring.* The director, Brian Brake, had asked Baxter to write the script and Douglas Lilburn to compose the music. After a month of persistent bad weather, he abandoned the project. Baxter's much-loved *Poem in the Matukituki Valley* came from the unfinished film script.[133]

In November 1909, Major Bernard Head from the Alpine Club in London and his New Zealand guides, Jack Clarke and Alex Graham, searched in vain for an ascent route from the Kitchener Valley in the East Matukituki Valley. They then decided to approach it from the West Matukituki Valley and established a high camp on French Ridge. Next day they crossed Quarterdeck Pass on the south flank of Mount French and accomplished the first ascent of Mount Aspiring/Tititea via its South Ridge.[134] Head named the Kitchener River after the famous British Army General. Another party of mountaineers named French Peak after the first commander of the British Army in World War I and Mount Joffre after French's French counterpart.

We followed a good track through tāwhai/beech woodland from Aspiring Hut to Shovel Flat, where a shovel blade stuck in a tree trunk used to mark the track's northern entry point. The belt of trees at the far end of Shovel Flat divided it from Pearl Flat, which was named after a packhorse. We forded the river there and slogged up a steep track to the cold, corrugated iron **French Ridge Hut (4)**, which was built near the tree line in 1940 and shifted to a higher, more exposed site where strong winds would prevent snowdrifts from building up around its walls (the Lucas-Trotter Memorial Hut later replaced it).

The cloud base descended during the night. In the morning I caught a glimpse of Gloomy Gorge through swirling mist as we cramponed up a shelf glacier to **Quarterdeck Pass (5)** on the southern shoulder of Mount French. We crested it in a white-out and then plugged steps up a soft snow slope until it flattened out on top of French Peak. Next day a storm associated with Cyclone Giselle kept us hut-bound. Unbeknown to us hurricane-force winds were driving the inter-island ferry *Wahine* onto rocks at the mouth of Wellington Harbour.

Eight months later I joined Ken, Bruce and Brenda Knight for another crack at climbing Mount Aspiring/Tititea. We tarried awhile on Quarterdeck Pass to absorb the panorama of that great peak and all the Main Divide peaks around the névé of the Bonar Glacier. We then roped up and trooped down the glacier. Bruce and I were ahead of the other

The glorious view across the Bonar Glacier of Mt Aspiring/Tititea (3,033m) on the Coxcomb Ridge when Brenda Knight, Bruce Mason, Ken Gousmet and I crossed Quarterdeck Pass from French Ridge Hut in January 1969.

The view across the névé of the
Bonar Glacier from Quarterdeck Pass
of Popes Nose (2,700m) where the
Coxcomb Ridge joins the Main Divide.

pair and strayed too close to the Breakaway Icefall between French
Peak and Mount Joffre. A snow bridge collapsed under my feet and my
large backpack became wedged in the mouth of a hidden crevasse. My
feet flailed helplessly in the air until I was extracted.

An hour later we climbed a snow slope to the old corrugated iron
Colin Todd Memorial Hut (6). The Otago Section of the New Zealand
Alpine Club had erected it in 1958 at an altitude of 1800 metres on
the Shipowner Ridge, which is an extension of the southwest ridge of
Mount Aspiring/Tititea. Two decades after our visit it was replaced by
a larger and well insulated hut.

We set off before dawn and cramponed up a frozen snow slope from
the névé of the Therma Glacier to the crest of the southwest ridge. The
sky was cloudless and the air was still. Fine weather fog filled the
Alpine valleys on the eastern side of the Main Divide, but not on the
western side. The square silhouette of Aoraki/Mount Cook was visible
on the northern horizon. Mounts Tūtoko and Earnslaw/Pikirakatahi
dominated the view to the south. I peered 2400 vertical metres down the

northwest face of Mount Aspiring/Tititea and saw the infant Waiatoto River emerge from Therma Glacier's terminal lake, which was dotted with little icebergs.

Many years later Duncan Williams and I left the bivouac rock at the head of the West Matukituki Valley, skirted a couple of waterfalls, and then plugged steps through fresh snow to the crest of **Hector Col (11)** on the southern side of Mount Bevan. Peering down the other side of the Main Divide I saw the lake-source of the Waipara tributary of the Arawhata River on the west coast. Two large blocks of ice had tumbled into it from the icefall-terminus of the Bonar Glacier, which overhung it. At 1498 metres above sea level, Hector Col at the head of the West Matukituki Valley is the lowest point on the portion of the Main Divide that bounds the Arawhata Catchment.

In February 1863 Otago's Provincial Geologist, James Hector, became the first person to wield an ice axe in New Zealand when he accomplished the first crossing of his namesake col with L. Raynor and Dunedin journalist John Sullivan.

Sullivan's newspaper report described Hector's party creeping down the gut on the northern side of this pass 'like flies on a wall' under constant danger from falling rocks. When they reached the tongue of the Bonar Glacier they followed the 'Waitautau' River, which issued from it, through a gorge to try to ascertain where it entered the sea. They retraced their steps after climbing 'Pigeon Hill' and observing that the river that they were following joined the 'Terrewhatta or Jackson River', which flowed into Jackson Bay/Ōkahu.[135] It was not the Awarua River that Otago's chief surveyor, John Thompson, had surmised in 1858 flowed from Mount Aspiring to Big Bay. That putative river had marked the west coast section of the Canterbury-Otago border since 1853.

In 1940 J.H. Christie and Allan Shannon crossed the Main Divide just south of Hector Col via a slightly higher but safer crossing point, which they named Matukituki Saddle, and then followed the Waipara and Arawhata Rivers all the way down to the sea.

Hector named the watershed between the Arawhata and Waiatoto Catchments after Canterbury's Provincial Geologist, Julius Haast. When Westland's chief surveyor Gerhard Mueller and his assistant Charlie

My first distant view of Hector Col (1,498m) on the Main Divide between Mt Barff and Mt Bevan when I tramped up the West Matukituki Valley.

Douglas explored the Waitautau Branch of the Arawhata Valley in February 1885 they indulged in a naming spree. Mueller renamed that river after the paddle steamer *Waipara*, which had sailed from Hokitika to Jackson Bay/Ōkahu for the official inauguration of the Jackson Bay Special Settlement in November 1874. My great-great-grandfather George Orams had the catering contract. The ship's passengers included the Superintendent of Westland Province, James Bonar. The name Shipowner Ridge commemorates SS *Waipara*'s three part-owners: Bonar, Bevan and Captain Bascand.[136] The Main Divide peak between Hector Col and Waipara Saddle, which communicates with the head of the Arawhata Valley, was named after Bonar's political ally, Edmund Barff. Four peaks on Haast Ridge were named after the topsails on a big windjammer: Mainroyal, Moonraker, Skyscraper, and Stargazer.

Light rain was falling when Brenda, Bruce, Ken and I returned to Pearl Flat in the West Matukituki Valley from Colin Todd Hut. After retrieving the bag of food that Ken had hung in a tree to deter hungry bush rats, we slogged up the other side of the valley via a steep track, which entailed climbing a tree trunk at one point. The sun came out just before we reached **Liverpool Bivouac (9)**, which the New Zealand Alpine Club's Otago Section had erected above the tree line in 1953.

Next day we stumbled over piles of avalanche snow and pulverised schist in the big cirque at the head of Liverpool Creek, then we ascended a diagonal snow slope at the back of that basin to a 1758-metre Main Divide pass between Mount Barff and Mount Liverpool named **Arawhata Saddle (10)**. Looking down the other side, I saw the infant Arawhata River begin its 60-kilometre journey to the Tasman Sea by plunging over a cliff from the concealed terminal face of the Snow White Glacier. A deep trough that had been vacated by the shrinking tongue of the Liverpool Glacier was the next hurdle that we had to cross. Getting into it was easier than getting out. Ken led the way and pulled up the packs with a climbing rope before the rest of us joined him. We then walked straight across the tongue of the Snow White Glacier and pitched our tent on the other side.

In the morning we roped up again and threaded a maze of crevasses where the Snow White Glacier turned sharply at the base of **Mystery Col (13)**. Once we were out of that minefield we made a beeline across the glacier's broad névé to **Whitbourn Saddle (12)**, which punctuates the Main Divide between Mount Maoriri and Pivot Peak at an altitude of 2233 metres. The snow was deep and firm enough to excavate a snow cave at the base of that saddle, so we spent the rest of the day digging an entry passage and constructing two sleeping platforms.

Otago surveyor Ernest Wilmot and his assistants, Frank Leonard and William Whitbourn, mapped the Dart/Te Awa Whakatipu Valley above Lake Wakatipu in the 1880s. In 1914 Leonard joined a party led by Major Bernard Head and Jack Clarke that scaled several peaks around the Dart Glacier and filled in some blank spaces on Wilmot's map. Head named Cascade Saddle after the adjacent waterfall and the three peaks on Governors Ridge (which he also climbed) after Governors Liverpool, Islington, and Plunket. He left New Zealand on a troopship shortly after that trip and died at Gallipoli. After climbing the peaks on either side of Whitbourn Saddle we crossed it and descended the Whitbourn Glacier to the Dart/Te Awa Whakatipu Valley and returned to the West Matukituki Valley via Cascade Saddle.

Thirty-seven years later I headed back to Whitbourn Saddle with Wānaka guide Russell Braddock and his friend Steve. Russell wanted to re-assess the route to it from Arawhata Saddle. From Whitbourn Saddle we skirted the base of Pivot Peak and descended its long northern spur to Mystery Col, which the Snow White Glacier had spilled across before 1950. I was shocked to see how much the glacier had shrunk since my last visit in 1969.

We skirted the big tarn on Mystery Col and descended the banks of Phantom Creek. When it entered a gorge, we climbed onto the broad tussock slopes between Phantom and Snowball Creeks where a stunning panorama unfolded of the Olivine-Arawhata Wilderness Area. At the head of the Joe branch of the Arawhata Valley I saw the heavily glaciated flanks of Climax and Destiny Peaks on the Olivine Range and the Joe Glacier's small névé on Mount Alfred, where the Olivine Range joins the Main Divide. The Snowball Glaciers decked the portion of the Main Divide between Mount Alfred and Whitbourn Saddle called the Snowdrift Range. We continued our descent through

A contrasting view of the tongue of the Snow White Glacier from Mystery Col when Russell Braddock guided me right down the Arawhata Valley in 2006.

The view of the Snow White Glacier
source of the Arawhata River below
Mystery Col when Brenda, Bruce, Ken
and I crossed Arawhata Saddle in 1969.

open tāwhairauriki/mountain beech woods in the rain shadow of
the Olivine Range. A young stag was grazing on the other side of the
Arawhata River when we emerged from the trees on Williamson Flat.
After pitching the tent we watched the setting sun gild the ice cap on
Mount Ionia (14) on the Waipara Range.

In 1863 Andy Williamson and his two companions sailed from
Otago to Jackson Bay/Ōkahu in the cutter *Nugget* and ventured up
the Arawhata Gorge, but failed to pan any gold there. In 1897 William
O'Leary (Arawhata Bill) reached Williamson Flat, which he called 'The
Thousand Acres' (actually 400 acres). He accomplished the first solo
alpine crossing between Jackson Bay/Ōkahu and Lake Wakatipu via
O'Leary Pass, and repeated that feat several times.

One fine day in 1885 Gerhard Mueller and his field assistant, Charlie
Douglas, surveyed the upper Arawhata Catchment from the summit of
Mount Ionia. Douglas named three prominent peaks on the Waipara
Range after ancient kingdoms in Asia Minor: Caria, Cilicia, and Ionia.
He later told Arthur Harper that it took him half a day to cut steps up
the icy slopes of Mount Ionia with a long-handled slasher. It was one

of the earliest ascents of a high peak in the Southern Alps/Kā Tiritiri o te Moana.

When I woke up the tent was enveloped in mist, which swiftly dissipated as the sun climbed into a clear blue sky. We forded the calf-deep Joe River and followed the true left bank of the Arawhata River into the McArthur Gorge between Cilicia Peak on the Waipara Range and Camp Oven Dome on a branch of the Olivine Range called the Five Fingers Range. My friend Ken Mason had found a rusty camp oven under a bivvy rock in this gorge, which I did not spot. When the gorge closed in, we climbed about 150 metres through mossy tāwhai/beech trees until we stumbled on a deer trail, which led to McArthur Flat. As soon as we emerged from the woods, we had to ford the wild Williamson River, which issues from the Andy Icefall at the eastern end of the Olivine Ice Plateau. We linked arms and shuffled past boulders in the cold, waist-deep river, then pitched the tent on a patch of bare sand amongst the clumps of toitoi by the river.

Next day we descended the infamous Ten Hour Gorge. Gerhard Mueller was not exaggerating when he reported that its boulders range in size from a gold digger's hut to a courthouse. It had begun to rain and the gorge closed in shortly after we forded Halfway Creek. A couple of times we were forced to sidle the steep, bush-clad slopes above the bare flood line and once, when we could find no alternative, we had to wriggle through a gap between two giant boulders, pushing our packs in front of us. It took us eight hours to traverse that gorge, which ended in a large pool. A short track from there led to Arawhata Bill's roomy rock bivouac in which two clay floors had been excavated; dry wood was stacked on the lower one. The upper 'bedroom' floor' had a clay shelf at the back, but was otherwise empty.[137]

The rain became heavier when we reached the top of the Arawhata Flats which, although 45 kilometres from Neils Beach, is only 80 metres above sea level and is very flood-prone. Accordingly, Russell picked an elevated campsite in case the river rose during the night. In the morning we heard the welcome sound of Maurice Nolan's jet boat coming up the river. After removing a stick that had jammed the steering mechanism, he whisked us down to the Arawhata Bridge.

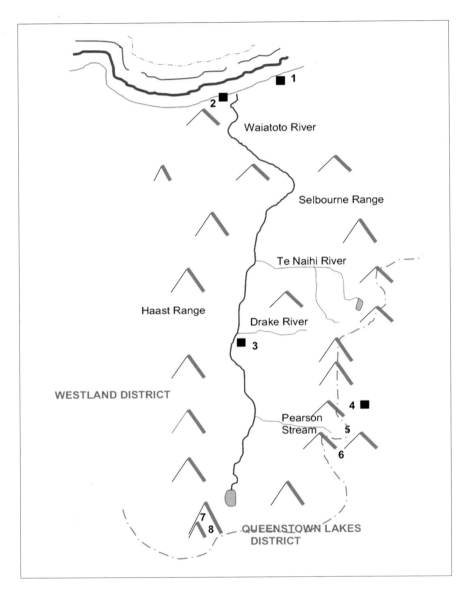

Legend

1. Waiatoto
2. Hannahs Clearing
3. Drake Hut
4. Top Forks Hut
5. Pearson Saddle
6. Rabbit Pass
7. Mt Aspiring/Tititea
8. Popes Nose

Chapter 12
The Waiatoto (Waitoto)

In December 2000 an Israeli tourist Oded Dvoskin, who had become a family friend, bravely agreed to explore the Wilkin Valley with me. We drove to Wānaka, then took SH6 to Makarora and boarded a Makarora Rivertours' jet boat, which whisked us up the Wilkin (Ōtokitaha – 'place of the adze'[138]) tributary of the Makarora River to Kerin Forks Hut on John Kerrin's old Jumboland run. A waggoner named Yankee Dan used to graze a horse named Jumbo on Jumboland Flat further up that valley.[139]

We followed a good track up the wooded true right bank of the Wilkin River to the new **Top Forks Hut (4)** at the top of Jumboland Flat and spent two nights there. On the way I saw two stoats run across the track and noted the absence of birdsong. The hut's intentions book

Pearson Saddle (1,409m) on the Main Divide below Picklehaube when Oded Dvoskin and I ascended the West Branch of the Wilkin Valley from Forks Hut.

contained an entry by a member of the American Society for Barefoot Living, who planned to cross Rabbit Pass without boots. We sat on the porch and watched the westering sun gild the snowy summits of Mounts Castor and Pollux and the Ice King Tops.

After breakfast we followed the Rabbit Pass Track through mossy tāwhai/silver beech woodland on the true right bank of the South Branch of the Wilkin River. We emerged from the woods in a grassy glen, at the far end of which rose the forbidding 150-metre Waterfall Face which, fortunately, was free of snow. A row of orange stakes marked the route up it.

At the far end of the head cirque of the East Wilkin Valley above the Waterfall Face lies **Rabbit Pass (6)**, which connects with the East Matukituki Valley. Two Main Divide peaks named Pickelhaube and

Taurus form the southern rim of this cirque. Between those two peaks lies **Pearson Saddle (5)**. At 1400 metres above sea level, the summit of that saddle is the lowest spot on the section of the Main Divide that bounds the Waiatoto Catchment.

After surmounting the Waterfall Face we climbed onto Pearson Saddle and peered into the deep cirque on its western side where the Pearson tributary of the Waiatoto River emerged from a tongue of avalanche snow and promptly disappeared into a gorge. Waitotō (water that gushes forth) is a plausible spelling of this river name. However, in 1897 William Wilson consulted Ngāti Mahaki elders who told him that it was named Waitoto after a man. Waitoto is inscribed on the 1860 Arahura Purchase deed map.

In February 1885 Charlie Douglas and Westland's chief surveyor, Gerhard Mueller, climbed Mount Hyperia on the Haast Range. From the summit they surveyed the Main Divide on the north-eastern side of the Waiatoto Valley.[140] Six years later, Mueller asked Douglas to explore the Waiatoto Valley and look for valuable minerals and a Main Divide Pass that would be a feasible route for a transalpine road or railway line.

In 1889 Mueller had put Charlie Douglas on the payroll of the Hokitika-based Westland Survey as its one and only 'explorer'. He was 49 years of age and had received a good classical education at an Edinburgh high school. He took a Greek New Testament and a copy of Homer (that must have included a map) on his long forays into the backcountry. In 1891 he undertook a four-week 'starve' all the way up the true right bank of the Waiatoto River to its source. He carried 100 pounds of food and a rifle and took two dogs to supplement his rations by catching kākāpō and weka. His quirky sense of humour was evident when he bestowed the ancient Greek name of Thessalonica, Therma (heat), upon the glacial source of the Waiatoto River.[141]

Douglas observed that rabbits had colonised the head of the Waiatoto Valley, but he failed to locate the 'Rabbit Pass' through which he presumed they had migrated from Central Otago via the Matukituki Valley. The two passes on that route were subsequently named by others Rabbit Pass and Pearson Saddle. Douglas went on to name the Pearson River the 'Lysander River' and the peak above its gorge 'Mount Thymbra' after an ancient city on the Trojan Plain. But when Mueller transferred to the General Survey Office Wellington in 1891 he subsequently renamed the Lysander River after the Commissioner of Crown Lands in Southland Province, Walter Pearson, who had retired from the Lands Department in 1889. Douglas criticized Mueller in a letter for naming too many peaks in the Landsborough Valley, one of which is Mount Pearson, after Survey Department officials and other employees. In his view sonorous Māori and classical Greek place names were far more appropriate in that Arcadian setting.[142]

But Mueller did occasionally look beyond civil servants for inspiration. For instance he renamed Mount Thymbra after the constellation Taurus or the block of wooded hills called Taunus (hedge) about 50 kilometres north of Darmstadt in the German State of Hessen, where he grew up - this peak is labelled Mount Taunus on one early map! He transferred the place name Pickelhaube ('spiked helm' – worn by Prussian soldiers after 1843), which Douglas had oddly attached to a glacier on Mount Pollux, to the sharp peak on the southern side of Pearson Saddle. Both men probably saw those peaks over the crest of the Haast Range when they climbed Mount Ionia in 1885 (see Page 195).

In the 1946 issue of the *New Zealand Alpine Journal*, John Sim reported a rumour he'd heard to the effect that Jack Matthews had crossed Pearson Saddle and floated down the Waiatoto Valley on a raft 'some years ago'. In May 1948, two government deer cullers, Trevor Carlton and Des Corboy, crossed that pass and scrambled down the steep and scrubby southern flanks of the Pearson Gorge to the Waiatoto Confluence, then retraced their steps to the Wilkin Valley. Later that year, Scott Gilkison, G. Goodyear, J. Hoskins and C. Kershaw tramped up the Waiatoto Valley and accomplished a full crossing of Pearson Saddle with the aid of the cullers' notes.[143] Early Māori travellers would surely have preferred to take the safer and shorter transalpine routes through the Taikawariki Mountains north of the Wilkin Valley.

Nine years later I drove to Wānaka and teamed up with Russell Braddock for a transalpine trip, over Pearson Saddle. When we reached that Main Divide pass an easterly breeze was blowing mist through it, but blue sky was visible above the Waiatoto Valley.

Russell led the way over a grassy knoll on the left and then down a

My first view of Mt Aspiring/Tititea
(3,033m) and the proglacial lake-source of
the Waiatoto River when Russell Braddock
guided me over Pearson Saddle in 2009.

gentle slope to a couloir filled with old avalanche snow. Amongst the
debris in this gully I spied some reddish rocks from a 'metavolcanic
horizon' like the reddish rocks that I had seen below Hector Col in the
West Matukituki Valley. We then sidled across a grassy slope below
a row of bluffs to a prominent bench at 1350-metre contour line then
climbed up to the base of a vertical reef of snow-white quartz, which I
mistook for a waterfall when I spotted it from Pearson Saddle.

We climbed a bit higher as we skirted the end of Beauty Ridge to
avoid a ravine that plunged into the Pearson Gorge. On the other side
of that ridge a wonderful panorama unfolded of the ice-capped Haast
Range and a murky lake below Stargazer Bluff. The Haast Range joined
the southwest ridge of **Mount Aspiring/Tititea (7)** above the shining
névé of the rapidly retreating Therma Glacier, which is the source of
the Waiatoto River. Its silt-laden melt water flowed through its former
proglacial lake and then disappeared from view in a maze of scrub-
covered terminal moraine ridges.

After lunch we cautiously descended the steep tussock face on the western side of Beauty Ridge to a bench not far above the tree line, which we followed southward until it ended on the lip of a hanging valley. The waterfall-source of the Bettne tributary of the Waiatoto River tumbled into that valley from a hidden snowfield. Russell picked a descent route through the trees to a small clearing beside the Bettne River and we pitched our tent there. Waking in the early hours, I lifted the tent flap to see an incredible number of stars.

In the morning we forded the Bettne River, climbed over the end of Wedge Spur, and headed further east through relatively open tāwhai/ silver beech woodland on an old lateral moraine bench around the 700-metre contour line. Like Charlie Douglas, we blundered into thickets of giant ongaonga/stinging nettles in not one, but two dank gullies. A bit further on I found a cast deer antler and heard a kea screech in the treetops. At the end of that bench, we forded the Graham River and then burrowed like rabbits through a 500-metre tract of dense tūpare/'leatherwood' scrub on a massive terminal moraine ridge.

Russell by the terminal lake of the Volta Glacier, which had retreated from sight under its Icefall on Mt Aspring/Tititea [3,033m] and Popes Nose [2,700m] where the Coxcombe Ridge joins the Main Divide.

Four hours after leaving our campsite we emerged from the scrub and walked across a bare outwash surface to the outlet of a two-kilometre lake. The Therma Glacier no longer extends into the middle of it as it did back in 1969 when I peered down the northwest face of Mount Aspiring/Tititea. The Therma Glacier source of the Waiatoto River is now 60 kilometres from the sea on top of a bluff at the base of Mount Aspiring/Tititea. In 1908 Ebenezer Teichelman stood on that glacier's great terminal moraine, which it then lapped, and likened its icefall over that bluff to the Hochstetter Icefall on Aoraki/Mount Cook. That glacier's retreat accelerated after it separated from the retreating Volta Glacier, which descends from an ice plateau on the southern side of Pickelhaube.

From the shore of that lake, which is only 663 metres above sea level, I had a unique top-to-bottom view of Mount Aspiring/Tititea. At 3033 metres above sea level, the summit of this great peak is the highest point in the water catchment areas of the Waiatoto and Arawhata Rivers. My eyes followed the Coxcombe Ridge from that summit to its junction with the Main Divide on the summit of **Popes Nose (8).** At 2700 metres above sea level, that subsidiary peak is the highest point on the section of the Main Divide that bounds the Waiatoto, Arawhata, and Clutha River/Mata-au Catchments. Gazing higher I noticed that a film of alto-stratus cloud had filled the sky. It thickened as we made our way back to our campsite. We sidled a bit too high and did not arrive there until dusk, by which time it was raining.

In 1907 the first General Manager of the Department of Tourism and Health Resorts, Thomas Donne, encouraged Hokitika surgeon and mountaineer Ebenezer Teichelman to prospect a route up Mount Aspiring/Tititea from the head of the Waiatoto Valley. Teichelman studied Charlie Douglas' reports and sailed to Okuru where he teamed up with Franz Josef-based guide Alex Graham and a local farmer, Dennis Nolan, who had re-cut the cattle track up the Waiatoto Valley for them. Three packhorses transported their food and equipment through the Waiatoto Ford above the Te Naihi Confluence and then up the true left bank to Bonar Flat.

From that point all their food and equipment had to be carried on their backs. To begin with they were holed up in a rock bivouac while a storm battered the area for a few days, after which they moved up to a high camp on the terminal moraine of the Therma Glacier. Graham failed to find a route onto the northwest ridge of Mount Aspiring/ Tititea – and time was running out. Teichelman had to catch the next scheduled sailing from Okuru to Hokitika in order to relieve his locum or face an arduous five-day horse trek home so a day trip up Guide Ridge had to suffice. They reached the summit of the peak that Douglas had named after Mount Cissus in Macedonia and discovered an unknown tributary of the Therma Glacier, which Teichelman named the Volta Glacier, possibly after the inventor of the battery. Mount Cissus had been renamed Snow Dome.[144]

In the spring of 1981, a massive rock fall into the terminal lake of the Therma Glacier sent a nine-metre wall of water rushing down the Waiatoto Valley causing all the cattle on the river flats to drown. A similar event occurred in December 2011, but fortunately, no one was in the valley on either occasion so no human life was lost.

It rained steadily, but not heavily all night. By dawn the rain appeared to have set in, so we packed up and made a determined effort to reach **Drake Hut (3)** further down the Waiatoto Valley by nightfall. We reasoned that it would be a better place to be trapped between raging side streams if the weather worsened. So following deer trails down the broad ridge between the Bettne and Pearson Gorges we reached the north bank of the Waiatoto River just below the maze of terminal moraine ridges and headed down the valley.

Pearson Stream was the first and deepest tributary that we had to ford. Linking arms, we inched across it below two big boulders, which split up the current. We were soaked to the waist when we stepped onto the opposite bank. The long open flats on the south bank of the Waiatoto River were tantalisingly close, but unreachable. We battled on through the dense, dripping-wet rainforest, clambering over fallen tree trunks and trying not to slip on greasy rocks. The river flats are smaller and scrubbier on the north bank and the mingimingi scrub was often laced with barbed tataramoa/'bush lawyer' vines, which snagged our packs. Near Stormwater Creek, four hinds darted across a small clearing and I saw the smooth schist face of Stocking Peak through a break in the clouds.

Charlie Douglas had scaled the 25-degree schist slabs on that peak in his socks, which gripped the rock better than his hobnailed boots. From the summit he peered into swirling mist and caught a glimpse of what he thought was a pass between Mounts Ragan and Arbela. Assuming it was the route over the Main Divide that rabbits were taking from Otago to the remote flats in this west coast valley, he named it 'Rabbitt Pass' (sic). The real Rabbit Pass was further east.

We reached Drake Hut just before dark and quickly got the fire roaring. Tomorrow was declared a bye-day so that we could dry our sodden gear. This shabby old hut, which two deer hunters had built in 1966, also received a tidy-up. Next day the going got progressively easier as the deer trails became wider, the flats became longer and the weather improved by the hour. Putrefying piles of deer entrails littered the next flat where hunters had gutted deer carcasses to lighten them so that more could be slung from a helicopter strop.

Charlie Douglas originally named the Te Naihi River after the Axius River in Macedonia. His old friend and fellow explorer Ruera Te Naihi ('Māori Bill') was the licenced Waiatoto ferryman from 1900 until 1907 when he drowned in a creek while cutting scrub. His wife, Ripeka, was Tūtoko's granddaughter. William O'Leary ('Arawhata Bill') was the next Waiatoto ferryman.

In 1877 August Eggeling moved from the failing Jackson Bay Settlement to a 50-acre freehold block on the north bank of the lower Waiatoto River, between Tom Casey's and George Nisson's farms. In the 1880s, George acquired the first grazing licence on the upper Waiatoto Flats and cut the first track up the north bank to Axius Flat; the Eggeling family has held that licence ever since. By the 1960s the wild deer population was so large that those flats had to be temporarily destocked. Following a huge deer cull the overgrown track to Axius Flat was reopened with a bulldozer and the flats were restocked with cattle in 1972.[145]

After fording the Te Naihi (or Axius) River in Axius Flat we picked up a bulldozed stock track and pitched the tent for the last time in Casey Flat, where Tom Casey had grazed his cattle in the nineteenth century. Next day we walked to the confluence of Palmer Creek where Russell had arranged a 10am rendezvous with the Waiatoto River Safaris' jet boat.

Once we were all on board, the jet boat driver took us for a spin through the rapids between Balustrade Bluff and the end of the

Selbourne Range before whisking us down to a waiting trailer at the ramp by the old south landing of the Waiatoto punt-ferry. We were then given a lift to Haast Village where we caught the midday shuttle bus back to Makarora.

Before I embarked on that trip down the Waiatoto River from source to sea, Evelyn and I had followed the Haast-Jackson Bay Road to a seaside settlement named **Hannahs Clearing (2)**. It was established in 1962 in conjunction with the joint opening of Carters Sawmill and the Wānaka-Haast Road over Haast Pass/Tiori Pātea, however the sawmill closed in 1978. When the area school in Haast village burned down, it was rebuilt in Hannahs Clearing.

The Waiatoto River mouth when Evelyn and I walked down the beach to this spot from Hannahs Clearing. My journey right down the Waiatoto Valley with Russell ended at the old ferry landing on the opposite bank.

We parked at the end of a short side road three kilometers south of Hannahs Clearing and then walked down the beach to the Waiatoto River Mouth. The air was warm and muggy. Steam was rising from patches of wet sand and a blanket of low cloud enveloped the summits of Mount McLean and Jackson Head. The long shore drift had lengthened the sand spit on the southern side of the river mouth, which forced the river to flow obliquely into the Tasman Sea. While we were there a pair of kōau/shags paddled across the bar, which had scarcely a ripple on it.

Telephone poles still line the old beach highway between the Okuru and Waiatoto Ferry Landings. A nearby creek was named after Bill Hindley, who had operated that ferry for 27 years after the 1873 Haast gold rush. The last gap in the Haast-Jackson Bay Road was closed when the Waiatoto Bridge replaced the Waiatoto Ferry in 1945.

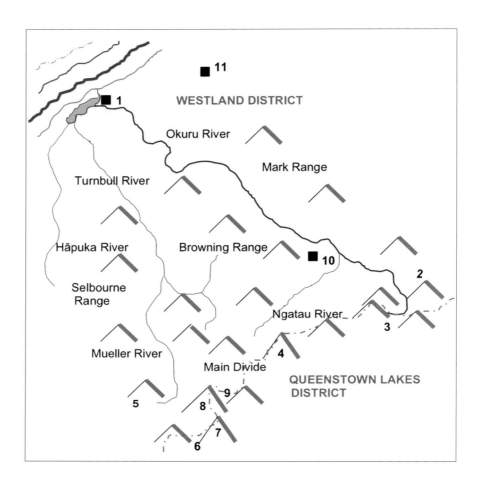

Legend

1. Okuru
2. Mueller Pass
3. Māori Saddle
4. Mt Doris
5. Mt Dispute
6. Newland Pass
7. Mt Alba
8. Trident Peak
9. Stewart Pass
9. Franklin Hut
10. Franklin Hutt
11. Haast Junction

Chapter 13
The Okuru/Ōpuka

In January 2001 I followed Haast-Jackson Bay Road from Haast Junction (11) down the south bank of the Haast River and then down the coast to a small settlement called Okuru (1) beside Okuru Lagoon. As I walked along its shore I met a local resident who was about to launch a dinghy. After inviting me to hop on board, he rowed us to a shingle island between the lagoon's two outlets, explaining that the river's original mouth had silted up several months ago and the banked-up lagoon had flooded several waterside properties. Westland District Council lowered the water level by bulldozing a new outlet. A big flood subsequently re-opened the old river mouth and created the island that we stood on. Ngāti Māhaki elders called this district Te Pūtaiwhenua (the rain-swept land).

The original mouth of the Okuru River, where this upriver story began. A local resident, Pat Trembeth, rowed me across Okuru (Ōpuka) Lagoon to the island that formed when a flood re-opened its old outlet after a new outlet had been dug.

The name that Captain Cook bestowed on the broad coastal indentation that he charted north of Cascade Point is preserved in the collective name, Open Bay Islands, for Taumaka and Ōpopotai, which lie five kilometres off the Okuru River mouth. In 1814 John Grono's schooner *Governor Bligh* hauled in there and rescued a forgotten gang of sealers that had been marooned on Taumaka for four years. They had skinned 11,000 seals and briefly visited the vacant Ōkura kāinga in two sealskin coracles.

The Okuru (or Ōkura) Lagoon is labelled Ōpuka (anchoring place[146]) on the 1860 Arahura Purchase deed plan. The Hāpuka and Turnbull/ Pūtakuru tributaries of the Okuru River flow into the head of this lagoon. Hokitika Harbourmaster Captain Thomas Turnbull sounded all the river bars in Open Bay and concluded that the Okuru River was the safest one to enter on the flood tide.

In 1874 John Browning surveyed a number of rural sections in the

Okuru Settlement.[147] By 1887 the Arawhata Settlement was virtually abandoned and nine families had moved to Okuru. A veteran of the 1873 Haast gold rush, Joseph Collyer, became the first Okuru ferryman, harbourmaster, and storekeeper. The Cuttance family held the grazing licence on the upper Okuru flats until 1907: the Eggeling family has held it ever since. A small hydroelectric power station was commissioned on the Turnbull/Pūtakuru River in 1974 to supply electricity to local households and the new sawmill in Hannahs Clearing.

The Waiatoto, Turnbull/Pūtakuru, and Okuru Rivers descend short rapids just before they cross the Alpine Fault. Those steps in their valley floors reflect how much uplift has occurred on the eastern side of the Alpine Fault since the last glaciation. The crests of the Selbourne and Browning Ranges between those rivers flatten off at the uniform height of 1450 metres above sea level, one kilometre east of their escarpments on that fault line. Beds of sand and water-worn pebbles on the flat tops of those mountain ranges indicate that they are raised remnants of a wave-cut platform. Assuming an average vertical uplift rate of 5 mm per year, then these tops would have been at sea level around 300,000 years ago. [148]

In March 2004 I embarked on a transalpine trip over Māori Saddle at the head of the Okuru (Okura) Valley with Andrew Taylor-Perry and his daughter Natasha. We drove down the west coast to the hotel at **Haast Junction (11)** where we spent the first night. I had obtained access permission to the valley from Kerry Eggeling and the hotel manager had allowed me to store my bicycle in a locked shed as I planned to catch a bus back from Makarora and then cycle to the Turnbull Road end where my car would be parked.

In the morning we drove to **Okuru (1)**, then followed Turnbull Road up the north bank of the Turnbull River/Pūtakuru. After leaving the car by the locked gate, we shouldered our packs and tramped a little way up the access road to the Turnbull Power Station, then along an old logging road at the base of the Browning Range to the Boil Hole below a long rapid in the Okuru River. A bulldozed cattle track continued up the true left bank of that river, which was running high after weeks of almost constant rain. We did not like the look of the ford in Moonlight

Flat and opted to bush-bash further up the true left bank until the cattle track recrossed the river.

A bit later a helicopter flew overhead with a small amphibious vehicle suspended underneath it in a cargo sling. When we entered a small clearing below Muster Flat, we met Don and Ian from the helicopter, who explained that they planned to use the vehicle we'd seen to cross the river. Ian asked us to pitch our tents near theirs to avoid spooking deer on the nearby flat. He told us a yarn about a hunter who was trapped in Spasm Hut on Moonlight Flat by a huge storm. His horse drowned and he had to lift a sheet of iron and sit on the roof to avoid the same fate.

We set off when Ian and Don returned from their morning stalk and forded the Okuru River twice at the top of Muster Flat. At the top of Franklin Flat, near **Franklin Hut (10)**, we forded the Okuru River again via a long shingle weir. Unfortunately, it ended about four metres from the opposite bank. As the water was clear and slow moving we carried on wading, but while I managed to keep my feet on the bottom Andrew and Natasha began to float and both had to be towed to the opposite bank. We passed an empty hunter's tent on the edge of the next clearing, which was called Graveyard Flat. Interestingly, a campsite was marked at that same spot on the map that Charlie Douglas had attached to his report about his seven-week survey of the Okuru Valley in 1885.[149] At the top of that flat we returned to the true left bank of the Okuru River above the confluence of the Ngātau River. Siberia Saddle between Mount Attica and **Mount Doris (4)** links the Ngātau branch of the Okuru Valley with the Siberia Branch of the Wilkin Valley.

We then entered the lower Okuru Gorge between Mount Action and Mount Actor. After clambering over countless boulders and rotting logs we recrossed the river at the recommended spot in *Moir's Guidebook* and camped on a sand bank. Next day we followed deer trails to the confluence of Princess Creek, then battled on through the upper Okuru Gorge, which curls around an outlier of Mount Actor called Mount Argos. We crawled over, under and around fallen trees and giant boulders until the valley widened, then forded the river and followed a well-used deer trail to a grassy glen where Natasha thought she heard the warning whistles of a deer – until we discovered the sound was made by two kōwhiowhio/blue ducks.

From his top camp at the head of the Okuru Gorge, Charlie Douglas had climbed onto a pass, which he named 'Maorie Saddle' (sic), between the low peak of Mount Citheron and a Main Divide peak called Mount Bertha. From that pass he looked down on the headwaters of what he thought was the Blue tributary of the Makarora River. It was actually the Howe tributary of the Burke River, which joins the Haast River/Awarua below the Haast Gorge. **Mueller Pass (2)** links the head of the Burke Valley with the Princess Branch of the Okuru Valley. Some travellers used that short cut between Okuru village and Haast Pass/Tiori Pātea. In a letter to Westland Survey Director Gerhard Mueller, Douglas explained that he had named 'Maorie Saddle' because he had been told that the Māori prospector known as Wakatipu Jack had crossed a Main Divide pass between the Okuru Valley and the Blue branch of the Makarora Valley.[150] The original name of the Blue tributary of the Makarora River was Waitaha.[151]

The name 'Maori Pass' first appeared on the 1881 South Island Counties map between the headwaters of the Blue and Okuru Rivers. Mrs E B Ewing of Makarora told Irvine Roxburgh that she remembered being told as a child that Māori parties preferred to cross a saddle at the head of the Blue Valley, instead of Haast Pass/Tiori Pātea.[152] On the second edition of the NZMS-1 topographical map, this pass was correctly identified and labelled Māori Saddle. The 'Maorie Saddle' that Douglas had climbed onto – and dismissed as a transalpine route – was re-named Douglas Saddle.[153] At 1245 metres above sea level, Māori Saddle is the lowest point on the section of the Main Divide that bounds the Okuru Catchment. Sherwood Roberts recorded its original name, Ōkahu Tarahaka.[154]

We pitched camp in the top flat and awoke to a sunny morning. **Māori Saddle (3)** was visible on the Main Divide at the head of the valley on the southern side of Mount Actor. Through it we could see the pointed peak that Douglas had named Mount Eyetooth. Taking a tip from *Moir's Guidebook*, we climbed a dry creek bed to avoid a lengthy tussle with subalpine scrub and returned to the rocky bed of the infant Okuru River at the base of a long grassy slope stretching up to Māori Saddle. The highest tributary, Atom Creek, trickled out of a small cirque on the other side of Mount Actor, about 45 kilometres from the sea.

My last view of the head cirque of the
Okuru Valley, where this river arises,
before Andrew Taylor-Perry and his
daughter Natasha and I crossed
Māori Saddle in swirling mist.

Māori Saddle (1,245m) on the Main
Divide from the head cirque of the
Blue branch of the Makarora Valley.

At that point we noticed that Māori Saddle consisted of two dips separated by a tall knob. On my NZMS-1 topographical map (second edition) the dip on the left was labelled Māori Saddle, however we decided to check the dip on the right first because it was closer and 100 metres lower. On the way up to it I peeked into a cavity between two large boulders and startled a kea. A cool sou'west breeze had sprung up and clouds were moving swiftly up the valley. When we reached the lower dip mist was swirling around us. Peering down the other side I saw a steep four-metre pitch of crumbly schist dotted with small ferns above a scree slope that funnelled into a shallow gully.

I dropped my pack and managed to inch down the slope, kicking my boots into it and gripping the bases of the small ferns for support. The higher dip was hidden in mist so I could not tell if it was a safer option. Andrew and Natasha failed to find a better descent route further south, so we decided to take the nearest one. I reprimanded myself for not bringing a long cord that we could have used to lower the packs. We also needed to get out of the cold wind.

Halfway down the steep pitch, Andrew lost his footing and wrenched his right knee when he landed on the scree. Fortunately he was able to walk, albeit slowly, using two Leki poles. We sidled into a tussock-filled gully below the high notch and then slowly descended to the head of the Blue Valley where Andrew insisted that we should carry on until we reached a good campsite below the tree line.

We took a high contour line to avoid the dense subalpine scrub, however we still had to cross several small gullies and skirt thickets of puniu/prickly shield fern and stunted whauwhi/eastern mountain ribbonwood trees. After a couple of hours, we encountered a bare avalanche track and followed it down to the tree line by the river. There we picked up a short track that led to a small grassy clearing on the opposite bank. During the afternoon the clouds had slowly thickened and drizzle set in as we pitched the tents. The Blue Valley Track was overgrown and poorly marked further down the valley.

Andrew's knee swelled during the night so that by morning it was obvious that he couldn't walk very far. I contacted the Canterbury Mountain Radio and requested an airlift. The helicopter arrived at noon with a Conservation Department officer who checked Andrew's knee and authorised the pilot to take him to the medical centre in Wānaka. He dropped me off at Makarora with the three packs.

I left the packs in a storeroom at the Mount Aspiring National Park's Makarora Base and caught the 1pm Intercity bus to **Haast Junction (10)** where I picked up my bicycle and began to pedal back to the car. As I passed the Haast Beach garage I spotted a parked police car and remembered that I had forgotten to bring a cycle helmet. A few minutes later a police officer pulled me over and wrote out an infringement notice. He then gave me a lift to the end of Turnbull Road, which enabled me to drive back to the Makarora before the office closed at 4pm. After picking up the packs, I drove on to Wānaka to meet Natasha and Andrew, whose knee was swaddled in thick bandages but had not required surgery.

In February 2000 Andrew and I embarked on a trip up the Newland branch of the Wilkin Valley and over **Newland Pass (6)** to climb **Trident Peak (8)** from the Waiatoto side. At 2088 metres above sea level, its summit is the highest point in the water catchment area of the Okuru River and on the portion of the Main Divide that bounds it because the Turnbull River/Pūtakuru, which drains its west flank, joins the Okuru River before it enters the sea.

A jet boat whisked us up the Wilkin/Ōtitaha tributary of the Makarora River to the Kerin (or Siberia) Forks Landing on the true left bank. We forded the Siberia River near its confluence and tramped up the true left bank of the Wilkin River to the confluence of the Newland River. After fording that tributary, we camped on the edge of a large expanse of sand and shingle that a '100-year flood' had deposited in 1994.

In the morning we climbed a steep wooded slope to a knoll on the flank of Mount Aeolus, which was named after Homer's Warden of the Winds, to avoid the deep gorge at the entrance to the Newland Valley. For the next three hours we clambered over and around fallen trees and giant boulders and pushed through thickets of saplings that had sprouted in the tracks of old rock and snow avalanches. Beyond the tree line we followed tussock and puniu/prickly shield fern leads through a broad scrub belt and camped on a patch of taru/carpet grass below a low terminal moraine near the head of the valley. We passed a dead fawn in a stream bed, but saw no other sign of wildlife.

In December 1950 Tom Barcham, Ashley Cunningham, Graham McCallum and Beryl Matthews from the Wellington-based Tararua Tramping Club pioneered the route that we planned to take over **Newland Pass (6)** between **Mount Alba (7)** and Mount Achilles.[155]

When we woke up the sky was clear, apart from a small cloud clinging to the summit of Mount Alba ('white mountain' in Latin; this peak was originally named Kahukura after an atua). We ascended the moraine ridge behind our campsite and a narrow ledge that soared at an oblique angle between smooth schist slabs to Newland Pass, employing the rope on the final pitch. Looking northward from this 1700-metre pass, I saw Mount Alba and **Trident Peak (8)** on the portion of the Main Divide between the Te Naihi and Siberia Valleys.

We shinned down a gully to the shrunken Axius Glacier, which descended towards Lake Axius from the misty heights of Mount Alba. The waterfall-outlet of that lake is the source of the Te Naihi (or Axius)

The view of Trident Pk (2,088m) on the
Main Divide when Andrew I crossed
Newland Pass to the head of the Te Naihi
branch of the Waiatoto Valley in 2000.

tributary of the Waiatoto River. On the far side of that glacier we sidled across partly snow-covered scree slopes to the vestigial Trident Glacier, crawled up a schist slab that bridged its bergschrund, and clambered up a short rock ridge to the summit of Trident Peak.

Lowering clouds clagged every peak except our perch. Peering down its north face I saw the crest of **Stewart Pass (9)** between Trident Peak and Mount Dreadful at the head of the South Branch of the Siberia Valley. At 1800 metres above sea level, it is the only pass on the five-kilometre portion of the Main Divide that bounds the water catchment area of the Turnbull River/Pūtakuru. Peter Barnes and Geoff Spearpoint managed to abseil its precipitous eastern flank in 2001.[156] On the western side of that pass I saw the Mueller tributary of the Turnbull River/Pūtakuru emerge from a vestige of the Dispute Glacier on **Mount Dispute (5)** and begin its journey to Okuru Lagoon. It was nearly dark and threatening to rain when we got back to Newland Pass so we spent an uncomfortable but dry night under an overhanging rock and descended to our campsite in the morning.

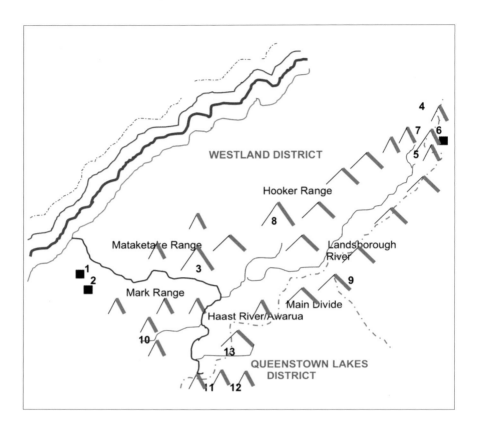

Legend

1. Haast Junction
2. Haast village
3. Mt MacFarlane
4. Mt Isabel
5. The Scissors
6. Barron Saddle Hut
7. Mt Burns
8. Mt Hooker
9. Brodrick Pass
10. Mueller Pass
11. Haast Pass/Tiori Pātea
12. Boundary Spur
13. Mt Brewster

Chapter 14
The Haast/Awarua

In January 2000 Evelyn, Sybil and I drove down the west coast from Greymouth, stopping at some interesting points on the way. Four kilometres north of the Haast Bridge we left SH6 and followed a dirt road through the grassy swale behind the beach and parked by the North Haast Beach Huts. From there we walked further south along a shingle spit to watch the Haast River/Awarua flow into the Tasman Sea. A flight of kōau/shags took off when we approached the tip of the spit, which was swept by breaking waves and a brisk sou'west breeze.

The Haast River/Awarua was renamed after Canterbury's Provincial Geologist, Julius Haast, who led an expedition from Lake Wānaka to the west coast via Haast Pass/Tiore Pātea in 1863 (see Page 146). On the deed plan attached to the 1860 West Coast Purchase document,

The mouth of the Haast River/Awarua,
where this upriver story began.

this river is labelled Awarua (two channels). On the 1880 Taiaroa map,
Whitirau (many crossings) is inscribed next to it.

During the first Haast Gold Rush in 1867, several hundred diggers
boarded the steamships *Alhambra*, *Bruce*, and *Claude Hamilton* in
Hokitika and disembarked on the bank of the Haast River/Awarua.[157]
The ships' helmsmen had to avoid the Alhambra Rock just outside the
river mouth and enter on the flood tide at the right angle, which was
ascertained by lining up the white flags on two shore beacons.[158] During
the second Haast gold rush, in 1873, William Harris opened a store
behind Haast Beach and John Marks opened another by the mouth of
the Haast River/Awarua. Marks also operated a ferry service across the
river and grazed cattle on its flats. After the gold rushes Adam Cron and
his family left the Jackson Bay Settlement and took over Marks' ferry
and grazing licences.[159]

The Makarora-Haast Stock Track was cut over Haast Pass/Tiori Pātea
between 1875 and 1881. Landsborough Station was stocked with cattle
via this track as early as 1876. It also enabled the struggling farmers

from the Jackson Bay Settlement to send stock to the Otago goldfields where their beef was in high demand. The Haast-Paringa Stock Track, which was cut between 1887 and 1890, gave them access to the Arahura Saleyard near Hokitika, which was 300 kilometres up the coast. From 1915 until 1958, the spring and autumn Haast cattle drives ended at the Whataroa saleyards.[160]

Fortnightly mail deliveries and the installation of a telephone line to Hokitika in 1910 helped to keep the isolated Haast community in touch with the outside world. In 1934, the bi-monthly Hokitika-Okuru shipping service was supplemented by New Zealand's first scheduled air service. Haast Aerodrome's three grass runways were constructed during World War II to refuel long-range coastal surveillance flights. The earthworks machinery was barged down from the North Island in 1941.

Construction of the Haast Highway commenced in 1928 (see Page 147). By 1958 it had reached Burke Flat at the bottom of the Haast Gorge and Haast cattle farmers began to truck their surplus stock from there to saleyards in Otago. The last section of the road, which opened in 1961, is vulnerable to landslides when storms strike this district. The closure of the last gap in SH6 between Lake Pāringa and Haast village in 1965 opened the tourist circuit of the South Island via this Blenheim-Invercargill highway and its east coast counterpart, SH1.

After visiting the river mouth, we drove across the 737-metre Haast Bridge to **Haast Junction (1)** and called in at the Department of Conservation's Haast Visitors' Centre. It opened in 1991 in conjunction with the UNESCO listing of the 2.6 million-hectare Waipounamu South-West New Zealand World Heritage Area, which covers ten per cent of New Zealand and extends from Abut Head to Puysegur Point. That listing protected the remaining conifer-broadleaf bush on the Haast Plain. The absence of a jetty at Jackson Bay/Okāhu before native timber exports were banned in the 1940s preserved that forest until the Wānaka-Haast Road opened in 1961. Loggers promptly moved in and sent trimmed logs from the Haast Plain to the Luggate sawmill while chilled deer carcasses went to Luggate Meat Packers.

Three kilometres east of **Haast Junction (1)**, SH6 passes through

Haast village (2). A bush-covered greywacke dome called Mosquito Hill rises in the middle of the big swamp on the opposite side of the river. The highway heads straight for a U-shaped gap in the wall of mountains to the east. The Mark Range to the south and the Mataketake (Kuramātakitaki – 'scarlet flowers' or 'easily seen hill'[161]) to the north flank this gap. Their western spurs have been pruned by the Alpine Fault, which 'unzips' every 150 to 350 years (291 years is the average interval according to the latest report by GNS Science).[162] The last event occurred in 1717. Major earthquakes on this strike-slip fault are magnitude 8 or more. The next 'big one' will probably push Mosquito Hill seven or eight metres north in relation to the fore-ranges of the Alps, which could rise up to one metre.

After leaving the coastal plain we followed SH6 up the south bank of the Haast River/Awarua at the base of the Mark Range. The prominent peak on the Thomas Range on the opposite side of the river was originally named Matapou (sharp post [163]); it was renamed **Mount MacFarlane (3)** after the Jackson Bay Settlement's Government Agent. Julius Haast named the Thomas Range after Canterbury's chief surveyor when he descended the river's true right bank from Pleasant Flat/Ōtoatahi (place of an aggressive male weka[164]) to the sea in 1863.

Behind Mount MacFarlane rises the Hooker Range culminating in **Mount Hooker (8)**, the original name of which was Rakai (standing up threateningly[165]). Haast renamed it after Joseph Hooker, who compiled the first catalogue of New Zealand flora. The Clarke River, named by Haast after the father of Australian geology, William Clarke, arises at the base of that peak. It nominally joined the Haast River/Awarua near Pleasant Flat/Ōtotahi until the Westland Survey downgraded it to a tributary of the Landsborough River.

Haast named two higher tributaries of the Haast River/Awarua after William Wills and Robert Burke, who died of thirst on the return leg of their 1860–61 'Victorian Exploratory Expedition' from Adelaide to the Gulf of Carpentaria; William Landsborough led the search party that discovered their bodies.

My first view of Haast Pass/Tiori Pātea (562m) on the Main Divide from Blue Duck Flat when I followed SH6 across it from the upper Haast/Awarua Valley.

After rounding Clarke Bluff we crossed the Haast/Awarua Bridge in Pleasant Flat/Ōtotahi, where my trip over **Brodrick Pass (9)** in 1970 had ended (see Page 128). Two kilometres further on I peered up the Burke Valley from Burke Flat and spotted **Mueller Pass (10)**. In the 1880s a branch of the Makarora-Haast Stock Track was cut over that pass to Okuru, but it was seldom used and soon became overgrown.

At the top of Burke Flat the highway entered the Haast Gorge between the Bealey Range and Hutchison Spur and crossed the Gates of Haast Bridge, which floods had destroyed twice. Above that gorge we drove across Blue Duck Flat in a long wooded glen and then up a short incline to the summit of **Haast Pass/Tiori Pātea (11)**. At 562 metres above sea level, it is the lowest spot on the portion of the Main Divide that bounds the water catchment areas of the Haast River/Awarua and the Clutha River/Mata-au.

At the top of Blue Duck Flat I peered through a gap in the belt of

Evelyn sitting by the Brewster
Glacier, source of Pyke Creek,
which is the principal source of the
upper Haast River/Awarua below
Mt Brewster, when we visited this
spot from Brewster Hut in 1997.

tāwhairauriki/mountain beech trees on the bank of the infant Haast
River/Awarua and saw a deeply eroded depression on the west flank
of the Main Divide a bit north of Haast Pass/Tiori Pātea where this
river begins its 100-kilometre journey to the sea. Hau mai tiketike
(wind blowing from the heights) is an old term for the section of the
Main Divide between this pass and **Mount Brewster (13)**, which Haast
named after a Scottish scientist.[166] The words 'Mt Tiori Patea' appear in
that position on the deed plan that Land Commissioner James Mackay
drew in 1860 and attached to the Arahura Purchase document. The
translation of Tiori Pātea on *Te Waipounamu Infomap circa 1840* is
'to hold up to view a particular cloak known as a pātea'. It could refer
to the Brewster Glacier on Mount Brewster, the sighting of which may
have been taken as a sign of favourable weather for an alpine crossing.

The largest tributary that joins the Haast River/Awarua in Blue Duck
Flat is Pyke Creek, which issues from the Brewster Glacier. A few years
earlier Evelyn and I had followed the Fantail Falls Track from Blue
Duck Flat to Brewster Hut at the base of Mount Armstrong. Next day we
sidled on short tussock at the base of that peak to the terminus of the
Brewster Glacier, which flows down the west flank of Mount Brewster.
During the Ōtira Glaciation it must have gouged out Haast Pass/Tiori
Pātea and merged with the Makarora Glacier.

The true master stream of the Haast River/Awarua River is the Landsborough River. It issues from the McKerrow Glacier at the base of **Mount Burns (7)** on the southern border of Aoraki/Mount Cook National Park and flows 65 kilometres through the Hooker-Landsborough Wilderness Area to its confluence with the Haast River/Awarua, which marks the northern boundary of Mount Aspiring National Park.

In December 1996 Andrew, Julian, and I drove from Christchurch to Aoraki/Mount Cook village and parked on the site of the old Hermitage Hotel at the base of White Horse Hill. We then lugged our packs up the steep tourist track to the Sealy Tarns and then up a zigzag line of boot prints on snow-covered scree to Mueller Hut on the northern tip of the Sealy Range, which offers a panoramic view of the Main Divide from Mount Burns to Aoraki/Mount Cook.

Next day we embarked on an overnight trip to **Barron Saddle Hut (6)**. On the way we climbed a minor peak named Mount Annette (after the second person to climb it) and then made a beeline across the Annette Plateau, which is the névé of the Metelille Glacier, to Sladden Saddle on the north ridge of Mount Sealy. The sun was nearing its zenith and the snow was turning into slush when we crested the saddle and crammed into a patch of shade under an overhanging rock.

A lone cross-country skier swished past as we descended the Sladden Glacier on the other side of the saddle. Following his ski tracks around the base of Mount Darby, we made our way to Barron Saddle Hut, which was half buried by a snowdrift. A converted grain silo that was set on its side and bolted onto the bedrock, it is about 50 metres below the crest of Barron Saddle, which connects with the Dobson Valley at the head of Lake Ōhau.

In 1977 hurricane force winds had hurled the forerunner of Barron Saddle Hut, the Canterbury Mountaineering Club's Three Johns Hut, off the crest of Barron Saddle and its four occupants were killed. We inspected the site of that hut and saw the frayed ends of its anchor cables, which were still bolted onto bedrock, and a crumpled sheet of orange corrugated iron on the cliff face below it. Current design standards for high altitude huts stipulate that they must be able to withstand 240-kilometres per hour wind gusts.

Mt Burns (2,746m) on the Main Divide
when Andrew Taylor-Perry and I climbed
The Scissors from Barron Saddle Hut
at the head of the Mueller Glacier.

The Sealy Range joins the Main Divide on the East Peak of **The Scissors (5)**. After talking to a couple of climbers who had just climbed it, Andrew and I decided to follow their tracks at first light next morning. We kicked steps up an increasingly steep snow slope beside the rock arête on the southwest side of Barron Saddle and belayed each other up the final pitch. An icy blast slapped me in the face when I stepped onto the summit and the view to the west was swiftly blotted out by swirling mist, which boiled up from the abyss on the other side of the Main Divide. My frozen fingers fumbled with the camera and I missed a fleeting opportunity to photograph the nascent Landsborough River tumbling down its rocky bed between tawny tussock terraces.

Beyond a deep notch named Fyfe Pass, which separates The Scissors from The Watchtower, the Main Divide soared to the summit of **Mount Burns (7)**. At 2746 metres above sea level, it is the highest point within the water catchment area of the Haast River/Awarua. I could see the route up the Welchman Glacier that Whitney Thurlow had chosen when he guided me up that peak from Barron Saddle Hut in 1995. Tom Fyfe and George Graham accomplished the first crossing of Fyfe Pass, which connects with the head to the Landsborough Valley in 1894. Snow lying on the dangerous 45-degree schist slabs on the far side of that pass is liable to avalanche at any time.

In 1888 South Canterbury surveyor Noel Brodrick and his field assistants mapped the Mueller Glacier and named Barron Saddle after Canterbury's chief surveyor. Brodrick named the McKerrow, Sladden and Welchman Glaciers after other colleagues and assistants, and the Metelille Glacier after his daughter.[167] His west coast colleague, George Roberts, named three Main Divide peaks above the névé of the Mueller Glacier, Mounts Bannie, Isabel, and Mildred, after the wife and daughters of Westland's chief surveyor, Gerhard Mueller. The director of Melbourne's Botanic Gardens, Baron Ferdinand von Mueller, after whom Julius Haast had named the glacier, was not related to him (see Page 133).

The highest peak on the portion of the Main Divide between the Waitaki and Haast/Awarua Catchments was provisionally labelled The Dwarf on Brodrick's first map of that area, presumably in reference to the old proverb that 'a dwarf on a giant's shoulders sees the farther of the two'. However Charlie Douglas had named it Mount Burns a year earlier when he and Gerhard Mueller explored the Landsborough Valley. The Poet Glacier on the south flank of Mount Burns confirms that it was named after the Scottish bard.

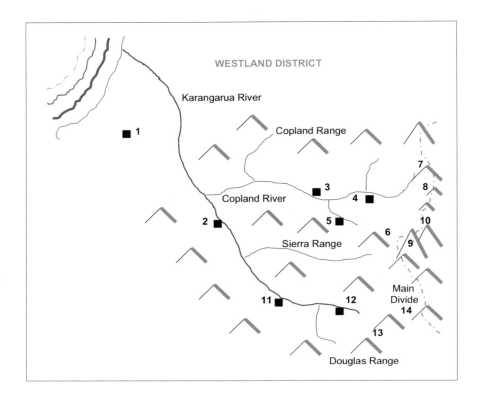

Legend

1. Manakaiaua
2. Cassell Flat Hut
3. Welcome Flat Hut
4. Douglas Rock Hut
5. Scott's Bivouac Rock
6. Welcome Pass
7. Lean Peak
8. Copland Pass

9. Mt Sefton/Kakiroa
10. The Footstool
11. Lame Duck Hut
12. Christmas Flat Hut
13. Karangarua Saddle
14. Douglas Pass
15. Hooker Hut

Chapter 15
The Karangarua

One summer I drove down the west coast with Evelyn and Sybil and parked near the outlet of Manakaiaua Lagoon at the end of the side road to Hunts Beach, which branches off SH6 near the Pine Grove Motel on the site of Adamson's homestead at Manakaiaua (1). The landowner not only gave us permission to camp there but also gifted us a bucket of fresh kutai/green lipped mussels. After slopping on lots of namu/sandfly repellent (gold-diggers back in the old days used camphorated lard), we forded the lagoon outlet on the ebb tide and hiked up the long beach between New Zealand's last extensive stand of kahikatea/'white pine' trees and the Tasman Sea/Te Tai o Rehua. I completed the ten-kilometre hike up Hunts Beach to the Karangarua River mouth on my own and watched an angler, who had passed me earlier on a quad bike, cast his line into the fast out-flowing current.

Like many other old west coast river names, Karangarua was a memento mori. Ngāti Māhaki elders in Bruce Bay/Mahitahi told William Wilson that the Karangarua (twice-related) River and all of its tributaries were named after a man who was killed there.

The low bush-covered lateral moraine called Jacobs Ridge/Tikitiki o Rehua (crown of Rehua [168]) on the southern side of Karangarua Flat ends at Jacobs Bluff, which separates Hunts Beach from Bruce Bay/Mahitahi. Pōrakiraki kāinga by the mouth of Jacobs River/Makaawhio (blue duck stream) at the northern end of that bay was founded in the fifteenth century and was once the largest in South Westland. One of its residents, Hakopa (Jacob) Kaapo, ferried gold-diggers across this river.

The Mahitahi River (one garment[169]), named after a woman who had died there, also flows into Bruce Bay/Mahitahi, which was renamed after the paddle steamer *Bruce*. According to local lore, Māui anchored his waka *Mahaanui* in the lee of its South Head/Heretaniwha (tied-up taniwha) and made his first landfall there. The rare blue stone called aotea/kyanite, which is occasionally cast up on its beach, represents one of Tama-ki-te-Raki's fugitive wives.[170]

The mouth of the Karangarua River, where this upriver story began.

Wild creatures called maeroero were said to haunt the Bannock Brae Range/Kahokahotere (scudding or swirling mist[171]) between the upper Mahitahi and Jacobs/Makaawhio Valleys. When David Monro and Frederick Tuckett explored the Catlins Coast in Murihiku in 1844 their Māori guide said that he saw a maeroero when he was a boy. Monro recorded his guide's description of that 'fearful wildfowl ... covered with coarse and long hair, which also flows down the back of his head nearly to his back. To compensate for this excessive quantity behind, his forehead is said to be bald.'[172] It could be a folk-memory of a moa, which stood on two legs like a man, had coarse hair-like feathers, and weighed up to 250 kilograms.

Mueller named the highest peaks on this mountain range Mount Herman and Mount Butzbach. Herman Borneman had bought 7000 acres in the Jacobs/Makaawhio Valley in 1879. The fact that Mueller did not use Borneman's surname implies that they were good friends and hints that they had discussed the likely setting of Wolfgang Goethe's poem Hermann und Dorothea, which was the old market town of Butzbach in the Grand Duchy of Hessen in Germany. By sheer coincidence it was where my father's grandfather was born.

Around 1820 Ngāi Tahu rangatira Tuarohe wrested control of the Makaawhio district from Ngāti Wairangi and settled in Pōrakiraki kāinga with relatives who belonged to the Ngāti Māhaki hapū of Ngāi Te Ruakihikihi. He and his kinsman Tūtoko, who died there in 1865, belonged to the Ngāti Kaipō hapū.[173] Te Rūnanga o Makaawhio, which is based in Bruce Bay/Mahitahi, holds manawhenua in Westland south of the Hokitika River. Hokitika-based Westland District Council has jurisdiction there.

An ephemeral gold-mining settlement sprang up at the southern end of Hunts Beach in 1865. Albert Hunt was rather unfairly blamed for a 'duffer' gold rush to Bruce Bay/Mahitahi earlier that year. Special techniques using copper plates and mercury were required to extract very fine gold particles from ilmenite-rich black sand deposits on South Westland beaches. Big waves could quickly 'cut' them and remove shallow deposits of fine gold particles.

Karangarua ferryman Archibald McBride lived on the ferry reserve by the Karangarua River mouth in the 1870s. One of the most dangerous fords on the old beach highway was near the mouth of Saltwater Creek/Ōhinetamatea, just south of Cook Bluff. Thomas Brunner's diary only records his crossing of the 'Manakaiaua River' between the 'Weheka' and Bruce Bay/Mahitahi, but he surely must have meant the Karangarua River instead.

In the late 1860s Andrew Scott drove a mob of sheep along those beaches and around the intervening bluffs and pastured them on Karangarua Flat. In 1870 the Waste Lands Board granted him a grazing licence; his descendants still run stock there. The Haast Cattle Track detoured away from the coast to avoid Cook Bluff and passed close to his homestead, which stood on the south side of the Karangarua Ford halfway up that flat. Andrew married the widow of Cook River/ Weheka ferryman, Robert McIntosh, who had drowned at the mouth of Saltwater Creek.[174] Scott's Accommodation House on the northern side of that ford has been replaced by Pine Grove Motel on SH6 at Manakaiaua, near the turn-off to Hunt's Beach.

In April 2003 Andrew and I stowed two packs and a bicycle in the boot of my van and then drove to Reefton to pick up Andrew's daughter, Natasha, before heading down the west coast. I dropped Andrew and Natasha off at the southern end of the Karangarua Bridge, parked my car at **Matakaiaua (1)** and then cycled back to the bridge. After hiding my bicycle in the bush, we tramped up the old stock track on the south bank of the Karangarua River. It had almost stopped raining at this point and as the clouds were beginning to lift I crossed my fingers and prayed that they would not descend again over the next two days.

It was the stag roaring season and so when we arrived at **Cassell Flat Hut (2)** the four deer hunters already ensconced there kindly offered us some fresh venison. The next day was fine and sunny and wisps of morning mist floated above the Karangarua River. Heading off, we saw five kōwhiowhio/blue ducks below the confluence of the Douglas River, which issues from the Douglas Glacier below **Mount Sefton/Kakīroa (9)**.

We forded Tui Creek at the top of Cassell Flat and found the first white permolat marker on the Karangarua Gorge Track, which climbed steadily through rātā–kāmahi bush on the northern flanks of the Rocky Range. The number of healthy rātā saplings in that area indicated that Australian brush-tailed possum numbers were comparatively low. We climbed in and out of dank gullies below a line of high bluffs until the track seemed to end on the rim of a huge chasm. At that point Natasha spotted a narrow ledge that angled up a nearby rock face and when we reached the top, we found that a chain has been attached to a tree trunk for climbers to grasp.

Picking up the track again above the bluff, we followed it under a dry overhang, which was littered with animal scat. After that detour around the chasm the track headed east through stunted manoao/silver pine bush in the upper Karangarua Valley. Mount Burns and the shining white névé of the McKerrow Glacier soared above Karangarua Saddle on the Douglas Range, which is contiguous with the Hooker Range.

After a short rest in **Lame Duck Hut (11)** we followed the track through the sole stand of tāwhairauriki/mountain beech trees in this valley. Their seeds are spread by the wind, which usually blows from the west. After the last glaciation the 'beech gap' between the Pāringa and Taramakau Rivers was rapidly colonised by podocarp and broadleaf specie because fruit-eating birds spread their seeds. We briefly lost the track on a revegetated slip but picked it up again by the confluence of the Troyte tributary of the Karangarua River.

We stumbled into **Christmas Flat Hut (12)** just before dark and were revived with shots of whiskey by two thar hunters. They had spent the day on Karangarua Saddle and told us how to get there. This hut actually comprises half of McCormick Hut, which was removed from Luncheon Rock by the Franz Josef Glacier/Ō Hine Hukatere in 1994 when an ice surge had threatened to crush it. The upper Karangarua Catchment was added to Westland/Tai Poutini National Park in 1983.

In December 1893, when Charlie Douglas was temporarily immobilised by arthritis, his assistant, Arthur Harper, and Ruera 'Bill' Te Naihi completed a reconnaissance survey of the Karangarua Valley. Harper cut the first track through the Karangarua Gorge, which followed a lower line than the present track, and named Lame Duck Flat after hearing Bill's account of an incident involving his three-legged dog Jack. Apparently the dog had disturbed a nesting kōwhiowhio/blue duck, which lured its persecutor away by pretending that it had a broken wing. The duck escaped and although the dog disappeared over a waterfall it survived unscathed. While Bill was fetching more food from the Scotts' homestead, Arthur blazed the route to Christmas Flat and spent Christmas Day there. His sole companions were a pair of weka, which became his Christmas dinner.[175]

The view of the source of the Karangarua
River below Karangarua Saddle on the
Douglas Range from Christmas Flat Hut.
The clouds descended onto it just before
Andrew Taylor-Perry and his daughter
Natasha and I reached its crest.

After Christmas the two explorers climbed onto the broad dip
on the Douglas Range and saw the McKerrow Glacier source of
the Landsborough River directly below them. Mounts Howitt and
Townsend on either side of that saddle were named after two men
who had drowned on the west coast in 1863. Harper and Te Naihi
descended a steep snow-filled gut to the McKerrow Glacier. Since then
the glacier's terminal face has retreated three kilometres to the base
of **Douglas Pass (14)** between Mount Howitt and Mount Isabel, where
the Douglas Range joins the Main Divide, and Karangarua Saddle has
become uncrossable via that direct route. George Roberts named Mount
Isabel after Gerhard Mueller's eldest daughter, and its neighbour,
Mount Bannie, after Mueller's wife Elizabeth Bannatyne McArthur.
When Charlie Douglas and Mueller explored the Landsborough Valley
in 1887 Douglas carried on alone and spied the glacial sources of the
Douglas River from Douglas Pass.

Steel-grey altostratus cloud had filled the sky overnight. We wasted no time in setting off for **Karangarua Saddle (13)** on the Douglas Range. An arm of the McKerrow Glacier at the head of the Landsborough Valley had clearly moved through it long ago. The cloud base lowered and began to envelop the neighbouring mountaintops as we ascended the Karangarua Riverbed.

After passing a waterslide down a long schist face, which appeared to be the main source of the river, we followed the hunters' advice and scrambled up a rubble-filled gut and then crossed what they had called a 'rock garden' by jumping over gaps between huge blocks of schist that had fallen off a row of bluffs, maybe during an earthquake. At the end of that obstacle course we ascended a grassy slope to the summit of Karangarua Saddle. The lowering clouds beat us to it, but I managed to catch a glimpse of the infant Landsborough River tumbling over boulders at the base of a 300-metre bluff.

As soon as we got back to Christmas Flat Hut we packed up and headed down to Lame Duck Hut, but the rain set in before we got there. Previous occupants of that dilapidated hut had slung a plastic sheet over the bunks to keep them dry, which had worked, but it was impossible to shut the door because the hut's timber frame was twisted. Its flat iron cladding was airdropped into a clearing when the hut was built in the 1960s (a new hut replaced it in 2008). Next day we pressed on to Cassell Flat Hut; however, the rain did not ease and it took us quite a while to find a safe place to ford Tui Creek.

Steady rain turned to intermittent heavy showers during the night. We set off early next morning, hoping to reach the road. Purcell and McTaggert Creeks were fordable, but a swollen side stream brought us to a halt within sight of the Karangarua Bridge. Natasha disappeared into the bush and found a fallen tree that spanned the stream. Three hours later we walked into the Fox Glacier Hotel bar and bumped into the two hunters whom we'd met in Christmas Flat Hut. One of them whipped out his video camera and showed us the stunning view that we had missed through Douglas Pass from Karangarua Saddle of Mount Sefton/Kakīroa and the huge shelf névé of the Douglas Glacier on the southern flanks of the Sierra Range, which met the Main Divide on **Mount Sefton/Kakīroa (9)**.

In January 1966 I joined two fellow members of the West Coast Alpine Club, Terry Sweetman and Chris Coll, on a circular trip around of Aoraki/Mount Cook via **Copland Pass (8)** and Graham Saddle. We left Greymouth a bit later than planned, consequently it was after 4pm when we were dropped off at the beginning of the track up the Copland branch of the Karangarua Valley. The old 1913 Architect Creek swing bridge was in a parlous state as minimal maintenance had been carried out on this track between World War II and the establishment of Westland National Park Board in 1960.

Chris tried to ford the rain-swollen creek on a rope, but the current was too strong so it was back to the bridge where Terry found that by standing on the wire rope on one side of the decrepit deck and using the wire rope on the other side as a handrail, he was able to cross. Chris and I followed suit. Unknown to us the 16-bunk **Welcome Flat Hut (3)**, which opened in 1913, was only an hour away when it became too dark to see the track. Dropping our packs, we pulled out our sleeping bags and enjoyed the sight of glow-worm lights twinkling in the bush all around us.

In 1892 Charlie Douglas and his assistant, Harry Cuttance, cut the first track up the true right bank of the Copland River to Welcome Flat. They carried on to Douglas Rock Bivouac and explored the headwaters of this river, which is the largest tributary of the Karangarua. Westland's Chief Surveyor, George Roberts, had asked Douglas to look for a Main Divide pass that pack mules could cross between the Copland Valley and The Hermitage for at least three months of the year. Douglas examined and dismissed the high passes at the heads of the Copland Valley and its Strauchon branch and noted that winter avalanches would destroy any tourist tracks in their vicinity.

In February 1896 a young English climber named Edward FitzGerald and his talented Swiss guide, Mattias Zurbriggen, accomplished the first ascent of **Mount Sefton/Kakīroa (9)** and the first crossing of Fitzgerald Pass. At 2109 metres above sea level, its crest is the lowest spot on the portion of the Main Divide that bounds the Karangarua Catchment. They set off from The Hermitage and reached that pass via a rock spur and the steep névé of the Stewart Glacier, then battled their way down the Copland Valley with the aid of a sketch map drawn by Charlie Douglas, which Fitzgerald subsequently gave to Arthur Harper.[176] A few weeks later Harper climbed the spur on the other side of Stewart Stream and crossed the Main Divide at a safer spot near the base of **Lean Peak (7)**. This so-called 'pass' is 41 metres higher than Fitzgerald Pass and one kilometre further north.

A saddle at the head of the Hooker Glacier had recently been named after Arthur Harper so George Roberts named the spot where Harper had crossed the Main Divide to the Copland Valley the Copland Pass.[177] Roberts probably named the Copland River after the surveyor and civil engineer, John Copland, whom he had trained under in Glasgow in the 1860s.[178] Roberts named the Strauchon tributary of the Copland River after Westland's Commissioner of Crown Lands and an adjacent col after Harry Cuttance.

After receiving Harper's negative report about Karangarua Pass, the Lands and Survey Department accepted Douglas' conclusion that a tourist track could be constructed to the head of the Copland Valley and that the alpine route from there to The Hermitage via Copland Pass should be marked by stone cairns. Douglas commented in a letter to George Roberts that 'it is not by trotting out of a comfortable hotel and back the same day that nature's wonders can really be seen.'[179] Between 1901 and 1913 the Te Koeti and Bannister families in Bruce Bay/Mahitahi constructed the Copland Track under a government contract up to Douglas Rock Bivouac (which a rock avalanche destroyed in 1968). **Douglas Rock Hut (4)** supplemented that bivvy rock in 1931.[180]

By 1910 the summer trip from Hooker Hut to Douglas Rock Bivouac via Copland Pass could be comfortably accomplished in one day. Over the next 30 years, Mount Cook Company guides escorted most of the parties that crossed Copland Pass. In 1944, the company's lease expired and the State-owned Tourist Hotel Corporation acquired The Hermitage Hotel and the Copland and Hooker Track huts, but few people walked the track until it was upgraded in the late 1960s.

Three hours up the Copland Track from Welcome Flat Hut we crossed Tekano Creek and stepped into Douglas Rock Hut. Our Park Service guides, Pat Sheridan and Lindsay Strang, arrived from The Hermitage just before dark. The weather next day was impeccable. After passing Douglas Rock Bivouac in the last grove of trees we followed a rough track across tussock-covered boulder fields and barren avalanche paths.

The track petered out on a long shingle scree above the farthest Main Divide source of the Karangarua River. Lindsay plugged steps up a snow slope at the top of that scree and stopped in a hollow just below the crest of Copland Pass. Looking southward along the Main Divide I saw the porcelain-white icecaps of **Mount Sefton/Kakīroa (9)** and **The Footstool (10)** soaring into the blue sky. Fine weather fog was beginning to fill the upper Copland Valley. On the other side of the Main Divide I saw glistening ice cliffs perched high above the Hooker Glacier on the south face of Aoraki/Mount Cook.

Kakīroa (long neck) was the original name of Mount Sefton, which appears to incline towards Aoraki/Mount Cook like Lean Peak, and which represents one of the passengers on the legendary waka *Arai Te Uru*.[181] Otago's Chief Surveyor John Thomson considered that it was located in his province in 1857 and renamed Kakīroa after Captain Stokes of HMSS *Acheron*, who had renamed Aoraki. Four years later the Otago-Canterbury border was revised and Julius Haast 're-renamed' Kakīroa after the Superintendent of Canterbury Province, William Sefton Moorhouse. At 3151 metres, the summit of that great peak is the highest point in the Karangarua Catchment.

Five years later a fellow member of the Alpine Club, Tony Parlane, climbed it with me from **Scott's Rock Bivouac (5)** near the source of Scotts Creek in the Copland Valley. We followed the crest of the Sierra Range from **Welcome Pass (6)** and gazed down on the Douglas Glacier source of the Douglas tributary of the Karangarua River and the short section of the Main Divide that it drains between Mount Isabel and Mount Sefton/Kakīroa. We had to belay off ice screws near the top and keep moving to stay warm.

Pat and Lindsay carefully guided us down the soft snow slope on the eastern side of the Copland Pass, and then down a long rock ridge and across Stewart Stream to the old **Hooker Hut (15)** on a sloping lateral moraine bench above the rubble-covered tongue of the Hooker Glacier. While we waited for the billy to boil, Lindsay entertained us with the

The striking view of The Footstool and Mt Sefton/Kakīroa (3,151m) on the Main Divide when Pat Sheridan and Lindsay Strang guided Chis Coll, Terry Sweetman and me over Copland Pass from Douglas Rock Hut in 1966.

hoary old yarn about Barney the ghost who rattles the door of that hut on dark stormy nights

In the 1980s the Hooker Glacier commenced its rapid retreat and an ever-expanding pro-glacial lake began to fill its vacated bed. Associated slumping of the western lateral moraine has destroyed the track that used to run along the grassy bench above the moraine wall and destabilised the site of Hooker Hut, which had been built in 1910. It was winched further and further up the slope in 1948, 1963, and 1994, and finally removed by helicopter in 2015.[182] Crossing Copland Pass nowadays entails a perilous descent and ascent of the Hooker Glacier's crumbling lateral moraine walls.

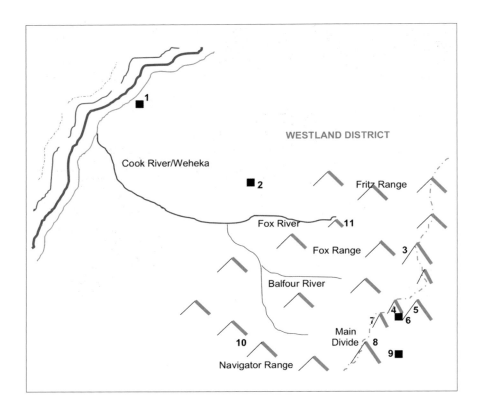

WESTLAND DISTRICT

Cook River/Weheka

Fritz Range

Fox River 11

Fox Range 3

Balfour River

4 5
7 6
Main
Divide 8
9
10
Navigator Range

Legend

1. Gillespies Beach
2. Fox Glacier/Weheka village
3. Mt Tasman/Horo Kōau
4. Harper Saddle
5. Aoraki/Mt. Cook
6. Empress Hut
7. Mt Sturdee
8. Mt La Perouse/Aroarokaehe
9. Gardiner Hut
10. Whale Saddle
11. Cone Rock

Chapter 16
The Cook/Weheka

In June 1991 Evelyn, Sybil and I drove to Fox Glacier/Weheka village (2) and spent Queen's Birthday weekend in the old Glacier Hotel. Next day we followed Gillespies Beach Road across Cook Flat and then over a bush-covered lateral moraine ridge to the seafront site of an old gold-mining township by the name of Gillespies Beach (1). Plump kererū/wood pigeons flapped overhead. Two elderly residents, John and Mark Shaw, invited us in for a cup of tea. John told us that they used to mine scheelite on a mountain behind Glenorchy. It became uneconomic in 1952 so they moved to Gillespie's Beach and extracted some gold from fresh black sand deposits on the beach. They had to truck in soil from Cook Flat to create their large vegetable garden. John said that fishing boats working too close to the shore had spoiled the surfcasting.

The mouth of the Cook River/Weheka,
where this upriver story began.

At the southern end of Gillespie's Beach we boulder-hopped around
Ōtūrokua Point to the mouth of the Cook River/Weheka and saw a
stunning spectacle. The highest peaks of the Southern Alps/Kā Tiritiri
o te Moana, culminating in the three-kilometre long and three-and-a-
half-kilometre high summit ridge of **Aoraki/Mount Cook (5)**, soared
into the clear blue sky like cumulus clouds. Many years later I followed
the steps of the gold diggers along Three Mile and Five Mile Beaches
between Ōkārito and the Waiho River mouth and along the old pack
track over Gillespies Point/Kōhaihai between Gillespies Beach and
Galway Bay, which is now only frequented by karoro/seagulls.

Ngāti Māhaki elders told William Wilson that Te Weheka (Te
Wehenga – 'the parting: one go one way, one go another') was the
original name of Cook Bluff on the southern side of the mouth of the
Cook River/Weheka as well as this big river and its master stream, the
Fox River, which issues from the huge Fox Glacier/Te Moenga o Tūawe.

Early gold prospectors thought that it flowed from Aoraki/Mount Cook and renamed it after that great peak.

Wilson was also told that Aoraki means 'above the clouds' or 'among the clouds'. The highest portion of the Southern Alps/Kā Tiritiri o te Moana was called 'Ngā Aotea' (the white clouds). Aotea was also the original name of Great Barrier Island, which is separated from the Coromandel Peninsula on Aotearoa (strictly the North Island) by a strait named Tai o Tea. Aotea and Aoraki may be contractions of Ao Rakiātea (the bright world of 'immense heaven' – Ra'iātea in Tahiti and Laniākea in Hawaii).

The original name of the highest peak between Aoraki/Mount Cook and Mount Sefton/Kakīroa, **Mount La Perouse/Aroarokaehe (8)**, means 'front of a whale's head'.[183] It resembles the head of a broaching whale.[184] The original name of the adjacent apex of the Main Divide, **Mount Tasman/Horokōau (3)**, means 'diving shag'. This great peak resembles a kōau/shag with outspread wings extending its neck to swallow a fish.[185] It perches on the port washboard of Te Waka a Aoraki near its gigantic commander, Aoraki (Aorangi), son of Rakinui (Ranginui).

After the 'duffer' gold rush to Bruce Bay in 1866 (see Page 235), hundreds of disgruntled prospectors trudged back up the old beach highway to Ōkārito, fossicking for gold on the way. James Gillespie struck it rich on the beach that bears his name just north of the mouth of the Cook River/Weheka. The site of the terminal face of the Weheka Glacier during the Ōtira Glaciation now lies offshore, however the northward longshore drift ensures that a lot of the gold that was deposited there is redeposited on this beach. When that gold rush peaked the township of Gillespies Beach had 11 stores, two butcheries, and two bakeries.[186]

Twenty-five years later, when Arthur Harper passed by, it had two stores, a hotel, a school, a church, and six or seven huts and houses – and an old '49er' named California Bill still operated the Cook River/Weheka ferry. Harper called it 'a godforsaken place' and noted that few of its residents were on speaking terms.[187] When Elsie Morton visited Gillespies Beach in 1931 its sole residents were the Bagley brothers. Later that year the virtually abandoned settlement briefly revived when an electric gold dredge began to excavate deep deposits of gold-bearing sand.[188]

Gillespies Beach butchers obtained fresh meat from Andrew

Scott on Karangarua Flat and Edward Ryan on Cook Flat. The broad shingle bed of the Cook River/Weheka was the only route to those two common grazing areas from Gillespies Beach until 1886, when Pat Sullivan and Fred Williams cut a bush track to their new homestead blocks on Cook Flat.

Pat Sullivan's sons built Glacier Hotel in 1928 on an 11-acre township reserve. Fox Glacier/ Weheka village sprang up there after the stock track over Ōmoeroa and Cook Saddles on the Fox Hills from Franz Josef/Waiho village was upgraded into an extension of the Main South Road from Hokitika. The first car arrived in 1929 and buses followed from 1936 onwards. Mick Sullivan employed a team of glacier guides headed by Frank Alack. Mike and Carol Browne took over the business in 1974 and renamed it Alpine Guides Fox Glacier.

In December 1969 three friends and I were holed up in **Fox Glacier/ Weheka** village **(2)** for two days due to rain-swollen rivers. When the rain stopped we drove up the old glacier access road on the south bank of the Fox River to the Chalet Lookout. In the 1930s, visitors could step straight onto the Fox Glacier/Te Moenga o Tūawe from that spot. We climbed a steep track to the summit of **Cone Rock (11)** and saw the Fox branch of the Cook River/Weheka gush out of the glacier's slowly retreating terminal face. A detached mound of 'dead ice' had been left behind in the middle of the riverbed.

The original name of the Fox Glacier/Te Moenga o Tūawe means either 'the bed of Tūawe' or 'the place where storm clouds stand still'.[189] Julius Haast renamed it after Queen Victoria's eldest son, Prince Albert (the future king Edward VII). A tributary glacier was named after Albert's sister Victoria. In 1872, Premier William Fox rode up the bed of the Cook River/Weheka from Gillespie's Beach to inspect this huge glacier, which was renamed in his honour.

Many years later Matt Wilkinson guided me to a point about 70 metres below the summit of Aoraki/Mount Cook. From there I spied the tongue of the La Perouse Glacier through Harper Saddle just before a blanket of fog moved up the valley and concealed it. That glacier is the most distant source of the Cook River/Weheka. Te Weheka was the original name of the Cook and Fox Rivers. Since the latter is the master

The view of the Fox Glacier/Te Moenga o Tūawe source of the Fox River, which is the master stream of the Cook River/Weheka, from Cone Rock in 1969.

stream of the Cook River/Weheka, the Fox Glacier/Te Moenga o Tūawe is its principal Main Divide source.

Pioneer Ridge and The Buttress divide the 36 square-kilometre névé of the Fox Glacier/Te Moenga o Tūawe into three snowfields called the Explorer, Albert, and Abel Janzoon Glaciers. The last-named snowfield reaches a height of 2800 metres at the base of the Heemskerk face of **Mount Tasman/Horo Kōau (3)**. The glacial ice that forms beneath those snowfields takes 60 years to reach the terminal face, which is only 240 metres above sea level. This glacier was 15 kilometres long when Harper and Douglas measured it in 1894. By 1994 it was much thinner and two kilometres shorter. A different weather pattern during the 1990s thickened this glacier's tongue and pushed it 500 metres forward. Since then, however, it has retreated faster than ever and collapsing lateral moraines are choking the riverbed with shingle. During the 'Little Ice Age', which began in the fifteenth century in the Pacific Region, it almost lapped the summit of Cone Rock.[190]

Abel Janzoon Tasman was the Captain Commander of the Dutch United East India Company's vessels *Heemskerk* and *Zeehaen*, which sailed across the Tasman Sea from Van Dieman's Land (Tasmania) in December 1642. When they were approximately 20 kilometres west of Punakaiki (Latitude 42 degrees 10 minutes South) Tasman sighted

The view of the La Perouse Glacier source of the Cook River/Weheka through Harper Saddle when Matt Wilkinson guided me up Aoraki/Mt Cook in 1996.

a 'groot hooch verheven landt (great high uplifted land)'[191]. Mount La Perouse/Aroarokaehe was renamed after French navigator Jean-François de Galaup Compte de La Pérouse. Five other peaks around the headwaters of the Cook River were also named after European navigators that explored the Pacific Ocean: Dampier, Hicks, Magellan, Torres, and Vancouver. Sticking to this maritime theme, Mounts Jellico and Sturdee were named after Royal Navy admirals in World War One.

When Charlie Douglas and Arthur Harper explored the upper Cook Valley in 1894, Harper was informed that a gold prospector named Harry 'The Whale' Vickers had fossicked up to the terminus of the Balfour Glacier, which has a small shelf névé beneath Mount Tasman/ Horo Kōau's Balfour face. Two other gold prospectors, 'Tony the Greek' and 'German Harry' Wolmer, had accompanied Vickers up the south bank of the Cook River to its La Perouse Glacier source. They bivvied under Tony's Rock and returned to Gillespies Beach via **Whale Saddle (10)** on the Copland Range, Architects Creek, and the Copland Valley.[192] In 1949 a track was cut to the head of the Cook Valley to enable an injured climber to be carried down to the road on a stretcher. The track has since disappeared and the upper Cook Valley is now designated a 'wilderness area'.

In December 1995 I set off from Aoraki/Mount Cook village with Gary Dickson from Alpine Guides Mount Cook with the original intention of climbing **Aoraki/Mount Cook (5)** from the head of the Hooker Glacier. A few days earlier a violent storm had dumped 445mm of rain in the upper Waitaki Catchment. The ensuing flood had partly destroyed the Hakataramea Bridge at Kurow. However, a thick carapace of water ice remained on the summit ridge of Aoraki/Mount Cook, which ruled out that objective.

We crossed the Hooker River via the footbridge below the terminal lake of the Mueller Glacier and then followed a rough track along a rock-studded lateral moraine bench beside the Hooker Glacier's proglacial lake. When the track began to climb towards Ball Pass on the Aoraki/Mount Cook Range we scrambled down a gully and walked up the Hooker Glacier.

We bypassed its icefall by scaling a big bluff called Pudding Rock at the bottom of the west ridge of the Low Peak of Aoraki/Mount Cook. The wire rope bolted onto the face of the bluff was a great help, but the effort of lugging my heavy pack up it was exhausting. We spent the first night in the second **Gardiner Hut (9)**, which was built on top of Pudding Rock in 1977. Katie Gardiner had opened the first hut on that old open bivouac site in 1934; a rock avalanche destroyed its replacement in 2014.

Next day we ascended the upper Hooker Glacier, which was partly covered by ice avalanche debris from the Empress Glacier on the western flank of Aoraki/Mount Cook. The next three nights were spent in New Zealand's highest building, the second **Empress Hut (6)**, which is situated 2530 metres above sea level on the toe of this mountain's Earle Ridge.

The Canterbury Mountaineering Club built the first Empress Hut on that old open bivouac site in 1953. The weather deteriorated after dark and about 10 centimetres of snow settled around the hut before the cold front moved away.

When the sky cleared we crossed the big snowfield called the Sheila Glacier between the Earle Ridge and Mounts Hicks and Dampier on the Main Divide to **Harper Saddle (4)** between Mount Hicks and **Mount Sturdee (7)**. At 2585 metres above sea level, the crest of this saddle is the lowest spot on the portion of the Main Divide that bounds the Cook River/Weheka Catchment. In the past the Sheila Glacier had clearly spilled through that gap into the head of the Cook Valley. Rising mist robbed us of a view of the Cook Valley from Mount Sturdee, however I saw the Fox Range rise out of the fog and soar up to the glistening ice cap of **Mount Tasman/Horo Kōau (3)**, which towered above its Balfour face at the head of the Balfour branch of the Cook Valley. I had seen the Heemskerk face of this great peak from West Hoe Pass in 1966 when Lindsay Strang guided Chris, Terry, and me over the Fritz Range between the névés of the Franz Josef Glacier/Kā Roimata o Hukarere and the Fox Glacier/Te Moenga o Tūawe.

At 3497 metres, the summit of Mount Tasman/Horo Kōau is the

Harper Saddle (2,585m) on the Main Divide when Gary Dickson guided me up the Hooker Glacier to Empress Hut en route to that saddle in 1995.

The spectacle across the névé of the Fox Glacier/Te Moenga o Tūawe of Mt Tasman/Horo Kōau (3,497m) on the Main Divide from West Hoe Pass on the Fritz Range when Lindsay Strang guided Chris Coll, Terry Sweetman and me over Graham Saddle on the Main Divide from De La Bêche Hut in 1966.

highest point in the Cook River/Weheka Catchment and on the South Island's entire Main Divide.

In December 1890 Arthur Harper and his cousin Reginald Blakiston ascended the Hooker Glacier to the saddle that was named after Harper and confirmed that Aoraki/Mount Cook was not in the Cook/Weheka Catchment and was entirely east of the Main Divide. In January 1905 Alex Graham, Henry Newton and Ebenezer Teichelmann accomplished the first crossing of Harper Saddle from a rock bivouac at the head of the Cook Valley. They scaled an unstable rock rib on the western side of this saddle and bivouacked on Pudding Rock en route to The Hermitage.[193]

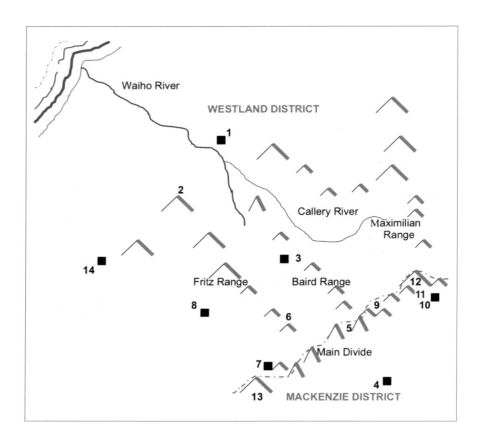

Legend

1. Franz Josef/Waiho village
2. Alex Knob
3. Almer Hut
4. De La Bêche Refuge Hut
5. Graham Saddle
6. West Hoe Pass
7. Pioneer Hut
8. Chancellor Hut
9. The Minarets
10. Tasman Saddle Hut
11. Mt Walter
12. Mt Elie de Beaumont
13. Mt Tasman/Horo Kōau
14. Fox Glacier/Weheka village

Chapter 17
The Waiho (Waiau)

In June 1993 I set off from Fox Glacier/Weheka village to visit the mouth of the Waiho River. After driving over the Fox Hills I left SH6 five kilometres south of the Waiho Bridge and followed Waiho Flat Road as far as the Docherty Creek Ford. I left my car there, forded the creek, and then followed an old logging road through the Waiho River Conservation Area (formerly Waikūkupa State Forest). A friendly pair of piwakawaka/fantails followed me past a regenerating grove of kahikatea/white pine trees. After skirting the head of a small lagoon, I walked up the beach and watched the Waiho (Waiau) River flow into the sea on the southern side of Waiho Bluff.

The flood tide had peaked and breaking waves sent ripples a short distance up the river, whose milky hue is due to 'rock flour' ground out

The mouth of the Waiho (Waiau) River,
where this upriver story began.

by its main source, the Franz Josef Glacier/Kā Roimata o Hine Hukatere,
which is only 25 kilometres from the sea. It looked like a giant waterfall
between two bush-clad spurs of the Main Divide and on this occasion
the high peaks behind its névé were enveloped in cloud.

When 'German Harry' Wolmer's prospecting days were over he
ran the Waiho Ferry on the old beach highway between Ōkārito and
Gillespies Beach. He is buried nearby.

Waiho is a corruption of the common river name Waiau ('strong
current' – danger!). To European ears at the time the diphthong *au*
sounded like *ho* and Aoraki sounded like 'Hauraki'.

My first trip up the glacier access road on the south bank of the
Waiho River to the Franz Josef Glacier/Kā Roimata o Hine Hukatere was
in 1964. It had shrunk and retreated two kilometres from the smooth
schist knob, which its terminal face reared above in a photograph taken
in 1867.

Its retreat stalls or temporarily reverses after strong El Niño events,
when greater quantities of snow accumulate on its 30-square kilometre
névé. After two decades of heavier than normal winter snowfalls
and relatively cool summers, which commenced in the late 1980s,

The Franz Josef Glacier/Kā Roimata
o Hine Hukatere source of the Waiho
(Waiau) River from the riverbank in 1996.

the glacier's tongue thickened and moved forward onto the riverbed, attaining a total length of 11.5 kilometres. Waves of ice moving up to four metres per day crushed scrub on the adjacent mountainsides. After thickening and advancing onto the Waiho Riverbed in the 1990s it has retreated faster than ever and the riverbed has risen at an average rate of 30 centimetres per year.

In the 1920s and 30s, Alex and Peter Graham guided clients up the Franz Josef Glacier/Kā Roimata o Hine Hukatere and over Graham Saddle to The Hermitage. A cantilevered walkway gave access to Roberts Point. From there climbers crossed the glacier to Defiance Hut, which Alex had built in the summer of 1912–13 with funding from the Department of Tourist and Health Resorts. Next day the guides led their clients up the glacier to Almer Hut on the spur of the Baird Range between the Almer Glacier (which was named after a Swiss guide) and the Geike Snowfield. On the following day, weather permitting, they would cross Graham Saddle to the rock bivouac or De La Bêche Refuge Hut by the Tasman Glacier. In 1959 local photographer Ralph Warburton did that trip with his dog Scott. In 1978 the old Defiance Hut was airlifted to the Westland/Tai Poutini National Park headquarters in **Franz Josef/Waiho village (1)** and a new hut was erected on the same site.[194]

The original name of the Franz Josef Glacier/Kā Roimata o Hine Hukatere refers to a local legend, which Murihiku Māori elders related to Herries Beattie.[195] When Hine Hukatere (Avalanche Maid) and Wawe (or Tūawe) tried to scale a steep mountainside, Hine's lover fell to his death and became the Fox Glacier/Te Moenga o Tūawe. Her roimata (tears) became the Franz Joseph Glacier/Kā Roimata o Hine Hukatere.[196]

In 1857 Leonard Harper renamed this glacier after Queen Victoria. Eight years later, Julius Haast decided to rename the glaciers and ridges in this area after the next generation of European monarchs, thus renaming the Victoria Glacier after the young Austrian Emperor, Franz Josef, and the Maxmillian Range on the northern rim of the Waiho Catchment after his brother, the ill-fated Emperor of Mexico. The Fritz and Victoria Glaciers on the southern side of the Fritz Range were named after the son and heir of King Friedrich I of Prussia and his wife Victoria, who was the eldest child of Queen Victoria. Unser Fritz ('our Fritz') Waterfall by the terminus of the Franz Josef Glacier/Kā Roimata o Hine Hukatere was named after Friedrich, who succeeded his father in 1888 to become Emperor Friedrich II of Germany. His death from cancer after a very brief reign dashed British hopes that the new German Empire would become a constitutional monarchy.

No New Zealand landmark commemorates Emperor Napoleon III of France, whom the historian Lewis Namier called Europe's first mountebank dictator. The 1870 Franco-Prussian war cost him his crown. George Roberts expressed his approval by naming four peaks on the Fritz Range after the architects of his downfall: Chancellor Bismarck and Generals Molke, Roon and Von Bulow. In 1883 Robert von Lendenfeld conducted a detailed topographical survey of the Tasman Glacier and named a large tributary the Kron Prinz Glacier after Franz Josef's son and heir, Rudolf, who committed suicide in 1889.

Ōkārito-based gold prospectors searched in vain for a 'mother lode' on the adjacent Burster Range and Tatare and Price Ridges. 'German Harry' climbed over the Burster Range and fossicked above the deep gorge of the Callery River, which was named after the first prospector to pan gold on its tiny beaches.[197]

In the late 1880s, the Public Works Department built a riding road from the port town of Ōkārito by the outlet of Ōkārito Lagoon to Waiho Flat, where the McFettrick brothers had a grazing licence. Hydraulic sluicing was still taking place on the alluvial terrace below the Callery Gorge when William and Emily Batson opened the first accommodation house there in 1896. The township site was initially called Waiho Gorge and is now Franz Josef/Waiho.

The first car reached Batson's Accommodation House in 1911. A year later, Jim Graham and his wife Rose bought this building and then shifted and enlarged it before renaming it the Franz Josef Hotel. Jim's brother, Alex Graham, trained and managed a group of glacier guides. Meanwhile, his other brother, Peter, had moved to The Hermitage in 1903 and eventually became its chief guide.[198] Jim's untimely death and the government's decision to lease The Hermitage to the Mount Cook Company prompted Peter to resign in 1921. He moved back to Waiho Gorge where he helped Alex manage the hotel and associated glacier guides. Peter's Pool by Sentinel Rock, **Alex Knob (2)** on the Fritz Range and Mount Graham between Mounts Silberhorn and Teichelman were all named after those two brothers.

The Tourist Hotel Corporation purchased Franz Josef Hotel in 1947, but seven years later it burned down and travellers had to forego accommodation here until 1965 when a new THC hotel (now Mueller

Hotel) opened at the northern end of the village in conjunction with the new Haast Highway. The headquarters of the 132,00-hectare Westland/ Tai Poutini National Park was built on the old hotel site, which unfortunately straddles the Alpine Fault.

In January 1966 Pat Sheridan and Lindsay Strang guided Chris Coll, Terry Sweetman, and me over Copland Pass to Aoraki/Mount Cook village. Two days later Lindsay met us at the Youth Hostel and shepherded us onto the bus to Ball Hut. There I saw the full extent of the Tasman Glacier and was astounded by its size.

We scrambled down the moraine wall to the chaotic surface of the Ball Glacier and then walked up the smooth centre line of the Tasman Glacier to **De La Bêche Refuge Hut (4)** on a lateral moraine bench by the confluence of the Rudolf and Tasman Glaciers. It supplemented the

The distant view of Graham Saddle (2,635m) on the Main Divide (just to the left of Mt De La Bêche and The Minarets) from Ball Hut in 1966.

big rock bivouac beside it where all the early mountaineers had slept. An hour after we arrived the sun sank behind Mount Haidinger on the Main Divide and the temperature suddenly dropped.

After Edward FitzGerald and his Swiss guide Mattias Zurbriggen accomplished the first ascent of Mount Sefton/Kakīroa, they crossed Fitzgerald Pass from the Hooker Valley and bush-bashed down the Copland Valley to Scott's homestead on Karangarua Flat. The Westland Survey granted Arthur Harper leave to accompany them back to the Hermitage. He led them up the Fox Glacier/Te Moenga a Tūawe and Victoria Glaciers to Zurbriggen Col on the Fritz Range, and then across the slopes of Mount Anderegg to the Melchior Glacier, which they named after another Swiss guide, Melchior Anderegg.

The trio then crossed the névé of the Franz Josef/Kā Roimata o Hine Hukatere and completed the first crossing of 'Crown Prince Saddle' to the Rudolf Glacier. At 2635 metres above sea level, it is the lowest negotiable pass on the portion of the Main Divide that bounds the Waiho Catchment.[199] It was renamed after George Graham, who had reached it first when he and Tom Fyffe had ascended Mount De La Bêche from the Rudolf Glacier in 1894.

Lindsay, Chris, Terry, and I were heading in the opposite direction. In the morning we ascended the lower Rudolf Glacier and then climbed the long snow slope between its icefall and De La Bêche Ridge. Once we had gained enough height, we crossed the névé of that glacier to **Graham Saddle (5)** between Mounts Rudolf and De La Bêche. Sheer cliffs bar access to a lower dip on the Main Divide just south of Mount Rudolf. Below the dazzling white névé of the Franz Josef/Kā Roimata o Hine Hukatere Glacier lay the verdant coastal plain and the blue sea.

After crossing a partially snow-filled bergschrund on the western side of Graham Saddle, we made a beeline for **West Hoe Pass (6)** on the Fritz Range, which meets the Main Divide on Mount Conway. The sun was blazing hot and my boots kept sinking into the rapidly softening snow. When we crested the pass a magnificent view unfolded of the three icefields that make up the névé of the Fox Glacier/Te Moenga o Tūawe: the Explorer, Albert, and Abel Janzoon Glaciers. Two short Main Divide spurs separate those icefields: Pioneer Ridge off Douglas Peak and The Buttress off **Mount Tasman/Horo Kōau (13)**. The Fox Range on the southern side of that huge névé joined the Main Divide on its shining icecap. In due course Lindsay guided us through a gap in Pioneer Ridge to the Alpine Club's new **Pioneer Hut (7)** below Mount Alack.

In 1953, the New Zealand Alpine Club built its first Pioneer Hut on a ledge just above the gap in Pioneer Ridge at an altitude of 2400-metres. A rock fall demolished it in 1963, killing one occupant and severely injuring another. The tiny three-bunk Katie Gardner Refuge Hut was swept off an adjacent ledge. Mick Sullivan's chief guide, Frank Alack, had built this particular hut after Katie and her three companions were rescued from the nearby crévasse that had sheltered them during a nine-day blizzard. The site of the hut we stayed in was subsequently found to be unstable so the hut was replaced by the third and fourth Pioneer Huts, which were built on the lowest section of Pioneer Ridge where the pioneer west coast climbers Ebenezer Teichelman, Henry Newton, and Alex Graham had pitched camp in 1904 and 1907.[200] The New Zealand Alpine Club marked its hundredth anniversary in 1991 by building Centennial Hut on Tusk Rock on the Franz Josef/Kā Roimata o Hine Hukatere Névé.

Next day we retraced our steps through the gap in Pioneer Ridge and negotiated a field of crevasses to Chancellor Ridge between the Fox Glacier/Te Moenga o Tūawe Icefall and the withered Victoria Glacier. A pair of inquisitive keas escorted us down that tussock-covered spur of the Bismarck Range to **Chancellor Hut (8)**, which was built by the Tourist Department in 1930 and still has separate male and female bunkrooms.

At the end of Chancellor Ridge we crossed smooth schist bedrock beside Alf Stream, which gushed from the terminus of the Victoria Glacier, and then disappeared underneath the Fox Glacier/Te Moenga o Tūawe. Crossing its relatively flat middle section below the icefall, we descended a rubble-filled gutter on the other side to bypass a zone of pressure ridges. When they diminished in size we climbed back onto the glacier's tongue and cramponed down to its terminus, where a van was waiting in the carpark to transport us to **Fox Glacier/Weheka village (14)**.

The view of Mt Élie de Beaumont
(3,109m) on the Main Divide above the
Spenser Glacier source of the long
Callery tributary of the Waiho River
from West Minaret, when I attended a
mountaineering course in January 1968.

Photo credit: R. Gooder

In February 1968 I took the inter-island ferry from Wellington to
Lyttelton and then a Railway Road Services bus to Aoraki/Mount Cook
village to attend a Mountain Instruction Limited course led by Geoff
Wyatt. As I had arrived a day early I took the opportunity to walk up to
Ball Hut where the course would begin.

Seven more participants arrived next morning and after lunch we
followed a track down to the Tasman Glacier and practised step cutting
on pressure ridges. The next day was drizzly so Geoff unlocked the
gear room and let each of us choose a pair of skis. These we carried up
a nearby spur and practised turns on the first snow slope, returning to
the hut via the Ball Glacier. On the way we practised rock-climbing
moves on a huge boulder and passed the remnants of a rope tow on
the old Ball Glacier ski area. On day three the clouds dispersed as we
trooped nine kilometres up the Tasman Glacier to **De La Bêche Refuge
Hut (4)**.

We got up before dawn and headed for **The Minarets (9)**. When we reached the snowline, I roped up with a fellow attendee, Ross Gooder, and ascended the snow slopes on the eastern side of De La Bêche Ridge, keeping close to the crest to avoid crevasses. Ross and I climbed the West Minaret from the small ice plateau at the top of the ridge and obtained a bird's-eye-view of the Callery Catchment and **Mount Elie de Beaumont (12)**. A sheet of altostratus cloud and the rising westerly wind indicated that the weather would soon change. Four years later I was shocked to learn that Ross had died while climbing in Italy.

In 1862, Julius Haast walked halfway up the Tasman Glacier and named the rocky peak between the Rudolf and Tasman Glaciers after the palaeontologist who became the first director of the Britain's Geological Survey, Henry De La Bêche. Haast may have also named the two symmetrical ice-capped summits alongside that peak The Minarets. The New Zealand Alpine Club erected De La Bêche Hut in 1931 after a young guide and his four clients died, probably from a lightning strike, when a violent nor-west storm overtook them on the Tasman Glacier.[201]

At 3109 metres above sea level, the summit of Mount Elie de Beaumont is the highest point in the water catchments of the Waiho and Whataroa Rivers and on the corresponding portions of the Main Divide. The Maximilian Ridge of that great peak separates the upper catchments of those rivers. The Burton Glacier behind the West Ridge of Mount Elie de Beaumont is the furthest source of the Callery River and hence the Waiho River; its largest source is the Franz Josef Glacier/ Kā Roimata o Hine Hukatere.

Julius Haast named that great peak after French geologist Léonce Élie de Beaumont, whose 'shrinking earth theory' likened mountain ranges to the wrinkles on the skin of a dried apple. Mount Walter was named after an English climber who belonged to the family that owned *The Times* newspaper in London. He visited this area in 1895 and named a tributary of the Spenser Glacier the Times Glacier.[202]

Early west coast travellers identified three lofty sections of the Main Divide north of Aoraki/Mount Cook with Aoraki's brothers (see Page 133). Their names may be clues to their identities: Rakiroa (long Raki) may be the section of the Main Divide culminating in Mount Haidinger between Mount Tasman/Horo Kōau and The Minarets, Rakirua (second Raki) may be Mount Elie de Beaumont, and Rārakiroa (long stretched-out line) may be the nigh impassable section of the Main Divide behind the headwaters of the Whataroa and Whanganui Rivers.

In January 1995 I flew in a ski plane to the head of the Tasman Glacier with Whitney Thurlow from Alpine Guides Mount Cook and spent three nights in Tasman Saddle Hut (10). This hut was erected in 1963 at an altitude of 2303 metres on the crest of a bluff in the middle of the Tasman Névé, halfway between Tasman and Lendenfeld Saddles. Mount Elie de Beaumont's standard ascent route via the Anna Glacier route was cut off by a deep crevasse so we took the alternative route up a steep snow arête and over the summit of Mount Walter (11). En route we spotted five climbers snoozing in their bivvy bags on the little ice plateau between Mounts Green and Walter.

The sky lightened when we reached the summit of Mount Walter. Whitney belayed me down the other side to an unnamed col on the Main Divide, after which we then cramponed up a steep rib of frozen snow until it flattened out on the broad summit of Mount Elie de Beaumont. Beneath its north face I saw the tip of the Burton Glacier source of the Callery River, which is the most distant source of the Waiho River. The huge névé of the Franz Josef Glacier/Kā Roimata o Hine Hukatere was visible beyond the jagged Baird Range on the southern side of the Spencer Glacier. A solitary cloud clung to the summit of Aoraki/Mount Cook.

We cautiously descended the upper Anna Glacier and then sidled onto the east ridge of Mount Elie de Beaumont, which descends to Lendenfeld Saddle. After skirting its brittle greywacke gendarmes for about an hour, Whitney belayed me down a snow slope that appeared to end on the saddle. The hot midday sun had softened the upper layer snow, which had an unnerving tendency to slide on the frozen base of the snow pack. I kicked the front points of my crampons into the deeper layers until a yawning bergschrund brought me to a halt. I backtracked a bit and then moved sideways to a rock outcrop where Whitney established an anchor point that enabled us to abseil the gap. An hour and a half later we were back in the hut.

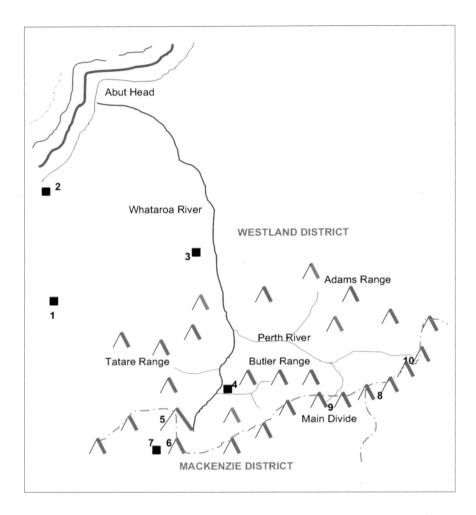

Legend

1. Franz Josef/Waiho village
2. Ōkārito
3. Whataroa
4. Butler Junction Hut
5. Mt Elie de Beaumont
6. Hochstetter Dome
7. Tasman Saddle Hut
8. Dennistoun Pass
9. Sealy Pass
10. Perth Col

Chapter 18

The Whataroa

In June 1993 I set off from Fox Glacier village to visit the Whataroa River mouth and drove northward over the Fox Hills, through Franz Josef/Waiho village (1), past Lakes Māpourika (Māpouriki) and Wahapō, and then over the Waitangi Taona (Waitangi Tahuuna – 'crying for water'[203]) Bridge to Whataroa village (3). I left SH6 there and drove westward on Whataroa Flat Road and Waitangi Taona Road to a boat landing on the south bank of the deep, slow-moving north branch of the Waitangi Taona, which flows through Waitangi Roto Lagoon and enters the sea near Waitahi Point. A year earlier, Evelyn and I had travelled down that river in a jet boat to see the only kōtuku/white heron nesting area in New Zealand, but this trip would be on shanks' pony. I followed the grassy true left bank for a couple

The mouth of the Whataroa River,
where this upriver story began.

of hours then waded a chest-deep ford, which was the only one that I could find, and scrunched up the pebbly beach to the Whataroa River mouth. The long bush-covered lateral moraine ridge called Whataroa on the northern side of that river ended abruptly on Abut Head.

Māori elders in Bruce Bay/Mahitahi told William Wilson that Whataroa (long elevated food storage platform) was the original name of Abut Head as well as of the river itself and also of a man who had died there; personal names can refer to places and many lives have been lost in west coast rivers. In 1865 Gerhard Mueller observed that the Waitangi Taona and Whataroa Rivers united before they entered the sea near Waitahi (one river) Point so their common outlet must have been the 'Waitaki (or Waitahi) River' that Leonard Harper was escorted across in 1857 by Tuhuru's eldest son, Tarapuhi Te Kaukihi.

The Waitangi Taona River drains the western slopes of Tatare Ridge, which usually receives 12 metres of rain each year. A massive deluge in the 1960s resulted in a permanent split in that river. Its new south branch flowed through the old Loan Block paddocks into Lake Wahapō and the hydroelectric power station on the Wahapō tributary of the Ōkārito River, which issues from Lake Mapourika and flows into a 2500-hectare lagoon called Ōkārito ('place of Kāriko' – 'young raupō/bulrush shoots' and a personal name). Wahahapō (Wahapō) and Mapourika (Mapouriki) were Kāriko's daughters.[204] Ōkārito Lagoon is the largest estuary on the west coast. It used to be a prodigious larder of tuna/eels, which feed on the mata/whitebait fry of the *galaxiid* fish inanga, kōaro, and kōkopu.

In 1863 Arthur Dobson surveyed the section of the 'West Canterbury' coast between the mouth of the Grey River/Māwheranui and Abut Head. Robert Bain and John Rochford surveyed the section between Abut Head and Big Bay. A few years later, columns of gold diggers, peddlers and packhorses were boulder hopping and dodging waves on the old trail as they made their way around Abut Head to the Whataroa Ferry. A pack track over the ridge behind that bluff eased their suffering until the road opened over Mount Hercules.

Two years later, in 1865, gold diggers flocked to Three Mile and Five Mile Beaches south of Ōkārito Lagoon where a bustling port town named **Ōkārito (2)** sprang up by the old kāinga site on the dry sandy flat between a large wetland and the lagoon's southern shore. Its population peaked at 4500 and then rapidly declined. Ōkārito was connected to Hokitika by a telegraph line in 1897 and continued to be the chief service centre for South Westland until 1909, when the Whataroa River was bridged and Whataroa become the district's new hub with a courthouse and cattle sale yards. Okarito's inevitable decline stalled in 1931, when a big gold dredge powered by Pelton wheels began to excavate Five Mile Beach. The last ship berthed at the Ōkārito wharf in 1939 and the town's last hotel burned down in 1956. Donovan's Store is the only building left in Ōkārito from its golden era.

In 1866 Ōkārito butcher Harry Friend began to graze cattle on Whataroa and Waiho Flats, which were then called common grazing areas. Whataroa Flat was cut up into farm blocks in 1901. When the Whataroa Bridge opened, Alex Gunn closed his ferry service, postal agency and accommodation house at Rōhutu on the south bank and moved to Whataroa. In the 1930s, unemployment relief workers confined the Waitangi Taona River between stop banks to protect Whataroa Flat.

The view of the Perth Glacier source of the Perth tributary of the Whataroa River when Andrew Taylor-Perry and I climbed onto Perth Col from the Clyde Valley in 1990.

In February 1998 Adam and I followed the West Coast Road from Christchurch to Kumara Junction and then headed south on SH6. I parked on the south bank of the Whataroa River by the piles of the first bridge where I had once panned for gold with Tom Nolan. From there we followed an old stock track up the Whataroa Valley under 150-metre gravel cliffs. They demonstrate how high the valley floor on the eastern side of the Alpine Fault has risen since the last glaciation. Two hours later we crossed the long Whataroa swing bridge.

Three years earlier, in 1995, Adam and I had crossed **Dennistoun Pass (8)** from the Rangitata Valley and descended the south bank of the Perth tributary of the Whataroa River to the Whataroa swing bridge (see Page 106). In 1990 Andrew and I had climbed onto **Perth Col (10)** from the Clyde Valley and seen the Perth River emerge from the shrivelled tongue of the Perth Glacier, which is the furthest source of the Whataroa River (see Page 114).

The first swing bridge at the bottom of the Whataroa Gorges was erected by a government contractor in 1906 to provide gold diggers with safe access to the beaches on the true right bank between the gorges above the Perth Confluence. Westland County Council replaced that bridge in the 1930s. After crossing the new Whataroa swing bridge we passed the junction of the Perth and Whataroa Tracks and followed the latter around three gorges and Reynolds and Scotts Beaches, which lay between them.

We then skirted the highest gorge before descending to Barrowmans Flat, which was once grazed by cattle. It is now covered with second-growth bush, but we did spot the stone chimneybreast of one of the huts that gold diggers, who received some financial support from the Unemployment Board's Gold Prospecting Subsidy Scheme, had built there during the Depression. Light rain was falling when we reached **Butler Junction Hut (4)**, which was built by the Forest Service in 1964.

The rain stopped before dawn, but low clouds continued to clag the mountains. After an early breakfast we crossed the swing bridge that had replaced Bill Barrowman's cage across the Butler tributary and followed Barrowman's Track through dense rātā-kāmahi bush to the new swing bridge over the Whataroa River. An avalanche had demolished the old one a couple of years earlier. Clambering over and around big boulders on the opposite bank, eventually we picked up

The view of the Whymper Glacier source of the Whataroa River when Whitney Thurlow guided me over Hochstetter Dome to Mt Aylmer from Tasman Saddle Hut in 1995.

a rough track over the scrub-covered terminal moraine ridge that the Whymper Glacier butted against before the 1960s. On the other side of that ridge the infant Whataroa River wandered across a long gravel outwash surface from the rubble-covered tongue of the Whymper Glacier below the mist-enshrouded flanks of **Mount Elie de Beaumont (5)**. We walked up to the glacier and returned to Butler Junction Hut just before dark.

In January 1995 I rendezvoused in Aoraki/Mount Cook village with Whitney Thurlow from Alpine Guides Mount Cook and flew to the head of the Tasman Glacier. We based ourselves for the next three nights in **Tasman Saddle Hut (7)**, which perched on top of a bluff not far from the highest landing area for ski planes. At three o'clock next morning we switched on our headlights and set off to climb **Hochstetter Dome (6)**. After weaving through a maze of crevasses we cramponed up a long icy slope and reached the crest in time to see an unearthly red glow suffuse the apex of the Whataroa Catchment, the 3,109 metre-high summit of **Mount Elie de Beaumont (5)**.

We followed the Main Divide eastward from Hochstetter Dome to Mount Aylmer. Beneath Mount Elie de Beaumount's huge Whymper Face I saw the Whataroa River issue from the terminus of the Whymper Glacier. Its rubble-covered tongue was augmented by the northern icefall-outlet of the névé of the Tasman Glacier, which poured through Lendenfeld Saddle between Hochstetter Dome and the east ridge of Mount Elie de Beaumont. An odd thing about the Whataroa Glacier is that it arises on an extension of the Malte Brun Range – a cross fault had helped it to breech the old Elie de Beaumont-Butler Range watershed.

On the southern side of Mount Aylmer an unbroken snow slope swooped down to Tasman Saddle, which connects with the névé of the Murchison Glacier. We cramponed down to that saddle and visited our neighbours in the new Kelman Hut, which is perched on a rock arête at the base of Mount Annan on the Malte Brun Range. A line of boot prints guided us back to our hut where we had a siesta while the hot midday sun turned the surrounding snowfields into slush.

In March 1883 Austrian naturalist Robert von Lendenfeld mapped the Tasman Glacier and named Hochstetter Dom (sic) after Ferdinand

The glorious view from Hochstetter
Dome of Mt Elie de Beaumont (3,109m)
on the Main Divide illuminated by the
ruby-red rays of the rising sun.

von Hochstetter. He arrived in New Zealand in 1858 with an Austrian
scientific expedition and had been commissioned to conduct geological
surveys of Auckland and Nelson Provinces. Lendenfeld accomplished
the first ascent of this peak with his wife and a porter named Dew. Julius
Haast had worked with Hochstetter in Nelson Province and named the
great icefall at the base of Aoraki/Mount Cook after his mentor when
he inspected it in 1862.

Noel Brodrick extended Lendenfeld's survey in 1889 and named the
peak on the eastern side of Hochstetter Dome, where the Malte Brun

Range meets the Main Divide, after his wife, Helen Aylmer. The saddle on the eastern side was named after Lendenfeld; the big glacier on the northern side of those mountains was named after Edward Whymper, who had led the first party to scale the Matterhorn in the Swiss Alps.

In 1897 Tom Fyfe and Malcolm Ross accomplished the first and only crossing of Lendenfeld Saddle with a death-defying descent of the icefall that plunges through this gap on the Main Divide to the Whymper Glacier. They bush-bashed down the south bank of the Whataroa River until sheer bluffs forced them to swim the last gorge. Their trials ended when they reached Gunn's Ferry at Rōhutu (native myrtle/*Neomyrtus pendunculata*) on the old Whataroa-Ōkārito Road.

In October 1992 I signed up for a Christchurch Tramping Club trip led by Alan Ross to the Godley Glaciers. We spent the first night by Tekapo village. Next day we drove up the dusty Lilybank Road along the eastern side of Lake Tekapo. The trip almost ended in a deep hole in the Macaulay riverbed, but the driver managed to back out his Isuzu Bighorn and find a better ford. On the other side of that river lay Lilybank Station, where Julius Haast saw kōpukapuka/*Ranunculus lyalli* or 'Mount Cook Lilies' flowering for the first time and realised that they were giant buttercups.

Julius Haast renamed the river that flows into the head of Lake Tekapo after the co-founder and first resident agent of the Canterbury Association, John Godley. Rawiri Te Maire told Noel Brodrick that its original name was Whimiahoa. An alternative name, Te Awa a Te Ruapū (the river of Te Ruapū) has also been recorded. The terminus of the Godley Glacier is the Waitaki River's most distant source from the sea.

Lilybank Station, which we needed to cross in order to reach our destination, was owned by the New Zealand Trophy Guides Company. Its manager, Gerard Olde-Olthof, had given us permission to drive across the homestead block to Lucifer (hot-as-hell) Flat and then follow rough wheel tracks up the east bank of the Godley River. About 25 kilometres up the Godley Valley we reached Separation Stream, which issues from the Separation Glacier below Twilight Col between Mounts D'Archiac and Forbes on the Two Thumbs Range. We left the vehicle on the southern side of that alpine torrent, linked arms to ford it, and then crossed the terminal moraine that the Godley Glacier abutted when Haast explored that area in 1862. Beyond that ridge stretched the murky proglacial lake of the Grey and Maud Glaciers, which had recently parted company. Miniature icebergs bobbed on wavelets along its southern shore.

The Grey Tributary of the Godley Glacier was named after New Zealand's third governor, George Grey. Canterbury mountaineer George Mannering named the adjacent tributary after his sister Maud, who had visited this area with him in 1891. The proglacial Maud-Grey Lake formed in the early 1950s when the Godley Glacier disengaged from those tributaries. Since then its terminal face has retreated at the average rate of 66 metres per year.[205]

The tongues of the Classen and Godley Glaciers almost touched each other when Julius Haast examined them in 1862. He named the former glacier after classics scholar Johannes Classen, and the mountain that it descended from after the famous German chemist, Justus von Liebig. A Main Divide peak near Classen Saddle was named after Noel Brodrick, who surveyed that area in more detail in 1889.

We skirted the eastern shore of the Maud-Grey Lake and ascended the banks of FitzGerald Stream, which tumbled through a gap in a lateral moraine wall. Behind that gap lay the small grassy terrace where early mountaineering parties had pitched their tents. The New Zealand Alpine Club erected Godley Hut there in 1935. Hanging on the wall was a framed photograph taken by Edgar Williams from Panorama Peak in 1918 that showed a sea of ice lapping that moraine wall. The bare trim line above that lake records the thickness of the Godley Glacier's tongue when Haast saw it 130 years ago.

In the 1930s, the owner of Lilybank Station sold the site of Godley Hut to the New Zealand Alpine Club. It lay just outside the boundary of the Mount Cook Recreational Reserve, which was established in 1895 and had been extended to incorporate the Godley Glaciers in 1927. From 1921 until 1944 that public reserve was leased to the Mount Cook Company, which exercised its right to manage all recreational facilities within it. Those included all of the alpine huts with the sole exception of De La Bêche Refuge beside the upper Tasman Glacier. Mountaineering clubs were not permitted to erect new huts or shelters in that recreational reserve until after World War II.

Next day we climbed over a bluff, cautiously descended a stone chute on the other side, and then boulder-hopped along the eastern shore of the proglacial lake of the Godley Glacier, which is the farthest source of the Waitaki River. It began to form when the Godley Glacier disengaged from the Grey Glacier in the 1960s, but stopped growing when the Godley Glacier's rapid retreat stalled at the confluence of the Ruth Glacier on the eastern side of Mount Wolseley. The weather was superb so we climbed onto the snow-covered glacier and ascended its bare medial moraine ridge until we reached the base of Mount Petermann, then sidled around its southern flank to the summit of **Sealy Pass (9)**. Gazing down the other side I saw the snowfield source of the Scone tributary of the Perth River.

Leonard Harper's account of his 1857 journey down the west coast states that his guide, the paramount Ngāti Waewae rangatira Tarapuhi Te Kaukihi, told him that a trail led up its banks to 'a good low pass to the East over some open flats'.[206] Richard Sherrin prospected the upper Whataroa Valley for gold with two Māori companions in 1963 and reported sighting 'the remarkable glacial saddle' that led to the east coast.[207] At 1,722 metres above sea level, the summit of Sealy Pass is the lowest spot on the portion of the Main Divide that bounds the Whataroa Catchment.

Sealy Pass cannot be spotted from the west until the bush line is reached in the Scone Valley. It is the only transalpine route between Whitcombe Pass and Brodrick Pass that competent early travellers could have taken in summer or early autumn. The Godley Glacier's medial moraine would have offered snow-free access to or from the Scone Valley by mid-summer.

In 1894 Alex Gunn provided Westland's chief surveyor, George Roberts, with topographical details of the Whataroa Catchment. In 1875 Gunn had explored the Perth Valley up to the Scone Confluence with two gold prospectors, Harry 'The Whale' Vickers and James Bettison, and presumably named that tributary after Scone in Perthshire where Scotland's early kings were crowned. Charlie Douglas named the lofty spur of the Main Divide between the Whataroa and Perth Valleys after a local farmer and road works overseer, John Butler.[208]

In 1869 South Canterbury surveyor and photographer Edwin Sealy ascended the Godley Glacier and reached the pass that Thomas Brodrick named Sealy Pass on his 1888 map of the upper Godley Valley. Sealy's influential 1880 pamphlet entitled *Are we to stay here?*

The view of Sealy Pass (1,722m) on the
Main Divide when I ascended the tongue
of the Godley Glacier from Godley Hut with
a tramping club party in October 1992.

helped to generate support for the Liberal Government's land reform
programme.

After two failed attempts, James and Thomas Pringle of Lilybank
Station and a companion named Blyth took advantage of a long spell
of fine weather in the late summer of 1892. In just three days they
ascended the Godley Glacier to Sealy Pass and then descended the
Perth and Whataroa Valleys to Gunn's Ferry at Rōhutu.[209] Alex Gunn's
son William subsequently blazed a track up the Perth and Scone
Valleys and accompanied Jim Dennistoun and Peter Graham on the
first recorded west-to-east crossing of Sealy Pass in 1908.

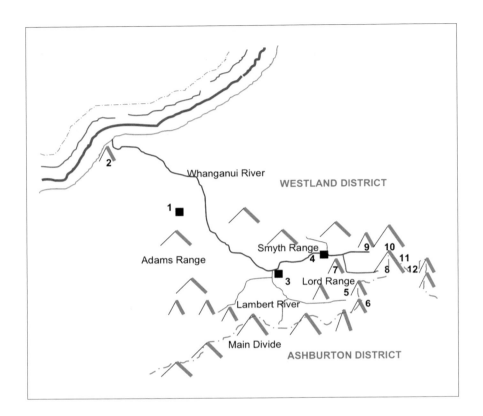

Legend

1. Harihari
2. The Doughboy/Mt Oneone
3. Hunter's Hut
4. Smyth Hut
5. Mt Lord
6. Strachan Pass
7. Mt Mueller
8. Mt Whitcombe
9. Red Lion Peak
10. Mt Evans
11. Full Moon Saddle
12. Amazons Breasts

Chapter 19
The Whanganui

In June 2004 Adam and I followed SH6 over Haast Pass/Tiori Pātea and spent a night in Franz Josef/Waiho village. Next day we drove further north through Whataroa, over the Whataroa Bridge, and along the base of a slip-scarred escarpment, where the Alpine Fault truncates the Adams Range. The next section of SH6 climbed over a heavily wooded ridge called Mount Hercules (Whataroa) to the Inter-Wanganui Flat between the Pōerua (or Little Whanganui) and (Big) Whanganui Rivers. Pukeko/ 'swamp hens' were stalking the paddocks alongside the road. Whanganui literally means 'big inlet' or 'big valley'. Ngāti Māhaki elders told William Wilson that it was a man's name in this instance.

Before we entered **Harihari (1)**, which is the hub of this farming

The view of the mouth of the
Whanganui River from the Doughboy,
where this upriver story began.

district, I turned left and followed Whanganui Flat and La Fontaine
Roads to an old sawmill site on the south bank of the Whanganui
River. We left the car there and followed the Harihari Coastal Walkway
southward along the embankment of an old logging tramway, which
crossed a large swampy clearing that was once full of huge kahikatea/
white pine trees. On the far side we climbed over a bush-clad lateral
moraine ridge and walked past some whitebaiters' huts beside the
estuary of the Pōerua River.

We then skirted the base of Pōerua Bluff and scrunched up a stony
beach to a 58-metre-high lateral moraine remnant called **The Doughboy/
Mount Oneone (2)**. Ngāti Māhaki elders told William Wilson that
Oneone was a corruption of Oue (tilted). The shaggy cloak of kiekie
vines on this landmark conceals the nesting burrows of titi/sooty
shearwaters. We climbed a long flight of steps to a viewing platform
on the summit and gazed across the Whanganui River mouth to the tip
of a massive lateral moraine ridge called Whanganui Bluff (or Cliffy
Head). The Harihari Coastal Walkway returns to the place where we
left the car via the bank of this river, which was lined with dismantled
whitebaiting stands.

The manawhenua of Te Rūnanga o Makaawhio extends to the
Hokitika River, however the manawhenua of Te Rūnanga o Ngāti

Waewae overlaps it north of the Pōerua (two nights) River. In April 1860 every able-bodied hapū leader on the west coast travelled to Taetae's pā by Pōerua Roto (Saltwater Lagoon), six kilometres south of the Pōerua River mouth, to debate the terms of the Crown's Arahura Purchase offer.[210]

Westland County Council began to license the operators of the ferries on all the major rivers within its jurisdiction in 1868. They also issued the first grazing licences on the Inter-Whanganui Flat, which was then a common grazing area. William Bell became the licensed ferry operator on the Whanganui Estuary and resided on the 25-acre ferry reserve on its northern shore. In 1847, Thomas Brunner and his Māori guides had spent a night there in a vacant whare (hut). Whanganui, means 'wide gap in seacliffs or mountains' and is a common place name in this country.

Ross butchers Henry Dietrich and Henry Karnbach ran cattle on every common grazing area between the Hokitika and Waiho Rivers until the 1877 Land Act allowed graziers to buy 50 to 100-acre blocks of land on these open flats under the Homestead Scheme.

The name Harihari (a song to make people pull together) was coined for the town that sprang up on the Inter-Whanganui Flat after the Whanganui River was bridged in 1909. It lies at the foot of the western escarpment of the Wilberg Range, which was named after a Westland Survey cartographer. Three streams pour off this escarpment and flow into the La Fontaine Swamp, which was drained and turned into fertile pastures on the western side of Harihari.

By 1878, a muddy inland bridle track had supplemented the Old Beach Highway from Ross to Ōkārito. Over the next 20 years this track was upgraded into a dray road. Peter Hende set up a ferry service at the base of the mountains when the road gang reached the Whanganui River. He and his wife Caroline lived on the 50-acre ferry reserve on the south bank and ran the adjacent post office and accommodation house until a long wooden trestle bridge replaced the Whanganui Ferry in 1908.[211] A two-lane concrete bridge replaced it in 1963.

In March 1999 I embarked on a transalpine trip from the Whanganui Valley to the Rakaia Valley with Andrew, Dave, Cam, and his daughter

Ruth. My daughter Janet drove us from Christchurch to Kumara Junction and then down SH6 to the northern end of the Whanganui Bridge where she turned left onto Quarry Road. This led to the Amethyst Creek hydroelectric power station, which opened in 1950 and was due to be upgraded to a six megawatt plant. Janet dropped us off at the end of the road, then we shouldered our heavy packs and began to follow meandering cattle tracks up scrubby riverside flats. It had been a dry autumn and Hendes Creek, which had been spanned by a footbridge since a hunter drowned there, was only ankle-deep. A recent cattle muster had turned the track over Annoyance Bluff into a quagmire. We dropped the idea of reaching the new **Hunter's Hut (3)** near the Lambert Confluence and instead pitched camp in Jones Flat at dusk. Next day we crossed the Whanganui River via the cage at the head of Jones Flat and carried on up the true left bank.

Above the confluence of Devastation Creek, the riverbed was choked with boulders and it was impossible to stick to the bank. After scouting around we picked up the overgrown track to Smyth Hut, but unfortunately it was so overgrown that it was often easier to thresh through the old growth scrub alongside it. From time to time, that so-called track dropped down to the riverbed and we had to scramble around and over huge boulders until we found the next section of the track. We spent the second night in recesses under two giant boulders with the unseen river roaring by in the dark. The only way to fill our billy with water was to climb onto a giant riverside boulder, attach the billy to the end of our climbing rope, and lower it until the rope slackened.

We resumed our slow progress up the true left bank of the Whanganui River shortly after daybreak. A couple of hours later we stumbled onto an excellent track from the riverbed to **Smyth Hut (4)**. The clearing next to it was evidently a helicopter pad. An entry in the hut book explained that the track led to some hot pools, so we rushed back to investigate but only found one pool that was warm enough to warrant taking our boots off and dipping our feet in. A nearby swing bridge (which was later destroyed by a flood) offered safe access to the County Branch of the Waitaha Valley via the Smyth Creek bed and a dip on the Smyth Range. J N Smyth was one of George Roberts' Westland Survey employees.

An active sou'west front was forecast to cross the island tomorrow. Since it would hold us up for a day, we had to sit it out closer to the Main

The view of the Essex Icefall source of the master stream of the Whanganui River, Vane Stream, when Andrew Taylor-Perry, Dave Clark, Cam Odlin and his daughter Ruth and I ascended its banks in 1999. The nominal source of the Whanganui River is the confluence of Vane Stream and the Evans River.

Divide if we were going to reach the road end in the Rakaia Valley in four days' time as we had planned. An entry in the hut book described a good bivvy site by Vane Stream that seemed to fit the bill. We bush-bashed up the true left bank of the Whanganui River for another hour until we found a dry flood channel that led to the boulder-strewn bed of Vane Stream. The nominal source of the Whanganui River is the confluence of its master stream, Vane Stream, and the Evans River, which issues from the Evans Glacier about 55 kilometres from the sea. The Hazard Glacier source of Vane Stream is the farthest one from the sea. We pitched camp on a patch of bare sand several metres above the bed of that tributary.

I should have realised that bare sand near an alpine river must have been deposited by running water. Rain set in at dusk and intensified during the night. At first light Andrew announced that the tent floor felt spongy and opened the flap. To our horror the tent was surrounded by water that was streaming off the tall drift terrace behind our tents.

The early morning view of Mt Whitcombe (2,650m) on the Main Divide and Snow Dome (on the left) above the Essex Glacier when Andrew, Dave, Cam, Ruth and I crossed Strachan Pass via Mt Lord on the Lord Range in 1999.

We built two rock platforms on the side of that terrace and lifted our tents onto them. By then the water was knee deep. The higher tent sites kept us dry, but were much less comfortable.

The sun came out in the morning and partly dried our gear before we set off up the banks of Vane Stream. We had to climb over a scrub-covered bluff at the base of **Mount Mueller (7)** and a large scree fan below the vestigial Wilberg Glacier on the northern side of Dan Peak. On the opposite side of the Vane Valley the extraordinary Essex Icefall poured over a cliff from the hidden Lornty (or Essex) Glacier below **Mount Whitcombe (8)** like toothpaste from a tube. The waterfall next to it issued from the hidden Dainty Glacier while Vane Stream tumbled out of a hanging valley above the far end of that cliff. We managed to lug our packs up a steep grassy slope beyond the Vane waterfall.

At the top of that slope we pitched our tents on the lip of a snow-filled hollow and filled our two billies with melt water. The Hazard Glacier source of Vane Stream was visible below Menace Gap, which punctuates the Main Divide between Mount Whitcombe and Mount Roberts. Fortunately there was enough daylight left for us to reconnoitre our planned route over **Mount Lord (5)** to **Strachan Pass (6)**. Clouds were still clinging to some mountain tops, however fine weather was forecast on the mountain radio.

At 2650 metres above sea level, the high peak of Mount Whitcombe is the highest point within the water catchment area of the Whanganui River and on the portion of the Main Divide that bounds it. In 1864, Canterbury Surveyor Henry Whitcombe and his assistant Jakob Lauper accomplished the first recorded coast-to-coast crossing of Whitcombe Pass (see Page 90). From Mount Whitcombe, the Main Divide runs southward to Menace Gap and then crosses Mount Roberts to Mount Lord. There it turns east and crosses the summit of Strachan Pass to Mount Westland. Strachan Pass connects the Lord Branch of the Lambert and Whanganui Valleys with the Clarke Branch of the Ramsay and Rakaia Valleys.

Since the 1980s, shrinkage of the Clarke Glacier has left it surrounded with high moraine walls. At 1729 metres above sea level, the summit of Strachan Pass is the lowest spot on the section of the Main Divide that bounds the Whanganui Catchment. George Roberts named it after his brother-in-law and foreman, Dan Strachan, who accomplished its first crossing in the summer of 1880–81.[212] Roberts also named Dan Peak after him; Mounts Lord and Mueller were respectively named after Westland's Public Works engineer and Chief Surveyor. Roberts and Strachan lugged a heavy Vernier theodolite and tripod along the Lord Range to their campsite on Camp Saddle between Dan Peak and Mount Mueller. They erected an iron trigonometrical station on the summit of Mount Mueller and took the bearings of beacon cairns topped with flagpoles that they had erected on the summits of Mount Lord and Mount Roberts on the adjacent section of the Main Divide.

Roberts then carried his theodolite up the Rakaia Valley and erected a trig station on Mount Butler on the eastern side of the Ramsey Glacier and again took the bearings of the flagged beacons on Mount Lord and Mount Roberts (see Page 92). Canterbury surveyor Warren Adams confirmed Roberts' geodesic measurements through Strachan Pass to within two metres and connected them with measurements from trig stations on Prospect Hill and other line-of-sight points all the way to the east coast. Roberts named Mount Adams and the Adams Range after his colleague.[213]

The sun climbed high into the clear blue sky the next day as we picked our way along the crest of the Lord Range to Mount Lord. Dave spotted the rusty blade of an old spade in the summit cairn; it must have been the one that Dan Strachan used to cut steps and remove a huge snowdrift that had covered the survey beacon. Looking down the Lord Valley on the other side of the Lord Range I saw Mounts Newton, Tyndall, and Lambert on the southern skyline. The white line beneath them was the névé of the Lambert Glacier, which is called the Garden of Allah.

We abseiled two steep pitches on the shady southeast side of Mount Lord and then cramponed down a vestige of the Lord Glacier to Strachan Pass. Unfortunately, no snow remained in the steep gullies on its eastern side and it took quite a long time to find a reasonably safe route down the high lateral moraine wall to the shrivelled tongue of the Clarke Glacier, which had separated from the Ramsay Glacier about 30 years ago.

We belayed each other down a knife-edge ridge between two gullies and pitched camp on a patch of fine gravel below the rubble-covered terminus of the Clarke Glacier. We set off again at first light and reached Reischek Hut by mid-afternoon. Andrew and Dave chose to spend the night there and used the mountain radio to arrange a pick-up at the road

The view of Strachan Pass (1,729m) on the Main Divide above the rapidly retreating Clarke Glacier from the Ramsay Glacier.

end at noon the next day while I had a plane to catch in the morning and needed to carry on. Cam and Ruth accompanied me to Glenfalloch Station, where Evelyn had agreed to pick us up. She had been waiting there for several hours when we turned up around midnight.

In January 2002, after a month of almost constant rain on the west coast, Andrew, Cam, Duncan and I were about to cancel a transalpine trip from the Whanganui Valley to the Rakaia Valley via **Full Moon Saddle (11)** and Erewhon Col when a big, slow-moving anticyclone headed towards the South Island. Shortly before sunrise on a cool, clear morning Cam's daughter Miriam drove us to Hokitika Airport where a Hughes 500 helicopter was waiting to fly all four of us and our heavy packs to the broad outwash surface below the Evans Glacier.

An eerie silence reigned after we were dropped off and the beat of the rotor blades had faded away. While the others boiled the billy and prepared a late breakfast, I trotted down the true left bank of the Evans River to inspect our old campsite by Vane Stream. A slip had obliterated the two rock platforms that had kept our tents above the rising floodwaters.

I caught up with the others on the Evans Glacier, which descends from Full Moon Saddle between the South Ridge of **Mount Evans (10)**

The view of the Evans Glacier source of
the Evans tributary of the Whanganui
River below Full Moon Saddle before
Andrew, Cam, Duncan Williams and
I ascended that glacier en route to
Mt Whitcombe in January 2002.

and a short spur of the Main Divide. Above the steep snow face on
the left I saw Red Lion Col between Mount Evans and **Red Lion Peak
(9)**. A waterfall tumbled over a long escarpment on the right at the
base of **Mount Whitcombe (8)**. We slogged up the Evans Glacier under
the blazing sun and pitched our tents on a rock knoll on the northern
side of Full Moon Saddle. At 2100 metres above sea level we had a
grandstand view of the Whanganui Valley and the peaks on either side
of the Evans Glacier. The crest of the Adams Range on the western
horizon glowed like hot embers as the sun slipped behind it.

Rising before dawn, we set off to climb Mount Whitcombe via
the safe but circuitous route that a friend had once described to me.
After crossing a snow-covered spur on the southern side of Full Moon
Saddle we had to descend about 700 metres to the floor of the huge
cirque above the escarpment on the southern side of the Evans Glacier.
We filled our water bottles with melt water before we scrambled up a
talus slope and then ascended the broad spur on the opposite rim of the
cirque to a western outlier of Mount Whitcombe called Snow Dome,
which was only 26 metres lower.

When we were halfway up that spur I noticed that a thick blanket of fine weather fog had formed above the floor of the Whanganui Valley. It slowly built up until it shrouded every mountainside below the 2000-metre contour line. The snow was rapidly softening and we had to take turns plugging steps along the ox-bow ridge that connected Snow Dome to the High Peak of Mount Whitcombe. From that vantage point I could peer down upon the Ramsay Glacier and over the tops of every mountain range in Mid Canterbury.

When we had finished taking photographs, we retraced our steps to Snow Dome. A sea of fog enveloped us shortly after we headed down its north spur. Condensing water vapour trickled off my jacket and visibility shrank to a few metres, but we somehow managed to stay on track and eventually found the scree that we had climbed onto the spur. We raced down it and wetted our dry whistles in a small melt stream at the bottom of the big cirque. The next challenge was to pick the right direction out of the fog-bound cirque between the sheer escarpment on the left and the crevasse field on the right. Cam failed to obtain a reliable GPS reading so we resorted to the trusty old method of spreading a topographical map out on the ground and oriented it with a compass. We emerged from the fog less than 100 metres from our campsite.

The fine weather persisted so next morning, instead of a bye day, we picked an easy objective: two small peaks on the Main Divide named the **Amazons Breasts (12)**. They were situated on the opposite side of the Bracken Snowfield, named after the composer of the words of New Zealand's national anthem, Thomas Bracken. It is not only the névé of the Evans Glacier but also the source of the Wilkinson tributary of the Whitcombe River, which is the main tributary of the Hokitika River. The view across that ice plateau from the North Amazons Breast was dominated by the jagged East Ridge of Mount Evans, which is the highest peak in the Hokitika Catchment.

Next day we crossed Erewhon Col and descended the Ramsay Glacier via the rock knoll at the base of Lauper Peak that Doug and I had reached from Lyell Hut 30 years earlier. In the morning I climbed Meins Knob with Duncan and saw the full extent of the transformations that climate change had wrought on the Lyell and Ramsey Glaciers since Julius Haast had sketched them from that spot in 1866.

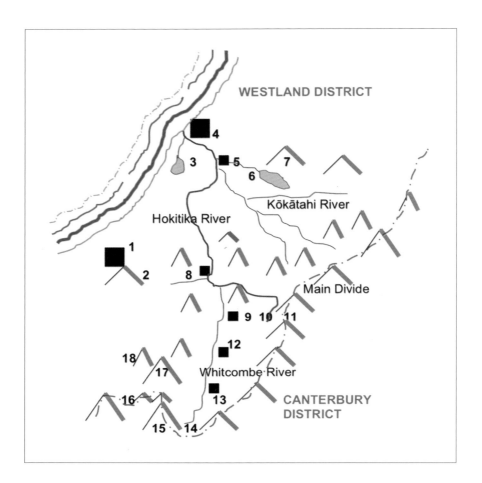

Legend

1. Ross
2. Mt Greenland
3. Lake Māhinapua
4. Hokitika
5. Kaniere
6. Lake Kaniere
7. Mt Tūhua
8. Rapid Creek Hut
9. Frews Hut
10. Frew Saddle
11. Mathias Pass
12. Price Hut
13. Neave Hut
14. Whitcombe Pass
15. Lauper Peak
16. Amazons Breasts
17. Mt Evans
18. Red Lion Peak

Chapter 20

The Hokitika

On a beautiful winter morning after my father died my mother and I walked along Gibson Quay to Sunset Point and watched the Hokitika River flow into the calm Tasman Sea. A flock of tarāpunga/red-billed seagulls had their beady eyes on it, too. Some battered ship's timbers and a replica of the schooner *Tambo*, which ran aground in 1866, had been set up on that point to commemorate the 42 shipwrecks on this river's treacherous bar and the associated loss of lives. In the distance a long procession of shining white peaks marched southward down the coast and disappeared over the horizon.

Hokitika (return by a direct route) alludes to Tama Āhua's legendary quest for his missing sister (or spouse) on the west coast. He returned to Taranaki after finding her body, which had turned into pounamu/

The mouth of the Hokitika River by Hokitika, where this upriver story begins.

nephrite, in the adjacent Arahura Valley. Hokitika also alludes to the Ngāi Tahu expedition that crossed the Alps around 1730 to procure pounamu/greenstone but had to turn back after crossing the Hokitika River when three high-ranking members, Tāne-tiki, son of Tū Ahuriri, Tute Pirirangi, and Tutaemaro, were killed in a clash with Ngāti Wairangi warriors near **Lake Māhinapua (3)**.[214]

Ngāti Wairangi's Māhinapua pā was defended on three sides by wild seas, the Hokitika River, and Māhinapua Creek/Tūwharewhare (house on a high bank). Around 1810 a Ngāi Tahu taua led by Wharekai destroyed that pā and built Poutini pā on the South Spit. Around 1834 it was seized by a Ngāti Rārua taua led by Te Niho, who captured the head of Ngāi Tahu's Ngāti Waewae hapū, Tuhuru, by the Kōkatahi tributary of the Hokitika River where he was fishing and ransomed him for a famous pounamu/nephrite mere.

In 1834 a resident of Poutini pā guided Te Puoho's Ngāti Tama taua over Haast Pass/Tiori Pātea to Central Otago on their ill-fated raid into Ngāi Tahu's southernmost domain.[215] Thomas Brunner spotted an old waka on the Hokitika riverbank and was told that the pā's residents used to take it out to sea on calm days to catch hapuku/groper.[216] The customary fishing areas of Rūnanga o Makaawhio and Ngāti Waewae Rūnanga overlap between the Pōerua and Hokitika River mouths.

Hokitika township sprang up in October 1864 around the canvas store that John Hudson and James Price had established by the ferry landing at the base of Sunset Point. Those entrepreneurs had taken two packhorses over Harper Pass/Nōti Taramakau to carry their wares down the old beach highway from the boat landing on the south bank of the Grey River/Māwheranui to the new Waimea, Kaniere, and Totara Diggings. Two months later Captain Samuel Leech steered the paddle steamer *Nelson* into the south channel of the Hokitika River preceded by Hokitika ferryman James Teer in his dinghy and the Provincial Agent, William Revell, pegged out the town's first streets. The south channel was subsequently blocked to push the river against the Gibson Quay wharf and deepen its berths.

On the basis of a report by the Provincial Harbourmaster, Frederick Gibson, Hokitika was declared an official port-of-entry for vessels weighing less than 250 tons and drawing less than eight feet. For a brief period it was the busiest port in New Zealand. In March 1865 John Rochford laid out a grid of new streets behind Revell Street, which had 84 hotels during Hokitika's heyday. Whenever sea conditions on the bar were favourable steamboats ferried passengers and freight to and from a line of tall sailing ships from Sydney, Melbourne, Dunedin, and Wellington that lay at anchor in the offshore 'roadstead'. Hokitika was connected to Christchurch and the Port of Lyttelton by road via Arthur's Pass in 1866 and by rail in 1923. Since 1980 the terminus of the Hokitika Branch Line has been the Westland Dairy Factory, which processes most of the west coast's milk production. The South Westland Shipping Company's vessels *Gael* and *Hauiti* serviced remote settlements until the Port of Hokitika closed in 1950.

In 1865 George (King) Sale was appointed Commissioner of the West Canterbury Goldfields. Complaints about his allegedly 'dictatorial' powers and the Provincial Council's use of goldfields revenue to construct the road over Arthur's Pass instead of upgrading the muddy tracks, flimsy footbridges, and punt ferries between the booming goldfield settlements in the West Canterbury District of Canterbury Province resulted in it becoming a semi-autonomous county called Westland in 1867. It was a fully fledged province from 1873 until

1876, when the area between the Taramakau River and the Grey River/ Māwheranui was apportioned to Grey County and Westland Province became Westland County. In 1989 Westland County became the Westland District of West Coast Region.

My four paternal great-grandparents immigrated though Dunedin and subsequently settled on the west coast. Gabriel Heinz came from the Grand Duchy of Hesse in Germany via Ballarat, where his father had a gold claim. In 1863 Gabriel followed his two older brothers to Dunedin and was apprenticed to a local tinsmith. In 1866 he sailed to **Hokitika (4)**, where his brothers had recently settled, and made billies and gold pans which his brother William sold in his hardware factory shop. He also joined the volunteer Fire Brigade and married the secretary's daughter, Martha Orams. She was born in Liverpool and sailed to Hokitika via Melbourne and Dunedin with her parents, who came from East Anglia and the Shetland Islands. Martha died when my grandfather, Gabriel II, was eight. He married Janet Duncan, the eldest daughter of Robert and Jessie Duncan, who came from East Lothian, Scotland; Robert died in the Brunner Mine explosion when she was 13. In 1922 Gabriel II became the works manager at the gas works in Hokitika, which was where my father, Angus Heinz, grew up. He met my mother, Kathleen Shillito, when she was nursing at Wellington's Karitane Hospital and he was stationed nearby at Rongotai Air Base. They lived in Hokitika for two years after World War II, then moved to Greymouth where I grew up.

The first Hokitika Bridge, which was built in 1878, spanned a narrow stretch of this river between Blue Spur and Seddon (or Rimu) Terrace where the west coast's last gold rush took place in 1890. During the Ōtira Glaciation the Hokitika Glacier's terminal face reared above Blue Spur and that big 'drift' terrace, which consists of a stack of outwash gravels. Each layer contained buried streambeds where heavy gold particles had accumulated in 'fluvo-glacial leads'. In the 1860s gold diggers postulated that an ancient river that flowed southward though the 'Great Valley' of the Alpine Fault had eroded a fabulously rich 'mother lode' in the Alps and deposited those gold-bearing 'drift' gravels. SH6 crossed the bridge between **Kaniere (5)** and Woodstock until the new Hokitika Bridge opened in 1989. The 1903 timber-truss Hokitika Road-Rail Bridge, which it replaced, was called the world's longest xylophone because its planks played a lively tune when a vehicle drove across it.

Most of the alluvial goldfields between the Tōtara River mouth south of Hokitika and the upper Grey River/Māwheranui lay on the 10-kilometre-wide Golden Line where streams and rivers emerged from the amalgamated tongues of all the glaciers that flowed west from the Alps during the Ōtira Glaciation. In the warm intervals between successive glaciations the sea level rose and gold-bearing beach sand was deposited on the rims of the drift terraces that flank the central west coast seaboard. A large melt stream carved the gap in Seddon Terrace that contains Grove Swamp. It drains into Lake Māhinapua, which is the source of Māhinapua Creek/Tūwharewhare. This deep, slow-moving channel is normally a small tributary of the Hokitika River but can become a flood channel.

In January 1988 Adam and I drove to Hokitika and then followed Kaniere Road up the north bank of the Hokitika River past the red lichen-covered tailings of the Kaniere Gold Dredge by Kaniere village to Kōkatahi village on the lush green flood plain of the Kaniere and Kōkatahi (one kōkako/crow) Rivers, which is a patchwork of dairy farms. We then followed Kowhitirangi Road and Whitcombe Valley Road past two granite knobs called Camelback/Kowhitirangi and The Doughboy/Kokirangi to the slip-scarred escarpment where the Alpine Fault has pruned the western end of the Dietrich Range.

Looking northward I spied the gap between **Mount Tūhua (7)** and the western end of the Newton Range that marks the course of the Alpine Fault. Tūhua is the name of a legendary waka and an island off the upper North Island. The Alpine Fault runs under **Lake Kaniere (6)**, which is the source of the Kaniere tributary of the Hokitika River. A hydroelectric power station on that river supplied electricity to Hokitika residents, de-watering pumps on the Ross Diggings, and a large electric gold dredge on Seddon Terrace.

A final gear check revealed that we had not brought any matches. After a quick trip to the Kōkatahi store to remedy that omission we followed a dirt road across Ryan Flat to the Hokitika River bed and walked up it until we found the benched track that led to the cage across the river. On the opposite bank we passed **Rapid Creek Hut (8)** and forded Rapid Creek near the confluence of the Hokitika and Whitcombe Rivers. The Hokitika River emerged from the Kākāriki (parakeet) Canyon, which is the last of the four deep gorges that it has carved between the Dietrich and Meta Ranges. The Whitcombe River emerged from the Collier Gorge between the tip of Cropp Spur and the Meta Range. Collier was an early gold prospector who had fossicked in that area. John and William Cropp helped Charlie Douglas cut a track up the Whitcombe Valley in 1896.

Nor'west winds propel moisture-laden clouds straight up the Whitcombe Valley. Cropp Spur makes those clouds rise rapidly and dump huge quantities of rain into the headwaters of Rapid Creek and the Cropp and Price Rivers, which drain the flanks of that lofty barrier.

Glaciologist Trevor Chin mapped the maximum rainfall belt in Westland and found that it is five kilometres east of the first 1200-metre contour line, where the Rapid and Cropp tributaries of the Whitcombe River arise.[217] The average rainfall in Hokitika is 2.8 metres per year; at the headwaters of Rapid Creek it is 12 metres per year; on the adjacent section of the Main Divide it is five metres per year. Frequent storm damage makes the Whitcombe Track expensive to maintain.

Record rainfall figures were recorded in the upper catchment of Rapid Creek (16,617mm in the 1998 calendar year and 18,442mm between October 29, 1997 and October 29, 1998) during the extreme El Niño event in 1998, which also raised air and water temperatures all around the world.[218] Major El Niño events are associated with incessant west or sou'west winds and 4000-cumec floods in the Hokitika River up to once a month. Hokitika's streets have not been inundated yet, but the Hokitika River briefly re-occupied its old flood channel through Grove Swamp and Māhinapua Creek/Tūwharewhare in 1963.

When the Hokitika River is in high flood enormous quantities of silt and stones are flushed out to sea. Some of that material settles on the bar as the current slackens; the rest of it drifts northward and ends up on beaches. Radar soundings beyond the bar have revealed an abyssal channel in the continental shelf called the Hokitika Canyon. Sediments that accumulate on the bar periodically avalanche down that groove and fan out on the floor of the Tasman Basin.

We forded Rapid Creek without much difficulty and boulder-hopped up the true left bank of the Whitcombe River until we found the first Whitcombe Track marker. The original track took a high line across the Collier Gorge's slip-scarred, north wall. At the top of the gorge we crossed a 15 metres high swing bridge and then forded Harry, Dick, and Tom Creeks to **Frew's Hut (9)**. The green slab of tangiwai/serpentine that I spotted in Dick Creek must have come from one of the small Pounamu Ultramafic outcrops on the Meta Range.

When we dumped our packs in the hut Adam noticed that his sleeping bag had fallen out. We retraced our steps until dusk but failed to find it so I gave Adam my sleeping bag and used a foam mattress as a duvet. We both slept so soundly that neither of us heard a mouse nibbling the contents of the packet of biscuits that I had left on the table.

In the morning we followed a good track up the spur between Tom and Frew Creeks. One of my uncles had told me to cast my eyes on the ground when I reached the first rise above the bush line and try to count the cartridge cases. We dropped our packs in Frew Saddle Bivouac, which the Forest Service had built in 1957, and walked up to the 1308-metre summit of **Frew Saddle (10)** on the Meta Range. From there we gazed eastward across a long grassy glen called Siberia to the 1458-metre summit of **Mathias Pass (11)** on the Main Divide. The Meta Range meets the Main Divide a bit further east on Mount Marion. The Hokitika River arises beneath that peak and flows northward though Siberia before it plunges into its four gorges. After lunch we crossed Siberia to Mathias Pass.

We reached the summit just before a bank of mist blotted out the narrow view down the Canyon Creek bed of the Mathias branch of the Rakaia Valley. After filling our water bottles at the source of the Hokitika River, which is 64 kilometres from the sea, we spent the last night in the two-bunk Frew Saddle Bivouac. When we reached the road end, I found a note tucked under one of my car's windscreen wipers. The writer had found Adam's sleeping bag and invited him to pick it up at his address in Hokitika!

Mathias Pass was originally named Ōtūtekawa after the first Ngāi Tahu chief to settle on the shore of Te Waihora /Lake Ellesmere.[219] Tūtekawa was the subject of a vendetta in the North Island and had sought refuge in the vicinity of this pass, which was later renamed after

The view of the source of the Hokitika River below Mathias Pass/Ōtūtekawa on the Main Divide and Comyns Pk when my son Adam and I crossed Frew Saddle from Frews Hut in the Whitcombe Valley in 1988.

the Archdeacon of Akaroa. In the summer of 1879–80 the Manuka Point run-holder's son and two shepherds ascended the Canyon Creek bed to look for summer pastures and a potential route for a new stock track to the Hokitika Saleyards. At the bottom of the grassy glen on the other side of Mathias Pass/Ōtūtekawa they crossed the upper Hokitika River and followed a gold prospectors' track on the slopes of the Dietrich Range above the Hokitika Gorges and reached Hokitika five days later. The following year Gerhard Mueller assessed that route and advised John Hall's government that a stock track could be constructed from Hororata to Hokitika via Mathias Pass and Meta Saddle on the Meta Range, which was named after a local map draftsman's daughter. Frew Creek and Frew Saddle were named after a Westland County engineer.

Arthur Dobson was supervising the construction of the Canyon Creek section of that track when the project was abandoned.

In the summer of 1897–98 one of those Manuka Point shepherds, Alfred Comyns, drove a thousand sheep up Canyon Creek and left them to graze in the glen at the head of the Hokitika Valley. After most of that flock perished in an unseasonal snowstorm, that glen was known as Siberia.[220] Two decades later red deer began to infiltrate the Hokitika Valley from Mount Algidus Station through Mathias Pass/Ōtūtekawa.

Whitcombe Pass (1,239m) and Lauper Pk (2,485m) on the Main Divide above the source of the Whitcombe River, which is the master stream of the Hokitika River, when Wayne Butt and I climbed onto this pass from Lauper Bivouac in the Rakaia Valley in 1985.
Photo credit: W. Butt

In January 2001 Andrew, Cam, Duncan, and I embarked on a transalpine trip to Hokitika via **Whitcombe Pass (14)**. Cam's daughter Miriam and her partner Ra drove us to Upper Lake Heron Station and dropped us off near Downs Hut. Given that unsettled weather had been forecast, I watched their Landrover disappear in the distance with mixed feelings as we plodded up Prospect Hill. After crossing that obstacle we passed a memorial plaque to a drowning tragedy in the Rakaia River. It was too high to cross so we stuck to the true right bank and spent the first night in Reischek Hut.

The westerly wind quickly strengthened as we approached the terminal lake of the Ramsay Glacier. One powerful gust nearly bowled us over. We agreed that it was too risky to boulder-hop around that icy lake or to ford its fast-flowing outlet so we built two stone windbreaks below a moraine ridge, pitched our tents behind them, and hunkered down until the storm passed.

The next day was initially calm and sunny. It took us a couple of hours to skirt the Ramsay Glacier's terminal lake and clamber over its rubble-covered tongue, after which we tramped around the tip of the Butler Range and then up the Lauper branch of the Rakaia Valley to Whitcombe Pass. At 1239 metres above sea level its boulder-strewn summit is the lowest spot on the portion of the Main Divide that bounds the Hokitika Catchment. As we approached it an ominous sheet of grey altostratus cloud spread across the sky.

The Sale Glacier source of the Whitcombe River on the northern side of that pass was concealed behind a large moraine ridge at the base of **Lauper Peak (15)**. A stony outwash surface extended from there to a similar moraine ridge at the base of the **Amazons Breasts (16)**, which concealed the tongue of the Barron Glacier. John Baker and Samuel Butler had turned back at that point when they examined Whitcombe Pass in 1861 and so did Wayne Butt and I in 1985. Julius Haast named the Sale Glacier after West Canterbury's first Goldfields Warden and Resident Magistrate, George Sale, when he examined Whitcombe Pass with Mount Algidus run-holder Frank Neave. Austrian taxidermist Andreas Reischek (who also had a hut, stream, glacier, and peak named after him) was another member of Haast's 1879 Rakaia expedition. In the 1890s George Roberts named the Barron Glacier after the manager of the Survey Department.

We carried on down the scrubby true right bank of the infant

The view across the Bracken Snowfield of Mt Evans (2,620m), with Andrew in the foreground, when he, Cam, Duncan and I climbed The Amazons Breasts from a campsite on Full Moon Saddle.

Whitcombe River and pitched camp in a clearing at nightfall. Drizzle set in at dusk. We packed up at first light and picked up the recently re-cut Whitcombe Track near two pillar-like remnants of a terminal moraine called The Gateway. Half an hour later we reached **Neave Hut (13)** by the confluence of Neave Stream and prepared to sit out the latest storm front, which was a bit colder than the last one. Andrew had brought a couple of chapters of his masters' thesis to proofread. He began to read a chapter to us and later asserted that we all fell asleep during the course of it.

In 1863 Canterbury surveyor Henry Whitcombe and his assistant Jakob Lauper took 13 days to cross Whitcombe Pass and descend the Whitcombe and Hokitika Valleys to the west coast. The small kāinga at the Hokitika and Arahura River mouths were unoccupied, however they managed to find some potatoes to eat. Whitcombe drowned in the rain-swollen Taramakau River when they headed back to Christchurch via Harper Pass/Nōti Taramakau (see Page 90).

Julius Haast presumed that the Hokitika River issued from the Sale Glacier on the northern side of Whitcombe Pass when he examined that area in 1879. George Roberts renamed it the Whitcombe River, although it is a larger river than the upper Hokitika and arises further away from the sea.

On day five we followed the Whitcombe Track through a two-kilometre gorge to Cave Camp Flat by the confluence of the Wilkinson River, which plummeted from the Bracken Snowfield between the Katzenbach Ridge and the northeast ridge of **Mount Evans (17)** in a giant waterfall. A small cloud stubbornly clung to the summit of that great peak. I peered into a tent-shaped cavity called Cave Camp between two huge rock slabs that were leaning against each other and saw a memorial plaque to Norman Dowling. He had died when his party was descending the Mackenzie Glacier in 1938 after they had accomplished the second ascent of Mount Evans.

In 2002 Andrew, Cam, Duncan, and I camped on Full Moon Saddle at the head of the Whanganui Valley and climbed the **Amazons Breasts (16)**. **Mount Evans (17)** dominated the view to the north across the Bracken Snowfield (see Page 289). At 2620 metres, the summit of Mount Evans is the highest point in the Hokitika Catchment. In the opposite direction we saw the highest and lowest points on the portion of the Main Divide that bounds the Hokitika Catchment: the summit of **Lauper Peak (15)**, which is 2485 metres above sea level and the adjacent **Whitcombe Pass (14)**, which is half that height.

The increased mean height of the Main Divide between Lauper Peak and Mount Burns on the southern boundary of Aoraki/Mount Cook National Park appears to be due to the rim of the Pacific Plate over-riding the adjacent rim of the Australian Plate and then back-thrusting, which has thickened this sector of Zealandia's continental crust.[221] The farthest source of every Alpine river between the Hokitika River and Haast River/Awarua to the south lie in that elevated zone.

George Roberts named Mount Evans, Evans Creek, and Evans Saddle near Lake Ianthe/Matahi after James Evans, who had prospected for gold along the banks of the Waitaha and upper Whanganui Rivers in the 1870s and grazed cattle on the Inter-Whanganui Flat. His father built the Red Lion Hotel on Gibson Quay in Hokitika in 1865.[222] **Red Lion Peak (18)** and Red Lion Col, which separates it from Mount Evans, were named after that relic of Hokitika's golden era. Its tavern bar finally closed in 2011.

In March 2005 Russell Braddock and I camped on Red Lion Col at the head of the County branch of the Waitaha Valley and climbed the south ridge of Mount Evans. It was almost snow-free but quite unstable near the summit. This peak's three equidistant ridges prop it up.

Andrew, Cam, Duncan and I crossed numerous side streams and landslips as we followed the Whitcombe Track from Camp Flat to Price Flat, which was named after a surveyor. Many southern rātā trees on the surrounding mountainsides were ablaze with crimson blossoms. Bone-white branches distinguished the rātā trees that had been heavily browsed by Australian possums and were slowly dying. Their hawser-like roots stabilise steep rain-drenched mountainsides on the western side of the Main Divide. After inspecting the dank pāhautea/cedar slab hut in Price Flat, which was built by the river in 1949 for Internal Affairs Department deer cullers, we dropped our packs in the new **Price Hut (12)**, which stood on higher ground where floods could not reach it.

During the night the latest sou'west front began to move up the west coast. Clouds thickened next morning as we tramped further down the valley and rain set in before we reached **Frews Hut (9)**. We decided to push on after reading some alarming entries in the hut book. The despondent writer was stuck there for several days when heavy rain made Rapid Creek impassable (it is now bridged). Three years after our trip a tremendous deluge sent a 12-metre surge down the river that wrecked the Collier Gorge swing-bridge.

Because the wet schist boulders in the Whitcombe Riverbed below the gorge were quite slippery, Cam lost his footing on one and hurt his shoulder. Rapid Creek had risen a bit, but we forded it safely and spent the last night in **Rapid Creek Hut (8)**. Next day we walked out to the road. A few minutes later the taxi that we had booked via the Canterbury Mountain Radio service arrived to take us to Hokitika.

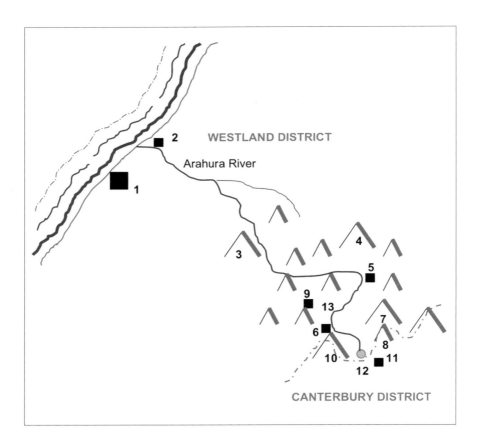

WESTLAND DISTRICT

Arahura River

CANTERBURY DISTRICT

Legend

1. Hokitika
2. Arahura
3. Mt Tūhua
4. Mt Tara o Tama
5. Mudflat Hut
6. Harman Hut
7. Mt Axis
8. Mt Harman/Kaniere
9. Grassy Flat Hut
10. Mt Beals
11. Gelignite Hut (ruin)
12. Browning Pass/Nōti Raureka
13. Styx Saddle

Chapter 21

The Arahura

Many years ago I drove across the old timber-truss Arahura road-rail bridge and stopped at a seaside dairy farm by Greyhound Corner, where the Greyhound Hotel had stood for a hundred years. After talking to the landowner, I walked across a paddock and then scrunched up the pebbly beach to watch the Arahura River flow into the remarkably calm Tasman Sea. The tide was out and the river was shallow enough to ford to Arahura (2). The Paparoa Range looked like a beached whale on the northern horizon.

The original Greyhound Hotel was built beside the west coast's first sheep and cattle sale yards on the southern side of the Arahura River mouth, where the Harper Pass Stock Track and the West Coast Road over Arthur's Pass joined the old beach highway. In the 1860s and 70s there

The mouth of the Arahura River,
where this upriver story begins.

was an insatiable demand for fresh meat on the booming goldfields around
Hokitika. Butchers paid high prices for livestock at the Arahura yards. In
1866 the number of sheep and cattle that were driven over Harper and
Arthur's Passes from Canterbury peaked at 4000 heads per month.[223]

The semi-mythical Kāhui a Rapuwai, also known as Te Pātea, were
said to have been the first permanent settlers in Arahura district.
Herries Beattie was informed that they had migrated to the west
coast, via Whakatū/Nelson from the Pātea district in Taranaki under
the leadership of Raumano. Native Reserve Commissioner Alexander
Mackay wrote that after 'the crew of the canoe Takitimu', whom he
presumed were the forbears of Waitaha, 'a branch of the Ngati Hau from
Whanganui, under a chief named Tauirapareko, were the next to arrive
in the Middle (South) Island; a section of whom called Ngati Wairangi,
with their chief Tawhirikakahu, settled at Arahura on the West Coast' —
sometime in the sixteenth century.[224]

After repulsing several Ngāi Tahu incursions across the Alps from
Kaikōura, Kaiapoi, and Ōtākou, Ngāti Wairangi were subjugated and

absorbed around 1810 by a strong taua from Kaiapoi led by Tuhuru and Wharetai. The thriving Arahura-Whakatū-Whanganui traffic in pounamu/nephrite was re-routed through Kaiapoi until 1828 when Te Niho and Takerei led a Ngāti Tama-Ngāti Rārua taua from Mohua/ Golden Bay down the west coast and captured its paramount chief, Tuhuru. Te Niho reinstated the northward pounamu/nephrite traffic route and controlled the Arahura district until 1835, when he made a tactical withdrawal after his powerful Ngāti Tama ally Te Puoho, was killed in Murihiku (see Page 144).

Arahura village was rebuilt in 1896 near the Arahura road-rail bridge on the 2000-acre Arahura Native Reserve on the northern side of the Arahura River mouth. Te Rūnunga o Ngāti Waewae has been based there since the death of Tuhuru's youngest son, Werita Tainui, in Māwhera pā. Its manawhenua extends from the Pōerua River in the south to Kahurangi Point in the north, overlapping the manawhenua of Te Rūnunga o Makaawhio between the Pōerua and Hokitika Rivers and, controversially, the manawhenua of Ngāti Tama, Ngāti Rārua, and Te Āti Awa rūnunga in Golden Bay/Mohua between the lower Buller River/Kawatiri and Kahurangi Point. The 1860 Arahura Purchase deed and the 1998 Ngāi Tahu Claims Settlement Act vested ownership of the Arahura Riverbed and its pounamu/nephrite resources in Ngāti Waewae rūnunga. It is the real Waipounamu (Wāhi Pounamu – 'place of pounamu/nephrite').

Arahura means 'path discovered' or 'to get up and look' (for pounamu/nephrite). Kahurangi is the most highly prized variety of that green stone, which ranges from dark 'kawakawa' to pale 'inanga'. There is a local tradition that if Waitiaki, the embodiment of the mauri (life force) of pounamu/nephrite, appears to its seeker in a dream then a fine piece will be found.

In 2009 the old timber truss Arahura Bridge was replaced and its southern approaches were straightened, which eliminated Greyhound Corner. A few years earlier I had hired a mountain bike in **Hokitika (1)**, put it my van and then driven up Arahura Valley Road, which joins SH6 at the southern end of the Arahura Bridge. The emerald meadows beside the road contrasted sharply with the piles of red lichen-covered stone tailings, which the Arahura Gold Dredge had deposited on the north bank in the 1950s. After passing the site of the 'Crooked Bridge', where the Old Christchurch Road via Blue Spur used to cross the Arahura River, I followed Humphries Gully Road to a locked gate at the bottom of Humphries Gully.

Evelyn drove the van back to Hokitika while I cycled further up the Arahura Valley on an old forestry road that ran through a *Pinus radiata* plantation. After a while it zigzagged up the side of a tall drift terrace and crossed a gorse-infested pākihi. Most of the trees on that terrace had been felled to make fluming for the Humphries Gully Water Race. I passed two men gathering sphagnum moss and ducked under the overhanging branches of giant gorse bushes until the old forestry road joined Milltown Road. It was then all downhill to the Hans Bay picnic area beside Lake Kaniere where Evelyn had parked the van.

By the 1880s sluicing for gold was more economic than tunnelling for it. A 19-kilometre water race was constructed from Mount Brown Creek below the First Arahura Gorge in the Arahura Valley to feed 'Monitor' sluice guns in Humphries Gully and a holding dam was constructed on the drift terrace below the terminal moraine that the vanished Arahura Glacier had deposited towards the end of the Ōtira Glaciation. The Milltown Road from Lake Kaniere follows the line of the race maintenance track around Mount Tūhua. An unemployment relief scheme during the Great Depression extended that water race ten kilometres further west to Tucker Flat, but it failed to produce much gold.[225]

Westland County Council built a benched pack track through the Arahura Gorges to the Wilberforce Quartz Reefs near **Browning Pass/ Nōti Raureka (12)**. An exploratory adit (entrance) was driven into the main reef, but gold assays from it were disappointing and mining activities ceased in that area at the start of World War I.[226]

In September 1988 Evelyn and I followed Milltown Road past **Mount Tūhua (3)** and across the new Milltown Bridge over the Arahura River to an old sawmill site on Milltown Flat. At the top of that flat the Alpine Fault prunes the western spurs of the McArthur Range as it strikes southwest from the Wainihinihi Branch of the Taramakau Valley towards an unnamed saddle between Mount Tūhua and Mount Brown at the western end of the Newton Range. We parked at the northern end of the Milltown Bridge and followed the Arahura Track through the short First Gorge between the Newton and McArthur Ranges, over the Cesspool swing bridge, and then into the Second Gorge.

Pounamu/nephrite cobbles and boulders in the Arahura River bed were regarded as a species of fish that turned into stone when they left the water. They were said to have had fled from their enemies in Hawaiki to Tūhua/Mayor Island in Te Tai o Toi/the Bay of Plenty but moved on when the matā-tūhua/obsidian tribe followed them to that island and settled there. The grinding sounds of the sharp teeth of Pourangahua's wife, Kanioro, and the sandstone woman, Hine Hoanga, deterred the pounamu/nephrite tribe from entering any rivers on the east coast of Te Ika a Māui/the North Island. The atua Ngahue sent his assistant, Poutini, there to escort the fugitives to a safe refuge in the Arahura Valley in Tai Poutini/the west coast of Te Waipounamu the South Island.

Poutini became besotted with Waitiaki, the beautiful wife (or sister) of the Pātea ancestor Tama Āhua, who often visited Tūhua/Mayor Island in those days. He abducted Waitiaki in the waka *Tūhua* and then imprisoned her in the Arahura Valley's Second Gorge by transforming her into a pounamu/nephrite reef in the bed of Waitiaki/Olderog Creek. Poutini's waka became Mount Tūhua on the southern side of the Arahura River, below the first gorge.[227] Hare Hongi said that Tama Āhua left his old home in Whangamatā in Te Tai o Toi and found Waitiaki by tracking the flight paths of his special implement, a tekateka (short javelin). It landed at Lake Taupō, Mount Taranaki, Onetahua/Farewell Spit and finally the remote Arahura Valley. **Mount Tara o Tama (4)** beside the Arahura River's second gorge, is the tip of his tekateka. Tama failed to break Poutini's enchantment and returned to Taranaki. Island Hill/Tumuaki between the Arahura and Kāwhaka Valleys represents his slave.[228] The forebears of Te Pātea and Ngāti Wairangi followed his giant footsteps to Tai Poutini.

The Arahura Track was in good condition, apart from a few washed-out sections where it crossed side creeks. In those places a chain attached to a tree trunk on the edge of the washout helped us to regain the track. High cloud thickened throughout the day and rain set in when we were halfway through the Third Gorge. We crossed the river via the Mud Flat swing bridge and followed a side track to **Mudflat Hut (5)**.

Heavy rain began to hammer on the hut's iron roof after dark and continued for much of the night. The roar of the river steadily increased and I wondered how long the deluge would last. All the side streams that we had crossed would have become raging torrents by dawn. The Styx Valley Track was probably the safest route back to the car. We set off at first light and followed the Arahura Track further up the valley to **Styx Saddle (13)**.

We turned right at the finger post and followed the Styx Track down the Styx Branch of the Hokitika Valley, which the south arm of the vanished Arahura Glacier had excavated right down to Lake Kaniere. The rain gradually eased and the Styx River's tributaries remained fordable, but the strong nor'west wind did not abate. Two deerstalkers greeted us when we approached the road and kindly gave us a lift back to our car. Next day the swollen Grey River/Māwheranui flooded Greymouth's riverside business district at high tide.

Several weeks of wet weather were coming to an end in November 1999 when my daughter Janet and I left Hokitika and drove eastward on Lake Kaniere Road. We parked by the Styx Bridge and followed the Styx Track up the true right bank of the Styx River. Last summer a landslip had swept a short section of the track into the river. A bit further on, a raging side stream brought us to a halt and we camped on the track. Fortunately, the stream dropped overnight and we pressed on at dawn to **Grassy Flat Hut (9)**.

As the Styx River had to be forded twice in Grassy Flat, we had breakfast in the hut before we tackled the second ford. Stumbling in the middle of it, I emerged wet to the waist (full immersion in the mythical Styx River in Hades was said to confer immunity from injury). Back on the true right bank we passed through a grove of ancient tōtara trees with the biggest girths that I had ever seen. We turned right at the fingerpost on **Styx Saddle (13)** and followed the Arahura Track through a belt of sub-alpine scrub at the base of Mount Browning, and then across the

The view of Mt Axis (1,979m) on the
Campbell Range when my daughter
Janet and I climbed Mt Harman/Kaniere
from Harman Hut via that peak in 1999.

Harman Creek swing bridge and an old terminal moraine ridge to the
six-bunk **Harman Hut (6)**, which had replaced the old stone Pyramid
Hut. Three Conservation Department employees arrived at the same
time by helicopter and promptly closed the bridge for maintenance
work. We sat on a grassy mound near the hut and picked a route up
Mount Axis (7) on the opposite side of the upper Arahura Valley.

Mount Axis is the apex of the Campbell Range, which is the eastern
section of the watershed between the Arahura Valley and Taipō Branch
of the Taramakau Valley. At 1979 metres above sea level, the summit
of Mount Axis is the highest point in the water catchment area of the
Arahura River.

The Campbell Range joins the Main Divide on **Mount Harman/
Kaniere (8)**. The Browning Range between the Styx and Kōkatahi
Branches of the Hokitika Valley joins the Main Divide on **Mount Beals
(10)**. It may have been named after mining engineer Latham Beal who

The view across Browning Pass/
Nōti Raureka of the Lake Browning/
Whakarewa source of the Arahura River
and Mt Beals (1,940m) on the Main
Divide from Mt Harman/Kaniere.

was a foundation member of the New Zealand Institute of Surveyors. At 1940 metres above sea level, the summit of Mount Beals is the highest point on the portion of the Main Divide that bounds the Arahura Catchment. The lowest point lies between those peaks: the 1411-metre summit of **Browning Pass/Nōti Raureka (12)**, which connects with the Rakaia Valley. The Arahura River begins its 56-kilometre journey to the sea from the outlet of Lake Browning/Whakarewa on top of this pass.

Next day we followed the Arahura Track a short distance up the Arahura Valley, then forded the river and scrambled up the banks of a steep side stream to the end of the west ridge of Mount Axis. We carried on up that ridge until it suddenly steepened, then sidled onto the big scree at the head of Sphinx Creek, which stretched up to the crest of the Campbell Range. A cold easterly wind stung my cheeks when we reached the snow-covered ridgeline and I began to plug a line of steps to the summit of Mount Axis.

From that vantage point I could see the mouths of the Arahura and Hokitika Rivers and the Main Divide from Mount Rosamond at the head of the Taipō branch of the Taramakau Valley to Mount Beals at the head of the Arahura Valley. We followed the watershed of the Campbell Range further east to Mount Harman/Kaniere, where we could gaze down on Popes Pass at the head of the Taipō Valley and Browning Pass/Nōti Raureka at the head of the Arahura Valley. A long glissade from there almost took us to the shore of Lake Browning/Whakarewa. We then followed the Arahura Track back to the hut, by which time the workmen had completed their jobs. Janet was invited to cut the hazard tape to officially re-open the footbridge.

In November 1993 Andrew and I embarked on the Three Pass Trip from Arthur's Pass village to Hokitika. My father's cousin, Bill Heinz, was the leader of the party that had pioneered that popular triple crossing of the Main Divide via Harman, Whitehorn, and Browning/Nōti Raureka Passes in December 1926. Dad always wished that he had done it.

In March 1865 Kaiapoi's Anglican missionary, James Stack, sent Canterbury's Secretary of Public Works, John Hall, a description of an ancient trail to the west coast that he had obtained from an old Māori parishioner. It ascended the Wilberforce/Waitāwhiri Valley to 'Kaniere Pass' beside a mountain named Kaniere and a lake called Whakarewa ('to melt' or 'to start flowing'), which was the source of the Arahura River, then descended an 'open valley' to the banks of the Hokitika River. Stack reported that 'Maoris heavily laden with provisions starting from the cave just east of Kaniere mountain reached the coast on the following day at noon'.[229] Kanieri was also a common spelling. The Campbell Range is labelled 'Kaniere' on the map that was attached to his report.

Felted tremolite fibres made pounamu/nephrite boulders very difficult to cut before the development of new abrasive sawing and scarfing techniques using whetted blades of kūrūpākāra/schist from the 'Kaniere Mountains' (kani means 'to saw') or kanimata/slate from Bold Head/Paramata near the Waitaha River mouth and local river sand containing tiny garnets. The increase in production of polished pounamu/nephrite items from the seventeenth century onwards was due in part to those new techniques, which were apparently attributed to Kanioro, the saw stone wife of Pourangahua.

In the sacred histories of some North Island iwi, Rongo-i-tuas's sons Hoaki and Tau-kata sailed from Hawaiki to Te Tai o Toi to search for their sister Kanioro. She had sailed to Whakatāne with Pourangahua then they moved to Tai Rāwhiti. Pou is also said to have dwelt in the Pātea district and is recorded as a Rapuwai ancestor.[230] Kanioro may have accompanied him to the Arahura district and helped him to cut pounamu/nephrite with her sharp teeth. Names and story lines can slowly alter. The Campbell Range/Kaniere Mountains could represent Kanioro and Mount Turiwhate on the northern side of Kāwhaka (to light a fire) Creek could represent her sister Tūturiwhata who burnt her breast in a fire. The tūturiwhata/red-breasted dotterel is named after her.[231]

In 1877 James Stack published a Ngāi Tahu legend about a high-ranking Ngāti Wairangi woman named Raureka who wandered up the Arahura Valley and pioneered the transalpine trail over Browning Pass/Nōti Raureka. She followed the banks of the Wilberforce/Waitāwhiri and Rakaia Rivers to the east coast and then headed south. Near Arowhenua she met some men who were trying to chip a waka hull out of a tree trunk with blunt uri/basalt adzes. She gave them a sharp pounamu/nephrite adze from her backpack, which performed a lot better.[232] William Taylor was told that she married an Arowhenua chief named Pūhou. He led the first Ngāi Tahu expedition over Nōti Raureka (Raureka's Pass) to obtain pounamu/nephrite and sacred lore, in which Ngāti Wairangi tohunga were said to be highly proficient. According to Sherwood Roberts, Browning Pass/Nōti Raureka was also called Nōti Hokitika. William Smart was told that travellers were prohibited from using that route after 20 people died on the pass when they were caught in a blizzard.

In the summer of 1864–65 teams of surveyors searched for a potential road line from Christchurch to the newly discovered goldfields near Hokitika. Canterbury road engineer Richard Harman, surveyor John Browning, and his friend R. Johnstone followed up Stack's report. They had explored the head of the Waimakariri Valley and found two Main Divide passes, which were provisionally named after Browning and

Harman. When they reached the head of the Wilberforce/Waitāwhiri Valley they met Edward Griffiths and his friend Otway, who told them that they had just found a Main Divide pass with a lake on the summit.[233]

The combined parties crossed that pass and followed the Arahura River down the other side, but the onset of rain in the first gorge that they entered and a shortage of food forced them to beat a retreat to their base camp. Harman, Johnstone and Otway returned to Christchurch, but Browning and Griffiths decided to stay put until the weather improved. In early May they re-crossed that pass, which was subsequently renamed after Browning, and followed the south bank of the Styx and Hokitika Rivers right down to Hokitika and caught a boat back to Christchurch.

When spring arrived, the Provincial Council awarded Walter Greenlaw a contract to build a stock track to Hokitika via **Browning Pass/Nōti Raureka (12)** to reduce stock numbers on the newly opened road over Arthur's Pass. A zigzag track had been constructed halfway up the eastern side of the pass when the project was cancelled. At least three mobs of sheep were driven over it to the Arahura Saleyards.[234] Browning Pass at the head of the Waimakariri Valley was renamed after one of the Campbell brothers that jointly bought Craigieburn Station in 1867. He had searched for unclaimed grazing land in this area after he arrived from Scotland in 1861.

The owner of the Alpine Motel in Arthur's Pass gave us a lift to Klondyke Corner near the Bealey Bridge and offered to pick us up by the Styx Bridge in three days' time. Keith was training for the Kepler Marathon and offered to pick us up after a run up to **Styx Saddle (13)** and back. We tramped up the Waimakariri Riverbed to Carrington Hut, forded the White River and entered the Taipōiti Gorge. After clambering over a huge pile of avalanche snow in the middle of the gorge we then climbed a grassy slope to Harman Pass, which punctuated the Main Divide between Mounts Campbell and Isobel.

We camped on the summit next to the Ariel Tarns, which are the source of the Mary tributary of the Taipō River. The long snow slope leading up to Whitehorn Pass was visible just beyond Mount Isobel. The topographer on the 1906 Geological Survey of the Hokitika Subdivision,

My first view of Browning Pass/Nōti Raureka (1,411m) on the Main Divide before Andrew Taylor-Perry and I crossed it from the Wilberforce/Waitawhiri Valley.

Reginald Greville, had named that pass after his chainman, Alfred Whitehorn.

In the morning we plugged steps up that soft snow slope to Whitehorn Pass. The summit was enveloped in cloud so we oriented ourselves on the map to avoid a hidden bluff, then walked 30 metres to the right and descended another long snow slope to the head of the Cronin branch of the Wilberforce/Waitāwhiri Valley. The Cronin Icefall on Mount Rosamond came into view when we emerged from the cloud base. Our next stop was the Canterbury Mountaineering Club's Park Morpeth Memorial Hut by the confluence of the Cronin Stream and the Wilberforce River/Waitāwhiri.

After lunch we headed up the stony bed of the Wilberforce River/ Waitāwhiri and ascended the unfinished benched track that zigzagged up the southern side of Browning Pass/Nōti Raureka. When it petered out we slogged up a long scree slope, which grew steadily steeper as we gained height. When we encountered snow and our boots began to lose traction we sidled onto the rock rib on the right, picked our way up it, and stepped onto the pass beside the ruins of **Gelignite Hut (11)**.

The contractor that had blasted part of the proposed stock track through the bluffs above Hall Creek to the left of the scree before the project was abandoned may have built that tiny stone hut to store explosives in. It may have been used for the same purpose by the hard rock miners that drove an adit into one of the Wilberforce Reefs at the base of Mount Harman/Kaniere.[235] Lake Browning/Whakarewa was covered with ice apart from a patch of open water around its outlet. We pitched our tent on a flat area next to that spot.

Our boots were inadvertently left outside the tent overnight so that in the morning they were frozen solid. When they had thawed out enough we followed the Arahura Track down through the bluffs on the northern side of the pass and along the true left bank of the infant Arahura River. On the way we watched a pair of kōwhiowhio/blue ducks shepherd five fluffy ducklings over the boulder-strewn riverbank. Keith jogged past us twice as we strode down the Styx Valley Track and was sitting in his car reading a book when we reached the road.

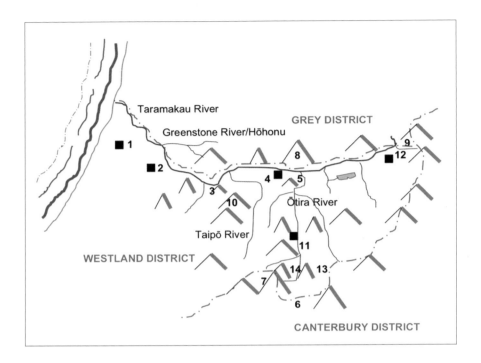

Taramakau River

Greenstone River/Hōhonu

GREY DISTRICT

■ 1

■ 2

3

10

4 ■ 5

8

Ōtira River

■ 12

9

Taipō River

■ 11

WESTLAND DISTRICT

7

14 13

6

CANTERBURY DISTRICT

Legend

1. Kumara Junction
2. Kumara
3. Wilsons Knob
4. Jacksons Hotel
5. Kellys Hill
6. Arthur's Pass
7. Mt Rolleston

8. Mt Alexander
9. Harper Pass/Nōti Taramakau
10. Mt Tara o Tama
11. Ōtira village
12. Number 4 (Locke Stream) Hut
13. Hills Peak
14. Mt Philistine

Chapter 22
The Taramakau

When Evelyn and I headed back to Christchurch after my cycling trip up the Arahura Valley we turned off SH6 about 17 kilometres north of Hokitika and followed Serpentine Road to a sandy car park beside the Taramakau River mouth. The flood tide had filled the shallow lagoon behind this picnic area, which is roughly where the south landing of the Taramakau punt ferry on the old beach highway was situated. The stone cairn by the car park is a memorial to Henry Whitcombe, who was swept out to sea near this spot in 1863 when he tried to cross the rain-swollen river in an old half rotten waka (see Page 301). Since then high seas have scoured away the site of Taramakau kāinga on the opposite side of the river mouth. Thousands of years ago high seas had cut escarpments on the seaward sides of the high 'drift' terraces between the Taramakau and Hokitika River mouths.

Evelyn and our daughter Sybil by the mouth of the Taramakau River, where this upriver story begins, in 1999.

Charles Heaphy and William Fox visited Taramakau kāinga in the winter of 1846 and counted 21 adult residents, some of whom had escaped the destruction of Kaiapoi pā in 1832. Every whare contained an axe and iron pot that had been procured on the east coast and a block of pounamu/nephrite that was being honed into a weapon or ornament using wet sand containing tiny red garnets, kūrūpākāra/schist saws from the Kaimatā and Kaniere Ranges, parahōanga/grindstones from the southern Paparoa Range, and matā/flint drill bits from a Paparoa sea cliff called Pāhutani.[236] Ngāti Māhaki elders told William Wilson that Taramakau was the name of a man who was killed there. This river name also alludes to 'te ara makau' (the husband's path), of Tama-nui-a-Raki who had followed its banks in pursuit of his runaway wife Rukutia (see Page 61).

Tama-ki-te-Raki sailed around this island in search of his runaway wives. Kokotakiwai was found at the entrance to Milford Sound/Piopiotahi, where she had turned into a reef of dark green takiwai/bowenite (see Page 176). Another wife had turned into the rare blue stone aotea/kyanite, which washes up on the shore of Bruce Bay/Mahitahi. A huge wave swept his waka *Tairea* up the Taramakau

River and deposited it in the bed of its Greenstone/Hōhonu tributary. Boulders of pounamu/nephrite in the beds of those rivers represent the shattered waka and its crew. Boulders of pale varieties of that treasured stone, inanga and kahurangi, represent the broken body of Tama's most beautiful wife.[237]

After watching the Taramakau River run into the sea we followed SH6 up a short rise onto the high drift terrace where SH73 joins SH6 by a railway crossing at **Kumara Junction (1)**. SH6 and the Greymouth-Hokitika Railway Line head north from there to the Taramakau Road-Rail Bridge, which was supplemented by a parallel two-land road bridge in 2018. When I was young I saw the crossing keeper cycle back and forth across it to shut and reopen the gate before and after a freight train or railcar crossed it.

Wagons and passenger coaches fitted with wide wheels travelled back and forth along the old beach highway between Greymouth and Hokitika until 1877, when a steam-powered 'bird cage' suspended from a steel cable replaced the punt ferry at the Taramakau River mouth. It connected the Paroa and Kumara horse trams, which transported passengers between Greymouth and the booming goldfields around **Kumara (2)**, which is pronounced 'kumaara' since it derives from kohimāra — white flowers on tataramoa/'bush lawyer' vines. Those tramlines closed when the steel truss Taramakau Road-Rail Bridge opened in 1888 and the advancing railhead of the Greymouth-Hokitika Line reached Kumara Junction. Beach Road between Kumara and the old beach highway became the 'Kumara Straight' section of SH73.

After the abolition of Provincial Governments in 1876 the Taramakau River from its Main Divide source near Harper Pass/Nōti Taramakau to the sea marked the boundary between Westland and Grey Counties and the new boundary between the Church of England's Nelson and Canterbury Dioceses, which had formerly mirrored the inter-provincial boundary (mediaeval dioceses and military provinces shared the same boundaries too).

We left SH6 at Kumara Junction and kept driving eastward on SH73, which arrowed across a huge gorse-infested pākihi to Kumara township. Long streets with many empty sections gave an indication of Kumara's size in the late nineteenth century. My great-great-grandfather, George Orams, was a boarding house keeper and nightwatchman in Kumara in the 1870s and 80s. I remember striding down the eight-kilometre 'Kumara Straight' with my father and brother to catch a bus at Kumara Junction after following the No-name Road from Marsden to Kumara. We had to ford the Greenstone/Hōhonu (deep) River because the bridge had been removed to enable the Taramakau Gold Dredge to excavate its bed.

No-name Road crosses a higher terrace on the opposite side of the Taramakau River called Nemona (No Name) Hill. A school friend had shown me the site of a Chinese settlement on the edge of that terrace. Amongst the broken bottles and pottery that littered that spot I found a grindstone and a tiny opium vial. Grey County Council constructed the No-name Road between Greymouth and the lucrative Greenstone Diggings beside the Greenstone/Hōhonu River in the 1870s. My father's cousin had located the untouched site of the Greenstone police station and found some gold in the underlying gravel. That ghost town's last building collapsed in the 1950s.

After driving through Kumara we made a detour down the Dillmanstown-Larrikins Road and followed a signposted track to the 3000-ton Londonderry Rock on one of the terminal moraines that the Taramakau Glacier had deposited during the Ōtira Glaciation. The pākihi that we had driven across from the coast was the coeval glacial outwash surface.

We rejoined SH73 in Dillmanstown where the Kumara gold rush had commenced in 1875. Two men who were looking for a secret spot to set up an illicit whisky still had found a gold lead in a gully on the adjacent rim of the Taramakau Gorge and news of it did not leak out for quite a while.[238] In its heyday Dillmanstown was criss-crossed with water races perched on 12–18 metre-high trestles. Sluicing companies bought up most of the land in that township and its residents shifted to Kumara.

The Taramakau River has carved its gorge through a stack of glacial outwash surfaces deposited one on top of the other during successive advances of the vanished Taramakau Glacier. Gold miners stopped digging when they reached the 'blue bottom' mudstone. In 1876 the National Government funded the construction of the Dillmans Water Race from a reservoir fed by Kapitea and Kāwhaka Creeks to hydraulic elevators and sluice guns on the gold diggings between Kumara and Dillmanstown. Underground sludge channels allowed washed-up tailings to be flushed into the gorge. Seven major gold-bearing leads were excavated through the Kumara Goldfield. The Dillmans Water Race was subsequently extended beyond its reservoir to tap the headwaters of the Wainihinihi tributaries of the Taramakau and Arahura Rivers via two tunnels. In 1978 this 21-kilometre race was diverted into the Loopline and Kapitea Reservoirs to drive the 3.8 MW Dillmans and the 6.0 MW Kumara Power Station.

Those costly race upgrades failed to reverse the decline in gold production in the Kumara goldfield. A cast iron siphon with flexible joints was placed in the bed of the Taramakau River to extend the piped Government-owned Dillmans Water Race across the gorge to a holding pond on Howes Terrace above the north bank to allow sluicing companies to excavate this isolated portion of the Kumara drift terrace between the Greenstone/Hōhonu and Taramakau Rivers. This scheme was commissioned in 1912 but failed to recoup its costs.

In the 1930s, the Arahura, Kaniere, and Ngahere Dredging Companies subsidised the extension of transmission lines over Arthur's Pass to drive large electric gold dredges that could access 26-metre-deep alluvial gold leads on the west coast. In 1956, the Kaniere Dredge was moved to the bed of the Greenstone/Hōhonu tributary of the Taramakau River. It worked its way down to the Taramakau Riverbed and recovered around 11,000 ounces of gold annually until it was decommissioned in 1982.

In April 1864 the Canterbury Provincial Council made the controversial announcement that Albert Hunt had won the reward that it had offered to the first person to find payable gold in West Canterbury. The site was five kilometres up the banks of the Greenstone/Hōhonu River at Māori Point. Actually, two prospectors from the Buller District, Michael French and William Smart, had struck gold there a month before Hunt, but filed their claim in Westport instead of Christchurch. The paramount Ngāti Waewae rangatira Tarapuhi Te Kaukihi had told them where to look when he visited Westport to buy tools to break up a pounamu/nephrite or 'greenstone' boulder in the bed of this river.[239] Mounts French and Smart on the Hōhonu Range are their memorials.

Three strong men could paddle or pole a waka up to the Greenstone/Hōhonu Confluence from the Taramakau River mouth. Residents of Taramakau kāinga ran a profitable freight service to the Greenstone Diggings in 1866. In earlier times parties of travellers bound for the east coast poled waka up to this confluence, then hiked up the banks of the Greenstone/Hōhonu River and Little Hōhonu Creek, over Ōhonu Saddle to the shore of Lake Brunner/Moana Kōtuku, and then crossed an open pākihi called Bruce's Paddock and forded the Taramakau River to Tauotikiranga pā on Rocky Point. Westbound parties built mōkihi (rafts) there and rode them down to the river mouth.

The first track from the old beach highway to the Greenstone Diggings was an extension of the track to the Waimea Diggings in the upper Waimea (Waimeha – 'insignificant') Valley between the Arahura and Taramakau Valleys. Within a year that 'mud and slush' track was upgraded into Stafford-Dilmanstown Road and Greenstone Road, linked by a punt ferry across the Taramakau River. Gorge Bridge replaced that ferry and Greenstone Road has become Lake Brunner Road. The West Coast Wilderness Cycle Trail follows the route of the Government Water Race between Kumara and Milltown Flat in the Arahura Valley.

The Greenstone Diggings were on the northern side of the huge outwash surface that formed between 18,000 and 24,000 years ago below the terminal moraine of the vanished Taramakau Glacier during the three phases of the Ōtira Glaciation, which were called the Kumara 1, 2 and 3 Advances on the west coast and the Blackwater 1 and 2 and Poulter Advances on the east coast. The Kumara Diggings were on the southern side of this surface. Older outwash surfaces associated with the Waimea, Waimaunga and Nemona Glaciations were largely erased by erosion.[240] Movements on the Alpine Fault simultaneously moved them north-westward at an average rate of 35mm per year in relation to the Southern Alps/Kā Tiritiri o te Moana, which means that the Arahura Glacier dropped the pounamu/nephrite boulders on Nemona (No Name) Hill around 360,000 years ago during the Nemona Glaciation.

The Kumara and Greenstone goldfields lay on the Golden Line, which marked the position of the terminus of the Taramakau component of the amalgamated tongues of the glaciers that emerged from alpine valleys during the Ōtira Glaciation. Heavy gold particles accumulated in fluvio-glacial leads or 'pay channels', which became buried along the 10-kilometre-wide Golden Line between Hukarere in the upper Grey/Māwheranui Valley and Hokitika (see Page 295).

After driving through Dillmanstown we followed SH73 through rimu-tōtara bush in the 341-hectare Ōkuku Scenic Reserve on the terminal moraine ridges that were deposited by the Taramakau Glacier during the Ōtira Glaciation. Further up the south bank of the Taramakau River we drove through the gap that the vanished glacier had carved between two granite plutons: Mount Turiwhate (Turiwhati – bad, rough[241]) and the Hōhonu Range. The heights of the U-shaped hanging valleys in the Hōhonu Range reveal the glacier's thickness.

The Taramakau and Paringa Rivers mark the northern and southern boundaries of the west coast's 'beech gap', which became deforested during the Ōtira Glaciation. When it ended, berry-eating birds spread the seeds of podocarp and broadleaf trees through that big gap before tāwhai/beech trees could gain a foothold – their seeds are spread by the wind.

The Old Christchurch (or Kawaka) Road joins SH73 between Ōkuku Creek and Blakes Creek on the eastern side of the vanished Taramakau Glacier's terminal moraine. Canterbury contractor Edwin Blake constructed the road over that bush-clad ridge and down the Kāwhaka Valley to the Arahura River mouth. The first coaches from Christchurch travelled down the Ōtira and Taramakau Riverbeds until they reached the Kawaka Roadend at Harris' Hotel by Turiwhate Creek. My grandfather said that coach horses used to gallop into Hokitika because they could smell their oats in the stable.

After skirting the base of Mount Turiwhate we crossed the Big Wainihinihi (Wainehenehe – 'bush stream') River, which flows northward along the trace of the Alpine Fault, and then followed the highway in the same direction along the base of the Griffin Range/Ōtahua.

A few years earlier I had walked up the bed of Harrington Creek near the old Griffin homestead until I reached the western escarpment of the Griffin Range/Ōtahua and then followed a zigzag track up to **Wilsons Knob (3)**. A local farmer, Paddy Fitzgerald, had told me that it had been cut to drive sheep onto the grassy tops and that if I headed south along the top of the escarpment, keeping the wind on my right shoulder, I would find the old serpentine quarry. He also told me that he had carved heat-resistant bricks to line railway locomotive fireboxes from talc boulders that he had collected in the bed of Rocky Creek.

I followed his directions and found the serpentine quarry in a big brown Pounamu Ultramafic outcrop. Peering down the western escarpment of the Griffin Range I saw a light green strip of second-growth bush. It marked the route of the cableway that had carried quarried slabs of serpentine down to a stone cutting workshop by Lynch Creek where they were turned into decorative facings. The German investors in this enterprise had to abandon it at the outbreak of World War I.

Waitiaki/Olderog Creek bed at the southern end of the Griffin Range/Ōtahua contains pounamu/nephrite boulders from another Pounamu Ultramafic outcrop in the Haast Schist Zone, which faces the Alpine Fault. It has risen from the base of the continental crust and contains highly metamorphosed olivine-rich intrusions from the earth's Mantle. Jade carving workshops sprang up in Hokitika and Greymouth in the 1960s when helicopters began to airlift pounamu/nephrite boulders from the bed of that creek. Poutini Ngāi Tahu rūnunga own all pounamu/nephrite resources within their rohe except pieces that the sea has cast onto a beach. Talc and serpentine boulders from a Pounamu Ultramafic outcrop eroded by Rocky Creek have been found in the bed of that tributary of the Taipō River.

In 1906, Geological Survey director James Bell examined the Taipō Catchment and found many small quartz reefs but no 'mother lode'. Most of the gold in the Kumara Goldfield came from quartz veins in the Greenland Greywacke basement rock around the silica-rich granite intrusions of the Hōhonu Batholith. Repeated advances of the Taramakau Glacier had removed most of that rock around the Hōhonu Range and its neighbours, Mount Turiwhate, and Mount Te Kinga. An arm of the Taramakau Glacier had moved through the wide gap between the Hōhonu Range and Mount Te Kinga and excavated the bed of Lake Brunner/Moana Kōtuku. In 1889 the Taramakau Gold Company built a track onto the Kelly Range and sampled two quartz reefs, but the assay reports disappointed its investors. A few gold diggers scratched a meagre living beside Seven Mile Creek, which drains the southern slopes of the Kelly Range and joins the Taipō River. The Dillon and Wilkinson brothers took over their claims and shot deer on the Taipō Flats until the 1960s.

Three kilometres past Harrington Creek we crossed the Taipō (Devil)/ Hopeakoa River. The cast iron piers of the Taipō Bridge were built to carry the Midland Railway Line before its route was changed. Prior to that bridge's opening, westbound coach passengers were holed up in the Taipō Hotel whenever that river was in flood. After rounding Rocky Point/Tauotikiranga at the end of the Bald Range, SH73 leaves the Alpine Fault Line and follows its Hope Branch into the upper Taramakau Valley. After driving through The Avenue Scenic Reserve we came to a farming settlement called Jacksons after the brothers who had opened **Jacksons Hotel (4)** in conjunction with the opening of the nearby Taramakau Rail Bridge in 1893; the parallel Stanley Gooseman Road Bridge opened in 1972.

Ten kilometres beyond Jacksons, the highway and railway leave the south bank of the Taramakau River at Aickens at the base of **Kellys Hill (5)**, where the Bald Range joins Kellys Range, and head south up the Ōtira Valley. In the 1880s a former roadman named William Aicken grazed cattle there and opened Aickens Accommodation House. Five kilometres up this big side valley we crossed Kellys Creek. Before the old accommodation house by that ford burned down in 1870 the sign outside it read 'Otira Hotel kept by Kelly where man and beast may fill their belly'. We tucked into fish and chips in the Terminus Hotel in **Ōtira village (11)** before crossing Arthur's Pass en route to Christchurch.

Arthur Dobson and two companions crossed his namesake pass in 1864 (see Page 82). A year later 1000 workmen constructed the west coast road over Arthur's Pass. A thrice-weekly coach service was inaugurated between Christchurch and Hokitika when that road opened in March 1866. Fit male passengers would walk behind the coach to lighten the load on the steepest section of the road over the pass. The two-storey Terminus Hotel opened when the advancing railhead from Greymouth reached this spot in 1901.

When the Ōtira Railway Tunnel opened in 1923, train passengers could buy hot pies, sandwiches and cups of tea in the Ōtira Railway

The view of Arthur's Pass (920m) on the Main Divide when my son Julian and I climbed Kellys Hill from the Ōtira Valley in 1999.

Station canteen while they waited for the powerful Kb steam locomotive that had hauled their carriages from Greymouth to be replaced by an Eo-class English Electric locomotive that could handle the 1 in 33 gradient in the Ōtira Tunnel. The steam locomotives were retired in 1968 and the electric locomotives were retired in 1997. Ōtira village had up to 100 residents before the 1980s, when the railways were privatised and the Railway Department houses were sold.

The road over Arthur's Pass is closed about six times a year due to snow or slips. In the 1890s Dutch artist Petrus van der Velden made several trips to Otira Gorge Hotel by Barrack Creek to capture this area's changeable moods in preliminary sketches for his acclaimed series of Ōtira Gorge paintings.[242] That hotel burned down in 1941; a flood had destroyed its forerunner in 1886. About 2000 years ago part of **Hills Peak (13)** collapsed into the upper Ōtira Gorge, probably due to an earthquake. The escarpment at the top of the resultant debris fan called the Otira Slip is close to the Scott Fault, which strikes southward through Arthur's Pass into the Bealey Valley. In 1999 a major upgrade

of the Ōtira Gorge Road culminated in the opening of the 440-metre
Otira Viaduct, which carries SH73 right over the Ōtira Slip.

In March 1998 a fine weather forecast gave Andrew and me the green
light for a tramping trip along the ancient Taramakau Trail. We boarded
a West Coast Shuttle bus in Christchurch. Over the crest of **Arthur's
Pass (6)** we had a bird's-eye view of the partly built Ōtira Viaduct from
the old road across the Ōtira Slip before it descended the infamous
zigzag into the Ōtira Gorge; the 440-metre Ōtira Viaduct across that
slip was still under construction. We alighted at Aickens and set off for
Harper Pass/Nōti Taramakau (9) at the head of the Taramakau Valley.

The Taramakau River resembles a Canterbury river as it flows
south-westward in braided channels along the crush zone of the Hope
Fault. In olden times the best route for porters carrying heavy loads of
pounamu/nephrite from Arahura to Kaiapoi lay up the broad shingle
bed of this river and over Harper Pass/Nōti Taramakau, which is 42
metres higher than Arthur's Pass, but much easier to cross on foot. Its
alternative name, Te Rau o Tama (the leaves that were ripped off Tama-
nui-a-Raki's rain cape), alludes to Tama's trials when he pioneered this
transalpine trail (see Page 61).

Early travellers stuck to the south bank of the Taramakau River beyond
Rocky Point/Tauotikiranga. They caught birds in the bush in the lower
Ōtira Valley and around Lake Kaurapataka (Kāurupātaka). A campsite
at the base of Harper Pass/Nōti Taramakau was called Whakamoemoe
(gone to sleep).[243] The original name of **Mount Alexander (8)** and the
mountain range that it crowns on the northern side of the Taramakau
Valley was Kaimatā (to eat stones or uncooked food[244]), which could
imply that it was one of the giant Kāhui Tipua who fell asleep there
(see Page 163); the old place names Te Tarahaka o Kaimatā (the pass of
Kaimatā) and Nōti Ōtira were probably attached to Arthur's Pass.

We followed a fence-line track from the Aitkens Conservation
Department base to the west bank of the Ōtira River, which was running
clear but higher than expected. It took a while to find a fordable shingle

The view of the source of the Taramakau
River below the junction of the Kaimatā
Range and the Main Divide when I
climbed Mt Drake from Harper Bivouac.

weir and we were both wet to the waist when we reached the other bank. A set of wheel tracks guided us across grassy flats to Pfeifer Creek. From there we gravel-bashed up the Taramakau riverbed, apart from a foray into the bush to find a safe place to ford the Ōtehake tributary. About six hours from Aitkens we reached **Number Four** (or Locke Stream) **Hut (12)**, where adze marks made by its builder in 1942 were visible in the pāhautea/cedar floorboards.

After a meal break in the hut we followed short tracks in and out of the bush between stints of boulder-bashing up the bed of the infant Taramakau River, about 75 kilometres from its mouth. We eventually picked up the old bridle track that zigzagged up to Harper Pass/Nōti Taramakau. Daylight was fading fast when we reached the summit. We used our headlights to negotiate a deep washout on the eastern side of the pass, but we failed to spot Harper Pass Bivouac, which is set back from the Hurunui River in a grove of whauwhi/eastern ribbonwood trees. In order to save weight we had chosen not to bring sleeping bags so we emptied our 80-litre packs, laid them out in a patch of fern, and used them as bivvy bags.

It was a warm, dry night, but sleep did not come easily. Instead, I listened to a pair of roa/great spotted roa kiwi whistling to each other in the dark. When we got up in the morning the orange roof of Harper Pass Bivouac was clearly visible just 20 metres away. Andrew reported that one of those kiwis had walked right over his pack! On the way down the Hurunui Valley we had a dip in the hot pool before breakfast, which we ate on a grassy mound called Dinner Hill. It is a relic of a terminal moraine ridge that the reinvigorated Hurunui Glacier had deposited after the Ōtira Glaciation.

A bit further on we picked up the Kiwi Saddle Track and followed it through magnificent stands of tāwhairaunui/red beech trees on the northern shore of Lake Sumner and then over Kiwi Saddle/Whakarewa between Macs Knob and the western end of the Glynn Wye Range to the Hope-Kiwi Lodge. There we enjoyed the simple luxuries of a warm fire, hot food, and foam mattresses to sleep on. The original name of Kiwi Saddle/Whakarewa, which appears on Edward Jollie's North Canterbury map, evidently refers to its identifier, Mount Longfellow at the western end of the Glynn Wye Range/Whakarewa. Andrew's wristwatch alarm roused us in time to tramp down the Hope Track along the north bank of the Hope River to Windy Point in the Boyle

Valley where we caught the Westport shuttle bus back to Christchurch, 48 hours after we were dropped off at Aitkens.

In October 1985 Adam and I drove to Pegleg Flat on **Arthur's Pass (6)** and climbed **Hills Peak (13)** via an exit gully on the southern side of the big Otira Slip at the head of the Ōtira Gorge. The panorama from that peak encompassed the watershed between the upper Ōtira and Rolleston Valleys from **Mount Philistine (14)** to **Mount Rolleston (7)** on the Main Divide, which my friend Terry and I had traversed two years earlier. We bypassed the final steep section by sidling onto the vestigial Waimakariri Glacier and shinning up an easier rock rib.

At 2275 metres above sea level, the High Peak of Mount Rolleston

The view across Arthur's Pass of Mt Rolleston (2,275m) on the Main Divide and Mount Philistine (on the right) when my son Adam and I climbed Hills Pk in 1985.

is the highest point in the Taramakau Catchment and on the portion of
the Main Divide that bounds it. At 920 metres Arthur's Pass between
Mount Rolleston and Phipps Peak is the lowest spot on that portion
of the Main Divide. In 1864 Arthur Dobson reported the existence
of his namesake pass to Canterbury's Chief Surveyor, Thomas Cass,
who named the adjacent peak Mount Rolleston after the Secretary
of Canterbury Province, William Rolleston. He also served as its last
Superintendent, from 1868 until 1876 (see Page 77).

Westland surveyor George Roberts erected the first trig station on
Hills Peak around 1880 and was using it to link the Westland and
Canterbury geodesic surveys (see Page 65) when he named the river
that arises at the base of Mount Rolleston the Rolleston River.[245] When
it was renamed the Ōtira River Rolleston's name was transferred to the
tributary of the Ōtira that arises below Waimakariri Col but it is still
attached to a tiny glacier on Mount Philistine, which is the highest
point on the spur of the Main Divide between the Ōtira and Rolleston
Valleys.

Marmaduke Dixon and Arthur Harper climbed that peak in about
1880 under the mistaken impression that it was Mount Rolleston,
which must have been shrouded in cloud. As soon as they realised
their error they renamed it Mount Philistine after the horse that had
hauled a cart filled with their climbing and camping equipment from
Christchurch to Arthur's Pass.

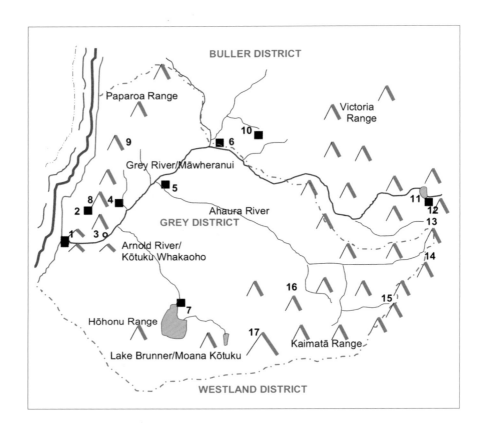

Legend

1. Greymouth
2. Dunollie
3. Brunner Mine
4. Blackball Mine
5. Ahaura
6. Ikamātua
7. Moana
8. Mt Davy
9. Mt Ryall
10. Waiuta Mine
11. Lake Christabel Hut
12. Mt Boscawen
13. Mt Baron
14. Amuri Pass/Nōti Waiheke
15. Hope Pass
16. Mt Bryan O'Lynn
17. Mt Alexander

Chapter 23

The Grey/Māwheranui

I grew up in a suburb of Greymouth (1) called Cobden on the north bank of the Grey River/Māwheranui. This river, the Tasman Sea, and Cobden Hill – the Twelve Apostles Range – bounded my childhood domain. My father enjoyed taking my brother and me for Sunday strolls along the disused railway track to the North Tip Head. As we stared in awe at the sea mounting up on this river's dangerous bar he would ask us the rhetorical question: 'What are the wild waves saying?' And then he would sing 'Many brave hearts lie asleep in the deep. Sailor beware! Sailor take care!'

The Cobden School bell was salvaged from the SS *Wonga Wonga*, which ran aground on Cobden Beach in 1866. The steel boilers of the *Kaponga* and *Abel Tasman*, which struck the North Tip in the 1930s,

The mouth of the Grey River/Māwheranui
and the North Tip Head by Cobden,
where this upriver story begins.

were visible at low tide. Four balls hanging from the signal station mast
on the South Tip meant 'safe to enter'; three balls meant 'bar dangerous';
two balls meant 'wait for high tide'; one ball meant 'dredge working'.
We always walked home via the beach to pick up knobs of dark red
rātā driftwood to put on the open fire and if we were very lucky, a dark
green pounamu/nephrite pebble.

Occasionally we walked over the Cobden Bridge and watched
a crane pluck a hopper from one of the Q wagons that shunters had
assembled in long lines beside the coaling berths on Māwhera Quay.
The crane swung the hopper over a coal ship's open hatch, then a catch
was released and eight tons of coal plunged into the ship's hold with
a loud roar. I was escorted on board the Harbour Board's bucket-line
dredge *Mawhera* a few times and saw sweating workers in her narrow
stoke hole toss shovel-loads of coal into the fire box under the boiler. I

also saw framing timber for the new hotel in Milford Sound/Piopiotahi being stacked on the deck of the *Hauiti*. That little ship sank in 1954; another regular visitor to this once busy river port, the *Kaitawa*, sank in 1966 with the loss of all hands.

Dad's parents lived in Cobden from 1904 until 1921, then moved to Hokitika. When my grandfather worked for the Greymouth Gas Company he laid the gas main across the Cobden Bridge and serviced gas streetlights and their automatic timers. My parents moved to Cobden in 1947 when Dad left the *Hokitika Guardian* and became a linotype operator on the *Grey River Argus*. After its demise in 1966 they moved to Wellington and he worked on *The Dominion*. My brother Douglas and I roamed through the dense bush on Cobden Hill and ventured further and further afield as we grew older. We caught sprats in the river and paddled a korari/'kladdie' (dry harakeke/flax flower stalk) raft down the lagoon to the 'Third Shingles' where a kōtuku/white heron was usually stationed.

A strong Ngāi Tahu taua from Kaiapoi led by the Ngāti Waewae chief Tuhuru and the Ngāi Tū Rakautahi chief Wharetai crossed the Alps and wrested control of the central west coast from Ngāti Wairangi around 1810. Tuhuru built Māwhera pā on the southern side of the Cobden Gap, which the Grey River/Māwheranui had carved between the Twelve Apostles Range/Rapahoe and Peter Ridge. A few years earlier a Ngāti Kuri party from Kaikōura had destroyed Aromahana (getting hot) pā on the northern side of the Cobden Gap. Ngāti Wairangi warriors exacted their revenge after trapping them in Ahaura pā.[246] The Oates Brothers piloted the first European ship to enter the Hokitika River and the Grey River/Māwheranui, the schooner *Emerald Isle*, on a gold prospecting trip in 1857. Three years later, in 1860, James Mackay concluded the Arahura Purchase negotiations in Māwhera pā.

In 1852 Governor Grey decreed that the mouths of the Hurunui and the lower Grey River/Māwheranui would mark the eastern and western ends of the boundary between Nelson and Canterbury Provinces. Ten years later Nelson's chief surveyor, Thomas Brunner, surveyed a port town on the north bank, which Nelson's Superintendent, Alfred Saunders, named after British politician Richard Cobden who was a fervent advocate of an imperial free trade zone. Its 250-foot wharf and adjacent ferryboat landing were built just below the Cobden Gap. Canterbury's Provincial Government responded by building a longer wharf on the south bank and a rock training wall that pushed the river's current against it. Cobden and Greymouth were separate boroughs until 1930.

In 1864 the steamer *Nelson* landed 40 gold prospectors and Westport storekeeper, Reuben Waite, on the south bank of the Grey River/ Māwheranui and a small settlement sprang up around Waite's store. In June 1865 John Rochford coined the name Greymouth and laid out its riverside streets on the 1000-acre Māwhera Native Reserve between Boundary Street and Māwhera pā. New Zealand Post recognises Māwhera as its alternative name. The 1870s-era embankment, which used to carry the railway line to the wharf, was raised after the rain-swollen river spilled over it twice in 1989. It has the second-largest water catchment area on the west coast and a mean flow of 337 cumecs.

Thomas Brunner renamed the Grey River/Māwheranui after Governor George Grey. Māwheranui is the short version of its original name, Kā Māwheratanga o kā kūwha o Tū te Raki Whānoa (the movement of the thighs of Tū te Raki Whānoa). Murihiku elders told Herries Beattie that the wriggling of that atua's thighs when he sat on the Paparoa Range created the Brunner Gorge and the Cobden Gap, which allowed that dammed-up river to flow into the sea. Above the confluence of the Little Grey River/Māwheraiti it was called the Big Grey River/Pōhaturoa (big stones). Its two afferents are the Brown Grey River, which arises in the Victoria Range, and the Blue (or Clear) Grey River, which arises on the Main Divide. Bruce Bay/Mahitahi elders told William Wilson that the Grey River/Māwheranui and its deep Arnold/Kōtuku Whakaoho (aroused by the call of the kōtuku/white heron) tributary were named after a man and his wife who were killed there.

In 1848, Nelson surveyor Thomas Brunner examined a thick coal seam in the Brunner Gorge between the Paparoa and Kaiata (early breakfast[247]) Ranges. In 1864, 40 tons of this bituminous coal were barged to the Cobden wharf and then shipped to Nelson. Horse-drawn barge traffic also served farming and gold mining settlements further up the river. The Nelson Government subsidised the **Brunner Mine (3)** until 1876, when provinces were abolished and the new railway line to the Greymouth wharf enabled the mine company to ramp up coal production. In 1896, 65 miners were killed when a pool of methane, or 'firedamp', in the bowels of that mine exploded. My great-grandfather, Robert Duncan, was among the dead.

The opening of the West Paparoa mines behind **Dunollie (2)** from 1904 onwards boosted coal traffic through the Port of Greymouth. Australian engineer Napier Bell designed the S-shaped Cobden Rail Bridge to those mines and improvements to the harbour-works, which in today's money cost the equivalent of 100 million dollars. The river mouth was narrowed to 500 feet to enable the current to scour it and maintain a 22-foot high water depth at the bar. Further harbour-work repairs and extensions were carried out from 1926 until 1948, when the railway line from Cobden Quarry to the North Tiphead closed. The first Cobden Road Bridge replaced the ferryboat in 1886; a footway with passing bays for prams was added in 1920. A two-lane concrete bridge replaced it in 1975.

The bare quartz sandstone surface on top of **Mount Davy (8)** on the Paparoa (broad back[248]) Range is a relic of the Waipounamu Erosion Surface (see Page 154) that has been stripped of its old covering strata, Brunner and Paparoa Coal Measures and Kaiata Mudstone, which appear in the Brunner Gorge, and Cobden Limestone, which appears in the Cobden Gap. Crustal compression raised that surface and tilted it away from the Inangahua Fault Zone below its eastern escarpment. Julius Haast renamed it after the English chemist Humphrey Davy who invented the miners' safety lamp and the first anaesthetic gas, nitrous oxide.

Coal was New Zealand's chief source of thermal energy until the 1960s, when offshore gas fields were tapped and the Cook Strait power cable and several new hydroelectric power stations were commissioned. Gasworks and steam-powered locomotives became obsolete and the demand for coal fell sharply. The Wallsend and Dobson Mines and the **Blackball Mine (4)**, which opened in 1893, had to close but the Roa Mine on the other side of Mount Davy stayed open. In 1966, a flood destroyed the 56-year-old Blackball Road-Rail Bridge. The closure of the Liverpool Mine and its fell railway on the west flank of Mount Davy dealt another blow to the local economy.

After the old colliers that called at the Port of Greymouth were scrapped most west coast coal was railed to the Port of Lyttelton, where bulk carriers could berth. Some coal was barged from Greymouth to the Portland Cement Works in Whangarei. In the 1990s, high demand for bituminous coal resulted in a short-lived mining boom. In 2010, 29 coal miners died when a methane gas explosion destroyed the new

Pike River Mine (9). The conversion of the Roa Mine into an open-cast pit in 2015 ended the underground mining era in Grey District.

One dry summer, when the rivers were low on the west coast, Adam and I drove to Greymouth and then followed SH7 up the south bank of the Grey River/Māwheranui. I showed Adam the memorial by the Kaiata Straight where Arthur Dobson's brother George was murdered by a bushranger and the mass grave in the Stillwater Cemetery where my great-grandfather and 64 fellow miners were buried. Their eldest daughter, who was my grandmother, grew up in Brunnerton and had to leave school at 13 to help her widowed mother. A year later one of her brothers fell off a canoe and drowned in the river.

Stillwater sprang up by the east landing of the ferry on the Arnold River/Kōtuku Whakaoho, which was bridged in 1872. This tributary issues from Lake Brunner/Moana Kōtuku (white heron sea) and was renamed after the poet Matthew Arnold.

The Stillwater Bridge over the Grey River/Māwheranui replaced the flood-damaged Blackball Road-Rail Bridge in 1978. The historic 1875 Brunner Suspension Bridge downriver is now a footbridge. **Ahaura** village **(5)** sprang up by the east landing of the Ahaura Ferry, which was replaced by a bridge in 1879. That tributary's name may be a corruption of Ōhauroa (long cliff; Ahaura pā was protected by its high east bank).[249]

After driving through Ahaura we followed SH7 across Ahaura and Totara Flats. At the far end of the Big Grey Bridge we turned right and headed south on Snowy Creek Road. It was flanked by red lichen-covered tailings deposited by the Snowy River gold dredge, which stopped working in 1957. We inspected the remains of the Waiuta Mine's powerhouse, quartz battery, and the cyanide tanks where gold was extracted from crushed-up quartz until 1951. A few kilometres further on we crossed the Alexander River near the sites of the powerhouse and battery of the Alexander Mine, which closed in 1943. James Hurley and local farmer Loftus McVicar found the last unexploited auriferous quartz reef in this region on a spur above this tributary of the Big Grey River/Pōhaturoa River in 1921.

Beneath the bush-covered Old Man Gravels and segments of outwash surfaces that formed below piedmont glaciers on the eastern side of the Grey-Inangahua Depression during successive glaciations lies Greenland Greywacke laced with auriferous quartz reefs. The 35-kilometre Lake Hochstetter and Nelson Creek Water Race was commissioned in 1878 to supply pressurised water to sluicing claims on this section of the Golden Line (see Page 295). The world's largest gold dredge, *Grey River No 1*, excavated the south bank of the Grey River/Māwheranui opposite Blackball Creeks in the 1890s. The Paparoa portion of the Grey Valley-Reefton Lodes began to be exploited in 1868.

Greymouth was not connected by road to the rich quartz mines in the Waimaunga (or Blackwater) branch of the Little Grey/Māwheraiti Valley until 1879. A road connection had previously been established to them from Reefton via Waimaunga (or Reefton) Saddle so they were apportioned to Inangahua County, instead of Grey County, when Westland and Nelson Provinces were dis-established in 1876.

In 1905 the rich Blackwater reef was discovered near the source of the Waimaunga (Blackwater) tributary of the Grey River/Māwheranui. It was located under a high drift terrace that formed more than 200,000 years ago during the Waimaunga Glaciation. Waiuta township sprang up by the first shaft, which was later used to ventilate the **Waiuta Mine (10)**. It was the country's second-richest gold mine until 1952, when the collapse of the old Blackwater Shaft forced it to close. After the last dance was held in Waiuta the dance hall was trucked to Cobden and converted to a Scout Den.

When I visited Waiuta in 1965, seven buildings were still standing. They included the hospital and the mine office by the poppet head above the mine's 879-metre Prohibition Shaft. The mine office was unlocked, the floor was littered with blank forms, and its big steel safe was open. Only one house was still standing three decades later when Andrew and I followed the miners' track from Waiuta to the site of the Big River gold mine in Big River Ecological Reserve. That mine opened in 1890 and closed in 1942 due to labour shortages. Although the hotel and mine office had disappeared a nearby hut had clearly been built with recycled timber. We inspected the mine's winches, boiler house, and the poppet head above the 537-metre mineshaft. Next day we followed a bush track to the upper Inangahua Valley section of SH7. On the way we passed the 10-head Golden Lead Battery, which had been sledged up the stony bed of Deep Creek by a team of bullocks.

Adam and I followed Snowy Road over a bush-clad ridge between Conical Hill and Gentle Annie Gorge to the O'Carroll homestead in McVicar Flat and obtained permission to camp further up the flat. After lunch we followed a bulldozed track through tāwhai/silver beech woods on the true right bank of the Big Grey River/Pōhaturoa to Newcombe Flat at the end of Palmers Road.

In January 1860 Governor Gore-Browne's Land Purchase Officer James Mackay and his three Māori guides walked from Nelson to Māwhera pā via the ancient west coast trail through the 'Great Valley' of the Alpine Fault between steep granite spurs of the Victoria Range and truncated schist spurs of the Southern Alps/Kā Tiritiri o te Moana. They blazed that trail over Mary-Maruia Saddle between the Maruia Valley and the confluence of the Blue (or Clear) and Brown Grey Rivers and then followed the true left bank of the Big Grey River/Pōhaturoa through Gentle Annie Gorge to the Waipuna Plain.

Mackay recognised the spot that he and his cousin Alexander had reached when Tarapuhi had guided them up the Grey River/ Māwheranui Valley in 1859 and found the depot of potatoes that Tarapuhi had left there two days ago as they had arranged. It was opposite the confluence of the tributary that James had named after his cousin, Alexander Mackay. Mackay's party caught up with Tarapuhi and his companion, John Rochford, and were ferried down to Māwhera pā in their waka. Julius Haast and James Burnett followed at a slower pace, examining rocks and plants, and mapping the landscapes that they passed through.

A few years later track-cutters cleared the Maruia-Grey Stock Track along the route of that ancient trail and drovers began to graze sheep and cattle on the open river flats that it crossed. In 1862 Major Richard Newcombe of Starborough Station and his partner, Alfred Dommet, took up the 70,000-acre Blue Grey Run, which included all the grassy flats above the Waipuna Plain, and stocked it with cattle from St James Station via Ada Pass and the upper Maruia Valley.

Samuel Mackley acquired the 4000-acre Waipuna Run on the grassy flat below Gentle Annie Gorge and stocked it with sheep via Amuri Pass and the Ahaura Valley.[250]

In January 1988 Adam and I drove over Lewis Pass to Springs Junction in the Maruia Valley, where SH65 peels off SH7 and heads north down the Maruia Valley towards its junction with SH6 in the Buller/ Kawatiri Valley. Next day we followed SH7 to the foot of Rahu Saddle on the Victoria Range, then turned left and followed Palmers Road over Mary-Maruia Saddle and down the true left bank of the Big Grey River/Pōhaturoa to Newcombes by the confluence of the Robinson River, which Mackay had named after the Superintendent of Nelson Province. I had a chat with the manager of Blue Grey Farm, who remarked that few visitors came up the valley; however, several years earlier a bulldozer had arrived after being driven through the bush on Nancy-Tass Saddle from the Kopara (kōparapara/bellbird) Settlement in the Ahaura Valley.

We drove back up the road to an empty grassy clearing called Palmers, parked the car by the northern end of the bridge over the Blue Grey River, which is the master stream of the Big Grey River/Pōhaturoa, and followed a good track through mixed tāwhai/silver beech and tāwhairaunui/red beech woodland on the river's true right bank in Waiheke State Forest (now Lake Christabel Conservation Area). A couple of hours from the road the track crossed the massive landslip that had dammed the river over 1000 years ago and created Lake Christabel. One hundred and twenty kilometres from the sea, it is full of large land-locked tuna/eels. Sediment is filtered out of the Blue [or Clear] Grey River as it percolates through that landslide, which excluded non-native fish until 1995, when trout were illegally introduced into this Fauna Reserve. The track skirted the northern shore of that lake and then crossed a flat covered with dead trees that had been killed when the lake level rose for a while. At the top of that flat we crossed the Rough Creek swing bridge to **Lake Christabel Hut (11)**.

Next day we forded the Blue Grey River and followed the Robinson Saddle Track up its true left bank. When it climbed above the sub-alpine scrub we descended to the banks of the infant river, which tumbled

The view of the source of the master
stream of the Grey River/Māwheranui,
the Blue (or Clear) Grey tributary of
the Big Grey/Pōhaturoa River, when
Adam and I climbed Mt Boscawen
from Lake Christabel Hut in 1988.

The view across the head cirque
of the Robinson Valley of Mt Baron
(1,806m) on the Main Divide (on
the right) from Mt Boscawen.

through a long grassy glen. We ascended it for a while, then climbed onto a dip in the Main Divide, which trampers call Boscawen Saddle.

The clouds lifted as we headed south along the Main Divide to the summit of **Mount Boscawen (12)**. Looking down I saw the Blue Grey River emerge from a small scree on the west flank of that peak. In 1872 a mob of stray cattle was driven up the Robinson Valley, over a dip on the Main Divide on the northern side of Mount Boscawen and then down the Doubtful, Hope, and Waiau Valleys to Culverden where the drover was arrested when he attempted to sell them.[251] **Mount Baron (13)** was distinguished by its small snow cap on the opposite side of the head cirque of the Robinson Valley, where the Hochstetter Range meets the Main Divide. At 1806 metres, its summit is the highest point on the portion of the Main Divide that bounds the Grey/Māwheranui Catchment and the tri-point where the boundaries of Westland, Nelson, and Canterbury Land Registration Districts meet.

Hugh Boscawen worked for the Lands and Survey Department

The first view of Hope Pass (951m) on the Main Divide when my son Julian and I climbed onto it from St Jacob Hut in the upper Hope Valley in 1994.

before he became Governor Onslow's private secretary and later toured the west coast with him in 1892. Mount Baron was originally named after the department's manager who was the Under-Secretary of Crown Lands at that time, Alexander Barron. Its name was presumably changed to Baron to avoid confusion with Mount Barron in the Ōtira Valley.

In April 1994 my son Julian and I took the Main North Road out of Christchurch and SH7 from Waipara to the Windy Point near the confluence of the Hope and Boyle Rivers. We left the car in the car park, crossed the adjacent footbridge over the Boyle River, and then followed the Hope Valley Track through honey-scented tāwhai/black beech woodland on the north bank of the Hope River. Four hours up the track we crossed the upper Hope River via a footbridge in its narrow gorge.

We left the Hope Track at the end of the footbridge and scrambled up to the farm track that skirts the gorge and descends to the long grassy flats in the section of the valley above the gorge called the St. Jacob Valley. Daylight was fading when we dropped our packs in the old

Forestry Hut at the southern end of St Jacob Flat. An entry in the hut book posed the question, 'Who was St. Jacob?' Gerald Ducarel bestowed biblical names on several valleys in this area during the 1860s. Being French he would have called James the disciple and Jacob the patriarch, Jacque.

In the morning we followed a bulldozed track to the northern end of St Jacob Flat, which was fringed by deciduous whauwhi/ eastern mountain ribbonwood trees. Their leaves had already turned yellow. We carried on up the true right bank of the infant Hope River until we spotted a stone cairn. It marked the start of a good track, which we followed through groves of kotukutuku/tree fuchsia and neinei/'pineapple trees' to the open summit of **Hope Pass (15)**. At 951 metres above sea level, it is the lowest spot on the portion of the Main Divide that bounds the Grey/Māwheranui Catchment.

Rain was moving up the Tūtaekuri (dog turd) Branch of the Ahaura Valley on the north-western side of the pass. The name of that valley implies that Māori travellers regarded that transalpine route as a poor alternative to the **Amuri Pass/Nōti Waiheke (14)** route. We beat a fast retreat, but the rain overtook us before we reached the hut. The run holder, John Shearer, arrived an hour later to muster his calves for a pre-winter sale. He said that Hope Pass was his 'open back door' and asked us if we had seen any stock near it.

In 1861 John Rochford and his Māori guide followed an old trail over the Nancy-Tass Saddle from the Big Grey River/Pōhaturoa Valley and ascended the bed of the Waiake (Waiheke – 'descending water') tributary of the Ahaura River to a Main Divide pass labelled 'Waiaki' (Nōti Waiheke) on the 1859 Kaikōura Purchase deed plan. Rochford's guide told him that the 'Waiaki' trail through the mountain ranges east of the Grey/Māwheranui Valley was never blocked by snow.

A year later Rochford and Isaac Freeth, who had leased part of Edward Lee's pastoral run on Ahaura Flat in the Grey/Māwheranui Valley, blazed the 'Waiaki Pass' route between the Grey and Amuri Districts of Nelson Province. Rochford renamed it Amuri Pass and reported that it was a viable route to drive sheep and cattle to the west coast. A month later Samuel Mackley cut a track over Amuri Pass from his run on Waipuna Flat. In September 1863 he and Henry Jacobsen drove 100 sheep and two heifers from Amuri District to Waipuna Station via that track.[252]

The view across the Taramakau Valley of
Mt Alexander (1,958m) on the Kaimatā
Range when Julian and I climbed Kellys
Hill from the Ōtira Valley in 1999.

When gold was discovered near Waipuna Station in 1868, Mackley
opened an accommodation house, store and bakery at **Ikamātua (6)**
near the confluence of the Big Grey River/Pōhaturoa and Little Grey
River/Māwheraiti. The Nelson Provincial Government upgraded the
Ahaura-Amuri Track around the same time, but 13 years later it was
reported to be overgrown and hardly ever used.

In 2009 Andrew and I followed the old stock track up the Doubtful
Valley and over Amuri Pass. Reconstruction of this track, with the

Backcountry Trust's support, had only advanced a few kilometres down the western side. As they had done on Arthur's Pass and Harper Pass, drovers had burned-off the flammable 'turpentine scrub'/*Dracophyllum longifolium* to clear the crest of Amuri Pass and encourage grass to grow on it to feed passing stock. We descended a steep side track to the Waiheke Riverbed and followed it down to Slatey Creek Hut. It was built by the Internal Affairs Department in 1952, shortly before the Forestry Department took over its deer control duties. Next day we tramped across long grassy flats, forded the fast-flowing Tūtaekuri River, and then followed a dirt extension of Ahaura-Amuri Road through head-high gorse to Waikiti Downs Station in the Kopara Farm Settlement, where Evelyn picked us up.

In Julian's last year at high school he and I drove to the Ōtira Valley and climbed Kelly Hill as I had done when I was his age. It gave us a grandstand view of **Mount Alexander (16)** at the western end of the Kaimatā Range, which is being squeezed up between the Clarence, Hope and Alpine Faults. I pointed out the ascent route up a steep stream bed that Terry and I had taken in 1984 and our campsite high on the south ridge where I fell asleep while Terry cooked dinner on the Primus. I had worked all night before we left Christchurch. At 1958 metres above sea level, the summit of Mount Alexander is the highest point in the Grey River/Māwheranui Catchment. John Rochford renamed that landmark after Alexander Mackay, who had crossed Harper Pass/Nōti Taramakau with him in May 1859 to assist his cousin, James Mackay, in the first round of the Arahura Purchase negotiations. Alexander was subsequently appointed Commissioner of Native Reserves in the South Island.

One of Rochford's Māori guides told him that this prominent peak was called Kaimatā ('to chew the hard stones'[253] or 'to eat raw food'[254]), which could imply that it is the tipua-guardian of this area and its important alpine passes (see Page 163). Julius Haast and Arthur Dobson spelled that name 'Kaimatau' and thought that it was the original name of Mount Rolleston. The mountain range on the northern side of the upper Arahura Valley may have represented another 'stone-eater', Kanioro (see Page 314). The thin kūrūpākāra/schist saws that Māori artisans used to cut grooves in slabs of pounamu/nephrite came from the Haast Schist Zone in the fastest rising portion of the Alps alongside the Alpine Fault.

Legend

1.	Charleston	10.	Mt Travers
2.	Westport	11.	Mt Franklin
3.	Denniston	12.	Mt Mackay
4.	Inangahua	13.	Blue Lake Hut
5.	Reefton	14.	Sabine Hut
6.	Murchison	15.	Wairau Pass/Maunga Tāwhai
7.	Mt Murchison/Tāhuatao	16.	Beebys Knob
8.	St Arnaud village	17.	Lewis Pass/Kopi o Kai Tāngata
9.	Upper Travers Hut		

Chapter 24
The Buller/Kawatiri

In January 1993 I drove Evelyn, three-year-old Sybil, and four teenagers from Christchurch to Karamea on the west coast. We followed SH7 over Lewis Pass/Kai o Tāngata (17) on the Main Divide and then Rahu Saddle on the Victoria Range to Reefton in the Inangahua Valley. That town sprang up in 1870 when the first rich gold-bearing quartz reef in this district was discovered nearby at the head of Murray Creek. Like many other west coast towns that were originally based on mining and forestry, Reefton has turned into a farming and tourist hub.

We left SH7 there and followed SH69 down the Inangahua Valley to **Inangahua village (4)** and then SH6 through the lower Buller/Kawatiri Gorge to Carters Beach Motor Camp. Next day we crossed the new

My daughter Sybil on the South
Breakwater at the mouth of the
Buller River/Kawatiri, where
this upriver story begins.

Buller Bridge to **Westport (2)** and then followed SH67 up the coast to
Karamea township by the Karamea (Kakara Taramea – a sweet scented
gum extracted from taramea/spear grass or 'wild Spaniard') River.[255]
After dropping the trampers off at the start of the Heaphy Track by the
Kōhaihai River mouth, Sybil and I returned to Westport

We had four days to fill in before it was time to pick up the trampers
at the northern end of the track in Golden Bay/Mohua. Before we left
Westport we drove to the end of South Tip Head Road and watched a
fishing boat cross the calm Buller River/Kawatiri bar. Looking eastward
across the narrow coastal plain, I spotted the lower Buller/Kawatiri
Gorge between Mount Rochford and the Buckland Peaks. The river had
evidently maintained its straight course to the sea by carving that gorge
through the slowly rising coastal ranges.

Kawatiri (Kawatere – 'deep fast-flowing river') was the original
name of this great river. With a mean flow of 417 cumecs and a 6350
square-kilometre water catchment area, it is the largest on the west
coast. Thomas Brunner and Charles Heaphy wanted to rename it after
the New Zealand Land Settlement Company's Nelson agent William

Fox, but Fox renamed it after Charles Buller, who was a director of that London-based company and a Liberal Member of Parliament.

Paparoa (broad back) was the original name of the flat-topped ridge that stretches north from Mount Rochford on the northern side of the lower Buller/Kawatiri Gorge. The name Paparoa was also attached to the southern extension of that ridge from the Buckland Peaks to Mount Davy on the northern side of the Brunner Gorge in the Grey/Māwheranui Valley.[256] The Karamea granite core of those ranges is being squeezed up like a pip between the longitudinal Inangahua and Cape Farewell Fault Zones. About 35 million years ago those parallel faults flanked a swamp-filled rift valley. The Buller Coalfield formed when its peat beds were buried beneath layers of sandstone and limestone and then submerged by the sea. The Inangahua Coalfield east of the Paparoa Range formed in an estuarine environment as this region emerged from the sea between 16 and 22 million years ago.

When Julius Haast and James Burnett completed their geological and topographical survey of the Grey District of Nelson Province in 1860, they turned their attention to the Buller District. John Rochford had begun that task a year earlier but had to abandon it when the canoe that his party was travelling in capsized in the Buller River/Kawatiri above its lower gorge. They lost all their food and spare clothes and had to retreat to the mouth of that river to await the return of the cutter *Supply*, which had dropped them off there. Rochford led them over the Paparoa Range on the northern side of the river, which he had surveyed from his namesake peak before the ill-fated canoe trip. When they descended the Waimangaroa (Waimangaroa – 'long black river'[257]) Riverbed he observed that it was littered with coal.

Haast followed up Rochford's discovery and found an eight-foot seam of bituminous coal at Burnett's Face above a branch of the Waimangaroa Valley, which Haast named Coalbrookdale. He named the plateau and peak above this valley after John Rochford and the granite peaks on the southern side of the Buller Gorge after English geologist William Buckland. In 1873 the 'Mount Rochford Plateau' was renamed after John **Denniston (3)** who had completed the preliminary survey of that coalfield by Haast and Burnett.

In 1965 the new geography teacher at Greymouth High School, John Waugh, took my class on a tour of coalmines in Buller and Murchison Counties. We spent two nights in Carters Beach Motor Camp and drove up to the Denniston Plateau on a fine sunny day. There I saw several metres of overburden being stripped off a thick coal seam and peered down the 47-degree Denniston Incline to its terminus in Waimangaroa, 1670 metres below on the narrow coastal plain. Railway wagons filled with seven tons of coal shot down that incline on a continuous wire rope, which pulled up the empty wagons on a parallel track.

Rochford spotted some gold flakes in the Waimangaroa Riverbed and in a side stream 25 miles up the Buller River/Kawatiri. The headwaters of those rivers erode auriferous quartz reefs in 450 million-year-old Greenland greywacke around Karamea Granite peaks in the Lyell Range, which Haast named after the famous Scottish geologist Charles Lyell. Māori prospectors from Golden Bay/Mohua had the Buller District of Nelson Province to themselves until news of their finds sparked the Buller gold rush in April 1861.

In June of that year Collingwood merchants Reuben Waite and T S Rogers entered the Buller River/Kawatiri in the ketch *Jane* and established Westport's first store in a vacant riverside hut. The shantytown that sprang up on the sandy flat between the river mouth and North Beach was the first Pākehā settlement on the west coast. In 1862 Thomas Brunner cut survey lines for a new township to be known as Westport at a safe distance from the sea and the river, which were encroaching on the sandy flat from both sides.

In November 1863 diggers rushed to the new 'Māori Diggings' by the Lyell tributary of the Buller River/Kawatiri, 15 kilometres above the Old Diggings in the lower Buller/Kawatiri Gorge, Supplies were barged through this gorge to the Inangahua Landing near the Lyell Confluence. It took three or four men four days to pole their broad-beamed boats upriver to that landing. Whenever they reached a rapid two horses were off-loaded to tow the boat up that section. In 1864 many Buller diggers abandoned their claims and rushed off to newly discovered goldfields in Central Otago and West Canterbury.

When Westport was founded it took at least 18 days to get there from Nelson via the Buller Valley Track. Two years later, improvements to the Porika and Braeburn sections of that track cut the average travel time to six days. The original track climbed over a huge obstacle in the lower gorge called Hawk Crag until 1869 when a contractor blasted a half tunnel in its sheer face. The river level is usually 15 metres below the road at that point, however enormous floods have inundated the half-tunnel several times. That difficult section of the Buller Valley Track did not become a coach road until 1878, however the coach road between Westport and **Charleston (1)** was completed in 1866. The bridle track that continued down the coast to Cobden opened in 1873 and became the Westport-Greymouth section of SH6 in the 1930s.

Westport's first wharf was built in 1877. Most of the output from the Buller Coalfields passed through it from then until 1943, when Westport was linked by rail to the Port of Lyttelton on the east coast. From 1879 until 1967, coal from Denniston Plateau mines was railed from Waimangaroa to Westport via the newly opened Mount Rochford Railway Line. In 1896 the Millerton Incline began to deliver coal from Stockton Plateau mines to bins on the line's new railhead in Granity.

In 1888 a timber truss railway bridge was built across the Buller River/Kawatiri to transport blocks of Karamea granite, which are studded with big pink feldspar crystals, from a quarry on Cape Foulwind to the North Tip Head. The river was dredged to allow larger colliers to berth in Westport. Its new breakwaters narrowed the river mouth to 300 metres and forced the current to scour the bar. When that project was finished the railway track was lifted and the rail bridge became a single-lane road bridge, which survived the largest flood that has ever been recorded in a New Zealand river. It measured 11,300 cumecs and inundated part of Westport in 1926.[258] A concrete two-lane bridge replaced the old one in 1976.

The first permanent settlers in Buller District were the semi-mythical Kāhui a Rapuwai (or Pātea) people who were said to have migrated from the Pātea district in Taranaki. Pakohe/indurated siltstone adzes from the D'Urville Island/Rangitoto ki te Tonga, matā tūhua/obsidian from Tūhua/Mayor Island, and a few pounamu/nephrite items from Arahura district that have been found in a fourteenth century settlement site by the mouth of the Buller River/Kawatiri. A gift exchange system had evidently been established around the shores of the inter-island strait by that time. Te Pātea were absorbed in the sixteenth century by two successive waves of migrants from the Whanganui district: Ngāti Tūmata Kōkiri settled in the Buller district and Ngāti Wairangi settled in the districts that lay south of the Paparoa Range.

Clashes between those tribes and Ngāi Tahu over hunting rights in the upper Waiau Valley incited Tuhuru and Te Wharekino, and their Ngāti Apa allies in Mohua/Golden Bay to launch a successful pincer attack on Ngati Tūmata Kōkiri's last stronghold by the mouth of the Karamea River. While Tuhuru's taua marched up the west coast, Te Wharekino's taua crossed the Alps from Kaiapoi (see Page 49). Tuhuru and Wharetai had seized control of the central and southern west coast around 1810. Seizure of the Karamea district enabled Tuhuru to extend his chiefdom further north to Kahurangi Point.

In 1828 the Ngāti Rārua rangatira, Te Niho, wrested the Tai Tapu district north of Kahurangi Point from Ngāti Apa and settled at Paturau by Whanganui/Westhaven Inlet. In 1832 he and his Ngāti Tama ally, Takerei, led a taua down the coast and captured Tuhuru near Hokitika, then ransomed him for an annual tribute of pounamu/nephrite. Two years after the death of Te Puoho in Murihiku, Te Niho retreated to Tai Tapu beyond Kahurangi Point and Ngāti Waewae rangatira re-asserted their authority in Buller and Karamea districts by attacking a Ngāti Rārua camp beside Ōtūkoroiti Point, planting kūmara/sweet potato gardens at intervals along the coastal trail, and establishing Ōmau nohoanga near Cape Foulwind.

In 1844 Joseph Thoms landed a sealing gang on Black Reef off Cape Foulwind and steered his schooner *The Three Brothers* into the Buller/Kawatiri River. Thoms found a sign written in English on the riverbank that instructed someone to follow the writer up the coast to Tai Tapu.[259] A few west coast residents had been taught to read and write at the Wesleyan mission station in Port Underwood. Alternatively, a sealer could have written that mysterious message. Thomas Brunner's guide Kehu said that two shipwrecked sealers had walked up the coast and were killed by Te Niho in Tai Tapu to avenge the abduction of his daughter by some other sealers.[260]

Thomas Brunner and Charles Heaphy had a hard job persuading Te Niho to allow them to cross Tai Tapu with Kehu en route to the west coast in 1846. The Top of the South tribes maintain that their rohe extended to the Arahura River in 1840. In 2007 the Waitangi Tribunal determined that their manawhenua and that of Ngāi Tahu overlap north of a line from the source of the Buller River/Kawatiri behind Lake Rotoiti to its mouth.[261] Governor Grey attempted to extinguish the native titles of Ngāti Rārua, Ngāti Tama, Te Āti Awa, and Ngāti Apa in the central and northern west coast with the 1853 Waipounamu Purchase. The Crown subsequently offered them further redress and accepted that their ancestral rohe included the upper Buller/Kawatiri Valley. It was excluded from the 1860 West Coast Purchase agreement with Poutini Ngāi Tahu, the borders of which are reflected in the borders of West Coast Region.

After watching the Buller River/Kawatiri flow into the sea, Sybil and I followed SH6 back through its lower gorge. Seven kilometres beyond Hawk Crag we stopped for lunch in the old Berlins Hotel. A notice on the wall explained that it was the upper floor of the Welcome Inn in Lyell until 1943, when it was dismantled and re-erected on the site of the Old Diggings Hotel, which John Berlin had opened in Berlins in 1874. A list of the 17 earthquakes that had rocked this district since the 1840s also caught my eye.

Twelve kilometres further on, by the confluence of the Buller/ Kawatiri and Inangahua (plentiful inanga/*galaxiidae* fish) Rivers, we passed the intersection of SH69 in **Inangahua (4)**. Werita Tainui told James Stack that Kōhanga Pōraka was its original name. A Road Services bus from Greymouth used to connect with the Newmans bus service from Westport to Nelson outside the Inangahua Hotel. In 1968 the magnitude 7.1 Inangahua earthquake wrecked every building in this village and generated almost three metres of uplift near its epicentre to the north near the Lyell Range. Charles Lyell was the first geologist to link earthquakes with active fault lines.

Fifteen kilometres past the Inangahua we crossed the Iron Bridge over the Buller River/Kawatiri, which replaced a punt ferry in 1890, and passed the site of Lyell's last building, the Post Office Hotel, which burned down in 1962. That town sprang up on the 'Maori Diggings' by the confluence of the Lyell River.

The Buller River/Kawatiri carved its middle gorge between the Lyell Range and the northern end of the Victoria Range. Those contiguous Paparoa Granite ranges run longitudinally across the Buller/Kawatiri Catchment and are being squeezed up at a mean rate of five millimetres per year between re-activated parallel fault lines just like the Paparoa Range.

I stopped to inspect the huge landslide that had briefly dammed the Buller River/Kawatiri in its middle gorge after the Inangahua Earthquake. I also stopped to read a plaque by the place where SH6 crosses the White Creek Fault near the epicentre of the 1929 magnitude 7.8 Murchison earthquake in which 17 people died. The road on the western side of that fault rose five metres and moved two and a half metres northward.

A bit further on we crossed Eight Mile (or Boundary) Creek, which marks the boundary between the jurisdictions of Buller District and West Coast Regional Councils and Tasman District Council. The latter includes the upper Buller/Kawatiri Catchment. Ngāti Apa ki Te Rā Tō holds manawhenua there.

Seven kilometres past the old coach stop and stables by the Newton River, which drains the peak that Haast named after Isaac Newton, we crossed the Buller River/Kawatiri above the confluence of the Maruia River via the O'Sullivan Bridge, which was named after a gold miner. In 1961 a heavily laden truck fell through the deck of the 1909 O'Sullivan Bridge in the upper Buller Gorge. For the next 14 years a bailey bridge kept SH6 open between there and Inangahua Junction until it was replaced by a new O'Sullivan Bridge in 1975, the opening ceremony for which was attended by the truck driver who had survived that accident.

At the southern end of that bridge we passed the junction of SH65 from Springs Junction, which bypasses a narrow section of the Maruia Valley via the Shenandoah and Rappahannock side valleys. We carried on up the south bank of the Buller River/Kawatiri to **Murchison (6)**, which was originally named Hampden after the English Civil War battlefield. It was the service centre of Murchison County before it was incorporated into Buller District and is the hub of the isolated farming settlement on the Four Rivers Plain/Mātakitaki (fine river view). The Maruia, Mātakitaki, Mangles/Tūtaki, and Matiri Rivers join the Buller River/Kawatiri in that large down-faulted basin, which is surrounded by ridges of near vertical Brunner Sandstone strata capped by a horizontal bed of Cobden limestone. Tāwhai/silver beech trees and pinus radiata plantations now cover many of their burnt-off northern faces.

In 1863 a prospector named George Moonlight, who had worked on the Californian goldfields, found alluvial gold in the Mātakitaki Valley. He also found a 22-kilometre short cut between the new track over the Braeburn Range and the upper Maruia Valley via the upper Mangles/

Tutaki Valley and Maruia Saddle. The Walker brothers acquired the first run in the upper Maruia Valley and used that short cut to stock it with cattle from Donald McGregor's Braeburn Run in the Mangles/Tutaki Valley. Moonlight's discovery of the richest goldfield in South-West Nelson District on the banks of Moonlight Creek in the Grey/Māwheranui Valley brought him fame but no fortune. He corresponded with his cousin Thomas, who was a general in the United States Army, and named two tributaries of the Maruia River after the Shenandoah and Rappahannock Valleys in East Virginia where Thomas had fought.[262]

In 1874 George Moonlight opened the first general store in Murchison, which was named Hampden in those days. He then bought the original Commercial Hotel and moved it from a flood-prone site by the Mātakitaki River to the village centre. Hampden was established on the south bank of the Buller River/Kawatiri in order to serve farms and gold diggings in the adjacent valleys of three north-flowing tributaries: the Maruia ('river fed by many streams' or 'shady river'), the Mātakitaki, and the Mangles/Tutaki, which was renamed after a New Zealand Company director. The south-flowing Matiri River is the fourth tributary that joins the Buller River/Kawatiri on the Four Rivers Plain/Mātakitaki. Thomas Brunner's guide Kehu called the prominent landmark at the head of that plain Tāhuatao. Haast renamed it **Mount Murchison (7)** after the Scottish geologist who had observed that gold-bearing quartz reefs in basement sedimentary rock were often associated with a granite intrusion. In 1883 Hampden (on-the-Buller) was renamed Murchison to avoid confusion with Hampden (by-the-sea) in Otago.

The original Buller Road stuck to the north bank of the Buller River and bypassed Murchison until the Longford and O'Sullivan Bridges respectively opened in 1900 and 1909. In 1923 Nuggety Point Bridge replaced the old timber truss Longford Bridge near the golf course. The founders of the Newman Brothers bus company, Harry and Tom Newman, drove the first mail coach from Nelson to the Four Rivers Plain/Mātakitaki in 1879. A packhorse carried the mailbag through the Long Ford to Hampden on the opposite bank of the Buller River/Kawatiri.[263] By 1883, contractors had pushed the road end through the upper Buller Gorges to Lyell.

After driving through Murchison we crossed the Mangles River/Tūtaki and the Nuggety Point Bridge over the Buller River/Kawatiri and then followed SH6 up the north bank towards Devil's Grip Gorge. Before we entered this gorge we crossed the Owen River, which drains a lofty range of marble mountains that Julius Haast named after British palaeontologist Richard Owen, and spotted lots of white boulders in its bed. In Devils Grip Gorge between the Hope Range and Mount Murchison/Tāhuatao, pale Separation Point granite appeared in roadside cuttings and landslip scars. It contacts dark 'mafic' magnesium-iron-rich Rotoroa (or Darran) diorite and gabbro magma (see Page 175) in the Muntz and Braeburn Ranges on either side of Lake Rotoroa. They were contiguous with the Darran Range in northern Fiordland before Alpine Fault movements dragged them far apart. The Separation Point 'batholith' formed 100 million years ago near the end of the 'Rangitata' mountain building era when an enormous bed of sediments deposited by ancient rivers on the converging Pacific plate compressed the rim of Gondwanaland until a down-fold of its greywacke basement rock melted and metamorphosed into silicon-rich granite. The parallel Hōhonu and Karamea batholiths formed in the same way about 350 million years ago in the 'Tūhua Orogeny' mountain building era.

Five kilometres beyond the confluence of the Gowan River, which issues from Lake Rotoroa, we left the banks of the Buller River/Kawatiri at Kawatiri Junction and followed SH6 up the Hope Valley en route to Nelson. Kawatiri Station was the terminus of the unfinished Nelson-Inangahua Railway Line from 1926 until 1931; Glenhope was its terminus from then until the line closed in 1955.

SH6 crosses Hope Saddle on the Pinchback Range, which David Clark found in 1863, between the Clark branch of the Motueka Valley and the Hope branch of the Buller/Kawatiri Valley. Glenhope is a blind side valley in northern England, however this one was probably named after the Secretary of State for the Colonies in Robert Peel's Ministry. The Nelson-Glenhope Railway Line followed a parallel route through Belgrove Tunnel in the Spooner Range and Tadmor Saddle on the Pinchback Range.

Before the forerunner of SH6 was constructed over Hope Saddle most westbound travellers followed the Wairau Track up the Motupiko branch of the Motueka Valley and then the Porika (Pōreke – 'parakeet') Track over the Muntz Range from Speargrass Flat to the outlet of Lake

Rotoroa, and then the Tūtaki Track over the Braeburn Range to the Mangles/Tūtaki Valley, which led to the Four Rivers Plain/Mātakitaki. Electricity transmission lines take the same route from the Kikiwa Substation in the Motupiko Valley to Murchison.

In 1866 a horse bridge replaced the hazardous ford below the outlet of Lake Rotoroa, which was named the Gowan River after a New Zealand Land Company director. It took five years to construct the road through Devil's Grip Gorge between the Hope and Braeburn Ranges to the Four Rivers Plain/Mātakitaki. Charles Heaphy coined that name in 1843 after dense scrub laced with thorny tataramoa/'bush lawyer' on jumbled boulders thwarted his first attempt to descend this gorge.

At the head of the Hope Valley we followed SH6 over the Pinchback Range to the Motueka Valley and then over the Spooner Range to the Waimea Plain and then up the eastern shore of Tasman Bay to Nelson. Two days later we followed SH60 westward along the shore of Te Tai o Aorere, over the marble-topped Pikikiruna Range and around Golden Bay/Mohua, to Collingwood by the mouth of the Aorere River. We then drove up the Aorere Valley to Browns Hut and found our five trampers waiting outside on the grass nursing their sore feet.

In January 1988 Evelyn and I drove over Lewis Pass to Springs Junction, then down the Maruia Valley and up the Buller/Kawatiri Valley to Kawatiri Junction. On that occasion I followed SH63 further up the banks of that river through Speargrass Flat/Te Ara and finally over a tāwhai/beech-covered terminal moraine ridge to **St Arnaud** village **(8)** on the shore of Kerr Bay at the northern end of Lake Rotoiti ('little roto/lake' – the word roto was imported from tropical Polynesia where it means 'a lagoon inside a coral reef'). The Buller River/Kawatiri nominally begins its 170-kilometre journey to the sea from the bay on the opposite side of the Brunner Peninsula. In 1846 it took Thomas Brunner 170 days to follow its north bank from Lake Rotoiti to the sea with Kehu and Pikiwate and their wives. I learned from a park ranger that the grassy mounds on the shore of Kerr Bay were kakahi/fresh water mussel shell middens. Brunner wrote that he liked them steam-cooked with raupo/bulrush roots in an umu/earth oven.

Speargrass Flat/Te Ara (the trail) was the outwash surface below the terminal moraine of the Travers Glacier during the Ōtira Glaciation. During the Waimaunga Glaciation, a similar flat had formed below the terminal moraine of the Sabine Glacier, which flowed down the Howard/Pukawini Valley before strike-slip movements on the Alpine Fault pushed that side valley out of alignment with the Sabine Valley. The Rotoroa Lakebed used to be occupied by the D'Urville Glacier and the Travers Valley, which contains Lake Rotoiti, used to be aligned with the Motupiko Valley.

In 1842 Nelson surveyors John Cotterill and Richard Peanter followed their Māori guide up the Motupiko Branch of the Motueka Valley to Lake Rotoiti. They climbed a peak on the St Arnaud Range, but failed to spot the inland plain that was rumoured to lie beyond the head of the Wairau Valley. A century later Jack Dumbleton climbed that peak, which he named Mount Cotterill, and then climbed a peak at the head of the Travers Valley, which he named after Brunner's guide Hone Mokekehu or 'Kehu'.[264] Cotterill died at Tuamarina during the 1843 Wairau Affray (see Page 22). William Fox renamed the Pukawini tributary of the Buller River/ Kawatiri after James Howard, who also died there on that tragic day.

In the spring of 1848 George McRae took up the Lake Rotoiti run, which stretched down to the Hope Confluence. He wintered his sheep in the woods around Speargrass Flat/Te Ara. Charles Muntz took up the Howard Run in 1866.[265] Kerr Bay was named after the fourth owner of Lake Rotoiti Station, who drowned in the lake. Rabbits invaded this area in the 1860s and red deer were introduced in the 1890s. Sheep were driven onto the St Arnaud (or 'No-Catchem') tops every summer and the lake head flats were grazed by cattle until 1956, when the 101,900-hectare Nelson Lakes National Park was established.

Evelyn and I spent the first night on this trip in the Kerr Bay camping ground at the northern end of Lake Rotoiti. A loud kōparapara/bellbird chorus roused us at first light. After breakfast we stuffed provisions for seven days into our packs and followed the track along the lake's eastern shore. We had lunch in Lakehead Hut, which offered some respite from the hot midday sun. On the far side of Lakehead Flat we picked up the Travers Valley Track and followed it in the welcome shade of tāwhairauriki/mountain beech trees to John Tait Hut.

Another fine day dawned the next morning so we decided to climb **Mount Travers (10)** on the way to Upper Travers Hut. When we reached Summit Creek we stashed our packs behind a fallen tree and ascended its lightly wooded true left bank. Above the tree line we carried on climbing through alpine grasslands and herb fields until we reached the creek's source at the base of the north face of Mount Travers. We scrambled up a steep rubble-filled couloir and then ascended a gentler slope to the tall trig station on top of Mount Travers. By that time a sheet of altostratus cloud had filled the sky and the summit was buffeted by a brisk westerly wind.

Looking southward along the Main Divide I spotted Mount Una and saw the East Sabine River flowing northward from the centre of the Spenser Knot in a deep U-shaped valley between **Mount Mackay (12)** on the Main Divide and **Mount Franklin (11)** on the snow-streaked Franklin Ridge. At 2340 metres above sea level, the summit of Mount Franklin is the highest point in the Buller/Kawatiri Catchment and Tasman District and merely two metre higher than Mount Travers (if one ignores the latter's trig station). At 2300 metres above sea level, the summit of Mount Mackay is the highest point on the portion of the Main Divide that bounds the Wairau and Buller Catchments (see Page 28).

Daylight was fading when Evelyn and I left the woods and crossed a grassy clearing to **Upper Travers Hut (9)** near the base of Kehu Peak. I nearly stepped on two people who were lying amongst the tussocks outside the hut. One of them sat up and introduced himself. That is how I met Dave Clark and his daughter Bridget; Dave said that they had been lying back admiring a crimson cloud that had appeared over Mount Travers. He invited us to have dinner with his family when we returned to St Arnaud in four days' time. We have been close friends ever since.

That lenticular cloud was a harbinger of the strong wind that we encountered next day on Travers Saddle between Mount Travers and the Main Divide. We dropped our packs behind a rock and strolled over some smooth rock knolls to the tarn-source of the Travers River, which is the ultimate source of the Buller River/Kawatiri. We then scrambled up a scree slope to Rainbow Col. Now and then an extra strong gust of wind made us stagger. Peering down the other side I saw dust clouds rising in the Rainbow Branch of the Wairau Valley.

We retrieved our packs and followed the track down the western

The view of Mt Mackay (2,300m) on the
Main Divide and Mt Franklin (2,340m) on
Franklin Ridge (on the right) when my wife
Evelyn and I climbed Mt Travers from John
Tait Hut in the Travers Valley in 1988.

side of Travers Saddle to the banks of the East Sabine River, however
the clouds opened before we reached the trees. The East Sabine River
was crossed before I realised that it must have been at the bottom of
a deep slit gorge under the short bridge on the valley floor. When we
reached the old Forks Hut one of the occupants told me that a gust of
wind had caught her off balance and she had cut her finger on a rock
that we had noticed in passing – because of the blood spatters – below
Travers Saddle. She had dressed the wound and planned to walk out to
the road in the morning.

The wind died and the sky cleared overnight so the next morning
we crossed the footbridges over the two branches of the Sabine River
just above their confluence and then followed the track up the true left
bank of the West Sabine River. After crossing an old avalanche path

The view of the tarn-source of the master
stream of the Buller River/Kawatiri, the
Travers River, on Travers Saddle, with
Mt Travers in the background, from
Rainbow Col when Evelyn and I crossed
that saddle from Travers Hut in 1988.

flanked by shattered tree trunks, we left the track and forded the river.
I foolishly opted to carry my boots to keep them dry and almost lost
them when I stumbled in midstream.

We then made a beeline through tāwhairauriki/mountain beech
woods to a stream that emerged from a huge scree fan on the west flank
of Mount Franklin. This was the route up Mount Franklin that I had
picked in the *Nelson Lakes National Park* handbook. However, it was
three steps forward and two steps back until we reached some ledges
that we could clamber up to the summit ridge. The summit cairn was
100 metres further on. Banks of mist drifted by on the light sou'west
breeze and between them we caught fleeting glimpses of Mount Mackay.
We also saw Brocken Spectres around the shadows of our heads when
the sun's rays cast them onto the mist.

After picking our way carefully over frost-shattered rocks on the other side of the summit, we then scrambled down a rubble-filled gully and enjoyed a long scree run down to the spot where we had left our packs. A pair of pīwauwau/rock wrens bobbed about on a big boulder eyeing us intently as we ate a few biscuits before we returned to the track. We reached **Blue Lake Hut (13)** just before dark to find a party of trampers had arrived an hour before us after crossing Waiau Pass. In the morning we carried mugs of tea down to the shore of Blue Lake and admired the reflections of trees and mountains in its gin-clear water, which has been judged the most translucent in New Zealand. Its inflow filters through the old landslide that dams Lake Constance at the head of this valley.

After breakfast we followed the Sabine Track down to Lake Rotoroa. On the way we saw lots of small white balls called strawberry fungi in the beds of side streams. They grow on the trunks of tāwhai/beech trees and related trees in southern Chile. When winds shake them off they roll down banks and end up in streams. We sat on a fallen tree trunk and watched a toutouwai/bush robin peck crumbs by our feet while we were eating lunch. The old **Sabine Hut (14)** at the head of Lake Rotoroa was full so we pitched our tent on a nearby beach and crawled inside to escape a horde of hungry namu/sandflies, which battered on the tent walls like raindrops.

Next day we followed the Howard Track over the Muntz Range to the upper Howard Valley. After a short rest in the Howard Shelter we followed the Speargrass Track over a kānuka–covered spur of Robert Ridge at the northern end of the Travers Range and then down the Speargrass/Te Horowai (the landslide stream) Valley to a car park halfway up Pourangahau/Mount Robert. From that vantage point I looked down on West Bay where the Buller River/Kawatiri issues from Lake Rotoiti and then straight along the Alpine Fault line from the Speargrass/Te Horowai Valley to Wairau Pass/Maunga Tāwhai at the northern end of the Main Divide.

Julius Haast climbed Mount Murchison/Tāhuatao on a clear day and saw the upper Buller/Kawatiri Catchment 'laid out like a map'.[266] He identified and named Mounts Newton and Owen and the jagged Lyell Range on the northern horizon, and Mounts Mackay and Franklin beyond the head of Lake Rotoroa, where it is crossed by the Alpine Fault. Haast named the Sabine Valley between those two peaks after British astronomer Edward Sabine, who had elected him to the Royal

The view across Lake Rotoiti of Wairau Pass (675m) on the Main Divide when Evelyn and I reached the car park on Pourangahau/Mt Robert after following the Speargrass Track from Sabine Hut at the head of Lake Rotoroa.

Society of London. Sabine had joined John Franklin's 1818 Arctic expedition. Franklin and every member of his 1845–47 expedition perished in the Arctic. His main objectives were to obtain data about the earth's magnetic field for Sabine and find a northwest passage to the Pacific Ocean.

Haast named two peaks on the Braeburn Range after the pioneer Scottish geologist, James Hutton, and his friend, John Playfair, who had published *Illustrations of the Huttonian Theory of the Earth* in 1802. Three decades after Hutton had deduced the great age of the earth from sedimentary strata on Siccar Point near Edinburgh, Charles Lyell revived his ideas in his famous book, *Principles of Geology*. Pourangahau/Mount Robert at the northern end of the Middle Range was renamed after Haast's eldest son who was living with his deceased wife's parents in Germany. William Travers renamed the Middle Range and its highest peak after his father, General Boyle Travers.

On the way home Evelyn and I stopped at the (third) Tophouse Hotel by the intersection of the Kotere-Tophouse Road and the old access road to Lake Rotoiti Station and had a cup of tea with the proprietors, Mike and Melody Nicholls. Mike told me that this old cob accommodation house was built beside the post office at this road junction in 1875. He had once shown us the site of the second Tophouse Hotel by the intersection of the Rainbow and Wairau Roads on the eastern side of Wairau Pass/Maunga Tāwhai. He then led us to the old cob cottage on the eastern side of the pass that had substituted for George McRae's homestead on Speargrass Flat/Te Ara in a television documentary about Thomas Brunner's epic exploration of the west coast. Mike was still searching for the site of the first Tophouse Hotel, which may have been Morse and Coopers first homestead, somewhere beside the original Wairau Track over **Wairau Pass/Maunga Tāwhai (15)** (see Page 22).

I stopped on top of that pass, where the Old Wairau Road joins SH63, and gazed down the Wairau Valley to the inter-island strait. These geographical journeys had come full circle and times had changed. Knowing the past we take heed for the future, ka muri ka mua.

GLOSSARY

Te Reo Māori
Ahi: fire
Ao: luminosity/cloud
Ara: trail
Ariā: epiphany of an atua or spirit of a great ariki
Ariki: paramount chief and spiritual head of an iwi
Atua: progenitor and protector of a part of whenua
Awa: river
Hapū: subdivision of an iwi
Hapua: hollow/lagoon
Hau: wind
Huka: white foam/snow
Iwi: tribe/hapū comprising the descendants of a great ancestor
Kāhui tipua: diverse group of remote ancestors
Kai: food/to eat
Kaitiaki: guardian of a tribal territory's natural resources
Kāinga/Kāika: unfortified village where the fires of occupation, ahi kā, burn
Kirikiri: expanse of stones

Koha/Oha/Oa: gift
Kopi: gorge
Mahinga kai/Mahika kai: food resource area
Mana: sense of honour /prestige/spiritual power or 'inner fire'
Manawhenua: mana derived from ancestral land
Manga/Maka: stream
Maripi: stone knife/scraper
Mātāpuna: real source of a river
Maunga/Mauka: mountain
Moana: sea
Mōkihi: raft
Motu: vegetated island/isolated grove of trees
Ngāti/Kāti, Ngāi/Kāi, Ngā/Kā, Nga Aitanga: the descendants
Nohoanga/Nohoaka: seasonal camp site
Nōti: mountain pass
Pā: fortified village or refuge
Pākihi: flat open land
Pari: cliff
Pēpeha: proverb
Pō: night/underworld
Puke: hill
Puna: spring
Pātu: hand weapon
Rae: headland
Rangatira: lord of a hapū
Rangi/Raki: day/the celestial world
Rarohenga: the underworld
Rohe: boundary/territory/ fishing net
Roto: lake
Rūnanga/Rūnaka: community council
Tāhuna: expanse of sand
Takiwa: tribal territory/chiefdom
Tāngata whenua: indigenous 'people of the land'
Taniwha: acquatic dragon
Tapu: hallowed/dangerous/reserved for the atua
Tara: peak
Tarahanga/Tarahaka: mountain pass
Tari: ridge
Taua: fighting force
Tipua/Tupua: remote ancestor with supernatural powers.
Tohunga: expert in tribal lore/conductor of religious rites
Toki: adze
Tōpuni: dog-skin cloak/an overlay of spiritual values
Umu: earth oven
Wai: water/watercourse
Wairua: spirit
Waka: canoe
Whānau: a family (the smallest unit of a hapū)
Whanga/Waka/Haka/Aka: an inlet or wide gap in a row of hills or sea cliffs
Whare: dwelling
Whenua: land/placenta/Nature, which nourishes us

Mountaineering Terms
Arête: a narrow mountain ridge
Batholith: an intrusion of igneous rock that extends to a great depth
Bergschrund: a deep crevasse at the head of a glacier

Cirque: a high basin at the head of a mountain valley
Col: a negotiable notch on a high ridge
Cornice: an unstable lip of snow on a mountain ridge
Couloir: a steep gully on a mountainside
Gendarme: a rock pinnacle on a mountain ridge
Névé: a snowfield at the head of a glacier
Serâc: an unstable ice pinnacle in a steep glacier

Geological Terms
Auriferous quartz: gold-bearing quartz – silicon oxide – a very
    common constituent of all continental crust rocks. It dissolves
    in superheated water and precipitates in rock fissures.
Batholith: an intrusion of igneous rock that extends to a great depth
Bowenite: a hard form of serpentine – a metamorphic
    magnesium silicate mineral of igneous origin
Cenozoic: modern zoological era
Chromite: an iron-chromium oxide mineral found in small percentages in Harzburgerite
Dunite: an ultramafic rock almost entirely composed of olivine – magnesium
    iron silicate – the main constituent of the earth's upper mantle
Granodiorite: an intrusive igneous rock similar to granite with light feldspar crystals
Harzburgerite: an ultramafic rock composed mainly of pyroxene and olivine
Ilmenite: a black iron-titanium oxide mineral of igneous origin
Indurated argillite: a sedimentary rock toughened by intrusions of tremolite fibres
Kyanite: a blue aluminium silicate mineral found in high-grade schist
Lithosphere: the earth's crust, which floats on the earth's mantle
Mesozoic: intermediate zoological era (300–65 million years ago)
'Metavolcanic horizon': a layer of volcanic ash that has been
    metamorphosed by extreme heat and pressure
Obducted: over-ridden
Oceanic ridge: a divergent plate boundary where oceanic crust is generated
Orogeny: uplift of mountain ranges
Palaeozoic: ancient zoological era
Piedmont glacier: an ice sheet composed of merged glaciers that
    have spread onto a plain from separate valleys
Proglacial: in front of a glacier
Serpentinite: hydrated ultramafic magma from a tectonic plate boundary
Scheelite: a calcium tungstate mineral
Silcrete: sand and gravel in hard siliceous cement
Strike-slip (sideways): horizontal direction of movement along a fault line
Subduction system: descent of one of the tectonic plates that comprise
    the earth's crust beneath another tectonic plate
Talus: a sloping mass of debris below a cliff
Terrane: part of a landmass that has a different origin to its other parts
Tectonic plate: one of the mobile segments that make up the earth's crust
Transform fault: a shear plane between two mobile tectonic plates
Tremolite: a metamorphic mineral – magnesium silicate – of sedimentary origin

Endnotes

Chapter One

1   *Marlborough Express*, August 25, 1950.

2   Skinner W H, *Ancient Maori Canals, Marlborough, New Zealand.*
(Journal of the Polynesian Society), v 21, p 105.

3   Elvy W J, *Kei Puta te Wairau* (Whitcombe and Tombs, 1957), p 45. Also Te Maiharoa
T (Beattie H, ed) *Folklore and Fairy Tales of the Canterbury Maoris* (Herries Beattie,
1957), p 27 and *Our Southernmost Maori* (Herries Beattie, 1954), p 81. Rawiri Te
Maire Tau published two versions of this story in *Ngā Pikitūroa o Ngāi Tahu. The
Oral Traditions of Ngāi Tahu* (Otago University Press, 2003), pp 206 and 267. East
Polynesian helmsmen setting out from Tahiti or Rarotonga would have followed
migrating flocks of kuaka/godwits and titi/sooty shearwaters, which may have been
characterised as the legendary Kāhui Tipua waka *Huruhurumanu* (bird feathers). By
night the helmsmen could have navigated by the southern lodestar, Atutahi (Canopus)
and Te Matau a Māui (Māui's fish hook' – the tail of Scorpio), which moves along the
ecliptic embedded in Te Ikanui a Te Rangi ('the great fish in the heavens', ie the Milky
Way). In Dominion Museum Monograph No 3, *The Astronomical Knowledge of the
Maori,* Elsdon Best noted that the tail of Scorpio also represented the Tane's celestial
waka, which transported the wairua (spirits) of deceased chiefs along the ecliptic called

Te Ara Whanui a Tāne. Best listed three of that waka's names: *Uruao, Te Wakaahua a Rangi* and *Te Waka a Tamarereti*. In Ngāi Tahu star lore the tail of Scorpio and Orion's Belt represented the tauihu (prow) and (taurapa) sternpost of the celestial waka *Uruao*.

4   Elvy W J, *Kei Puta te Wairau* (Whitcombe and Tombs, 1957), p 14. Also Stack J, *Remarks on Mr Mackenzie Cameron's Theory respecting the Kahui Tipua* (Transactions and Proceedings NZ Institute, 1880), v 12, p 163, and McFadgen, B, *Hostile Shores: Catastrophic Events in Prehistoric New Zealand and their Impact on Maori Coastal Communities* (Auckland University Press, 2007) pp. 93 and 186-189. Whanganui elders told Richard Taylor (*Te Ika a Maui*, 1855, p 117) that Kupe's adze blows were responsible for 'severing the two islands asunder' and 'cutting off New Zealand from Hawaiki, to which it is said to have been previously united'.

5   Travers W T L., *On the Life and Times of Te Rauparaha* (Transactions. and Proceedings. NZ Institute, 1872), p 81.

6   Insull H A H, *Marlborough Place Names* (A H and A W Reed, 1952), p 58.

7   Humphries E and Mitchell S A, Geology, doi.org/xpt (2014).

8   Mackay A A, *Compendium of Native Affairs in the South Island* (Gov Printer, 1873), v 2, p 50.

Chapter Two

9   Gardner W G, *The Amuri. A County History* (Amuri County Council, 1965), p 36.

10   Chorlton R, *Mount Mackay and the Spensers* in *Tararua Tramper* (Tararua Tramping Club, 1949), p 58.

11   Op cit note 11, p 6.

12   Sherrard J, *In the Heart of the Kaikouras* (*Journeys,* South Island Publicity Assoc, 1956), No 61, p 27.

13   Chinn T, *Glaciers and the glacial inventory* in the *New Zealand Alpine Journal* (NZ Alpine Club, 1988), v 41, p 96.

14   Kennington A L, *The Awatere, A District and its People* (Marlborough District Council, 1978), p 202.

15   Andersen J, *Maori Place-names* (Polynesian Society, 1942), p 136.

16   Halbert R W, *Horouta* (Reed Books, 1999), p 30.

Chapter Three

17   Andersen J, *Maori Place-names* (Polynesian Society, 1942), p 136.

18   Roberts W S H, *Maori Nomenclature*, *Otago Daily Times*, 1912, p 63.

19   Mackay A A, *Compendium of Native Affairs in the South Island* (Gov Printer, 1873), v 1, p 45.

20   Hindmarsh W, *Tales of the Golden West* (Whitcombe and Tombs, 1906), p 88.

21   *Nelson Examiner*, March 14, 1860.

Chapter Four

22   Tikao T (Beattie H ed), *Tikao Talks* (A H and A W Reed, 1939), p 104.

23   Cowan J, in Herries Beattie, *Maori Place-names in Otago* (Herries Beattie, 1944), p 16.

24   Harper A P, *The First crossing of the Southern Alps* (NZ Alpine Journal, 1921), v3, p 75. The name of Harper's companion has also been recorded as Edwin Lock.

25   Tau R Te Maire and Anderson A (eds), *Ngāi Tahu A Migration History* (Bridget Williams Books, 2008), p 247 and White J, *Ancient History of the Maori* (Government Printer, 1887), v2, p 37. Otago missionary Charles Creed sent John White a transcript of the South Island myth about Tama-nui-a-Raki. That 'great wanderer … was addicted to female slave hunting and stealing and plundering property … (and) first discovered and revealed to his people the road to Poutiri (Tai Poutini – the west coast) while chasing the ships that had taken many females away … some of the mountains which we now see were ships in days gone by'. Tama-nui-a-Raki (Tama-nui-a-Rangi) is a poetic name for Te Rā (the sun); his westward journey and descent to the underworld echoes its journey. The tales about the travels of Tama-ki-te Raki and Tama Āhua gave directions

for early seafarers that were heading to the west coast from opposite directions about where to find precious stones. In the Whanganui version of the Kupe saga, that traveller eloped with his friend Hoturapa's wife Kuramarotini to the west coast of the North Island, which he barricaded with wild seas on one side and thorny vegetation on the other (Motif 400 in the Aarne-Thompson index: Man on a Quest for his Lost Wife).

26   Taylor W A, *Lore and History of the South Island Maori* (Bascands, 1952), p 177.

27   *Lyttelton Times,* October 23, 1861.

28   May P R, *The West Coast Gold Rushes* (Pegasus Press, 1962), p 81.

29   Suggate R P, *The Alpine Fault Bends and the Marlborough Faults* (Royal Society of NZ Bulletin 18, 1977), p 69.

30   Cresswell D., *Squatter and Settler* (Waipara County Council, 1952), p.61.

31   Beckett T N, *The Poulter Watershed and Harper Pass* (The Canterbury Mountaineer, 1944), no 13, p 35. *See also* the editor's note in The Canterbury Mountaineer (1932), no 1, p 46.

Chapter Five

32   Beattie H, *The Maoris and Fiordland* (Herries Beattie, 1949), p 8. Christine Tremewan published a different origin-myth of Banks Peninsula/Horomaka in *Traditional Stories from Southern New Zealand* (Macmillan Brown Centre for Pacific Studies, 2002, p 99) a garbled local version of an old myth jotted down by a French whaler. It probably declared that Banks Peninsula/Horomaka was the body of a giant tuna/eel that Māui had decapitated.

33   McFadgen B, *Hostile Shores Catastrophic Events in Prehistoric New Zealand and their Impact on Maori Communities* (Auckland University Press, 2007) p 192.

34   Beattie H, *Traditions and legends collected from the natives of Murihiku,* Part III (Journal of the Polynesian Society, 1918), p 46.

35   Gage M, *Late Pleistocene Glaciations of the Waimakariri Valley, Canterbury, New Zealand* (NZ Journal of Geology and Geophysics, 1958), v1, p 23 and Murray Cage, *Geology of Arthur's Pass National Park*, National Park Scientific Series No 7 (Department Of Conservation, 1987) p 37.

36   Beattie H (ed), *Folklore and Fairy Tales of the Canterbury Maoris,* Told by Taare Te Maiharoa to Maud Goodenough Hayter (Mrs T Moses) (Herries Beattie, 1957), p 12.

37   Andersen J, *Maori Place-names* (Polynesian Society, 1942), p 136.

38   Odell R S, *Handbook of Arthur's Pass National Park* (Whitcombe and Tombs, 1935), p 57

39   Mee D, *An Early Greymouth Climbing Group* (The Canterbury Mountaineer, 1991), No 56, p 59.

40   McLennon V, *Coaching Days and Accommodating Ways* (Hilton Press), p. 53 and Tom Beckett's article *O'Malley's Track* in The Canterbury Mountaineer, 1942, No 11, p 8. The George O'Malley who built this track was presumably James' brother.

41   Cave M, *Geology of Arthur's Pass National Park*, National Park Scientific Series, No. 7 (Dept of Conservation, 1987), p 49.

42   Canterbury Progress League, *The Story of the Midland Railway* (Canterbury Progress League, 1923), p 155.

43   Herries H, *Maori Places-names of Canterbury* (Herries Beattie, 1945), p 87 and Beattie H, *Our Southernmost Maoris* (Herries Beattie, 1954), p 126.

44   Dobson A D, *Reminiscences of Arthur Dudley Dobson Engineer 184–1930* (Whitcombe and Tombs, 1930), p 77.

45   Skinner H D, *Maori Life on the Poutini Coast* (Journal of the Polynesian Society, 1912), v 21, p 142. This paper was based on William Wilson's notes of his interviews with Māori elders in South Westland, which reside in the Alexander Turnbull Library.

Chapter Six

46   E, *The Southern Districts of New Zealand* (Longman, Brown, Green and Longmans, London, 1851), p 100.

47   Shortland E, *The Southern Districts of New Zealand* (Longman, Brown, Green, and Longmans, London, 1851), p 100.

48 Taylor W A, *Lore and History of the South Island Maori* (Bascands, 1952), p 100.
49 ibid, p.94
50 Pascoe J D, *Unclimbed New Zealand* (George Allen and Unwin, London, 1939), p 81.
51 Lauper J (ed J Pascoe), *Over the Whitcombe Pass. The Narrative of Jakob Lauper. Reprinted from the Canterbury Gazette, July 1863.* (Whitcombe and Tombs, 1960). Also Deryck Morse's article (op cit note 7) and Hilary Low's improved translation of Lauper's report (*Pushing His Luck*, Canterbury University Press, 2010).
52 Beattie H, *Maori Lore of Lake, Alp and Fiord* (Herries Beattie, 1945), p 62.
53 Acheson J, *Mr Surveyor Roberts* (NZ Alpine Journal, 1973) v 26, p 109.
54 Wall A, *Long and Happy. An autobiography* (A.H. and A.W. Reed, 1965), p 107.
55 Galloway D, *Julius von Haast's botanical explorations* (NZ Alpine Journal, 1976) v 28, p 88.
56 Andersen J, *Maori Place-names* (Journal of the Polynesian Society, 1942), p 137.

Chapter Seven
57 Kerr P, *From the Beginning* (Strathallen County Council, 1979), p 61.
58 Andersen J *Maori Place-names* (Journal of the Polynesian Society, 1942), p 137.
59 Beckett T N, *The Mountains of Erewhon* (A H and A W Reed, 1978), p 44.
60 Beattie H, *Maori Lore of Alp, Lake and Fiord* (Herries Beattie, 1945), p. 96.
61 ibid p 59.
62 J B A Acland, *Early Explorations at the Headwaters of the Rangitata River* (NZ Alpine Club Journal, 1892), v 1, p 29.
63 Op cit note 62, p 59. The Māori names of the Havelock and Clyde Rivers appear on the 1880 'Taiaroa' Map of the South Island, that resides in Canterbury Museum.
64 Pascoe J D, *The Perth Glaciers* (Canterbury Mountaineer, 1934–35), v 4, p 33 and Priestley Thomson's obituary for John Pascoe in the 1973 issue of the NZ Alpine Club Journal, v 26, p 115.
65 Teichelmann E J, *The Relation of the Rakaia and Rangitata on the East to the Wanganui and Whataroa on the West* (NZ Alpine Club Journal, 1923), v 3, p 187.
66 Op cit note 61, p 110.

Chapter Eight
67 Taylor W A, *Lore and History of the South Island Maori* (Bascands, 1952), p 103.
68 Barrett G (ed), *Queen Charlotte Sound. The Traditional and European Records, 1820* (Carlton University Press, Ottawa, 1987), p 166.
69 The final resting place of the *Uruao,* the ancestral waka of the Waitaha people, is described in the Proposed Timaru District Plan (Timaru District Council, October 1995), p 15
70 Beattie H, *Maori Place-names of Otago* (Herries Beattie, 1944), p 11. The earliest spelling is Ohamaru. There is another Oamaru on the east coast of the North Island.
71 Anderson A, *The Welcome of Strangers* (University of Otago Press, 1998), p 107.
72 Op cit note iv, p 26.
73 Tikao T (Beattie H ed). *Tikao Talks* (A H and A W Reed, 1939), p 112. Tikao added that after losing his precious firebrand, Te Ahi a Ūe, Tamatea and his companions were chilled by a cold wind on Te Poho o Tamatea (Mount Vernon) on the Port Hills beside Lyttelton Harbour/Whakaraupō. Tamatea summoned volcanic fire from the central North Island and a ball of fiery embers rolled down the Whanganui Valley from Mount Ngarahoe to Cook Strait/Te Moana a Raukawa, then flew through the air to Banks Peninsula/Horomaka. It scorched a band of red rock called Te Poho o Tamatea near Tamatea's feet and sparked wildfires on the plains. Tikao called the hot pools at Hanmer Springs Te Whakatakanga o te ngarehu o te ahi a Tamatea (the falling of the embers of the fire of Tamatea). In her book *Hawaiki. A new approach to Maori tradition,* Margaret Orbell noted that a Tahitian atua who presided over fire was named Tamatea. A Tai Rāwhiti elder told William Colenso that 'the Moas all perished through the fire of Tamatea … when Tamatea arrived, he burnt up the tangled mass of herbage and scrub from the surface, then it was that man, possessing useful land, dwelt and lived well'.

(*On the Moa*, in Transactions and Proceedings of the NZ Institute, 1879, v 12, p 81). East coast woodlands were repeatedly burnt to flush out game birds, foster the growth of aruhe/bracken fern and tī/kouaka/cabbage trees, the roots of which were baked and eaten, and enlarge the grassy habitats of weka and kākāpō. The island in Foveaux Strait named Rarotoka (Raotonga) and the southern-most district on Rarotonga in the Cook Islands named Takitimu are indicative of the origin of Murihiku's earliest settlers.

74 Beattie H, *Early Tribes* (Journal of the Polynesian Society, 1916) v 25, p 12.

75 Cowan J, *Maori Place-names with Special Reference to the Great Lakes and Mountains of the South Island* (Transactions and Proceedings of the NZ Institute, 1905), v 38, p 113.

76 Mikaere B, *Te Maiharoa and the Promised Land* (Reed Books, 1988), p 69. James Mackay noted that his Māori guide called the Main Divide in the vicinity of Harper Pass 'Te Ao Mārama'.

77 Mills A D, *Oxford Dictionary of English Place-names*, 2nd ed (Oxford University Press, 1998), p 221.

78 Beattie H, *Moriori* (Herries Beattie, 1941), p 28.

79 Beattie H, *Maori Lore of Lake, Alp and Fiord* (Herries Beattie, 1945), p 55.

80 Wilson J, *A Border 'Battle' Long Ago* in *Historic Places in New Zealand* (Historic Places Trust, 1985), no 8, p 26.

81 Beattie H, *Maori Place-names of Canterbury* (Herries Beattie, 1945), p 28.

82 Taylor W A, *Lore and History of the South Island Maori* (Bascands, 1951), p 94.

83 Mueller G, *Appendices* to the *Journals of the House of Representatives* (1887), C-2, p 12 and Gilkison W S and Stevenson H J, *The Ohau Valleys* in *The New Zealand Alpine Journal* (NZ Alpine Club, 1956), v 16, p 438.

84 Brodrick T N, *Appendices* to the *Journals of the House of Representatives* (1896), C-1, p 107.

85 Op cit note xiii, p 58.

86 Op cit note iv, p 53 and Ngāi Tahu's tōpuni statement in the 2001 Aoraki/Mount Cook National Park Management Plan.

87 A stationary white cloud (ao-tea) on the horizon was a heavenly sign to Polynesian navigators that an island with a high mountain lay underneath it. Hikurangi (tail of the heavens) was a proverbial name for such a peak – at least three locations on the east coasts of these islands bore that name, notably the prominent peak near East Cape. Aoraki's celestial waka sailed all the way down to Murihiku (tip of the tail) in the deep south but could not return to the heavens.

88 Andersen J, *Maori Place-names* (Polynesian Society, 1942), p 137.

89 Op cit note 81, p 54. Edward Shortland also recorded this myth in his book *The Southern Districts of New Zealand* (Longman, Brown, Green and Longmans, London, 1851) p 163.

90 Wilson W, *Nomenclature, Legends, etc. as supplied by the Maoris of South Westland, 1987* (Johannes Andersen Papers MS 112, Alexander Turnbull Library).

91 Haleakalā National Park brochure published by the National Park Service, US Dept. of the Interior in association with the Mountain Institute.

92 Te Maiharoa T (Beattie H ed), *Folklore and Fairy Tales of the Canterbury Maoris* (Herries Beattie, 1957), p 28. Tane's son Takapotiri was the ancestor of birds. It has been suggested that Takapō was an abbreviation of his name.

93 Cox S C and Findlay R H, *The Main Divide Fault and its role in formation of the Southern Alps, New Zealand* (NZ Journal of Geology and Geophysics, 1995), v 38, p 489.

Chapter Nine

94 Beattie H, *Maori Lore of Lake, Alp and Fiord* (Herries Beattie, 1945), p 49.

95 ibid, p. 71.

96 Beattie H and Tikao T, *Tikao Talks* (A H and A W Reed, 1939), p 106.

97 Cowan J, *Travel in New Zealand* (Whitcombe and Tombs, 1926), v 2, p 97.

98 Haast H F, *Life and Times of Sir Julius von Haast* (Avery Press, 1948), p 276.

99 Beattie H, *Maori Place-names of Otago* (Herries Beattie, 1944), p 29.

100 Hall-Jones J, *John Turnbull Thomson* (McIndoe, 1992), p 16.

101 Op cit note 102, p 32.
102 *The Press* December 3, 2014.
103 Op cit note 102, p 32. In the Ngāti Kahungunu *Takitimu* saga recorded by J
    H Mitchell (A H and A W Reed, 1944), Kopuwai was the slave-attendant of
    Tamatea's wife Turihuka, who died on Breast Hill/Turihuka by Lake Hāwea.
104 Wishart S, *Night moves* (NZ Geographic, Jan–February 2012), p 55.
    Northland's flora and fauna have the highest rate of endemicity in New
    Zealand and botanical and zoological connections with New Caledonia.
105 Ross, D, Scottish Place-names (Berlinn, Edinburgh, 2001).
106 Waite F, *Port Molyneaux. A Centennial History* (Clutha County Council), 1940, p 6.
107 Beattie H, *Moriori* (Herries Beattie, 1941), p 37 and Beattie H, *Traditions
    and Legends* (Journal of the Polynesian Society 1916), v 25, p 62.
108 Griffiths G, *Names and Places in southern New Zealand*
    (Otago Heritage Books, 1990), p 60.
109 Waite F, *Port Molyneaux. A Centennial History* (Clutha County Council, 1840), p 46.
110 Op cit note 103, p 106.
111 Tikao T, (Beattie H ed *Tikao Talks* (A H and A W Reed, 1939), p 106. Also
    The Southern Maori and Greenstone (Transactions and Proceedings of the
    NZ Institute, 1919) v 52, p 51. Alternatively, this obscure lake name may be a
    contraction of Whaka a Tipua (hollow of the tipua). Herries Beattie discussed the
    various meanings and pronunciations of Wakatipu in *The Southern Maori and
    Greenstone* (Transactions and Proceedings of the NZ Institute, 1919, v 52, p 51).
112 Andersen J, *Maori Place-names* (Polynesian Society Journal, 1942), p 103.
    Since *namu* is the Tahitian word for 'green', Cook's Tahitian interpreter
    Tupa'ia must have inferred that *pounamu* meant 'green stone'.
113 Beattie H, *Maori Lore of Lake, Alp and Fiord* (Herries Beattie, 1945), p 29. Beattie
    translated the alternative form of this place-name, Pua Here, as 'bundle of bird snares'
    and Pua Hiri as either 'foaming vigorously' or 'bundle tied in a twisted manner'.
114 Soons J M and Selby M J, *Landforms of New Zealand* (Longman Paul, 1982), p 470.

Chapter Ten
115 Beattie H, *The Maoris and Fiordland* (Hearries Beattie, 1949), p 67.
116 Beattie H, *Far-famed Fiordland* (Herries Beattie, 1950), p 119.
117 Beattie H, *Maori Lore of Lake, Alp and Fiord* (Herries Beattie, 1945), p 144.
118 Pickering M, *The Southern Journey* (Mark Pickering, 1993), p 113.
119 Davies T, Pettinga J, et al, *The Press*, (April 13, 2012), p A17 and Gorman P, *The
    Press* (June 29, 2012), p A3. Investigations of an 8000-year sequence of sedimentary
    layers beside Hokuri Creek, which flows into Lake McKerrow/Whakatipu Waitai,
    came up with an inferred mean rupture recurrence rate of 329 years on the section
    of the Alpine Fault that this stream dissects. The last rupture of that fault occurred
    in 1717 A.D. Ruptures do not appear to involve more than two thirds of the
    fault's 600-kilometre length and they can spread northwards or southwards.
120 Op cit note 118, p 43 and Beattie H, *The Southern Maori and Greenstone* (Transactions
    and Proceedings of the NZ Institute, 1919), v 52, p 46. The *takiwai*/bowenite outcrop
    at Anita Bay was said to be the metamorphosed body of Hine Kokotakiwai, the fugitive
    wife of Tama-ki-te-Raki, who pursued her in the waka *Tairea*. Her children were
    metamorphosed into the Matakirikiri Hills just south of Anita Bay. Tama's pōkeka (rain
    cape made of long leaves) was torn to shreds when he scrambled around the shores of
    the fiords in search of his missing wives. The dense vegetation in this rain-drenched
    region was said to have sprouted from the leaves that fell off Tama's rain cape.
121 Johannes Andersen noted that 'koko' was an old term for
    ear pendants, hence the name Kokotakiwai.
122 Op cit note 118, p 12.
123 Op cit note 118, p 43. The last sighting of this bird was
    in 1902 and it is presumed to be extinct.
124 Hall-Jones J, *Martins Bay* (Craig Printing Co, 1987), p 13.

125 ibid, p 10.

126 Beattie H *Moriori* (Herries Beattie, 1941), p 10

127 Op cit note 118, p 65.

128 Tremewan C (ed), *Traditional Stories from Southern New Zealand* (University of Canterbury Press, 2002), p 267 and Andersen J, *Maori Place-names* (Journal of the Polynesian Society, 1942), p 34. In the southern version of the Tama-nui-a-Raki myth recorded by Charles Creed, Te Kohiwai is the name of Tama's daughter who went to live with her grandfather Tū-mauka after her father headed for the west coast in pursuit of her mother, Rukutia, and her father's erstwhile friend, Tū Te Koropānga. The names of two streams in the Taieri Gorge, Te Mimi o Kohiwai and Te Mimi o Tū, imply that in the southern version of this myth Te Kohiwai embarked on her journey from the Ōtākou district and followed the tracks of Tū Te Koropānga and Rukutia, up the Taieri Valley en route to the west coast. Percy Smith recorded a Taranaki cosmology that ranked Tū Mauna with Tāne and Tangaroa (*History and Traditions of the Taranaki Coast*) (Journal of the Polynesian Society, 1910) v 18, p 25).

129 Ngāi Tahu Claims Settlement Act 1998, Schedule 93, p 422.

130 Hall-Jones J *Fiordland Place-names* (Fiordland National Park Board), 1979, p 27.

Chapter Eleven

131 Wilson W, *Nomenclature, legends etc. as supplied by the Maori in South Westland, 1897*, in the Johannes Anderson papers MS 112, Alexander Turnbull Library.

132 Beattie, H, *Maori Lore of Lake, Alp and Fiord* (Herries Beattie, 1945), p 73 and Ngāi Tahu Claims Settlement Act 1998, Schedule 62, p 360.

133 O'Brien G, *High country weather* in *New Zealand Listener* (June 3–9, 2006), p 34. This poem was published in the June 1950 issue of *The New Zealand Alpine Club Journal*.

134 Graham A and Wilson J, *Uncle Alec and the Grahams of Franz Josef* (John McIndoe, 1983), p 98 and *The Press* (Christchurch), December 18, 1909.

135 Reports of this expedition appear in the *Otago Daily Times* February 9–18 and March 19–20, 1863.

136 Simmons F F, *The Waipara: a gem of nomenclature* (NZ Alpine Journal, 1950), v 13, p 283.

137 Dougherty I, *Arawhata Bill* (Exisle Publishing, 1996), p 36.

Chapter Twelve

138 Beattie H, *Maori Lore of Lake, Alp and Fiord* (Herries Beattie, 1945), p 69.

139 Gilkison W S and Craigie A R, *Wilkin Wanderings* (NZ Alpine Journal, 1942), v 9, p 138 and correction in NZ Alpine Journal, 1943, v 10 p. 65.

140 Mueller G, *Reconnaissance survey of the headwaters of the Arawata and Waiatoto Rivers, Westland* (Appendix to Journal of House of Representatives, 1885), v 1, C-1A, p 25. Douglas' sketch map of the Waiatoto Valley was reproduced by Phillip Temple in *New Zealand Explorers* (Whitcoulls, 1985), p 149.

141 Pascoe J (ed), *Mr Explorer Douglas* (A H and A W Reed, 1957), p 134.

142 Op cit note 144, p 14.

143 Gilkison W S, *Waiatoto Approach* (NZ Alpine Journal, 1949), v 13, p 29 and John Breen's book *River of Blood* (Longacre, 2009), p 172.

144 Teichelman E, *The Waiatoto Valley* (NZ Alpine Journal, 1935) v 6, p 18. Also Graham A and Wilson J, *Uncle Alec and the Grahams of Franz Josef* (John McIndoe, 1983), p 81.

145 Breen J, *River of Blood* (Longacre, 2009), p 79.

Chapter Thirteen

146 Madgwick P, *Aotea. A History of the South Westland Maori* (Paul Madgwick, 1992), p 97. Ngāti Māhaki elders at Bruce Bay/Mahitahi told George Roberts' son-in-law William Wilson that Okuru is a mis-spelling of Ōkura, which would mean 'place of the red glow' if it was an after-naming of Ōakura on the west coast of Taranaki.

147 Roxburgh I, *Jacksons Bay. A Centennial History.* (A H and A W Reed, 1976), p 188.

148 Cooper A.F. and Bishop D.C., *Uplift Rates and High Level Marine*

Platforms Associated with the Alpine Fault at Okuru River, South Westland (Royal Society of NZ Bulletin 18, 1979), p 35.

149 Pascoe J (ed), *Mr Explorer Douglas* (A H and AW Reed, 1957), p 101.
150 Ibid. A reproduction of Douglas' map, showing all his campsites, is reproduced in John Pascoe's book *Exploration New Zealand* (Reed Books, 1971), p 103. The man that Douglas called 'Whakatipu Jack' was probably Teone Te Wa or 'Māori Jack', who had guided Vincent Pyke's party over Haast Pass/Tiori Pātea in 1863. In his unpublished compendium entitled *Nomenclature, Legends, etc. as supplied by the Maoris in South Westland, 1897*, William Wilson noted that 'Big Jack' had travelled from Central Otago to the west coast via a pass at the head of the Okuru Valley.
151 Beattie H, *Maori Lore of Alp, Lake and Fiord* (Herries Beattie, 1945), p 70.
152 Op cit note 151, p 11. A string of ancient campsites has been discovered in the Okuru Valley.
153 Letter from J Thomson in FMC (Federated Mountain Clubs) Bulletin, No 171, p 11 and op cit note 151, p 103, which contains a reproduction of Douglas' map of this area.
154 Roberts W S H, *Maori Nomenclature* (*Otago Daily Times*, 1912), p 5.
155 Barcham H T, W*est of the Wilkin* (NZ Alpine Club Journal, 1951), v 14, p 7 and an article by Ashley Cunningham in FMC Bulletin, No 177, p 56.
156 The Climber (NZAC, Winter 2001), v 36, p 6.

Chapter Fourteen
157 May. P R, *The West Coast Gold Rushes* (Pegasus Press, 1962), p 222.
158 Bishop J and Walker M, *Westland County. A Centennial Album* (Westland County Council, 1977), p 20.
159 Roxburgh I, *Jacksons Bay. A Centennial History*. (A H and A W Reed, 1976), p 93.
160 Nolan W D, *The Droving Days* (Bill Nolan, 1998), p. 3.
161 Madgwick P, *Aotea. A History of the South Westland Maori* (Paul Madgwick, 1992), p 97.
162 *The Press,* March 7, 2017, A2.
163 Op cit note 163, p 70.
164 Ibid.
165 Op cit note 105 and Galloway D, *Julius von Haast's Botanical Explorations* (NZ Alpine Club Journal, 1976), v 29, p 88.
166 Op cit note 167.
167 Riley G, M*ount Cook National Park place names and their origin* (NZ Alpine Club Journal, 1967) v 22, p 111.

Chapter Fifteen
168 Beattie H, *Maori Lore of Lake, Alp and Fiord* (Herries Beattie, 1945), p 96.
169 Wilson W, *Nomenclature, Legends, etc. as supplied by the Maoris of South Westland 1897* (Johannes Andersen papers MS 112, Alexander Turnbull Library).
170 ibid.
171 Madgwick P, *Aotea. A Hisory of the South Westland Maori* (Paul Madgwick, 1992), p 54.
172 Tyrrell A R, *Catlins Pioneering* (Otago Heritage Books, 1989), p 10. The place name Puke Maeroero also occurs near Waikouaiti Bay, Lake Wakatipu, Lake Te Anau and Bruce Bay/Mahitahi on the west coast. Herries Beattie recorded more maeroero lore in *Traditions and Legends* (Journal of the Polynesian Society, 1918), v 26, p.153. They arrived on the mythical waka *Hururumanu* with the ancestors of many other birds.
173 Op cit note 176, p 43.
174 Scott S, in *Women of Westland and Their Families* (Westland Branch of the National Council of Women, 1977), v 2, p 295.
175 Harper A P, *Pioneer Work in the Alps of New Zealand* (T Fisher Unwin, London, 1896), p. 204
176 Op cit note 173, p 237.
177 Op cit note 179, p 280.
178 Copland J personal com and Riley G, *Mount Cook Place Names and*

their Origin (NZ Alpine Club Journal, 1967), v. 22, p 128

179 Pascoe J D (ed), *Mr. Explorer Douglas* (A H and A W Reed, 1957), p 167.

180 Ross T M, *One Hundred Years of Mountaineering. The West Coast Story* (*West Coast Times*, 1991), p 9.

181 Op cit note 173, p 54 and Cowan J, *Maori Place-names: with special reference to the Great Lakes and Mountains of the South Island* (Transactions and Proceedings of the NZ Institute, 1905) v 38, p 113.

182 *The Press,* May 23, 2015, p A9.

Chapter Sixteen

183 Beattie H, *Maori Lore of Lake, Alp and Fiord* (Herries Beattie, 1945) p. 53.

184 Andersen J, *Maori Place-names* (Journal of the Polynesian Society, 1942), p 140.

185 Op cit, note 188, p 55 (quoting James Cowan's sources).

186 May P R, *The West Coast Gold Rushes* (Pegasus Press, 1967), p 185.

187 Harper A P, *Pioneer Work in the Alps of New Zealand* (T Fisher Unwin, London, 1896), p 82.

188 Morton E K, *A Tramper in South Westland* (J E Jenkins and Co, 1951), p 31.

189 Beattie H *Our Southernmost Maoris* (Herries Beattie, 1954), p 106.

190 Sara W A, *Glaciers of Westland National Park* (NZ Geological Survey, 1974), p 35 and his paper *Franz Josef and Fox Glaciers, 1951–1967* (NZ Journal of Geology and Geophysics, 1968), v11, p 768. Also *Global warming has no recent parallel* New Scientist No 3241, August 3, 2019, p 19.

191 Mantell B D, *Captain Commander Abel Janzoon Tasman, the VOC and early voyages of discovery* (Brent Mantell, 1991), p 11.

192 Op cit note 192, p 126.

193 Graham A and Wilson J, *Uncle Alec and the Grahams of Franz Josef* (John McIndoe, 1983), p 48.

Chapter Seventeen

194 Kelly M, *Westland Huts* (NZ Historic Places, 1992), No 37, p 11.

195 Beattie H, *The Maoris and Fiordland* (Herries Beattie, 1949), p 13.

196 Beattie H, *Our Southernmost Maoris* (Herries Beattie, 1954), p 106.

197 Graham P (ed Hewitt H E), *Peter Graham: Mountain Guide* (A H and A W Reed, 1965), p 30.

198 Graham A and Wilson J, *Uncle Alec and the Grahams of Franz Josef* (John McIndoe, 1983), p 28.

199 Harper A P, *Pioneer Work in the Alps of New Zealand* (T Fisher Unwin, London, 1896), p 270.

200 Bamford D, *Eighty years of high living* (NZ Alpine Club Journal, 1984) v 37, p 105.

201 Mannering G E, *The Disaster on the Tasman Glacier* (NZ Alpine Club Journal 1930) v 4, p 119. The old hut was dismantled in 1979. Its replacement was removed in 2012 due to avalanche hazards.

202 Riley G, *Mount Cook National Park Place names and their origin* (NZ Alpine Club Journal, 1967) v 22, p 123.

Chapter Eighteen

203 Wilson W, *Nomenclature, Legends, etc. as supplied by the Maoris of South Westland, 1897* (Johannes Andersen Papers MS 112, Alexander Turnbull Library).

204 ibid.

205 Chinn T, *The proliferating glacial lakes* (NZ Alpine Club Journal, 2002) v 54, p 114.

206 Harper A P, *The First Crossing of the Southern Alps* (NZ Alpine Club Journal, 1921), v3, p 79. Leonard Harper's first account of this journey (in the *Lyttelton Times*, January 20, 1858) states that he estimated that he had walked 'ninety miles' down the west coast from Mawhera Pā to the Waitangi River, which is approximately the distance to Ōkārito. Arthur Harper stated in this book *Pioneer Work in the Alps of New Zealand* (p 211) that his father had reached the Haast River and that Tarapuhi had pointed out to

him the route over Haast Pass/Tiori Pātea. However, he also stated in that book that Bill Te Naihi had told him that when he was a boy his father had taken him up the coast to meet a pākehā at Ōkārito who had walked down the west coast with Tarapuhi. That statement implies that Harper's journey ended at Ōkārito and that the Waitangi River and the open flats that Tarapuhi was referring to were those between the Waitangi Taona and Whataroa Rivers. The only straightforward transalpine route from that area is via Sealy Pass, which communicates with the Waitaki (Waitangi) Valley on the east coast.

207 May P R, *The West Coast Gold Rushes* (Pegasus Press, 1967) p 89. Herries Beattie recorded a possible east coast reference to Sealy Pass in his book *Maori Lore of Lake, Alp and Fiord* (p 68).

208 Cotter E M, *Spotlight on the Whataroa* (NZ Alpine Club Journal 1954) v 15, p 507 and Westland Survey Field Book No. 639.

209 *Alpine Notes* (NZ Alpine Club Journal 1892) v 1, p121 and McCormack T, *A History of Surveying and Mountaineering in South Westland* (Lands and Survey Dept., Hokitika, 1986), p 29.

Chapter Nineteen

210 Taylor W A *Lore and History of the South Island Maori* (Bascands, 1952), p 193 and Ngāi Tahu Claims Settlement Act 1998, Schedule 53 (where this lagoon name is spelt Pouerua).

211 Berry V, *Goa Way Back* (Vic Berry, 1986), p. 16.

212 Acheson J, *Mr Surveyor Roberts* (NZ Alpine ClubJournal, 1973), v 26, p 108 and *A History of Surveying and Mountaineering in South Westland* by Trish McCormack, p. 17.

213 ibid, p. 106 and Geoff Spearpoint's article, *The Adams Wilderness,* in FMC Bulletin (June 2002), No 148, p. 16.

Chapter Twenty

214 Tau Te M and Anderson A (eds), *Ngāi Tahu: A Migration History* (Bridget Williams Books, 2008), p 120.

215 Smith S P, *History and Traditions of the Taranaki Coast* (Journal of the Polynesian Society, 1910) v 18, p 197.

216 Taylor N M, *Early Travellers in New Zealand* (Oxford, London, 1959), p 286.

217 Chinn T J, *How wet is the wettest of the wet West Coast* (NZ Alpine Club Journal, 1979), v 32, p 85.

218 NZ Official Yearbook 2010, p 9.

219 Beattie H, *Maori Lore of Lake, Alp and Fiord* (Herries Beattie, 1945), p 63

220 Pickering M.,, *Huts. Untold Stories from Backcountry New Zealand* (Canterbury University Press, 2010), p 97. Mueller's report was published in the *West Coast Times*, March 10, 1981, p 2.

221 *The Press*, September 3, 2015, p A3.

222 Logan H, *Great Peaks of New Zealand* (John McIndoe and the 1990 New Zealand Alpine Club Journal, p 139.

Chapter Twenty-one

223 Berry V, *Goa Way Back* (Vic Berry, 1986), p 13.

224 Mackay A, *Compendium of Native Affairs in the South Island* (Government Printer, 1872), Vol 1, p 39.

225 Bishop J and Walker M *Westland County* (Westland County Council and Pegasus Press, 1977), p 80.

226 Cropp A, *Kokatahi and Kowhiterangi on the West Coast* (A J Cropp, 2010) p 71.

227 Best E, *Maori Religion and Mythology* Part 2, (Dominion Museum Bulletin 11, 1982), p 455 and Wilson W, *Nomenclature, Legends etc as supplied by the Maoris in South Westland 1897* (Johannes Andersen papers, MS 112, Alexander Turnbull Library). Two of his informants said that Tūhua was the captain of the waka *Poutini* but his other informants said that the waka was named *Tūhua* and that Poutini was its captain. Te Akaaka o Poutini (Poutini's mooring place) is the name of a lagoon at the mouth

of the Grey River/Māwheranui. One of John White's correspondents informed him,
figuratively, that Tama-nui-a-Raki had discovered the route to Tai Poutini 'when in
chase of the ships which had taken many females away' and that what were called
'ships were islands or mountains, which went along in the ocean while Tama-ki-te-
raki went by land'. Tūhua, Rangitoto, and Aotea are the names of islands off the upper
North Island and mountains on the west coast; perhaps they had similar profiles when
seen from offshore. Tūhua is also the ancient name of Me'etia Island near Tahiti.

228   Hare Hongi, Journal of the Polynesian Society, 1896, v 5, p 234 and (in the same issue)
Te Kumeroa A, p 235. Black specks in kawakawa pounamu/nephrite were said to
be smuts that fell off a kokako/crow that Tama Ahua's's slave Tumuaki had dropped
into a fire. Tama turned him into Island Hill/Tumuaki. Kāwhaka (to light a fire) Creek
arises on the saddle between this hill and Mount Turiwhate. In another version of that
folktale, Tama-ki-te-Raki's fugitive wives Hine Tangiwai, Hine Hauhunga (frost) also
known as Inanga or Kahurangi, Hine Kawakawa, and Hine Aotea, sought sanctuary
on the west coast (pp 58 and 366) and metamorphosed into the corresponding
varieties of pounamu/nephrite. The hero's quest for his beloved who had been
abducted and imprisoned in a hard-to-find place is a worldwide folktale motif.

229   Taylor W A, Lore and History of the South Island
Maori (Bascands, 1952), pp 170 and 188.

230   Reed A W, Reed Book of Polynesian Mythology (Reed Publishing, 2004), pp 312
and 356 and Journal of the Polynesian Society (1912) v 21, p 152, and Te Maire
Tau R, Ngā Pikitūroa o Ngāi Tahu. The Oral Traditions of Ngāi Tahu (University
of Otago Press, 2003), p 169. Herries Beattie recorded the Rapuwai whakapapa.

231   Kanioro may be represented by Mount Harman/Kaniere. According to East
Cape traditions, Kanioro's spouse Pourangahua (or Pou) and her brother Hoaki
sailed back to Hawaiki in the waka Te Aratawhao (which corresponds to
the Arai Te Uru in southern traditions) to fetch seed kumara/sweet potatoes.
J H Mitchell noted in his book Takitimu that Kanioro and Pou had arrived
in Aotearoa in the waka Tūtara-kauika (leader of a school of whales).

232   Stack J, Sketch of the Traditional History of the South Island Maoris
(Transactions and Proceedings of the NZ Institute, 1877), v 10, p 86.

233   Pascoe J, Great Days in New Zealand Exploration (A H and A W Reed, 1959), p 116.

234   ibid

235   Keene H, Going for Gold (Department of Conservation, 1995), p 87.

Chapter Twenty-two

236   Adams N M, Early Travellers in New Zealand (Oxford
University Press, London, 1959), p 236.

237   Tikao T, (Beattie H, ed) Tikao Talks (A H and A W Reed, 1939), p 60. Tikao added
that the matā (flint) and hoanga (sandstone) peoples had arrived in several vessels,
one of which was the Arai Te Uru. They were the eternal foes of the pounamu
(greenstone) tribe. Māori artisans sought their assistance to grind blocks of
pounamu/nephrite into tools, weapons, and ornaments. After fleeing from their
foes in the North Island the pounamu folk avoided the sites on the east coast
of the South Island where passengers on the Arai Te Uru had come ashore and
sought refuge in remote gorges on the wild west coast. A Ngāi Tahu elder told
Herries Beattie that the waka Tairea became a submerged block of pounamu/
nephrite in the Arahura Gorge. (Beattie H, Traditional Lifeways of the Southern
Maori, edited by Atholl Anderson, University of Otago Press, 1994, p 523).

238   Heinz W F, New Zealand's Last Gold Rush (A H and A W Reed, 1977), p 4.

239   May P R, The West Coast Gold Rushes (Pegasus Press, 2nd edition., 1967), p 93.

240   Gage M, Legends in the Rocks (Whitcoulls, 1980), p 256 and Suggate
R P, Late Pleistocene Geology in the Northern Part of the South Island,
New Zealand (NZ Geological Survey Bulletin 77, 1965), p 48.

241   Wilson W, Nomenclature, Legends, etc. as supplied by the Maoris of South
Westland (Johannes Andersen papers MS 112, Alexander Turnbull Library).

242 Adams G, *Jack's Hut* (A H and A W Reed, 1968), p 89.
243 Taylor W A, *Lore and History of the South Island Maori* (Bascands, 1952), p 177.
244 Evison H C, *The Ngai Tahu Deeds* (Canterbury University
     Press, 2006) p 254 and Op cit note 247.
245 Odell R S, *Handbook of Arthur Pass National Park* (Whitcombe and Tombs, 1935), p 71.

Chapter Twenty-three
246 Dobson, A D, *Reminiscences of Arthur Dudley Dobson*
     (Whitcombe and Tombs, 1930), p 51.
247 Wilson W, *Nomenclature, Legends, etc. as supplied by the Maoris of South Westland
     1897* (Johannes Andersen papers MS 112, Alexander Turnbull Library).
248 Ibid. G G M Mitchell noted in his book *Place-names in Buller County* that the
     place name Paparoa referred to Mount Rochford and the Denniston Plateau.
     The Paparoa Range was evidently viewed as the southern extension of it.
249 Reed A W, *The Reed Dictionary of New Zealand Place Names* (Reed Books, 2002), p 4.
250 Hawker E, *Centennial Survey of Grey County 1877–1977* (Grey County Council), p 65.
251 Hawker V, *Historical Survey of the Grey County* (Grey County Council, 1960), p 73.
252 Op cit note 257, p 65.
253 Op cit note 254.
254 Evison H C, *The Ngai Tahu Deeds* (Canterbury University Press, 2006), p 254
     and Acheson J, *'Kaimatau' and 'Tera Tama'* in the NZ Alpine Club Journal
     (NZAC 1993), v 46, p 106. Haast and Dobson initiated a long debate about the
     location of 'Kaimatau'. John Acheson produced convincingly evidence that
     it was Mount Alexander. Kaimata is also an old Taranaki place name.

Chapter Twenty-four
255 Mitchell G G M, *Maori Place Names in Buller County* (A H. and A W Reed, 1948), p 31.
256 Halkett Millar J, *High Noon for Coaches* (A H and A W Reed, 1965), p 41.
257 Op cit note 262, p 40.
258 Poole A L, *Catchment Control in New Zealand* (Ministry
     of Works and Development, 1983), p 116.
259 ibid p 204.
260 ibid p 212 and p 222.
261 *The Press,* December 14, 2001, p 9 and September 4, 2007, p A3.
262 Moonlight I J, personal comm.
263 Op cit note 263, p 34.
264 Mitchell H and J, *Kehu* (Nelson Historical Society. Journal) 1996,
     p 3 and NZ Alpine Club Journal, 1948, v 12, p 190.
265 McConochie N, *Early Development of Upper Buller*
     (Newton McConochie, 1971), pp 21 and 31.
266 Haast J, *Report on a Topographical and Geographical Exploration of the
     Western District of Nelson Province* (Nelson Provincial Government, 1861).